T0228710

Computer Engineering:
Software and Hardware Systems

Computer Engineering:
Software and Hardware Systems

Editor: Stan Fulcher

New York

Published by NY Research Press
118-35 Queens Blvd., Suite 400,
Forest Hills, NY 11375, USA
www.nyresearchpress.com

Computer Engineering Software and Hardware Systems
Edited by Stan Fulcher

International Standard Book Number: 978-1-64725-374-5 (Hardback)

Cataloging-in-publication Data

Computer engineering : software and hardware systems / edited by Stan Fulcher.
   p. cm.
Includes bibliographical references and index.
ISBN 978-1-64725-374-5
1. Computer engineering. 2. Computer software. 3. Computer input-output equipment.
4. Computers. 5. Computer engineering--Data processing. 6. Computer systems.
I. Fulcher, Stan.
TK7885 .C66 2023
004--dc23

Contents

Preface

The main aim of this book is to educate learners and enhance their research focus by presenting diverse topics covering this vast field. This is an advanced book which compiles significant studies by distinguished experts in the area of analysis. This book addresses successive solutions to the challenges arising in the area of application, along with it; the book provides scope for future developments.

Computer engineering is a subfield of electrical engineering that combines the fields of electronics engineering and computer science required for creating computer software and hardware. The set of instructions that is stored and helpes run the hardware comprise the software components. The physical parts of a computer such as mouse, the central processing unit (CPU), storage, and printer are the hardware components. The main activities of computer engineering include designing, developing and testing computer hardware and software. They also analyze and evaluate the results of computer testing, and update the outdated equipment so that it can become compatible to be utilized with new software or hardware. Computer engineering is further subdivided into various sub-areas including machine intelligence, embedded systems, automation, cybersecurity, networking, and software engineering. This book aims to shed light on the various software and hardware systems used in computer engineering. It traces the progress of this field and highlights some of its key concepts and applications. Those in search of information to further their knowledge will be greatly assisted by this book.

It was a great honour to edit this book, though there were challenges, as it involved a lot of communication and networking between me and the editorial team. However, the end result was this all-inclusive book covering diverse themes in the field.

Finally, it is important to acknowledge the efforts of the contributors for their excellent chapters, through which a wide variety of issues have been addressed. I would also like to thank my colleagues for their valuable feedback during the making of this book.

Editor

Q3B: An Efficient BDD-based SMT Solver for Quantified Bit-Vectors

Martin Jonáš[✉] and Jan Strejček

Masaryk University, Brno, Czech Republic
{xjonas,strejcek}@fi.muni.cz

Abstract. We present the first stable release of our tool Q3B for deciding satisfiability of quantified bit-vector formulas. Unlike other state-of-the-art solvers for this problem, Q3B is based on translation of a formula to a BDD that represents models of the formula. The tool also employs advanced formula simplifications and approximations by effective bit-width reduction and by abstraction of bit-vector operations. The paper focuses on the architecture and implementation aspects of the tool, and provides a brief experimental comparison with its competitors.

1 Introduction

Advances in solving formula *satisfiability modulo theories* (SMT) achieved during the last few decades enabled significant progress and practical applications in the area of automated analysis, testing, and verification of various systems. In the case of software and hardware systems, the most relevant theory is the *theory of fixed-sized bit-vectors*, as these systems work with inputs expressed as bit-vectors (i.e., sequences of bits) and perform bitwise and arithmetic operations on bit-vectors. The quantifier-free fragment of this theory is supported by many general-purpose SMT solvers, such as CVC4 [1], MathSAT [7], Yices [10], or Z3 [9] and also by several dedicated solvers, such as Boolector [21] or STP [12]. However, there are some use-cases where quantifier-free formulas are not natural or expressive enough. For example, formulas containing quantifiers arise naturally when expressing loop invariants, ranking functions, loop summaries, or when checking equivalence of two symbolically described sets of states [8,13,17,18,24]. In the following, we focus on SMT solvers for *quantified* bit-vector formulas. In particular, this paper describes the state-of-the-art SMT solver Q3B including its implementation and the inner workings.

Solving of quantified bit-vector formulas was first supported by Z3 in 2013 [25] and for a limited set of *exists/forall* formulas with only a single quantifier alternation by Yices in 2015 [11]. Both of these solvers decide quantified formulas by *quantifier instantiation*, in which universally quantified variables in the Skolemized formula are repeatedly instantiated by ground terms until the resulting quantifier-free formula is unsatisfiable or a model of the original formula is found.

In 2016, we proposed a different approach for solving quantified bit-vector formulas: by using binary decision diagrams (BDDs) and approximations [14]. For evaluation of this approach, we implemented an experimental SMT solver called Q3B, which outperformed both Z3 and Yices. Next solver that was able to solve quantified bit-vector formulas was Boolector in 2017, using also an approach based on quantifier instantiation [22]. Unlike Z3, in which the universally quantified variables are instantiated only by constants or subterms of the original formula, Boolector uses a counterexample-guided synthesis approach, in which a suitable ground term for instantiation is synthesized based on the defined grammar. Thanks to this, Boolector was able to outperform Q3B and Z3 on certain classes of formulas. More recently, in 2018, support of quantified bit-vector formulas has also been implemented into CVC4 [20]. The approach of CVC4 is also based on quantifier instantiation, but instead of synthesizing terms given by the grammar as Boolector, CVC4 uses predetermined rules based on invertibility conditions, which directly give terms that can prune many spurious models without using potentially expensive counterexample-guided synthesis. The authors of CVC4 have shown that this approach outperforms Z3, CVC4, and the original Q3B. However, Q3B has been substantially improved since the original experimental version. In 2017, we extended it with simplifications of quantified bit-vector formulas using unconstrained variables [15]. Further, in 2018, we added the experimental implementation of abstractions of bit-vector operations [16]. With these techniques, Q3B is able to decide more formulas than Z3, Boolector, and CVC4. Besides the theoretical improvements, Q3B was also improved in terms of stability, ease of use, technical parts of the implementation, and compliance with the SMT-LIB standard. This tool paper presents the result of these improvements: Q3B 1.0, the first stable version of Q3B.

We briefly summarize the SMT solving approach of Q3B. As in most of modern SMT solvers, the input formula is first simplified using satisfiability-preserving transformations that may reduce the size and complexity of the formula. The simplified formula is then converted to a binary decision diagram (BDD) that represents all assignments satisfying the formula, i.e., the *models* of the formula. If the BDD represents at least one model, we say that the BDD is *satisfiable* and it implies satisfiability of the formula. If the BDD represents the empty set of models, we say that it is *unsatisfiable* and so is the formula. Unfortunately, there are formulas for which the corresponding BDD (or some of the intermediate BDDs that appear during its computation) is necessarily exponential in the number of bits in the formula. For example, this is the case for formulas that contain multiplication of two bit-vector variables [5]. To be able to deal with such formulas, Q3B computes in parallel also BDDs underapproximating and overapproximating the original set of models, i.e., BDDs representing subsets and supersets of the original set of models, respectively. The approximating BDDs may be much smaller in size than the precise BDD, especially if the approximation is very rough. Still, they can be used to decide satisfiability of the original formula. If an overapproximating BDD is unsatisfiable, the original formula is also unsatisfiable. If the overapproximating BDD is satisfiable, we take one of its models, i.e., an assignment to the top-level existential variables of the formula, and check whether it is a model of the original formula. If the answer is positive, the original formula is satisfiable. In the other case, we build a more precise overapproximating BDD. Underapproximating BDDs are utilized analogously. The only difference is that for unsatisfiable underapproximating BDD, we check the validity of a countermodel, i.e., an assignment to the top-level universal variables that makes the formula unsatisfiable. The approach is depicted in Fig. 1.

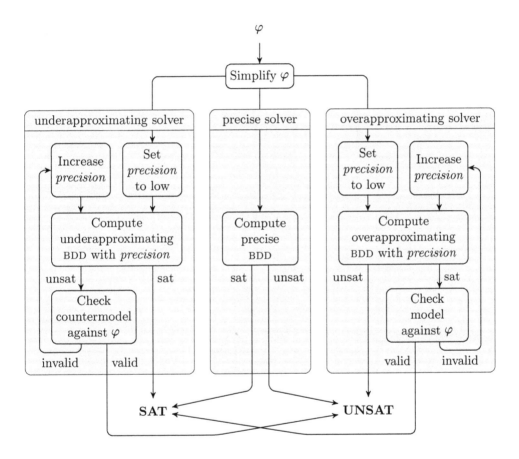

Fig. 1. High-level overview of the SMT solving approach used by Q3B. The three shaded areas are executed in parallel and the first result is returned.

Q3B currently supports two ways of computing the approximating BDDs from the input formula. First of these are *variable bit-width approximations* in which the *effective bit-width* of some variables is reduced. In other words, some of the variables are represented by fewer bits and the rest of the bits is set to zero bits, one bits, or the sign bit of the reduced variable. This approach was originally used by the SMT solvers UCLID [6] and Boolector [21]. Q3B extends this approach to quantified formulas: if bit-widths of only existentially quantified variables are reduced, the resulting BDD is underapproximating; if bit-widths of only universally quantified variables are reduced, the resulting BDD is overapproximating. The second way to obtain an approximation is *bit-vector operation abstraction* [16], during which the individual bit-vector operations may not compute all bits of the result, but produce some *do-not-know bits* if the resulting BDDs would exceed a given number of nodes. An underapproximating BDD then represents assignments that satisfy the formula for all possible values of these do-not-know bits. Analogously, an overapproximating BDD represents all assignments that satisfy the formula for some value of the do-not-know bits. Q3B also supports a combination of these two methods, in which both the effective bit-with of variables is reduced and the limit on the size of BDDs is imposed. During an approximation refinement, either the effective bit-width or the size limit is increased, based on the detected cause of the imprecision.

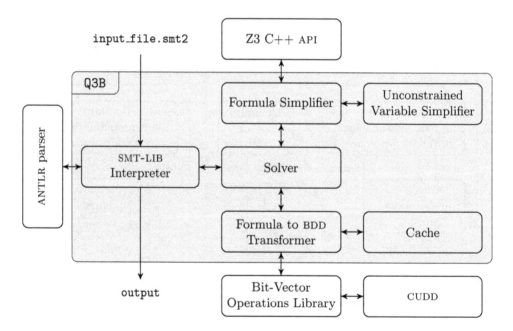

Fig. 2. Architecture of Q3B. Components in the shaded box are parts of Q3B, the other components are external.

2 Architecture

This section describes the internal architecture of Q3B. The overall structure including internal and external components and the interactions between them is depicted in Fig. 2. We explain the purpose of the internal components:

SMT-LIB Interpreter (implemented in `SMTLIBInterpreter.cpp`) reads the input file in the SMT-LIB format [3], which is the standard input format for SMT solvers. The interpreter executes all the commands from the file. In particular, it maintains the assertion stack and the options set by the user, calls solver when `check-sat` command is issued, and queries `Solver` if the user requires the model with the command `get-model`.

Formula Simplifier (implemented in `FormulaSimplifier.cpp`) provides interface for all applied formula simplifications, in particular miniscoping, conversion to negation normal form, pure literal elimination, equality propagation, constructive equality resolution (CER) [14], destructive equality resolution (DER) [25], simple theory-related rewriting, and simplifications using unconstrained variables. Most of these simplifications are implemented directly in this component; only CER, DER, and majority of the theory-related rewritings are performed by calling Z3 API and simplifications using unconstrained variables are implemented in a separate component of Q3B. The simplifier also converts top-level existential variables to uninterpreted constants, so their values are also included in a model. Some simplifications that could change models of the formula are disabled if the user enables model generation, i.e., sets `:produce-models` to `true`.

Unconstrained Variable Simplifier (implemented in `UnconstrainedVariableSimplifier.cpp`) provides simplifications of formulas that contain unconstrained variables, i.e., variables that occur only once in the formula. Besides previously published unconstrained variable simplifications [15], which were present in the previous versions of Q3B, this component now also provides new *goal-directed* simplifications of formulas with unconstrained variables. In these simplifications, we aim to determine whether a subterm containing an unconstrained variable should be minimized, maximized, sign minimized, or sign maximized in order to satisfy the formula. If the subterm should be minimized and contains an unconstrained variable, the term is replaced by a simpler term that gives the minimal result that can be achieved by any value of the unconstrained variable. Similarly for maximization, sign minimization, and sign maximization.

Solver (implemented in `Solver.cpp`) is the central component of our tool. It calls formula simplifier and then creates three threads for the precise solver, the underapproximating solver, and the overapproximating solver. It also controls the approximation refinement loops of the approximating solvers. Finally, it returns the result of the fastest thread and stores the respective model, if the result was `sat`.

Formula to BDD Transformer (implemented in the file `ExprToBDDTransformer.cpp`) performs the actual conversion of a formula to a BDD. Each subterm of the input formula is converted to a vector of BDDs (if the subterm's sort is a bit-vector of width n then the constructed vector contains n BDDs, each BDD represents one bit of the subterm). Further, each subformula of the input formula is converted to a BDD. These conversions proceed by a straightforward bottom-up recursion on the formula syntax tree. The transformer component calls an external library to compute the effect of logical and bit-vector operations on BDDs and vectors of BDDs, respectively. Besides the precise conversion, the transformer can also construct overapproximating and underapproximating BDDs. Precision of approximations depends on parameters set by the solver component.

Cache (implemented as a part of `ExprToBDDTransformer.cpp`) maintains for each converted subformula and subterm the corresponding BDD or a vector of BDDs, respectively. Each of the three solvers has its own cache. When an approximating solver increases precision of the approximation, entries of its cache that can be affected by the precision change are invalidated. All the caches are internally implemented by hash-tables.

3   Implementation

Q3B is implemented in C++17, is open-source and available under MIT license on GitHub: https://github.com/martinjonas/Q3B. The project development process includes continuous integration and automatic regression tests.

Q3B relies on several external libraries and tools. For representation and manipulation with BDDs, Q3B uses the open-source library CUDD 3.0 [23]. Since CUDD does not support bit-vector operations, we use the library by Peter Navrátil [19] that implements bit-vector operations on top of CUDD. The algorithms in this library are inspired by the ones in the BDD library BuDDy[1] and they provide a decent performance. Nevertheless, we have further improved its performance by several modifications. In particular, we added a specific code for handling expensive operations like bit-vector multiplication and division when arguments contain constant BDDs. This for example considerably speeds up multiplication whenever one argument contains many constant zero bits, which is a frequent case when we use the variable bit-width approximation fixing some bits to zero. Further, we have fixed few incorrectly implemented bit-vector operations in the original library. Finally, we have extended the library with the support for do-not-know bits in inputs of the bit-vector operations and we have implemented abstract versions of arithmetic operations that can produce do-not-know bits when the result exceeds a given number of BDD nodes.

For parsing the input formulas in SMT-LIB format, Q3B uses ANTLR parser generated from the grammar[2] for SMT-LIB 2.6 [2]. We have modified the grammar to correctly handle bit-vector numerals and to support `push` and `pop` commands without numerical argument. The parser allows Q3B to support all bit-vector operations and almost all SMT-LIB commands except `get-assertions`, `get-assignment`, `get-proof`, `get-unsat-assumptions`, `get-unsat-core`, and all the commands that work with algebraic data-types. This is in sharp contrast with the previous experimental versions of Q3B, which only collected all the assertions from the input file and performed the satisfiability check regardless of the rest of the commands and of the presence of the `check-sat` command. The reason for this was that the older versions parsed the input file using the Z3 C++ API, which can provide only the list of assertions, not the rest of the SMT-LIB script. Thanks to the new parser, Q3B 1.0 can also provide the user

---

[1] https://sourceforge.net/projects/buddy/.
[2] https://github.com/julianthome/smtlibv2-grammar.

with a model of a satisfiable formula after calling `get-model`; this important aspect of other SMT solvers was completely missing in the previous versions.

On the other hand, C++ API of the solver Z3 is still used for internal representation of parsed formulas. The Z3 C++ API is also used to perform manipulations with formulas, such as substitution of values for variables, and some of the formula simplifications. Note that these are the only uses of Z3 API in Q3B during solving the formula; no actual SMT- or SAT-solving capabilities of Z3 are used during the solving process.

Some classes of Q3B, in particular `Solver`, `FormulaSimplifier`, and `UnconstrainedVariableSimplifier`, expose a public C++ API that can be used by external tools for SMT solving or just performing formula simplifications. For example, `Solver` exposes method `Solve(formula, approximationType)`, which can be used to decide satisfiability by the precise solver, the underapproximating solver, or the overapproximating solver. `Solver` also exposes the method `SolveParallel(formula)`, which simplifies the input formula and runs all three of these solvers in parallel and returns the first result as depicted in Fig. 1.

4   Experimental Evaluation

We have evaluated the performance of QB3 1.0 and compared it to the latest versions of SMT solvers Boolector (v3.0), CVC4 (v1.6), and Z3 (v4.8.4). All tools were used with their default settings except for CVC4, where we used the same settings as in the paper that introduces quantified bit-vector solving in CVC4 [20], since they give better results than the default CVC4 settings. As the benchmark set, we have used all 5751 quantified bit-vector formulas from the SMT-LIB repository. The benchmarks are divided into 8 distinct families of formulas. We have executed each solver on each benchmark with CPU time limit 20 min and RAM limit of 8 GiB. All the experiments were performed in a Ubuntu 16.04 virtual machine within a computer equipped with Intel(R) Core(TM) i7-8700 CPU @ 3.20 GHz CPU and 32 GiB of RAM. For reliable benchmarking we employed BENCHEXEC [4], a tool that allocates specified resources for a program execution and precisely measures their usage. All scripts used for running benchmarks and processing their results, together with detailed descriptions and some additional results not presented in the paper, are available online[3].

Table 1 shows the numbers of benchmarks in each benchmark family solved by the individual solvers. Q3B is able to solve the most benchmarks in benchmark families *2017-Preiner-scholl-smt08*, *2017-Preiner-tptp*, *2017-Preiner-UltimateAutomizer*, *2018-Preiner-cav18*, and *wintersteiger*, and it is competitive in the remaining families. In total, Q3B also solves more formulas than each of the other solvers: 116 more than Boolector, 83 more than CVC4, and 139 more than Z3. Although the numbers of solved formulas for the solvers seem fairly similar, the cross-comparison in Table 2 shows that the differences among the individual solvers are actually larger. For each other solver, there are at least

---

[3] https://github.com/martinjonas/q3b-artifact.

Table 1. For each solver and benchmark family, the table shows the number of benchmarks from the given family solved by the given solver. The column *Total* shows the total number of benchmarks in the given family. The last line provides the total CPU times for the benchmarks solved by all four solvers.

Family	Total	Boolector	CVC4	Q3B	Z3
2017-Preiner-keymaera	4035	4022	3998	4009	**4031**
2017-Preiner-psyco	194	193	190	182	**194**
2017-Preiner-scholl-smt08	374	312	248	**319**	272
2017-Preiner-tptp	73	69	**73**	**73**	**73**
2017-Preiner-UltimateAutomizer	153	152	151	**153**	**153**
20170501-Heizmann-UltimateAutomizer	131	30	**128**	124	32
2018-Preiner-cav18	600	553	**565**	**565**	553
wintersteiger	191	163	174	**185**	163
Total	5751	5494	5527	**5610**	5471
CPU time [s]		7794	5877	19853	**4055**

Table 2. For all pairs of the solvers, the table shows the number of benchmarks that were solved by the solver in the corresponding row, but not by the solver in the corresponding column. The column *Uniquely solved* shows the number of benchmarks that were solved only by the given solver.

	Boolector	CVC4	Q3B	Z3	Uniquely solved
Boolector	0	123	69	78	8
CVC4	156	0	60	171	6
Q3B	185	143	0	208	25
Z3	55	115	69	0	6

143 benchmarks that can be solved by Q3B but not by the other solver. We think this shows the importance of developing an SMT solver based on BDDs and approximations besides the solvers based on quantifier instantiation.

5   Conclusions and Future Work

We have described the architecture and inner workings of the first stable version of the state-of-the-art SMT solver Q3B. Experimental evaluation on all quantified bit-vector formulas from SMT-LIB repository shows that this solver slightly outperforms other state-of-the-art solvers for such formulas.

As future work, we would like to drop the dependency on the Z3 API: namely to implement our own representation of formulas and reimplement all the simplifications currently outsourced to Z3 API directly in Q3B. We also plan to extend some simplifications with an additional bookkeeping needed to construct a model of the original formula. With these extensions, all simplifications could be used even if the user wants to get a model of the formula. We would also like to implement production of unsatisfiable cores since they are also valuable for software verification.

References

1. Barrett, C., et al.: CVC4. In: Gopalakrishnan, G., Qadeer, S. (eds.) CAV 2011. LNCS, vol. 6806, pp. 171–177. Springer, Heidelberg (2011). https://doi.org/10.1007/978-3-642-22110-1_14
2. Barrett, C., Stump, A., Tinelli, C.: The SMT-LIB Standard: Version 2.6. Technical report, Department of Computer Science, The University of Iowa (2017). www.SMT-LIB.org
3. CBarrett, C., Stump, A., Tinelli, C.: The SMT-LIB standard: version 2.0. In: Gupta, A., Kroening, D. (eds.) Proceedings of the 8th International Workshop on Satisfiability Modulo Theories, Edinburgh, UK (2010)
4. Beyer, D., Löwe, S., Wendler, P.: Benchmarking and resource measurement. In: Fischer, B., Geldenhuys, J. (eds.) SPIN 2015. LNCS, vol. 9232, pp. 160–178. Springer, Cham (2015). https://doi.org/10.1007/978-3-319-23404-5_12
5. Bryant, R.E.: On the complexity of VLSI implementations and graph representations of boolean functions with application to integer multiplication. IEEE Trans. Comput. **40**(2), 205–213 (1991)
6. Bryant, R.E., Kroening, D., Ouaknine, J., Seshia, S.A., Strichman, O., Brady, B.A.: An abstraction-based decision procedure for bit-vector arithmetic. STTT **11**(2), 95–104 (2009)
7. Cimatti, A., Griggio, A., Schaafsma, B.J., Sebastiani, R.: The MathSAT5 SMT solver. In: Piterman, N., Smolka, S.A. (eds.) TACAS 2013. LNCS, vol. 7795, pp. 93–107. Springer, Heidelberg (2013). https://doi.org/10.1007/978-3-642-36742-7_7
8. Cook, B., Kroening, D., Rümmer, P., Wintersteiger, C.M.: Ranking function synthesis for bit-vector relations. Form. Methods Syst. Des. **43**(1), 93–120 (2013)
9. de Moura, L., Bjørner, N.: Z3: an efficient SMT solver. In: Ramakrishnan, C.R., Rehof, J. (eds.) TACAS 2008. LNCS, vol. 4963, pp. 337–340. Springer, Heidelberg (2008). https://doi.org/10.1007/978-3-540-78800-3_24
10. Dutertre, B.: Yices 2.2. In: Biere, A., Bloem, R. (eds.) CAV 2014. LNCS, vol. 8559, pp. 737–744. Springer, Cham (2014). https://doi.org/10.1007/978-3-319-08867-9_49
11. Dutertre, B.: Solving exists/forall problems with Yices. In: Workshop on satisfiability Modulo Theories (2015)
12. Ganesh, V., Dill, D.L.: A decision procedure for bit-vectors and arrays. In: Damm, W., Hermanns, H. (eds.) CAV 2007. LNCS, vol. 4590, pp. 519–531. Springer, Heidelberg (2007). https://doi.org/10.1007/978-3-540-73368-3_52
13. Gulwani, S., Srivastava, S., Venkatesan, R.: Constraint-based invariant inference over predicate abstraction. In: Jones, N.D., Müller-Olm, M. (eds.) VMCAI 2009. LNCS, vol. 5403, pp. 120–135. Springer, Heidelberg (2008). https://doi.org/10.1007/978-3-540-93900-9_13
14. Jonáš, M., Strejček, J.: Solving quantified bit-vector formulas using binary decision diagrams. In: Creignou, N., Le Berre, D. (eds.) SAT 2016. LNCS, vol. 9710, pp. 267–283. Springer, Cham (2016). https://doi.org/10.1007/978-3-319-40970-2_17
15. Jonáš, M., Strejček, J.: On simplification of formulas with unconstrained variables and quantifiers. In: Gaspers, S., Walsh, T. (eds.) SAT 2017. LNCS, vol. 10491, pp. 364–379. Springer, Cham (2017). https://doi.org/10.1007/978-3-319-66263-3_23

16. Jonáš, M., Strejček, J.: Abstraction of bit-vector operations for BDD-based SMT solvers. In: Fischer, B., Uustalu, T. (eds.) ICTAC 2018. LNCS, vol. 11187, pp. 273–291. Springer, Cham (2018). https://doi.org/10.1007/978-3-030-02508-3_15

17. Kroening, D., Lewis, M., Weissenbacher, G.: Under-approximating loops in C programs for fast counterexample detection. In: Sharygina, N., Veith, H. (eds.) CAV 2013. LNCS, vol. 8044, pp. 381–396. Springer, Heidelberg (2013). https://doi.org/10.1007/978-3-642-39799-8_26

18. Mrázek, J., Bauch, P., Lauko, H., Barnat, J.: SymDIVINE: tool for control-explicit data-symbolic state space exploration. In: Bošnački, D., Wijs, A. (eds.) SPIN 2016. LNCS, vol. 9641, pp. 208–213. Springer, Cham (2016). https://doi.org/10.1007/978-3-319-32582-8_14

19. Navrátil, P.: Adding support for bit-vectors to BDD libraries CUDD and Sylvan. Bachelor's thesis, Masaryk University, Faculty of Informatics, Brno (2018)

20. Niemetz, A., Preiner, M., Reynolds, A., Barrett, C., Tinelli, C.: Solving quantified bit-vectors using invertibility conditions. In: Chockler, H., Weissenbacher, G. (eds.) CAV 2018. LNCS, vol. 10982, pp. 236–255. Springer, Cham (2018). https://doi.org/10.1007/978-3-319-96142-2_16

21. Niemetz, A., Preiner, M., Wolf, C., Biere, A.: BTOR2, BtorMC and Boolector 3.0. In: Chockler, H., Weissenbacher, G. (eds.) CAV 2018. LNCS, vol. 10981, pp. 587–595. Springer, Cham (2018). https://doi.org/10.1007/978-3-319-96145-3_32

22. Preiner, M., Niemetz, A., Biere, A.: Counterexample-guided model synthesis. In: Legay, A., Margaria, T. (eds.) TACAS 2017. LNCS, vol. 10205, pp. 264–280. Springer, Heidelberg (2017). https://doi.org/10.1007/978-3-662-54577-5_15

23. Somenzi, F.: CUDD: CU Decision Diagram Package Release 3.0.0. University of Colorado at Boulder (2015)

24. Srivastava, S., Gulwani, S., Foster, J.S.: From program verification to program synthesis. In: Proceedings of the 37th ACM SIGPLAN-SIGACT Symposium on Principles of Programming Languages, POPL 2010, Madrid, Spain, 17–23 January 2010, pp. 313–326 (2010)

25. Wintersteiger, C.M., Hamadi, Y., de Moura, L.M.: Efficiently solving quantified bit-vector formulas. Form. Methods Syst. Des. **42**(1), 3–23 (2013)

Sound Approximation of Programs with Elementary Functions

Eva Darulova[1]([⊠]) and Anastasia Volkova[2]

[1] MPI-SWS, Saarland Informatics Campus,
Saarbrücken, Germany
eva@mpi-sws.org
[2] Inria, Lyon, France
anastasia.volkova@inria.fr

Abstract. Elementary function calls are a common feature in numerical programs. While their implementations in mathematical libraries are highly optimized, function evaluation is nonetheless very expensive compared to plain arithmetic. Full accuracy is, however, not always needed. Unlike arithmetic, where the performance difference between for example single and double precision floating-point arithmetic is relatively small, elementary function calls provide a much richer tradeoff space between accuracy and efficiency. Navigating this space is challenging, as guaranteeing the accuracy and choosing correct parameters for good performance of approximations is highly nontrivial. We present a fully automated approach and a tool which approximates elementary function calls inside small programs while guaranteeing overall user given error bounds. Our tool leverages existing techniques for roundoff error computation and approximation of individual elementary function calls and provides an automated methodology for the exploration of parameter space. Our experiments show that significant efficiency improvements are possible in exchange for reduced, but guaranteed, accuracy.

1 Introduction

Numerical programs face an inherent tradeoff between accuracy and efficiency. Choosing a larger finite precision provides higher accuracy, but is generally more costly in terms of memory and running time. Not all applications, however, need a very high accuracy to work correctly. We would thus like to compute the results with only as much accuracy as is needed, in order to save resources.

Navigating this tradeoff between accuracy and efficiency is challenging. First, estimating the accuracy, i.e. bounding roundoff and approximation errors, is nontrivial due to the complex nature of finite-precision arithmetic which inevitably occurs in numerical programs. Second, the space of possible implementations is usually prohibitively large and thus cannot be explored manually.

Today, users can choose between different automated tools for analyzing accuracy of floating-point programs [7,8,11,14,18,20,26] as well as for choosing between different precisions [5,6,10]. The latter tools perform mixed-precision tuning, i.e. they assign different floating-point precisions to different operations, and can thus improve the performance w.r.t. a uniform precision implementation. The success of such an optimization is, however, limited to the case when uniform precision is just barely not enough to satisfy a given accuracy specification.

Another possible target for performance optimizations are elementary functions (e.g. `sin, exp`). Users by default choose single- or double-precision `libm` library function implementations, which are fully specified in the C language standard (ISO/IEC 9899:2011) and provide high accuracy. Such implementations are, however, expensive. When high accuracy is not needed, we can save significant resources by replacing `libm` calls by coarser approximations, opening up a larger, and different tradeoff space than mixed-precision tuning. Unfortunately, existing automated approaches [1,25] do not provide accuracy guarantees.

On the other hand, tools like Metalibm [3] approximate *individual* elementary functions by polynomials with rigorous accuracy guarantees given by the user. They, however, do not consider entire programs and leave the selection of its parameters to the user, limiting its usability mostly to experts.

We present an approach and a tool which leverages the existing whole-program error analysis of Daisy [8] and Metalibm's elementary function approximation to provide both *sound whole-program guarantees* as well as *efficient* C implementations for floating-point programs with elementary function calls. Given a target error specification, our tool automatically distributes the error budget among uniform single or double precision arithmetic operations and elementary functions, and selects a suitable polynomial degree for their approximation.

We have implemented our approach inside the tool Daisy and compare the performance of generated programs against programs using `libm` on examples from literature. The benchmarks spend on average 38% and up to 50% of time for evaluation of the elementary functions. Our tool improves the overall performance by on average 14% and up to 25% when approximating each elementary function call individually, and on average 17% and up to 31% when approximating compound function calls. These improvements were achieved solely by optimizing approximations to elementary functions and illustrate pertinence of our approach. These performance improvements incur overall whole-program errors which are only 2–3 magnitudes larger than double-precision implementations using `libm` functions and are well below the errors of single-precision implementations. Our tool thus allows to effectively trade performance for larger, but guaranteed, error bounds.

Contributions. In summary, in this paper we present: (1) the first approximation technique for elementary functions with sound whole-program error guarantees, (2) an experimental evaluation on benchmarks from literature, and (3) an implementation, which is available at https://github.com/malyzajko/daisy.

Related Work. Several static analysis tools bound roundoff errors of floating-point computations [7,18,20,26], assuming `libm` implementations, or verify the correctness of several functions in Intel's `libm` library [17]. Muller [21] provides a good overview of the approximation of elementary functions. Approaches for improving the performance of numerical programs include mixed-precision tuning [5,6,10,16,24], and autotuning, which performs low-level real-value semantics-preserving transformations [23,27]. These leverage a different part of the trade-off space than libm approximation and are thus orthogonal. Herbie [22] and Sardana [7] improve accuracy by rewriting the non-associative finite-precision arithmetic, which is complementary to our approach. Approaches which approximate entire numerical programs include MCMC search [25], enumerative program synthesis [1] and neural approximations [13]. Accuracy is only checked on a small set of sample inputs and is thus not guaranteed.

2   Our Approach

We explain our approach using the following example [28] computing a forward kinematics equation and written in Daisy's real-valued specification language:

```
def forwardk2jY(theta1: Real, theta2: Real): Real = {
  require(-3.14 <= theta1 && theta1 <= 3.14 && -3.14 <= theta2 && theta2 <= 3.14)
    val l1: Real = 0.5; val l2: Real = 2.5
    l1 * sin(theta1) + l2 * sin(theta1 + theta2)
} ensuring(res => res +/- 1e-11)
```

Although this program is relatively simple, it still presents an opportunity for performance savings, especially when it is called often, e.g. during the motion of a robotics arm. Assuming double-precision floating-point arithmetic and library implementations for sine, Daisy's static analysis determines the worst-case absolute roundoff error of the result to be 3.44e-15. This is clearly a much smaller error than what the user requested (1e-11) in the postcondition (ensuring clause).

The two elementary function calls to sin account for roughly 40.7% of the overall running time. We can save some of this running time using polynomial approximations, which our tool generates in less than 6 min. The new double precision C implementation is roughly 15.6% faster than one with libm[1] functions, i.e. using around 40% of the available margin. This is a noteworthy performance improvement, considering that we optimized uniquely the evaluation of elementary functions. The actual error of the approximate implementation is 1.56e-12, i.e. roughly three orders of magnitude higher than the libm error. This error is still much smaller than if we had used a uniform single precision implementation, which incurs a total error of 1.85e-6.

We implement our approach inside the Daisy framework [8], combining Daisy's static dataflow analysis for bounding finite-precision roundoff errors, Metalibm's automated generation of efficient polynomial approximations, as well as a novel error distribution algorithm. Our tool furthermore automatically selects a suitable polynomial degree for approximations to elementary functions.

---

[1] There are various different implementations of libm that depend on the operating system and programming language. Here when referring to libm we mean the GNU libc implementation.

Unlike previous work, our tool *guarantees* that the user-specified error is satisfied. It soundly distributes the overall error budget among arithmetic operations and libm calls using Daisy's static analysis. Metalibm uses the state-of-the art minimax polynomial approximation algorithm [2] and Sollya [4] and Gappa [12] to bound errors of their implementations. Given a function, a target relative error bound and implementation parameters, Metalibm generates C code. Our tool does not guarantee to find the most efficient implementation; the search space of implementation and approximation choices is highly complex and discrete, and it is thus infeasible to find the optimal parameters.

The input to our tool is a straight-line program[2] with standard arithmetic operators $(=, -, *, /)$ as well as the most commonly used elementary functions $(\sin, \cos, \tan, \log, \exp, \sqrt{})$. The user further specifies the domains of all inputs, together with a target overall absolute error which must be satisfied. The output is C code with arithmetic operations in uniform single or double precision, and libm approximations in double precision (Metalibm's only supported precision).

Algorithm. We will use 'program' for the entire expression, and 'function' for individual elementary functions. Our approach works in the following steps.

Step 1 We re-use Daisy's frontend which parses the input specification. We add a pre-processing step, which decomposes the abstract syntax tree (AST) of the program we want to approximate such that each elementary function call is assigned to a fresh local variable. This transformation eases the later replacement of the elementary functions with an approximation.

Step 2 We use Daisy's roundoff error analysis on the entire program, assuming a libm implementation of elementary functions. This analysis computes a real-valued range and a worst-case absolute roundoff error bound for each subexpression in the AST, assuming uniform single or double precision as appropriate. We use this information in the next step to distribute the error and to determine the parameters for Metalibm for each function call.

Step 3 This is the core step, which calls Metalibm to generate a (piecewise) polynomial approximation for each elementary function which was assigned to a local variable. Each call to Metalibm specifies the local target error for each function call, the polynomial degree and the domain of the function call arguments. To determine the argument domains, we use the range and error information obtained in the previous step. Our tool tries different polynomial degrees and selects the fastest implementation. We explain our error distribution and polynomial selection further below.

Metalibm generates efficient double-precision C code including argument reduction (if applicable), domain splitting, and polynomial approximation with a guaranteed error below the specified target error (or returns an error). Metalibm furthermore supports approximations with lookup tables, whose size the user can control manually via our tool frontend as well.

---

[2] All existing approaches for analysing floating-point roundoff errors which handle loops or conditional branches, reduce the reasoning about errors to straight-line code, e.g. through loop invariants [9,14] or loop unrolling [7], or path-wise analysis [7,9,15].

Step 4 Our tool performs roundoff error analysis again, this time taking into account the new approximations' precise error bounds reported by Metalibm. Finally, Daisy generates C code for the program itself, as well as all necessary headers to link with the approximation generated by Metalibm.

Error Distribution. In order to call Metalibm, Daisy needs to determine the target error for each `libm` call. Recall that the user of our tool only specifies the *total* error at the end of the program. Hence, distributing the total error budget among arithmetic operations and (potentially several) elementary function calls is a crucial step. Consider again our running example which has two elementary function calls. Our tool distributes the error budget as follows:

$$|f(x) - \tilde{f}(\tilde{x})| \leq |f(x) - \hat{f}_1(x)| + |\hat{f}_1(x) - \hat{f}_2(x)| + |\hat{f}_2(x) - \tilde{f}(\tilde{x})|$$

where we denote by f the real-valued specification of the program; $\hat{f}_1$ and $\hat{f}_2$ have one and two elementary function calls approximated, respectively, and arithmetic is considered exact; and $\tilde{f}$ is the final finite-precision implementation.

Daisy first determines the budget for the finite-precision roundoff error ($|\hat{f}_2(x) - \tilde{f}(\tilde{x})|$) and then distributes the remaining part among `libm` calls. At this point, Daisy cannot compute $|\hat{f}_2(x) - \tilde{f}(\tilde{x})|$ exactly, as the approximations are not available yet. Instead, it assumes `libm`-based approximations as baseline.

Then, Daisy distributes the remaining error budget either equally among the elementary function calls, or by taking into account that the approximation errors are propagated differently through the program. This error propagation is estimated by computing the derivative w.r.t. to each elementary function call (which gives an estimation of the conditional number). Daisy computes partial derivatives symbolically and maximizes them over the specified input domain.

Finally, we obtain an error budget for each `libm` call, representing the total error due to the elementary function call *at the end of the program*. For calling Metalibm, however, we need the *local* error at the function call site. Due to error propagation, these two errors can differ significantly, and may lead to overall errors which exceed the error bound specified by the user. We estimate the error propagation using a linear approximation based on derivatives, and use this estimate to compute a *local* target error from the total error budget.

Since Metalibm usually generates approximations with slightly tighter error bounds than asked for, our tool performs a second roundoff analysis (step 4), where all errors (smaller or larger) are correctly taken into account.

Polynomial Degree Selection. The polynomial degree significantly and in a discrete way influences the efficiency of approximations, so that optimal prediction is infeasible. Hence, our tool performs a linear search, using the (coarse) estimated running time reported by Metalibm (obtained with a few benchmarking runs) to select the approximation with the smallest estimated running time. The search stops either when the estimated running time is significantly higher than the current best, or when Metalibm times out.

We do not automatically exploit other Metalibm's parameters, such as minimum subdomain width for splitting, since they give fine-grained control that is not suitable for *general* automatic implementations.

3   Experimental Evaluation

We evaluate our approach in terms of accuracy and performance on benchmarks from literature [9, 19, 28] which include elementary function calls, and extend them with the examples rodriguesRotation[3] and ex2* and ex3_d, which are problems from a graduate analysis textbook. While they are relatively short, they represent important kernels usually employing several elementary function calls[4]. We base target error bounds on roundoff errors of a libm implementation: middle and large errors, each of which is roughly three and four orders of magnitudes larger than the libm-based bound, respectively. By default, we assume double 64 bit precision.

Our tool provides an automatic generation of benchmarking code for each input program. Each benchmarking executable runs the Daisy-generated code on 10^7 random inputs from the input domain and measures performance in the number of processor clock cycles. Of the measured number of cycles we discard the highest 10%, as we have observed these to be outliers.

Experimental Results. By default, we approximate individual elementary function calls separately, use equal error distribution and allow table-based approximations with an 8-bit table index. For large errors we also measure performance for: (i) default settings but with the derivative-based errors distribution; (ii) default settings but without table usage; (iii) default settings but with compound calls with depth 1 and depth ∞ (approximation 'as much as possible').

Table 1 shows the performance improvements of approximated code w.r.t. libm based implementations of our benchmarks. We compare against libm only, as no approximation or synthesis tool provides error guarantees. By removing libm calls in initial programs we roughly estimate the elementary function overhead (second column) and give an idea for the margin of improvement. Figure 1 illustrates the overall improvement that we obtain for each benchmark (the height of the bars) and the relative distribution of the running time between arithmetic (blue) and elementary functions (green), for large errors with default settings but approximate compound calls with depth = ∞.

Our tool generates code with significant performance improvements for most functions and often reduces the time spent for the evaluation of elementary functions by a factor of two. As expected, the improvements are overall better for larger errors and vary on average from 10.7% to 13.8% for individual calls depending on the settings, and reach 17.1% on average when approximating compound calls as much as possible. However, increasing the program target error (for equal error distributions Metalibm target error increases linearly with it) does not necessarily lead to better performance, e.g. in case of axisRotationY and rodriguesRotation. This is the result of discrete decisions concerning the approximation degrees and the domain splittings inside Metalibm.

---

[3] https://en.wikipedia.org/wiki/Rodrigues27_rotation_formula.

[4] Experiments are performed on a Debian Linux 9 Desktop machine with a 3.3 GHz Intel i5 processor and 16 GB of RAM. All code for benchmarking is compiled with GNUs g++, version 6.3.0, with the -O2 flag.

Table 1. Performance improvements (in percent) of approximated code w.r.t. a program with libm library function calls.

precision		double						single
	elem. func.	middle	large errors					middle
benchmark	overhead	equal	equal	deriv	no table	depth 1	depth ∞	equal
sinxx10	20.8	7.6	7.7	7.7	7.7	7.6	7.7	4.7
xu1	49.3	13.9	25.8	18.0	26.6	25.7	27.3	8.1
xu2	53.6	4.6	12.4	13.0	12.6	12.5	26.0	-1.4
integrate18257	52.8	15.2	19.4	15.1	-4.5	22.4	31.7	2.1
integStoutemyer	42.1	-1.0	6.5	1.4	0.4	4.8	21.9	6.4
axisRotationX	38.0	17.2	17.3	18.1	17.4	17.6	17.3	-10.5
axisRotationY	37.9	17.6	12.8	21.5	12.9	12.8	12.8	-14.1
rodriguesRotation	28.9	14.9	11.6	13.6	13.8	13.8	13.9	-7.6
pendulum1	24.4	-4.6	-2.9	-4.3	-4.2	11.0	11.7	-9.7
pendulum2	50.3	9.6	11.4	6.2	-0.8	20.2	20.5	-0.5
forwardk2jX	43.7	15.1	15.4	15.5	15.0	15.0	15.0	-10.2
forwardk2jY	40.7	10.7	15.6	15.6	15.6	15.6	15.6	7.4
ex2_1	34.6	12.8	12.8	12.3	12.3	12.3	12.1	8.4
ex2_2	34.9	5.9	14.8	15.4	15.1	15.0	15.3	3.6
ex2_3	42.1	23.5	24.5	24.5	24.1	24.8	24.3	3.9
ex2_4	31.8	11.9	12.5	12.5	12.6	14.3	14.3	7.9
ex2_5	40.6	22.5	24.4	24.5	24.4	24.4	24.3	10.2
ex2_9	35.0	7.2	7.1	7.4	7.2	7.0	9.4	-10.1
ex2_10	41.5	20.6	21.7	8.9	20.5	21.3	21.4	8.3
ex2_11	30.9	-6.8	-2.3	-4.9	-2.4	-4.8	-2.8	17.9
ex3_d	39.3	10.3	20.9	19.9	-1.1	19.9	20.3	4.9
average	38.7	10.9	13.8	12.5	10.7	14.9	17.1	1.4

Somewhat surprisingly, we did not observe an advantage of using the derivative-based error distribution over the equal one. We suspect that is due to the nonlinear nature of Metalibm's heuristics.

Table 1 further demonstrates that usage of tables generally improves the performance. However, the influence of increasing the table size must be studied on a case-by-case basis since large tables might lead to memory-bound computations.

We observe that it is generally beneficial to approximate 'as much as possible'. Indeed, the power of Metalibm lies in generating (piece-wise) polynomial approximations of compound expressions, whose behavior might be much simpler to evaluate than its individual subexpressions.

Finally, we also considered an implementation where all data and arithmetic operations are in single precision apart from the double-precision Metalibm-generated code (whose output is accurate only to single precision). We observe that slight performance improvements are possible, i.e. Metalibm can compete even with single-precision libm-based code, but to achieve performance improvements comparable to those of double-precision code, we need a single-precision code generation from Metalibm.

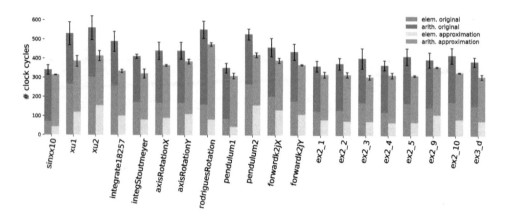

Fig. 1. Average performance and standard deviation. For each benchmark, the first bar shows the running time of the libm-based implementation and the second one of our implementation. Even relatively small overall time improvements are significant w.r.t. the time portion we can optimize (in green). Our implementations also have significantly smaller standard deviation (black bars). (Color figure online)

Analysis Time. Analysis time is highly dependent on the number of required approximations of elementary functions: each approximation requires a separate call to Metalibm whose running time in turn depends on the problem definition. Daisy reduces the number of calls to Metalibm by common expression elimination which improves the analysis time. Currently, we set the timeout for each Metalibm call to 3 min, which leads to an overall analysis time which is reasonable. Overall, our tool takes between 15 s and 20 min to approximate whole programs, with the average running time being 4 min 40 s per program.

4   Conclusion

We presented a fully automated approach which improves the performance of small numerical kernels at the expense of some accuracy by generating custom approximations of elementary functions. Our tool is parametrized by a user-given whole-program absolute error bound which is guaranteed to be satisfied by the generated code. Experiments illustrate that the tool efficiently uses the available margin for improvement and provides significant speedups for double-precision implementations. This work provides a solid foundation for future research in the areas of automatic approximations of single-precision and multivariate functions.

Acknowledgments. The authors thank Christoph Lauter for useful discussions and Youcef Merah for the work on an early prototype.

References

1. Bornholt, J., Torlak, E., Grossman, D., Ceze, L.: Optimizing synthesis with metasketches. In: POPL (2016)

2. Brisebarre, N., Chevillard, S.: Efficient polynomial L-approximations. In: ARITH (2007)
3. Brunie, N., de Dinechin, F., Kupriianova, O., Lauter, C.: Code generators for mathematical functions. In: ARITH (2015)
4. Chevillard, S., Joldeş, M., Lauter, C.: Sollya: an environment for the development of numerical codes. In: Fukuda, K., Hoeven, J., Joswig, M., Takayama, N. (eds.) ICMS 2010. LNCS, vol. 6327, pp. 28–31. Springer, Heidelberg (2010). https://doi.org/10.1007/978-3-642-15582-6_5
5. Chiang, W.F., Baranowski, M., Briggs, I., Solovyev, A., Gopalakrishnan, G., Rakamarić, Z.: Rigorous floating-point mixed-precision tuning. In: POPL (2017)
6. Damouche, N., Martel, M.: Mixed precision tuning with salsa. In: PECCS, pp. 185–194. SciTePress (2018)
7. Damouche, N., Martel, M., Chapoutot, A.: Improving the numerical accuracy of programs by automatic transformation. Int. J. Softw. Tools Technol. Transfer **19**(4), 427–448 (2017)
8. Darulova, E., Izycheva, A., Nasir, F., Ritter, F., Becker, H., Bastian, R.: Daisy - framework for analysis and optimization of numerical programs (tool paper). In: Beyer, D., Huisman, M. (eds.) TACAS 2018. LNCS, vol. 10805, pp. 270–287. Springer, Cham (2018). https://doi.org/10.1007/978-3-319-89960-2_15
9. Darulova, E., Kuncak, V.: Towards a compiler for reals. ACM TOPLAS **39**(2), 8 (2017)
10. Darulova, E., Sharma, S., Horn, E.: Sound mixed-precision optimization with rewriting. In: ICCPS (2018)
11. De Dinechin, F., Lauter, C.Q., Melquiond, G.: Assisted verification of elementary functions using Gappa. In: ACM Symposium on Applied Computing (2006)
12. de Dinechin, F., Lauter, C., Melquiond, G.: Certifying the floating-point implementation of an elementary function using Gappa. IEEE Trans. Comput. **60**(2), 242–253 (2011)
13. Esmaeilzadeh, H., Sampson, A., Ceze, L., Burger, D.: Neural acceleration for general-purpose approximate programs. In: IEEE/ACM International Symposium on Microarchitecture (2012)
14. Goubault, E., Putot, S.: Static analysis of finite precision computations. In: Jhala, R., Schmidt, D. (eds.) VMCAI 2011. LNCS, vol. 6538, pp. 232–247. Springer, Heidelberg (2011). https://doi.org/10.1007/978-3-642-18275-4_17
15. Goubault, E., Putot, S.: Robustness analysis of finite precision implementations. In: Shan, C. (ed.) APLAS 2013. LNCS, vol. 8301, pp. 50–57. Springer, Cham (2013). https://doi.org/10.1007/978-3-319-03542-0_4
16. Lam, M.O., Hollingsworth, J.K., de Supinski, B.R., Legendre, M.P.: Automatically adapting programs for mixed-precision floating-point computation. In: ICS (2013)
17. Lee, W., Sharma, R., Aiken, A.: On automatically proving the correctness of math.h implementations. In: POPL (2018)
18. Magron, V., Constantinides, G., Donaldson, A.: Certified roundoff error bounds using semidefinite programming. ACM Trans. Math. Softw. **43**(4), 34 (2017)
19. Merlet, J.P.: The COPRIN examples page. http://www-sop.inria.fr/coprin/logiciels/ALIAS/Benches/
20. Moscato, M., Titolo, L., Dutle, A., Muñoz, C.A.: Automatic estimation of verified floating-point round-off errors via static analysis. In: Tonetta, S., Schoitsch, E., Bitsch, F. (eds.) SAFECOMP 2017. LNCS, vol. 10488, pp. 213–229. Springer, Cham (2017). https://doi.org/10.1007/978-3-319-66266-4_14
21. Muller, J.M.: Elementary Functions - Algorithms and Implementation, 3rd edn. Birkhäuser, Basel (2016)

22. Panchekha, P., Sanchez-Stern, A., Wilcox, J.R., Tatlock, Z.: Automatically improving accuracy for floating point expressions. In: PLDI (2015)
23. Püschel, M., et al.: Spiral - a generator for platform-adapted libraries of signal processing alogorithms. IJHPCA **18**(1), 21–45 (2004)
24. Rubio-González, C., et al.: Precimonious: tuning assistant for floating-point precision. In: SC (2013)
25. Schkufza, E., Sharma, R., Aiken, A.: Stochastic optimization of floating-point programs with tunable precision. In: PLDI (2014)
26. Solovyev, A., Jacobsen, C., Rakamarić, Z., Gopalakrishnan, G.: Rigorous estimation of floating-point round-off errors with Symbolic Taylor Expansions. In: Bjørner, N., de Boer, F. (eds.) FM 2015. LNCS, vol. 9109, pp. 532–550. Springer, Cham (2015). https://doi.org/10.1007/978-3-319-19249-9_33
27. Vuduc, R., Demmel, J.W., Bilmes, J.A.: Statistical models for empirical search-based performance tuning. Int. J. High Perform. Comput. Appl. **18**(1), 65–94 (2004)
28. Yazdanbakhsh, A., Mahajan, D., Esmaeilzadeh, H., Lotfi-Kamran, P.: AxBench: a multiplatform benchmark suite for approximate computing. IEEE Des. Test **34**(2), 60–68 (2017)

Invertibility Conditions for Floating-Point Formulas

Martin Brain[3,4], Aina Niemetz[1], Mathias Preiner[1(✉)],
Andrew Reynolds[2], Clark Barrett[1], and Cesare Tinelli[2]

[1] Stanford University, Stanford, USA
preiner@cs.stanford.edu
[2] The University of Iowa, Iowa City, USA
[3] University of Oxford, Oxford, UK
[4] City, University of London, London, UK

Abstract. Automated reasoning procedures are essential for a number of applications that involve bit-exact floating-point computations. This paper presents conditions that characterize when a variable in a floating-point constraint has a solution, which we call invertibility conditions. We describe a novel workflow that combines human interaction and a syntax-guided synthesis (SyGuS) solver that was used for discovering these conditions. We verify our conditions for several floating-point formats. One implication of this result is that a fragment of floating-point arithmetic admits compact quantifier elimination. We implement our invertibility conditions in a prototype extension of our solver CVC4, showing their usefulness for solving quantified constraints over floating-points.

1 Introduction

Satisfiability Modulo Theories (SMT) formulas including either the theory of floating-point numbers [12] or universal quantifiers [24,32] are widely regarded as some of the hardest to solve. Problems that combine universal quantification over floating-points are rare—experience to date has suggested they are hard for solvers and would-be users should either give up or develop their own incomplete techniques. However, progress in theory solvers for floating-point [11] and the use of expression synthesis for handling universal quantifiers [27,29] suggest that these problems may not be entirely out of reach after all, which could potentially impact a number of interesting applications.

This paper makes substantial progress towards a scalable approach for solving quantified floating-point constraints directly in an SMT solver. Developing procedures for quantified floating-points requires considerable effort, both foundationally and in practice. We focus primarily on establishing a foundation for lifting to quantified floating-point formulas a procedure for solving quantified bit-vector formulas by Niemetz et al. [26]. That procedure relies on so-called *invertibility conditions*, intuitively, formulas that state under which conditions an argument of a given operator and predicate in an equation has a solution. Building on this concept and a state-of-the-art expression synthesis engine [29], we generate invertibility conditions for a majority of operators and predicates in the theory of floating-point numbers. In the context of quantifier-free floating-point formulas, floating-point invertibility conditions may enable us to lift the propagation-based local search approach for bit-vectors in [25] to the theory of floating-point numbers.

This work demonstrates that invertibility conditions exist and show promise for solving quantified floating-point constraints. More specifically, it makes the following contributions:

- In Sect. 3, we present invertibility conditions for the majority of operators and predicates in the SMT-LIB standard theory of floating-point numbers.
- In Sect. 4, we present a custom methodology based on syntax-guided synthesis and decision tree learning that we developed for the purpose of synthesizing the invertibility conditions presented here.
- In Sect. 5, we present a quantifier elimination procedure for a fragment of the theory that is based on invertibility conditions, and give experimental evidence of its potential, based on quantified floating-point problems coming from a verification application.

Related Work. To our knowledge, no previous work specifically discusses techniques for solving universally quantified floating-point formulas. Brain et al. [11] provide a comprehensive review of decision procedures for quantifier-free bit-exact floating-point using both SMT-based as well as other approaches. They identify four groups of techniques: bit-blasting approaches that use floating-point circuits to generate bit-vector formulas [13,16,20,33], interval techniques that use partitioning and interval propagation [10,22,23,31], optimization and numerical approaches that work with complete valuations [4,7,18,21], and axiomatic techniques that use partial or total axiomatizations of the theory of floating-point numbers in other theories such as real arithmetic [14,15].

On the other hand, approaches for universal quantification have been developed in modern SMT solvers that target other background theories, including linear arithmetic [8,17,29] and bit-vectors [26,27,32]. At a high level, these approaches use model-based refinement loops that lazily add instances of universal quantifiers until they reach a conflict at the quantifier-free level, or otherwise saturate with a model.

2　Preliminaries

We assume the usual notions and terminology of many-sorted first-order logic with equality (denoted by $\approx$). Let Σ be a *signature* consisting of a set Σ^s of sort symbols and a set Σ^f of interpreted (and sorted) function symbols. Each function symbol f has a sort $\tau_1 \times ... \times \tau_n \to \tau$, with arity $n \geq 0$ and $\tau_1, ..., \tau_n, \tau \in \Sigma^s$. We assume that Σ includes a Boolean sort Bool and the Boolean constants $\top$ (true) and $\bot$ (false).

We further assume the usual definition of well-sorted terms, literals, and (quantified) formulas with variables and symbols from Σ, and refer to them as Σ-terms, Σ-atoms, and so on. For a Σ-term or Σ-formula e, we denote the *free variables* of e (defined as usual) as $FV(e)$ and use $e[x]$ to denote that the variable x occurs free in e. We write $e[t]$ for the term or formula obtained from e by replacing each occurrence of x in e by t.

A *theory* T is a pair (Σ, I), where Σ is a signature and I is a non-empty class of Σ-interpretations (the *models* of T) that is closed under variable reassignment, i.e., every Σ-interpretation that only differs from an $\mathcal{I} \in I$ in how it interprets variables is also in I. A Σ-formula φ is *T-satisfiable* (resp. *T-unsatisfiable*) if it is satisfied by some (resp. no) interpretation in I; it is *T-valid* if it is satisfied by all interpretations in I. We will sometimes omit T when the theory is understood from context.

We briefly recap the terminology and notation of Brain et al. [12] which defines an SMT-LIB theory T_{FP} of floating-point numbers based on the IEEE-754 2008 standard [3]. The signature of T_{FP} includes a parametric family of sorts $\mathbb{F}_{\varepsilon,\sigma}$ where ε and σ are integers greater than or equal to 2 giving the number of bits used to store the exponent e and significand s, respectively. Each of these sorts contains five kinds of constants: normal numbers of the form $1.s * 2^e$, subnormal numbers of the form $0.s * 2^{-2^{\sigma-1}-1}$, two zeros ($+0$ and -0), two infinities ($+\infty$ and $-\infty$) and a single not-a-number (NaN). We assume a map $v_{\varepsilon,\sigma}$ for each sort, which maps these constants to their value in the set $\mathbb{R}^* = \mathbb{R} \cup \{+\infty, -\infty, \text{NaN}\}$. The theory also provides a rounding-mode sort RM, which contains five elements $\{\text{RNE}, \text{RNA}, \text{RTP}, \text{RTN}, \text{RTZ}\}$.

Table 1 lists all considered operators and predicate symbols of theory T_{FP}. The theory contains a full set of arithmetic operations $\{|...|, +, -, \cdot, \div, \sqrt{}, \max, \min\}$ as well as rem (remainder), rti (round to integral) and fma (combined multiply and add with just one rounding). The precise semantics of these operators is given in [12] and follows the same general pattern: $v_{\varepsilon,\sigma}$ is used to project the arguments to $\mathbb{R}^*$, the normal arithmetic is performed in $\mathbb{R}^*$, then the rounding mode and the result are used to select one of the adjoints of $v_{\varepsilon,\sigma}$ to convert the result back to $\mathbb{F}_{\varepsilon,\sigma}$. Note that the full theory in [12] includes several additional operators which we omit from discussion here, such as floating-point minimum/maximum, equality with floating-point semantics (fp.eq), and conversions between sorts.

Theory T_{FP} further defines a set of ordering predicates $\{<, >, \leq, \geq\}$ and a set of classification predicates $\{\text{isNorm}, \text{isSub}, \text{isInf}, \text{isZero}, \text{isNaN}, \text{isNeg}, \text{isPos}\}$. In the following, we denote the rounding mode of an operation above the operator symbol, e.g., $a \overset{\text{RTZ}}{+} b$ adds a and b and rounds the result towards zero. We use the infix operator style for isInf ($... \approx \pm\infty$), isZero ($... \approx \pm0$), and isNaN ($... \approx \text{NaN}$) for conciseness. We further use $\min_n/\max_n$ and $\min_s/\max_s$ for floating-point constants representing the minimum/maximum normal and subnormal numbers, respectively. We will omit rounding mode and floating-point sorts if they are clear from the context.

3   Invertibility Conditions for Floating-Point Formulas

In this section, we adapt the concept of invertibility conditions introduced by
Niemetz et al. in [26] to our theory T_{FP}. Intuitively, an invertibility condition ϕ_c
for a literal $l[x]$ is the exact condition under which $l[x]$ has a solution for x, i.e.,
ϕ_c is equivalent to $\exists x.\, l[x]$ in T_{FP}.

Definition 1 *(Floating-Point Invertibility Condition).* Let $l[x]$ be a Σ_{FP}-literal.
A quantifier-free Σ_{FP}-formula ϕ_c is an *invertibility condition* for x in $l[x]$ if
$x \notin FV(\phi_c)$ and $\phi_c \Leftrightarrow \exists x.\, l[x]$ is T_{FP} -*valid*.

As a simple example of an invertibility condition, given literal $|x| \approx t$ where
$|x|$ denotes the absolute value of x, a solution for x exists if and only if t is
not negative, i.e., if $\neg\mathsf{isNeg}(t)$ holds. We introduce additional terminology for
the sake of the discussion. We define the *dimension* of an invertibility condition
problem $\exists x.\, l[x]$ as the number of free variables it contains. For example, if s
and t are variables, then the dimension of $\exists x.\, x + s \approx t$ is two, the dimension of
$\exists x.\, \mathsf{isZero}(x+s)$ is one, and the dimension of $\exists x.\, \mathsf{isZero}(|x|)$ is zero. A literal $l[x]$
is *fully invertible* if its invertibility condition is $\top$. A term e is an (unconditional)
inverse for x in $l[x]$ if $l[e]$ is equivalent to $\top$. For example, the literal $-x \approx t$
is fully invertible and $-t$ is an inverse for x in this literal. We say that e is a
conditional inverse for $l[x]$ if $l[e]$ is an invertibility condition for $l[x]$.

Our primary goal in this work is to establish invertibility conditions for all
floating-point constraints that contain exactly one operator and one predicate.
These conditions collectively suffice to characterize when any literal $l[x]$ containing exactly one occurrence of x, the variable to solve for, has a solution. In
total, we were able to establish 167 out of 188 invertibility conditions (counting commutative cases only once) using a syntax-guided synthesis framework
which we describe in more detail in Sect. 4. In this section, we present a subset
of these invertibility conditions, highlighting the most interesting cases where

Table 1. Considered floating-point predicates/operators, with SMT-LIB 2 syntax.

Symbol	SMT-LIB syntax	Sort
isNorm, isSub	fp.isNormal, fp.isSubnormal	$\mathbb{F}_{\varepsilon,\sigma} \to$ Bool
isPos, isNeg	fp.isPositive, fp.isNegative	$\mathbb{F}_{\varepsilon,\sigma} \to$ Bool
isInf, isNaN, isZero	fp.isInfinite, fp.isNaN, fp.isZero	$\mathbb{F}_{\varepsilon,\sigma} \to$ Bool
$\approx, <, >, \leq, \geq$	=, fp.lt, fp.gt, fp.leq, fp.geq	$\mathbb{F}_{\varepsilon,\sigma} \times \mathbb{F}_{\varepsilon,\sigma} \to$ Bool
$\lvert\ldots\rvert, -$	fp.abs, fp.neg	$\mathbb{F}_{\varepsilon,\sigma} \to \mathbb{F}_{\varepsilon,\sigma}$
rem	fp.rem	$\mathbb{F}_{\varepsilon,\sigma} \times \mathbb{F}_{\varepsilon,\sigma} \to \mathbb{F}_{\varepsilon,\sigma}$
$\sqrt{\ }$, rti	fp.sqrt, fp.roundToIntegral	RM $\times\, \mathbb{F}_{\varepsilon,\sigma} \to \mathbb{F}_{\varepsilon,\sigma}$
$+, -, \cdot, \div$	fp.add, fp.sub, fp.mul, fp.div	RM $\times\, \mathbb{F}_{\varepsilon,\sigma} \times \mathbb{F}_{\varepsilon,\sigma} \to \mathbb{F}_{\varepsilon,\sigma}$
fma	fp.fma	RM $\times\, \mathbb{F}_{\varepsilon,\sigma} \times \mathbb{F}_{\varepsilon,\sigma} \times \mathbb{F}_{\varepsilon,\sigma} \to \mathbb{F}_{\varepsilon,\sigma}$

we succeeded (or failed) to establish an invertibility condition. Due to space restrictions, we omit the conditions for the remaining cases.[1]

Table 2. Invertibility conditions for floating-point operators (excl. fma) with $\approx$.

Literal	Invertibility condition
$x \overset{R}{+} s \approx t$	$t \approx (t \overset{RTP}{-} s) \overset{R}{+} s \vee t \approx (t \overset{RTN}{-} s) \overset{R}{+} s \vee s \approx t$
$x \overset{R}{-} s \approx t$	$t \approx (s \overset{RTP}{+} t) \overset{R}{-} s \vee t \approx (s \overset{RTN}{+} t) \overset{R}{-} s \vee (s \not\approx t \wedge s \approx \pm\infty \wedge t \approx \pm\infty)$
$s \overset{R}{-} x \approx t$	$t \approx s \overset{R}{+} (t \overset{RTP}{-} s) \vee t \approx s \overset{R}{+} (t \overset{RTN}{-} s) \vee s \approx t$
$x \overset{R}{\cdot} s \approx t$	$t \approx (t \overset{RTP}{\div} s) \overset{R}{\cdot} s \vee t \approx (t \overset{RTN}{\div} s) \overset{R}{\cdot} s \vee (s \approx \pm\infty \wedge t \approx \pm\infty) \vee (s \approx \pm 0 \wedge t \approx \pm 0)$
$x \overset{R}{\div} s \approx t$	$t \approx (s \overset{RTP}{\cdot} t) \overset{R}{\div} s \vee t \approx (s \overset{RTN}{\cdot} t) \overset{R}{\div} s \vee (s \approx \pm\infty \wedge t \approx \pm 0) \vee (t \approx \pm\infty \wedge s \approx \pm 0)$
$s \overset{R}{\div} x \approx t$	$t \approx s \overset{R}{\div} (s \overset{RTP}{\div} t) \vee t \approx s \overset{R}{\div} (s \overset{RTN}{\div} t) \vee (s \approx \pm\infty \wedge t \approx \pm\infty) \vee (s \approx \pm 0 \wedge t \approx \pm 0)$
$x \operatorname{rem} s \approx t$	$t \approx t \operatorname{rem} s$
$s \operatorname{rem} x \approx t$	?
$\sqrt[R]{x} \approx t$	$t \approx \sqrt[R]{(t \overset{RTP}{\cdot} t)} \vee t \approx \sqrt[R]{(t \overset{RTN}{\cdot} t)} \vee t \approx \pm 0$
$\lvert x \rvert \approx t$	$\neg \operatorname{isNeg}(t)$
$-x \approx t$	$\top$
$\overset{R}{\operatorname{rti}}(x) \approx t$	$t \approx \overset{R}{\operatorname{rti}}(t)$

Table 2 lists the invertibility conditions for equality with the operators $\{+, -, \cdot, \div, \operatorname{rem}, \sqrt{\ }, \lvert \ldots \rvert, -, \operatorname{rti}\}$, parameterized over a rounding mode R (one of RNE, RNA, RTP, RTN, or RTZ). Note that operators $\{+, \cdot\}$ and the multiplicative step of fma are commutative, and thus the invertibility conditions for both variants are identical.

Each of the first six invertibility conditions in this table follows a pattern. The first two disjuncts are instances of the literal to solve for, where a term involving rounding modes RTP and RTN is substituted for x. These disjuncts are then followed by disjuncts for handling special cases for infinity and zero. From the structure of these conditions, e.g., for $+$, we can derive the insight that if there is a solution for x in the equation $x \overset{R}{+} s \approx t$ and we are not in a corner case where $s = t$, then either $t \overset{RTP}{-} s$ or $t \overset{RTN}{-} s$ must be a solution. Based on extensive runs of our syntax-guided synthesis procedure, we believe this condition is close to having minimal term size. From this, we conclude that an efficient yet complete method for solving $x \overset{R}{+} s \approx t$ checks whether $t - s$ rounding towards positive or negative is a solution in the non-trivial case when s and t are disequal, and otherwise concludes that no solution exists. A similar insight can be derived for the other invertibility conditions of this form.

---

[1] Available at https://cvc4.cs.stanford.edu/papers/CAV2019-FP.

We found that t is a conditional inverse for the case of $\overset{R}{\mathrm{rti}}(x) \approx t$ and $x \operatorname{rem} s \approx t$, that is, substituting t for x is an invertibility condition. For the latter, we discovered an alternative invertibility condition:

$$|\overset{RTP}{t + t}| \leq |s| \vee |\overset{RTN}{t + t}| \leq |s| \vee \mathrm{ite}(t \approx \pm 0, s \not\approx \pm 0, t \not\approx \pm\infty) \tag{1}$$

In contrast to the condition from Table 2, this version does not involve rem. It follows that certain applications of floating-point remainder, including those whose first argument is an unconstrained variable, can be eliminated based on this equivalence. Interestingly, for $s \operatorname{rem} x \approx t$, we did not succeed in finding an invertibility condition. This case appears to not admit a concise solution; we discuss further details below.

Table 3 gives the invertibility conditions for $\geq$. Since these constraints admit more solutions, they typically have simpler invertibility conditions. In particular, with the exception of rem, all conditions only involve floating-point classifiers.

When considering literals with predicates, the invertibility conditions for cases involving $x + s$ and $s - x$ are identical for every predicate and rounding mode. This is due to the fact that $s - x$ is equivalent to $s + (-x)$, independent from the rounding mode. Thus, the negation of the inverse value of x for an equation involving $x + s$ is the inverse value of x for an equation involving $s - x$. Similarly, the invertibility conditions for $x \cdot s$ and $s \div x$ over predicates $\{<, \leq, >, \geq, \mathsf{isInf}, \mathsf{isNaN}, \mathsf{isNeg}, \mathsf{isZero}\}$ are identical for all rounding modes.

For all predicates except $\{\approx, \mathsf{isNorm}, \mathsf{isSub}\}$, the invertibility conditions for operators $\{+, -, \div, \cdot\}$ contain floating-point classifiers only. All of these conditions are also independent from the rounding mode. Similarly, for operator fma over predicates $\{\mathsf{isInf}, \mathsf{isNaN}, \mathsf{isNeg}, \mathsf{isPos}\}$, the invertibility conditions contain

Table 3. Invertibility conditions for floating-point operators (excl. fma) with $\geq$.

Literal	Invertibility condition
$x + s \overset{R}{\geq} t$	$(\mathsf{isPos}(s) \vee \mathrm{ite}(s \approx \pm\infty, (t \approx \pm\infty \wedge \mathsf{isNeg}(t)), \mathsf{isNeg}(s))) \wedge t \not\approx \mathsf{NaN}$
$x - s \overset{R}{\geq} t$	$\mathrm{ite}(\mathsf{isNeg}(s), t \not\approx \mathsf{NaN}, \mathrm{ite}(s \approx \pm\infty, (t \approx \pm\infty \wedge \mathsf{isNeg}(t)), (\mathsf{isPos}(s) \wedge t \not\approx \mathsf{NaN})))$
$s - x \overset{R}{\geq} t$	$(\mathsf{isPos}(s) \vee \mathrm{ite}(s \approx \pm\infty, (t \approx \pm\infty \wedge \mathsf{isNeg}(t)), \mathsf{isNeg}(s))) \wedge t \not\approx \mathsf{NaN}$
$x \cdot s \overset{R}{\geq} t$	$(\mathsf{isNeg}(t) \vee t \approx \pm 0 \vee s \not\approx \pm 0) \wedge s \not\approx \mathsf{NaN} \wedge t \not\approx \mathsf{NaN}$
$x \div s \overset{R}{\geq} t$	$(\mathsf{isNeg}(t) \vee t \approx \pm 0 \vee s \not\approx \pm\infty) \wedge s \not\approx \mathsf{NaN} \wedge t \not\approx \mathsf{NaN}$
$s \div x \overset{R}{\geq} t$	$(\mathsf{isNeg}(t) \vee t \approx \pm 0 \vee s \not\approx \pm 0) \wedge s \not\approx \mathsf{NaN} \wedge t \not\approx \mathsf{NaN}$
$x \operatorname{rem} s \geq t$	$\mathrm{ite}(\mathsf{isNeg}(t), s \not\approx \mathsf{NaN}, (|\overset{RNE}{t + t}| \leq |s| \wedge t \not\approx \pm\infty)) \wedge s \not\approx \pm 0$
$s \operatorname{rem} x \geq t$	?
$\sqrt[R]{x} \geq t$	$t \not\approx \mathsf{NaN}$
$|x| \geq t$	$t \not\approx \mathsf{NaN}$
$-x \geq t$	$t \not\approx \mathsf{NaN}$
$\overset{R}{\mathrm{rti}}(x) \geq t$	$t \not\approx \mathsf{NaN}$

only floating-point classifiers. All of these conditions except for $\mathsf{isNeg}(\mathsf{fma}(x, s, t))$ and $\mathsf{isPos}(\mathsf{fma}(x, s, t))$ are also independent from the rounding mode.

For all floating-point operators with predicate isNaN, the invertibility condition is $\top$, i.e., an inverse value for x always exists. This is due to the fact that every floating-point operator returns NaN if one of its operands is NaN, hence NaN can be picked as an inverse value of x. Conversely, we identified four cases for which the invertibility condition is $\bot$, i.e., an inverse value for x never exists. These four cases are $\mathsf{isNeg}(|x|)$, $\mathsf{isInf}(x \operatorname{rem} s)$, $\mathsf{isInf}(s \operatorname{rem} x)$, and $\mathsf{isSub}(\mathsf{rti}(x))$. For the first three cases, it is obvious why no inverse value exists. The intuition for $\mathsf{isSub}(\mathsf{rti}(x))$ is that integers are not subnormal, and as a result if x is rounded to an integer it can never be a subnormal number. All of these cases can be easily implemented as rewrite rules in an SMT solver.

For operator fma, the invertibility conditions over predicates $\{\mathsf{isInf}, \mathsf{isNaN}, \mathsf{isNeg}, \mathsf{isPos}\}$ contain floating-point classifiers only. For predicate isZero, the invertibility conditions are more involved. Equations (2) and (3) show the invertibility conditions for $\mathsf{isZero}(\mathsf{fma}(x, s, t))$ and $\mathsf{isZero}(\mathsf{fma}(s, t, x))$ for all rounding modes R.

$$\overset{R}{\mathsf{fma}}(-(t \overset{\mathsf{RTP}}{\div} s), s, t) \approx \pm 0 \vee \overset{R}{\mathsf{fma}}(-(t \overset{\mathsf{RTN}}{\div} s), s, t) \approx \pm 0 \vee (s \approx \pm 0 \wedge t \approx \pm 0) \quad (2)$$

$$\overset{R}{\mathsf{fma}}(s, t, -(s \overset{\mathsf{RTP}}{\cdot} t)) \approx \pm 0 \vee \overset{R}{\mathsf{fma}}(s, t, -(s \overset{\mathsf{RTN}}{\cdot} t)) \approx \pm 0 \quad (3)$$

These two invertibility conditions contain case splits similar to those in Table 2 and indicate that, e.g., $-t \overset{\mathsf{RTP}}{\div} s$ is an inverse value for x when $\overset{R}{\mathsf{fma}}(-(t \overset{\mathsf{RTP}}{\div} s), s, t) \approx \pm 0$ holds.

As we will describe in Sect. 4, an important aspect of synthesizing these invertibility conditions was considering their visualizations. This helped us determine which invertibility conditions were relatively simple and which exhibited complex behavior.

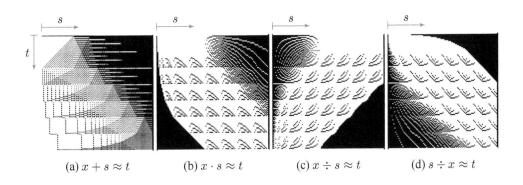

(a) $x + s \approx t$ (b) $x \cdot s \approx t$ (c) $x \div s \approx t$ (d) $s \div x \approx t$

Fig. 1. Invertibility conditions for $\{+, \cdot, \div\}$ over $\approx$ for $\mathbb{F}_{3,5}$ and rounding mode RNE.

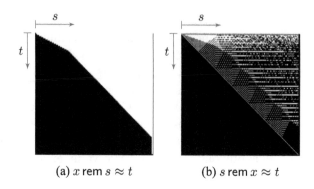

(a) $x \operatorname{rem} s \approx t$ (b) $s \operatorname{rem} x \approx t$

Fig. 2. Invertibility conditions for rem over $\approx$ for $\mathbb{F}_{3,5}$.

Figure 1 shows the visualizations of the invertibility conditions for operators $\{+, \cdot, \div\}$ over $\approx$ from Table 2 for sort $\mathbb{F}_{3,5}$ with rounding mode RNE (each of the literals is two-dimensional). We use 227×227 pixel maps over all possible values of s and t, where the pixel at point (s, t) is white if the invertibility condition is true, and black if it is false.[2] The values of s are plotted on the horizontal axis and the values of t are plotted on the vertical axis. The leftmost two columns (resp. topmost two rows) give the value of the invertibility condition for $s = \pm 0$ (resp. $t = \pm 0$); the rightmost column (resp. bottom row) gives its value for NaN; the next two columns left of (resp. next two rows on top of) NaN give its value for $\pm\infty$; the remainder plots the values of the subnormal and normal values of s and t, left-to-right (resp. top-to-bottom) in increasing order of their absolute value, alternating between positive and negative values. These visualizations give an intuition of the complexity of the behavior of invertibility conditions, which is a consequence of the complex semantics of floating-point operations.

Figure 2 gives the invertibility condition visualizations for remainder over $\approx$ with sort $\mathbb{F}_{3,5}$ and rounding mode RNE. The visualization on the left hand shows that solving for x as the first argument is relatively easy. It suggests that an invertibility condition for this case involves a linear inequality relating the absolute values of s and t, which we were able to derive in Eq. (1). Solving for x as the second argument, on the other hand, is much more difficult, as indicated by the right picture, which has a significantly more complex structure. We conjecture that no simple solution exists for the latter problem. The visualization of the invertibility condition gives some of the intuition for this: the diagonal divide is caused by the fact that output t will always have a smaller absolute value than the input s. The top-left corner represents subnormal/subnormal computation, this acts as fixed-point and behaves differently from the rest of the function. The stepped blocks along the diagonal occur when s and t have the same exponent and thus the pattern is similar to the invertibility condition for $+$ shown in Fig. 1. Portions right of the main diagonal appear to exhibit random behavior.

---

[2] Notice that we consider all possible $(2^{\sigma-1}-1)*2$ NaN values of T_{FP} as one single NaN value. Thus, for sort $\mathbb{F}_{3,5}$ we have 227 floating-point values (instead of $2^8 = 256$).

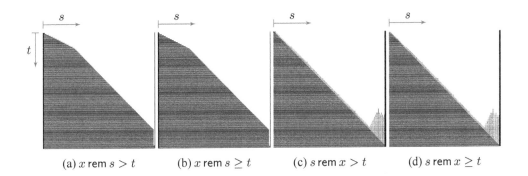

(a) x rem $s > t$ (b) x rem $s \geq t$ (c) s rem $x > t$ (d) s rem $x \geq t$

Fig. 3. Invertibility conditions for rem over inequalities for $\mathbb{F}_{3,5}$.

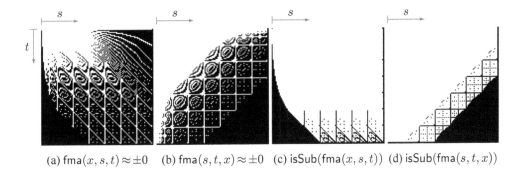

(a) fma$(x, s, t) \approx \pm 0$ (b) fma$(s, t, x) \approx \pm 0$ (c) isSub(fma(x, s, t))   (d) isSub(fma(s, t, x))

Fig. 4. Invertibility conditions for fma over {isZero, isSub} for $\mathbb{F}_{3,5}$ and rnd. mode RNE.

We believe this is the result of repeated cancellations in the computation of the remainder for those values, which suggests a behavior that we believe is similar to the Blum-Blum-Shub random number generator [9].

For remainder with inequalities, we succeeded in determining invertibility conditions for $\leq$ and $\geq$ if x is the first argument. However, for x rem s over $\{<, >\}$, and s rem x over $\{\geq, \leq, <, >\}$ we did not. This is particularly surprising considering that the invertibility conditions for non-strict and strict inequalities are nearly identical (varying only by a handful of pixels), as shown in Fig. 3. Note that for x as the first argument, all variations of the concise invertibility conditions for non-strict inequality we considered failed as solutions for the strict inequality. This behavior is representative of the many subtle corner cases we encountered while synthesizing these conditions.

Figure 4 shows visualizations for invertibility conditions involving fma. The left two images are visualizations for the invertibility conditions for isZero. The corresponding invertibility conditions are given in Eqs. (2) and (3) above. We were not able to determine invertibility conditions for operator fma over predicate isSub, which are visualized in the rightmost two pictures in Fig. 4. Finally, we did not succeed in finding invertibility conditions for fma with binary predicates, which are particularly challenging since they are three-dimensional. Finding solutions for these cases is ongoing work (see Sect. 4 for a more in-depth discussion).

4   Synthesis of Floating-Point Invertibility Conditions

Deriving invertibility conditions in T_{FP} is a highly challenging task. We were unable to derive these conditions manually despite our substantial background knowledge of floating-point numbers. As a consequence, we developed a custom extension of the syntax-guided synthesis (SyGuS) paradigm [1] with the goal of finding invertibility conditions automatically, which resulted in the conditions from Sect. 3. While the extension was optimized for this task, we stress that our techniques are theory-agnostic and can be used for synthesis problems over any finite domain. Our approach builds upon the SyGuS capabilities of the SMT solver CVC4 [5,29], which has recently been extended to support reasoning about the theory of floating-points [11]. We use the invertibility condition for floating-point addition with equality here as a running example.

Establishing an invertibility condition requires solving a synthesis problem with *three* levels of quantifier alternation. In particular, for floating-point addition with equality, we are interested in finding a solution for predicate IC that satisfies the conjecture:

$$\exists \mathsf{IC}. \forall s, t. (\mathsf{IC}(s, t) \Leftrightarrow (\exists x. x \overset{\mathsf{R}}{+} s \approx t)) \qquad (4)$$

for some rounding mode R. In other words, this conjecture states that $\mathsf{IC}(s,t)$ holds exactly when there exists an x that, when rounding the result of adding x to s according to mode R, yields t. Furthermore, we are interested in finding a solution for IC that holds *independently of the format* of x, s, t. Note that SMT solvers are not capable of reasoning about constraints that are parametric in the floating-point format. To address this challenge, following the methodology from previous work [26], our strategy for establishing (general) invertibility conditions first solves the synthesis conjecture for a fixed format $\mathbb{F}_{\varepsilon,\sigma}$, and subsequently checks whether that solution also holds for other formats. The choice of the number of exponent bits ε and significand bits σ in $\mathbb{F}_{\varepsilon,\sigma}$ balances two criteria:

1. ε, σ should be large enough to exercise many (or all) of the behaviors of the operators and relations in our synthesis conjecture,
2. ε, σ should be small enough for the synthesis problem to be tractable.

In our experience, the best choices for (ε, σ) depended on the particular invertibility condition we were solving. The most common choices for (ε, σ) were $(3,5)$, $(4,5)$ and $(4,6)$. For most two-dimensional invertibility conditions (those that involve two variables s and t), we used $(3,5)$, since the required synthesis procedures mentioned below were roughly eight times faster than for $(4,5)$. For one-dimensional invertibility conditions, we often used higher precision formats. Since floating-point operators like addition take as additional argument a rounding mode R, we assumed a fixed rounding mode when solving, and then cross-checked our solution for multiple rounding modes.

Assume we have chosen to synthesize the invertibility condition for conjecture (4) for format $\mathbb{F}_{3,5}$ and rounding mode RNE. Notice that current SyGuS solvers [2, 29] support only two levels of quantifier alternation. However, we can expand the innermost quantifier in this conjecture to obtain the conjecture:

$$\exists \text{IC. } \forall st. \, (\text{IC}(s,t) \Leftrightarrow (\bigvee_{i=0}^{226} i \stackrel{\text{RNE}}{+} s \approx t)) \tag{5}$$

where for simplicity of notation we use $i = 0, \dots, 226$ to denote the values of $\mathbb{F}_{3,5}$. This methodology was also used in Niemetz et al. [26], where invertibility conditions for bit-vector operators were synthesized for bit-width 4 by giving the conjecture of the above form to an off-the-shelf SyGuS solver. In contrast to that work, we found that the synthesis conjecture above is too challenging to be solved efficiently by current state-of-the-art enumerative SyGuS solvers. The reason for this is twofold. First, the smallest viable floating-point format is $3 + 5 = 8$ bits, which requires the body of (5) to have a significantly large number of disjuncts (227), which is more than ten times larger than the 16 disjuncts required when synthesizing 4-bit invertibility conditions for bit-vectors. Second, floating-point formulas are much harder to solve than bit-vector formulas, due to the complexity of their bit-blasted encodings. Thus, a significantly challenging satisfiability query must be solved *for each* candidate considered within the SyGuS solver.

To address the above challenges, we perform a more extreme preprocessing step on our synthesis conjecture, which computes the input/output behavior of the invertibility condition on all points in the domain of s and t. In other words, we rephrase our synthesis conjecture as:

$$\exists \text{IC. } \bigwedge_{i=0}^{226} \bigwedge_{j=0}^{226} (\text{IC}(i,j) \Leftrightarrow c_{i,j}) \tag{6}$$

where each $c_{i,j}$ is a Boolean constant (either $\top$ or $\bot$) determined by a quantifier-free satisfiability query. In particular, for each pair of floating-point values (i,j), constant $c_{i,j}$ is $\top$ if $x + i \approx j$ is satisfiable, and $\bot$ if it is unsatisfiable. In practice, we represent the above conjecture as a 227×227 table, which we call the *full I/O specification* of invertibility condition IC. In our experiments, computing this table for most two-dimensional invertibility conditions of sort $\mathbb{F}_{3,5}$ required 15 min (for $227 * 227 = 51,529$ quantifier-free queries), and 2 h for sort $\mathbb{F}_{4,5}$ (requiring $483 * 483 = 233,289$ queries). This process was accelerated by first applying random sampling over possible values of x to quickly test if a query was satisfiable. For some operators, notably remainder, this required significantly more time than for others (up to a factor of 2). Due to the high cost of this preprocessing step, we generated a database with the full I/O specifications for *all* invertibility conditions from Sect. 3 using a cluster of 50 nodes with Intel Xeon E5-2637 with 3.5 GHz and 32 GB memory, and then shared this database among multiple developers. Computing the full I/O specifications for $\mathbb{F}_{3,5}$, $\mathbb{F}_{4,5}$, and $\mathbb{F}_{4,6}$ required a total of 459 days of CPU time (6.1 for $\mathbb{F}_{3,5}$, 54.7 for $\mathbb{F}_{4,5}$, and

398.5 for $\mathbb{F}_{4,6}$). Despite the heavy cost of this step, it was crucial for accelerating our framework for synthesizing invertibility conditions, described next.

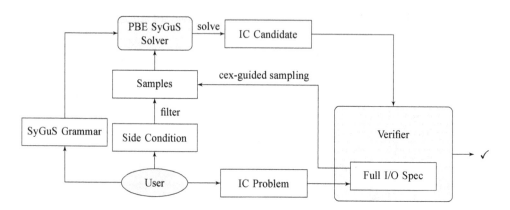

Fig. 5. Architecture for synthesizing invertibility conditions for floating point formulas.

Figure 5 summarizes our architecture for solving synthesis conjectures of the above form. The user first selects an invertibility condition problem to solve, where we assume the full I/O specification has been computed using the afore-mentioned techniques. At a high level, our architecture can be seen as an *inter-active synthesis environment*, where the user manages the interaction between two subprocedures:

1. a SyGuS solver with support for decision tree learning, and
2. a solution verifier storing the full I/O specification of the invertibility condition.

We use a counterexample-guided loop, where the SyGuS solver provides the solution verifier with candidate solutions, and the solution verifier provides the SyGuS solver with an evolving subset of sample points taken from the full I/O specification. These points correspond to counterexamples to failed candidate solutions, and are sampled in a uniformly random manner over the domain of our specification. To accelerate the speed at which our framework converges on a solution, we configure the solution verifier to generate multiple counterexample points (typically 10) for each iteration of the loop. The process terminates when the SyGuS solver generates a candidate solution that is correct for all points according to its full I/O specification.

We give the user control over both the solutions and counterexample points generated in this loop. First, as is commonly done in syntax-guided synthesis applications, the user in our workflow provides an input grammar to the SyGuS solver. This is a context-free grammar in a standard format [28], which contains a guess of the operators and patterns that may be involved in the invertibility condition we are synthesizing. Second, note that the domain of floating-point numbers can be subdivided into a number of subdomains and special cases (e.g. normal, subnormal, not-a-number, infinity), as well as split into different clas-sifications (e.g. positive and negative). Our workflow allows the user to provide a *side condition*, whose purpose is to focus on finding an invertibility condition that is correct for one of these subdomains. The side condition acts as a filtering mechanism on the counterexample points generated by the solution verifier. For example, given the side condition isNorm$(s) \wedge$ isNorm(t), the solution verifier checks candidate solutions generated by the SyGuS solver only against points (s, t) where both arguments are normal, and consequently only communicates counterexamples of this form to the SyGuS solver. The solution verifier may also be configured to establish that the current candidate solution generated by the SyGuS solver is *conditionally* correct, that is, it is true on all points in the domain that satisfy the side condition.

There are several advantages to the form of the synthesis conjecture in (6) that we exploit in our workflow. First, its structure makes it easy to divide the problem into sub-cases: our synthesis workflow at all times sends only a subset of the conjuncts of (6) for some (i, j) pairs. As a result, we do not burden the underlying SyGuS solver with the entire conjecture at once, which would not scale in practice. A second advantage is that it is in *programming-by-examples* (PBE) form, since it consists of a conjunction of concrete input-output pairs. As a consequence, specialized algorithms can be used by the SyGuS solver to generate solutions for (approximations of) our conjecture in a way that is highly scalable in practice. These techniques are broadly referred to as decision tree learning or unification algorithms. As a brief review (see Alur et al. [2] for a recent SyGuS-based approach), a decision tree learning algorithm is given as input a set of good examples $c_1 \mapsto \top, \ldots, c_n \mapsto \top$ and a set of bad examples $d_1 \mapsto \bot, \ldots, d_m \mapsto \bot$. The goal of a decision tree algorithm is to find a predicate, or *classifier*, that evaluates to true on all the good examples, and false on all the bad examples. In our context, a classifier is expressed as an if-then-else tree of Boolean sort. Sampling the space of conjecture (6) provides the decision tree algorithm with good and bad examples and the returned classifier is a candidate solution that we give to the solution verifier. The SyGuS solver of CVC4 uses a decision-tree learning algorithm, which we rely on in our workflow. Due to the scalability of this algorithm and the fact that only a small subset of our conjecture is considered at any given time, candidate solutions are typically generated by the SyGuS solver in our framework in a matter of seconds.

Another important aspect of the SyGuS solver in Fig. 5 is that it is configured to generate *multiple* solutions for the current set of sample points. Due to the way the SyGuS-based decision-tree learning algorithm works, these solutions tend to become *more general* over the runtime of the solver. As a simple example (assuming exact integer arithmetic), say the solver is given input points $(1, 1) \mapsto \top, (2, 0) \mapsto \top, (1, 0) \mapsto \bot$ and $(0, 1) \mapsto \bot$ for (s, t). It enumerates predicates over s and t, starting with simplest predicates first, say $s \approx 0$, $t \approx 0$, $s \approx 1$, $y \approx 1$, $s + t > 1$, and so on. After generating the first four predicates, it constructs the solution ite$(s \approx 1, t \approx 1, t \approx 0)$, which is a correct classifier for the given set of points. However, after generating the fifth predicate in this list, it returns $s + t > 1$ itself as a solution; this can be seen as a generalization of the previous solution since it requires no case splitting.

Since more general candidate solutions have a higher likelihood of being actual solutions in our experience, our workflow critically relies on the ability of users to manually terminate the synthesis procedure when they are satisfied with the last generated candidate. Our synthesis procedure logs a list of candidate solutions that satisfy the conjecture on the current set of sample points. When the user terminates the synthesis process, the solution verifier will check the last solution generated in this list. Users have the option to rearrange the elements of this list by hand, if they have an intuition that a specific candidate is more likely to be correct—and so should be tested first.

Experience. The first challenging invertibility condition we solved with our framework was addition with equality for rounding mode RNE. Initially, we used a generic grammar that contained the entire floating-point signature. As a first key step towards solving this problem, the synthesis procedure suggested the single literal $t \approx s \overset{\text{RNE}}{+} (t \overset{\text{RNE}}{-} s)$ as candidate solution. Although counterexamples were found for this candidate, we noticed that it satisfied over 98% of the specification, and a visualization of its I/O behavior showed similar patterns to the invertibility condition we were solving for. Based on these observations, we focused our grammar towards literals of this form. In particular, we used a function that takes two floating-points x, y and two rounding modes R_1, R_2 as arguments and returns $x \overset{R_1}{+} (y \overset{R_2}{-} x)$ as a builtin symbol of our grammar. We refer to such a function as a *residual* computation of y, noting that its value is often approximately y. By including various functions for residual computations, we focused the effort of the synthesizer on more interesting predicates. The end solution involved multiple residual computations, as shown in Table 2. Our initial solution was specific to the rounding mode RNE. After solving for several other rounding modes, we were able to construct a parametric solution that was correct for all rounding modes. In total, it took roughly three days of developer time to discover the generalized invertibility condition for addition with equality. Many of the subsequent invertibility conditions took a matter of hours, since by then we had a good intuition for the residual computations that were relevant for each case.

Invertibility conditions involving rem, fma, isNorm, and isSub were challenging and required further customizations to the grammar, for instance to include constants that corresponded to the minimum and maximum normal and subnormal values. Three-dimensional invertibility conditions (which in this work is limited to cases of fma with binary predicates) were especially challenging since the domain of their conjecture is a factor of 227 larger for $\mathbb{F}_{3,5}$ than the others. Following our strategy for solving the invertibility conditions for specific formats and rounding modes, in ongoing work we are investigating solving these cases by first solving the invertibility condition for a fixed value c for one of its free variables u. Solving a two-dimensional problem of this form with a solution φ may suggest a generalization that works for all values of u where all occurrences of c in φ are replaced by u.

We found the side condition feature of our workflow important for narrowing down which subdomain was the most challenging for the conjecture in question.

For instance, for some cases it was very easy to find invertibility conditions that held when both s and t were normal (resp., subnormal), but very difficult when s was normal and t was subnormal or vice versa.

We also implemented a fully automated mode for the synthesis loop in Fig. 5. However, in practice, it was more effective to tweak the generated solutions manually. The amount of user interaction was not prohibitively high in our experience.

Finally, we found that it was often helpful to visualize the input/output behavior of candidate solutions. In many cases, the difference between a candidate solution and the desired behavior of the invertibility condition would reveal a required modification to the grammar or would suggest which parts of the domain of the conjecture to focus on.

4.1 Verifying Conditions for Multiple Formats and Rounding Modes

We verified the correctness of all 167 invertibility conditions by checking them against their corresponding full I/O specification for floating-point formats $\mathbb{F}_{3,5}$, $\mathbb{F}_{4,5}$, and $\mathbb{F}_{4,6}$ and all rounding modes, which required 1.6 days of CPU time. This is relatively cheap compared to computing the specifications, since checking is essentially constant evaluation of invertibility conditions for all possible input values. However, this quickly becomes infeasible with increasing precision, since the time required for computing the I/O specification roughly increases by a factor of 8 for each bit.

As a consequence, we generated quantified floating-point problems to verify the 167 invertibility conditions for formats $\mathbb{F}_{3,5}$, $\mathbb{F}_{4,5}$, $\mathbb{F}_{4,6}$, $\mathbb{F}_{5,11}$ (Float16), $\mathbb{F}_{8,24}$ (Float32), and $\mathbb{F}_{11,53}$ (Float64) and all rounding modes. Each problem checks the T_{FP}-unsatisfiability of formula $\neg(\phi_c \Leftrightarrow \exists x. l[x])$, where $l[x]$ corresponds to the floating-point literal, and ϕ_c to its invertibility condition. In total, we generated

---

$\mathsf{QE_{FP}}(\exists x. P(t_1, \ldots, t_j[x], \ldots, t_n))$, where $x \notin FV(t_i)$ for $i \neq j$:

If $t_j[x] = x$, return $\mathsf{getIC}(x, P)$.
Otherwise, $t_j[x] = \diamond(s_1, \ldots, s_k[x], \ldots s_m)$ where $m > 0$, $x \notin FV(s_i)$ for $i \neq k$.
Let $Q[y] = P(t_1, \ldots, t_{j-1}, \diamond(s_1, \ldots, s_{k-1}, y, s_{k+1}, \ldots, s_m), t_{j+1}, \ldots, t_n)$ where y is a fresh variable.
Return $\mathsf{getIC}(y, Q[y]) \wedge \mathsf{QE_{FP}}(\exists x. s_k[x] \approx y)$.

Fig. 6. Recursive procedure $\mathsf{QE_{FP}}$ for computing quantifier elimination for x in the unit linear formula $\exists x. P(t_1, \ldots, t_j[x], \ldots, t_n)$. The free variables in this formula and the fresh variable y are implicitly universally quantified. Placeholder $\diamond$ denotes a floating-point operator from Table 1.

3786 problems ($116 * 5 + 51^3$ for each floating-point format) and checked them using CVC4 [5] (master 546bf686) and Z3 [16] (version 4.8.4).

We consider an invertibility condition to be verified for a floating-point format and rounding mode if at least one solver reports unsatisfiable. Given a CPU time limit of one hour and a memory limit of 8 GB for each solver/benchmark pair, we were able to verify 3577 (94.5%) invertibility conditions overall, with 99.2% of $\mathbb{F}_{3,5}$, 99.7% of $\mathbb{F}_{4,5}$, 100% of $\mathbb{F}_{4,6}$, 93.8% of $\mathbb{F}_{5,11}$, 90.2% of $\mathbb{F}_{8,24}$, and 84% of $\mathbb{F}_{11,53}$. This verification with CVC4 and Z3 required a total of 32 days of CPU time. All verification jobs were run on cluster nodes with Intel Xeon E5-2637 3.5 GHz and 32 GB memory.

5   Quantifier Elimination for Unit Linear Floating-Point Formulas

Based on the invertibility conditions presented in Sect. 3, we can define a quantifier elimination procedure for a restricted fragment of floating-point formulas. The procedure applies to *unit linear* formulas, that is, formulas of the form $\exists x.\, P[x]$ where P is a Σ_{FP}-literal containing exactly one occurrence of x.

Figure 6 gives a quantifier elimination procedure $\mathsf{QE_{FP}}$ for unit linear floating-point formulas $\exists x.\, P[x]$. We write $\mathsf{getIC}(y, Q[y])$ to indicate the invertibility condition for y in $Q[y]$, which amounts to a table lookup for the appropriate condition as given in Sect. 3. Note that our procedure is currently a partial function because we do not have yet invertibility conditions for some unit linear formulas. The recursive procedure returns a conjunction of conditions based on the path on which x occurs in P. If x occurs beneath multiple nested function applications, a fresh variable y is introduced and used for referencing the intermediate result of the subterm we are currently solving for. We demonstrate this in the following example.

Example 2. Consider the unit linear formula $\exists x.\, (x \mathbin{\overset{R}{\cdot}} u) \mathbin{\overset{R}{+}} s \geq t$. Invoking the procedure $\mathsf{QE_{FP}}$ on this input yields, after two recursive calls, the conjunction

$$\mathsf{getIC}(y_1, y_1 \mathbin{\overset{R}{+}} s \geq t) \wedge \mathsf{getIC}(y_2, y_2 \mathbin{\overset{R}{\cdot}} u \approx y_1) \wedge \mathsf{getIC}(x, x \approx y_2)$$

where y_1 and y_2 are fresh variables. The third conjunct is trivially equivalent to $\top$. This formula is quantifier-free and has the properties specified by the following theorem.

Theorem 1. *Let $\exists x.\, P$ be a unit linear formula and let $\mathcal{I}$ be a model of T_{FP}. Then, $\mathcal{I}$ satifies $\neg \exists x.\, P$ if and only if there exists a model $\mathcal{J}$ of T_{FP} (constructible from $\mathcal{I}$) that satisfies $\neg \mathsf{QE_{FP}}(\exists x.\, P)$.*

---

[3] 116 invertibility conditions from rounding mode dependent operators and 51 invertibility conditions where the operator is rounding mode independent (e.g., rem).

Niemetz et al. [26] present a similar algorithm for solving unit linear bit-vector literals. In that work, a counterexample-guided loop was devised that made use of Hilbert-choice expressions for representing quantifier instantiations. In contrast to that work, we provide here only a quantifier elimination procedure. Extending our techniques to a general quantifier instantiation strategy is the subject of ongoing work. We discuss our preliminary work in this direction in the next section.

6 Solving Quantified Floating-Point Formulas

We implemented a prototype extension of the SMT solver CVC4 that leverages the results of the previous section to determine the satisfiability of quantified floating-point formulas. To handle quantified formulas, CVC4 uses a basic model-based instantiation loop (see, e.g., [30,32] for instantiation approaches for other theories). This technique maintains a quantifier-free set of constraints F corresponding to instantiations of universally quantified formulas. It terminates with the response "unsatisfiable" if F is unsatisfiable, and terminates with "satisfiable" if it can show that the given quantified formulas are satisfied by a model of T_{FP} that satisfies F. For T_{FP}, the instantiations are substitutions of universally quantified variables to concrete floating-point values, e.g. $\forall x.\, P(x) \Rightarrow P(0)$, which can be highly inefficient in the worst case for higher precision.

We extend this basic loop with a preprocessing pass that generates theory lemmas based on the invertibility conditions corresponding to literals of quantified formulas $\forall x.P$ with exactly one occurrence of x, as explained in the example below.

Example 3. Suppose the current set S of formulas contains a formula φ of the form $\forall x.\, \neg((x \cdot u) + s \geq t \wedge Q(x))$ where u, s and t are ground terms; then we add the following formula to S where y_1 and y_2 are fresh (free) variables:

$$(\mathsf{getIC}(y_1, y_1 + s \geq t) \Rightarrow y_1 + s \geq t) \wedge (\mathsf{getIC}(y_2, y_2 \cdot u \approx y_1) \Rightarrow y_2 \cdot u \approx y_1)$$

The addition of this lemma is satisfiability preserving because, if the invertibility condition holds for $y_1 + s \geq t$ (resp., $y_2 \cdot u \approx y_1$), then y_1 (resp., y_2) a solution for that literal. We then add the instantiation lemma $\varphi \Rightarrow \neg((y_2 \cdot u) + s \geq t \wedge Q(y_2))$. Although x is not necessarily linear in the body of φ, if both invertibility conditions hold, then the combination of the above lemmas implies $(y_2 \cdot u) + s \geq t$, which together with the instantiation lemma allows the solver to infer that the remaining portion of the quantified formula Q cannot hold for y_2. An inference of this form may be more productive than enumerating the possible values of x in instantiations.

Evaluation. We considered all 61 benchmarks from SMT-LIB [6] that contained quantified formulas over floating-points (logic FP), which correspond to verification conditions from the software verification competition that use a floating-point encoding [19]. The invertibility conditions required for solving their literals include floating-point addition, multiplication and division (both arguments) with equality and inequality. We implemented all cases of invertibility conditions for solving these cases. We extended our SMT solver CVC4 (GitHub master 5d248c36) with the above preprocessing pass (GitHub cav19fp 9b5acd74), and compared its performance with (configuration CVC4-ext) and without (configuration CVC4-base) the above preprocessing pass enabled to the SMT solver Z3 (version 4.8.4). All experiments were run on the same cluster mentioned earlier, with a memory limit of 8 GB and a 1800 s time limit. Overall, CVC4-base solved 35 benchmarks within the time limit (with no benchmarks uniquely solved compared to CVC4-ext), CVC4-ext solved 42 benchmarks (7 of these uniquely solved compared to the base version), and Z3 solved 56 benchmarks. While CVC4-ext solves significantly fewer benchmarks than Z3, we believe that the improvement over CVC4-base is indicative that our approach for invertibility conditions shows potential for solving quantified floating-point constraints in SMT solvers. A more comprehensive evaluation and implementation is left as future work.

7   Conclusion

We have presented invertibility conditions for a large subset of combinations of floating-point operators over floating-point predicates supported by SMT solvers. These conditions were found by a framework that utilizes syntax-guided synthesis solving, customized for our problem and developed over the course of this work. We have shown that invertibility conditions imply that a simple fragment of quantified floating-points admits compact quantifier elimination, and have given preliminary evidence that an SMT solver that partially leverages this technique can have a higher success rate on floating-point problems coming from a software verification application.

For future work, we plan to extend techniques for quantified and quantifier-free floating-point formulas to incorporate our findings, in particular to lift previous quantifier instantiation approaches (e.g., [26]) and local search procedures (e.g., [25]) for bit-vectors to floating-points. We also plan to extend and use our synthesis framework for related challenging synthesis tasks, such as finding conditions under which more complex constraints have solutions, including those having multiple occurrences of a variable to solve for. Our synthesis framework is agnostic to theories and can be used for any sort with a small finite domain. It can thus be leveraged also for solutions to quantified bit-vector constraints. Finally, we would like to establish formal proofs of correctness of our invertibility conditions that are independent of floating-point formats.

References

1. Alur, R., et al.: Syntax-guided synthesis. In: Formal Methods in Computer-Aided Design, FMCAD 2013, Portland, 20–23 October 2013, pp. 1–8. IEEE (2013). http://ieeexplore.ieee.org/document/6679385/

2. Alur, R., Radhakrishna, A., Udupa, A.: Scaling enumerative program synthesis via divide and conquer. In: Legay, A., Margaria, T. (eds.) TACAS 2017. LNCS, vol. 10205, pp. 319–336. Springer, Heidelberg (2017). https://doi.org/10.1007/978-3-662-54577-5_18
3. IEEE Standards Association 754-2008 - IEEE standard for floating-point arithmetic (2008). https://ieeexplore.ieee.org/servlet/opac?punumber=4610933
4. Barr, E.T., Vo, T., Le, V., Su, Z.: Automatic detection of floating-point exceptions. SIGPLAN Not. **48**(1), 549–560 (2013)
5. Barrett, C., et al.: CVC4. In: Gopalakrishnan, G., Qadeer, S. (eds.) CAV 2011. LNCS, vol. 6806, pp. 171–177. Springer, Heidelberg (2011). https://doi.org/10.1007/978-3-642-22110-1_14
6. Barrett, C., Stump, A., Tinelli, C.: The satisfiability modulo theories library (SMT-LIB) (2010). www.SMT-LIB.org
7. Ben Khadra, M.A., Stoffel, D., Kunz, W.: goSAT: floating-point satisfiability as global optimization. In: FMCAD, pp. 11–14. IEEE (2017)
8. Bjørner, N., Janota, M.: Playing with quantified satisfaction. In: 20th International Conferences on Logic for Programming, Artificial Intelligence and Reasoning - Short Presentations, LPAR 2015, Suva, 24–28 November 2015, pp. 15–27 (2015)
9. Blum, L., Blum, M., Shub, M.: A simple unpredictable pseudo-random number generator. SIAM J. Comput. **15**(2), 364–383 (1986)
10. Brain, M., Dsilva, V., Griggio, A., Haller, L., Kroening, D.: Deciding floating-point logic with abstract conflict driven clause learning. Formal Methods Syst. Des. **45**(2), 213–245 (2014)
11. Brain, M., Schanda, F., Sun, Y.: Building better bit-blasting for floating-point problems. In: Vojnar, T., Zhang, L. (eds.) TACAS 2019, Part I. LNCS, vol. 11427, pp. 79–98. Springer, Cham (2019). https://doi.org/10.1007/978-3-030-17462-0_5
12. Brain, M., Tinelli, C., Rümmer, P., Wahl, T.: An automatable formal semantics for IEEE-754 floating-point arithmetic. In: 22nd IEEE Symposium on Computer Arithmetic, ARITH 2015, Lyon, 22–24 June 2015, pp. 160–167. IEEE (2015)
13. Brillout, A., Kroening, D., Wahl, T.: Mixed abstractions for floating-point arithmetic. In: FMCAD, pp. 69–76. IEEE (2009)
14. Conchon, S., Iguernlala, M., Ji, K., Melquiond, G., Fumex, C.: A three-tier strategy for reasoning about floating-point numbers in SMT. In: Majumdar, R., Kunčak, V. (eds.) CAV 2017. LNCS, vol. 10427, pp. 419–435. Springer, Cham (2017). https://doi.org/10.1007/978-3-319-63390-9_22
15. Daumas, M., Melquiond, G.: Certification of bounds on expressions involving rounded operators. ACM Trans. Math. Softw. **37**(1), 1–20 (2010)
16. De Moura, L., Bjørner, N.: Z3: an efficient SMT solver. In: Ramakrishnan, C.R., Rehof, J. (eds.) TACAS 2008. LNCS, vol. 4963, pp. 337–340. Springer, Heidelberg (2008). https://doi.org/10.1007/978-3-540-78800-3_24
17. Dutertre, B.: Solving exists/forall problems in yices. In: Workshop on Satisfiability Modulo Theories (2015)
18. Fu, Z., Su, Z.: XSat: a fast floating-point satisfiability solver. In: Chaudhuri, S., Farzan, A. (eds.) CAV 2016. LNCS, vol. 9780, pp. 187–209. Springer, Cham (2016). https://doi.org/10.1007/978-3-319-41540-6_11
19. Heizmann, M., et al.: Ultimate automizer with an on-demand construction of Floyd-Hoare automata. In: Legay, A., Margaria, T. (eds.) TACAS 2017, Part II. LNCS, vol. 10206, pp. 394–398. Springer, Heidelberg (2017). https://doi.org/10.1007/978-3-662-54580-5_30
20. Lapschies, F.: SONOLAR, the solver for non-linear arithmetic (2014). http://www.informatik.uni-bremen.de/agbs/florian/sonolar

21. Liew, D.: JFS: JIT fuzzing solver. https://github.com/delcypher/jfs
22. Marre, B., Bobot, F., Chihani, Z.: Real behavior of floating point numbers. In: SMT Workshop (2017)
23. Michel, C., Rueher, M., Lebbah, Y.: Solving constraints over floating-point numbers. In: Walsh, T. (ed.) CP 2001. LNCS, vol. 2239, pp. 524–538. Springer, Heidelberg (2001). https://doi.org/10.1007/3-540-45578-7_36
24. de Moura, L., Bjørner, N.: Efficient e-matching for SMT solvers. In: Pfenning, F. (ed.) CADE 2007. LNCS, vol. 4603, pp. 183–198. Springer, Heidelberg (2007). https://doi.org/10.1007/978-3-540-73595-3_13
25. Niemetz, A., Preiner, M., Biere, A.: Precise and complete propagation based local search for satisfiability modulo theories. In: Chaudhuri, S., Farzan, A. (eds.) CAV 2016, Part I. LNCS, vol. 9779, pp. 199–217. Springer, Cham (2016). https://doi.org/10.1007/978-3-319-41528-4_11
26. Niemetz, A., Preiner, M., Reynolds, A., Barrett, C., Tinelli, C.: Solving quantified bit-vectors using invertibility conditions. In: Chockler, H., Weissenbacher, G. (eds.) CAV 2018, Part II. LNCS, vol. 10982, pp. 236–255. Springer, Cham (2018). https://doi.org/10.1007/978-3-319-96142-2_16
27. Preiner, M., Niemetz, A., Biere, A.: Counterexample-guided model synthesis. In: Legay, A., Margaria, T. (eds.) TACAS 2017, Part I. LNCS, vol. 10205, pp. 264–280. Springer, Heidelberg (2017). https://doi.org/10.1007/978-3-662-54577-5_15
28. Raghothaman, M., Udupa, A.: Language to specify syntax-guided synthesis problems, May 2014
29. Reynolds, A., Deters, M., Kuncak, V., Tinelli, C., Barrett, C.: Counterexample-guided quantifier instantiation for synthesis in SMT. In: Kroening, D., Păsăreanu, C.S. (eds.) CAV 2015, Part II. LNCS, vol. 9207, pp. 198–216. Springer, Cham (2015). https://doi.org/10.1007/978-3-319-21668-3_12
30. Reynolds, A., King, T., Kuncak, V.: Solving quantified linear arithmetic by counterexample-guided instantiation. Formal Methods Syst. Des. **51**(3), 500–532 (2017)
31. Scheibler, K., Kupferschmid, S., Becker, B.: Recent improvements in the SMT solver iSAT. MBMV **13**, 231–241 (2013)
32. Wintersteiger, C.M., Hamadi, Y., de Moura, L.M.: Efficiently solving quantified bit-vector formulas. Formal Methods Syst. Des. **42**(1), 3–23 (2013)
33. Zeljić, A., Wintersteiger, C.M., Rümmer, P.: Approximations for model construction. In: Demri, S., Kapur, D., Weidenbach, C. (eds.) IJCAR 2014. LNCS (LNAI), vol. 8562, pp. 344–359. Springer, Cham (2014). https://doi.org/10.1007/978-3-319-08587-6_26

4

Reachability Analysis for AWS-Based Networks

John Backes[1], Sam Bayless[1,4], Byron Cook[1,2], Catherine Dodge[1],
Andrew Gacek[1(✉)], Alan J. Hu[4], Temesghen Kahsai[1], Bill Kocik[1],
Evgenii Kotelnikov[1,3], Jure Kukovec[1,5], Sean McLaughlin[1], Jason Reed[6],
Neha Rungta[1], John Sizemore[1], Mark Stalzer[1], Preethi Srinivasan[1],
Pavle Subotić[1,2], Carsten Varming[1], and Blake Whaley[1]

[1] Amazon, Seattle, USA
gacek@amazon.com
[2] University College London, London, UK
[3] Chalmers University of Technology, Gothenburg, Sweden
[4] University British Columbia, Vancouver, Canada
[5] TU Wien, Vienna, Austria
[6] Semmle Inc, San Francisco, USA

Abstract. Cloud services provide the ability to provision virtual networked infrastructure on demand over the Internet. The rapid growth of these virtually provisioned cloud networks has increased the demand for automated reasoning tools capable of identifying misconfigurations or security vulnerabilities. This type of automation gives customers the assurance they need to deploy sensitive workloads. It can also reduce the cost and time-to-market for regulated customers looking to establish compliance certification for cloud-based applications. In this industrial case-study, we describe a new network reachability reasoning tool, called TIROS, that uses off-the-shelf automated theorem proving tools to fill this need. TIROS is the foundation of a recently introduced network security analysis feature in the *Amazon Inspector* service now available to millions of customers building applications in the cloud. TIROS is also used within Amazon Web Services (AWS) to automate the checking of compliance certification and adherence to security invariants for many AWS services that build on existing AWS networking features.

1 Introduction

Cloud computing provides on-demand access to IT resources such as compute, storage, and analytics via the Internet with pay-as-you-go pricing. Each of these IT resources are typically networked together by customers, using a growing number of virtual networking features. Amazon Web Services (AWS), for example, today provides over 30 virtualized networking primitives that allow customers to implement a wide variety of cloud-based applications.

Correctly configured networks are a key part of an organization's security posture. Clearly documented and, more importantly, verifiable network design is important for compliance audits, *e.g.* the Payment Card Industry Data Security Standard (PCI DSS) [10]. As the scale and diversity of cloud-based services grows, each new offering used by an organization adds another dimension of possible interaction at the networking level. Thus, customers and auditors increasingly need tooling for the security of their networks that is accurate, automated and scalable, allowing them to automatically detect violations of their requirements.

In this industrial case-study, we describe a new tool, called TIROS, which uses off-the-shelf automated theorem proving tools to perform formal analysis of virtual networks constructed using AWS APIs. TIROS encodes the semantics of AWS networking concepts into logic and then uses a variety of reasoning engines to verify security-related properties. Tools that TIROS can use include SOUFFLÉ [17], MONOSAT [3], and VAMPIRE [23]. TIROS performs its analysis statically: it sends no packets on the customer's network. This distinction is important. The size of many customer networks makes it intractable to find problems through traditional network probing or penetration testing. TIROS allows users to gain assurance about the security of their networks that would be impossible through testing.

TIROS is used directly today by AWS customers as part of the Amazon Inspector service [11], which currently checks six TIROS-based network reachability invariants on customer networks. The use of TIROS is especially popular amongst security-obsessed customers, *e.g.,* the world's largest hedge fund Bridgewater Associates, an AWS customer, recently discussed the importance of network verification techniques for their organization [6], including their usage of TIROS.

Related Work. Several previous tools using automated theorem proving have been developed in an effort to answer questions about software defined networks (SDNs) [1,2,5,12,13,16,19,25]. Similar to our approach, these tools reduce the problems to automated reasoning engines. In some cases, they employ over-approximative static analysis [18,19]. In other cases, they use general purpose reasoning engines such as Datalog [12,15], BDD [1], SMT [5,16], and SAT Solvers [2,25]. VeriCon [2], NICE [8], and VeriFlow [19] verify network invariants by analyzing software-defined-network (SDN) programs, with the former two applying formal software verification techniques, and the latter using static analysis to split routes into equivalence classes. SecGuru [5,16] uses an SMT solver to compare the routes admitted by access control lists (ACLs), routing tables, and border gateway protocol (BGP) policies, but does not support full-network reachability queries. In our approach we employ multiple encodings and reasoning engines. Our SMT encoding is similar in design to Anteater [25] and ConfigChecker [1]. Anteater performs SAT-based bounded model checking [4], while ConfigChecker uses BDD-based fixed-point model checking [7]. Previous work has applied Datalog to reachability analysis in either software or network contexts [12–14,24]. The approach used in Batfish [13,24] and SyNET [12] is similar to our Datalog approach; they allow users to express general queries about whole-network reachability properties using an expressive logic language.

Batfish presents results for small but complex routing scenarios, involving a few dozen routers. SyNET [12] also uses a similar Datalog representation of network reachability semantics, but rather than verifying network reachability properties, they provide techniques to synthesize networks from a specification. The focus in TIROS's encoding is expressiveness and completeness; it encodes the semantics of the entire AWS cloud network service stack. It scales well to networks consisting of hundreds of thousands of instances, routers, and firewall rules.

2   AWS Networking

AWS provides customers with virtualized implementations of practically all known traditional networking concepts, *e.g.* subnets, route tables, and NAT gateways. In order to facilitate on-demand scalability, many AWS network features focus on elasticity, *e.g.* Elastic Load Balancers (ELBs) support autoscaling groups, which customers configure to describe when/how to scale resource usage. Another important AWS networking concept is that of Virtual Private Cloud (VPC), in which customers can use AWS resources in an isolated virtual network that they control. Over 30 additional networking concepts are supported by AWS, including Elastic Network Interfaces (ENIs), internet gateways, transit gateways, direct connections, and peering connections.

Figure 1 is an example AWS-based network that consists of two subnets "Web" and "Database". The "Web" subnet contains two instances (sometimes called virtual machines) and the "Database" subnet contains one instance. Note that these machines are in fact virtualized in the AWS data center. The "Web" subnet's route table has a route to the internet gateway, whereas the "Database" subnet's route table only has local routes (within the VPC). In addition, each of the subnets has an ACL that contains security access rules. In particular, one of the rules forbids SSH access to the database servers.

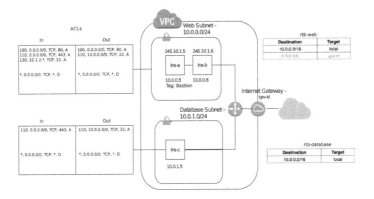

Fig. 1. An example VPC network

AWS-based networks frequently start small and grow over time, accumulating new instances and security and access rules. Customers or regulators want to make sure that their VPC networks retain security invariants as their complexity grows. A customer may ask *network configuration questions* such as:

1. *"Are there any instances in subnet 'Web' that are tagged 'Bastion'?"* or *network reachability questions* such as:
2. *"Are there any instances that can be accessed from the public internet over SSH (TCP port 22)?"*

To answer such questions we must reason about which network components are accessible via feasible paths through the VPC, either from the internet, from other components in the VPC, or from other components in a different VPC via a peering connection or transit gateway.

3   AWS Networking Semantics as Logic

TIROS statically builds a model of an AWS network architecture to check reachability properties. The model of the network consists of two parts, the *formal specification* and the *snapshot* of the network. The specification formalizes the semantics of the AWS networking components, *e.g.*, how a route table directs traffic from a subnet, in which order a firewall applies rules in a security group, and how load balancers route traffic. The snapshot describes the topology and details of the network. For example, the snapshot contains the list of instances, subnets, and their route tables in a particular VPC (or set of VPCs). To answer reachability questions, TIROS combines the formal specification, the snapshot, and a query into a formula that represents the answer. Tiros uses up to three reasoning engines to answer queries: the Datalog solver SOUFFLÉ [17], the SMT solver MONOSAT [3], or the first-order theorem prover VAMPIRE [23]. Due to the differing limitations and capabilities of each of these tools, we maintain three independent encodings of network semantics into logic, one for each of solver.

Datalog Encoding. In the Datalog encoding, a network model is a set of Datalog clauses (stratified, possibly recursive or negated Horn clauses without function symbols) using the theory of bit vectors to describe ports, IPv4 addresses, and subnet masks. The *specification* part of the network model contains types, predicates, constants, and rules that describe the semantics of the networking components in Amazon VPCs. The specification of Amazon VPC networks maps to approximately 50 types, 200 predicates, and over 240 rules. For example, a specification of the semantics of SSH tunneling is defined recursively: An instance can SSH tunnel to another instance iff it can either SSH to it directly, or through a chain of intermediate instances. We express this with predicates *canSshTunnel* and *canSsh*, of the type Instance × Instance, and rules:

$$canSshTunnel(I_1, I_2) \leftarrow canSsh(I_1, I_2).$$
$$canSshTunnel(I_1, I_2) \leftarrow canSshTunnel(I_1, I_3) \wedge canSshTunnel(I_3, I_2).$$

The *snapshot* part of the network model contains constants and *facts* (ground clauses with no antecedents) that describe the configuration of a specific AWS network. Constants have the form type$_{id}$. For example, the snapshot of a network with an instance with id 1234 in a subnet with id web consists of the constants instance$_{1234}$ and subnet$_{web}$, and the fact $hasSubnet$(instance$_{1234}$, subnet$_{web}$).

We illustrate the Datalog encoding using examples from Sect. 2. The network configuration question, $q(I)$, is encoded as $q(I) \leftarrow hasSubnet(I, \text{subnet}_{web}) \wedge hasTag(I, \text{tag}_{bastion})$. The network reachability question, $r(I, E)$, is encoded as:

$$r(I, E) \leftarrow hasEni(I, E) \wedge isPublicIP(Address) \wedge$$
$$reachPublicTcpUdp(\text{dir}_{ingress}, \text{proto}_6, E, \text{port}_{22}, Adress, \text{port}_{40000}).$$

In our Datalog encoding, we use the theory of bitvectors to reason about ports, IP addresses, and CIDRs. We use SOUFFLÉ as our Datalog solver, but in principle other Datalog solvers could also be used, so long as they also support bitvectors. We direct the reader to our co-author's dissertation (cf. Chapter 7 [28]) for a more detailed explanation of the Datalog encoding.

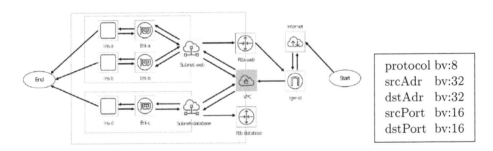

Fig. 2. (Left) The symbolic graph corresponding to the VPC in Fig. 1. (Right) A simplified symbolic packet, composed of bitvectors.

SMT Encoding. Our SMT encoding models network reachability as a *symbolic graph* of network components, along with one or more symbolic packet headers consisting of bitvectors for the source and destination addresses and ports. A symbolic graph consists of a set of nodes and directed edges, where the edges may be traversable or untraversable. Predicate $edge(u, v)$, where u and v are nodes, is true iff the corresponding edge is traversable. The assignment of the $edge(u, v)$ atoms in the formula determines which paths exist in the graph.

Figure 2 shows a symbolic graph corresponding to the VPC from Fig. 1. In our encoding, nodes represent networking components (such as instances, network interfaces, subnets, route tables, or gateways), and edges represent possible paths that packets may take between those components (such as between an instance and its network interface). Constraints between edge atoms and bitvectors in the packet headers define the routes that a packet can take.

For example, our encoding introduces an edge between each network interface node, Eni-a, and its containing Subnet-web node, $edge$(Eni-a, Subnet-web). As shown in Fig. 3, we also introduce constraints that force $edge$(Eni-a, Subnet-web) to be false if the packet's source address does not match the ENI's IP address. This ensures that packets leaving the ENI must have that ENI's IP address as their source address. Similar constraints ensure that packets entering the ENI must have that ENI's IP address as their destination address.

We encode reachability constraints into this graph using the SMT solver MONOSAT [3], which supports a theory of finite graph reachability. Specifically, we add a *start* and *end* node to the graph, with edges to the source components of the query and from the destination components of the query, and then we enforce a graph reachability constraint $reaches(start, end)$, which is true iff there is a start-end path under assignment to the edge literals. To encode the query "Are there any instances that can be accessed from the public internet over SSH?", we would add an edge from the *start* node to the internet, and from each EC2 instance to the *end* node. Additionally, we would add bitvector constraints forcing the protocol of the symbolic packet to be exactly 6 (TCP), and the destination port to be exactly 22.

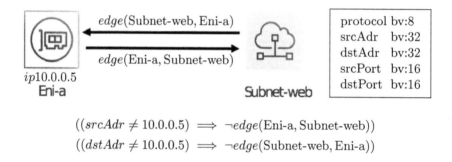

$$((srcAdr \neq 10.0.0.5) \implies \neg edge(\text{Eni-a}, \text{Subnet-web}))$$
$$((dstAdr \neq 10.0.0.5) \implies \neg edge(\text{Subnet-web}, \text{Eni-a}))$$

Fig. 3. A small portion of the VPC graph, with constraints over the edges between an ENI and its subnet enforcing that packets entering or leaving the ENI have that ENI's source or destination address.

The SMT encoding described above is intended specifically for answering network reachability queries, and does not currently take into account other properties (such as tags) that would be required to model the more general network configuration queries supported by our datalog encoding.

First-Order Encoding. In our encoding for superposition solvers such as VAMPIRE [23], we translate each network configuration question into a many-sorted first order logic problem that is unsatisfiable iff the answer to the question is true, and each network reachability question into a FOL problem that only has finite models, each corresponding to an answer to the question. For this encoding, we assume that network configuration questions have strictly yes/no answers, while network reachability questions return lists of solutions. In addition to its default saturation mode, VAMPIRE implements a MACE-style [26] finite model builder for many-sorted first-order logic [27]. Thus we use VAMPIRE both as a saturation-based theorem prover and a finite model builder, running both modes in parallel and recording the result of the fastest successful run.

Our encoding begins with the same set of facts as were generated from the network model by our Datalog encoding, represented here by the symbols $(A_1, A_2, \ldots)$. From there, we handle network configuration and network reachability questions differently, with network-configuration encodings optimized for proof-by-contradiction, while reachability configurations are optimized for model-building. Proof-by-contradiction for yes/no questions is potentially faster than model-building, as intermediate variables need not be enumerated.

We encode a network configuration question φ in negated form: $A_1 \wedge \ldots \wedge A_n \Rightarrow \neg\varphi$. If VAMPIRE can prove a contradiction in the negated formula, then φ holds. We encode a network reachability question φ into a formula of the form $A_1 \wedge \ldots \wedge A_n \wedge (\forall \bar{z})(q(\bar{z}) \Leftrightarrow \varphi) \Rightarrow (\forall \bar{z})q(\bar{z})$, where q is a fresh predicate symbol, and $\bar{z}$ are free variables of the network question φ. Each substitution of $\bar{z}$ that satisfies q corresponds to a distinct solution to the reachability question.

Our encoding targets VAMPIRE's implementation of many-sorted first-order logic with equality, extended with the theory of linear integer arithmetic, the theory of arrays [22], and the theory of tuples [20]. We encode types, constants, and predicates using Clark completion [9]. We direct the reader to our co-author's dissertation (cf. Chapter 5 [21]) for a more detailed explanation of the VAMPIRE encoding, including a detailed analysis of the performance trade-offs considered in this encoding.

4 Usage and Performance

In this section we describe the performance of the various solvers when used by TIROS in practice. Recall that our MONOSAT implementation can only answer reachability questions, whereas the other implementations also answer more general network configuration questions (such as the examples in Sect. 2).

In our experiments with VAMPIRE, we found that the first order logic encoding we used does not scale well. As we were not able to obtain good performance from our VAMPIRE-based implementation, in what follows we only present the experimental results for MONOSAT and SOUFFLÉ. We explain the poor performance of the VAMPIRE encoding mainly by the fact that large finite domains, routinely used in network specifications, are represented as long clauses coming from the domain closure axioms. Saturation theorem provers, including VAMPIRE, have a hard time dealing with such clauses.

Amazon Inspector. To compare the performance of SOUFFLÉ and MONOSAT in the context of the TIROS-based Amazon Inspector feature we randomly selected 10,000 network snapshots evaluated in December 2018. On these queries SOUFFLÉ required 4.1 s in the best-case, 45.1 s in the worst case, with 50th-percentile runtime of 5.1 s and 90th-percentile runtime of 5.5 s. MONOSAT required 0.8 s in the best case, 2.6 s in the worst case, with a 50th-percentile runtime of 1.39 s and 90th-percentile runtime of 1.79 s. To give the reader an idea of the relative size of the constraint systems solved, in the smallest case our SOUFFLÉ encoding consisted of 2,856 facts, and the MONOSAT encoding consisted of 609 variables, 21 bitvectors, and 2,032 clauses. In the largest case, our SOUFFLÉ encoding consisted of 7517 facts, and the MONOSAT encoding consisted of 2,038 variables, 21 bitvectors, and 17,731 clauses.

Scalability Tests. MONOSAT and SOUFFLÉ scale to all queries evaluated using Amazon Inspector. To help understand the limits of the SOUFFLÉ and MONOSAT-based backends on larger networks, in Fig. 4 we compare the performance of the solvers on a series of artificially generated networks of increasing size, with 100, 1000, 10,000, and 100,000 instances. In each case, the query is *"list all open paths from the Internet to any instance in the VPC"*. We can see from the figure that neither approach dominates. In most cases the Datalog encoding is able to scale to 10,000 instances, but in no cases can it scale to 100,000 instances. In most cases the SMT encoding is able to scale to networks with 100,000 instances, but for the 'benchmark-2' networks, MONOSAT requires almost a full hour to solve the 10,000 instance network that SOUFFLÉ solves in 81 s. The SMT encoding performs poorly on 'benchmark-2' because that benchmark has a vast number of distinct feasible paths through the network, each requiring a separate SMT solver call. Other benchmarks have fewer distinct paths.

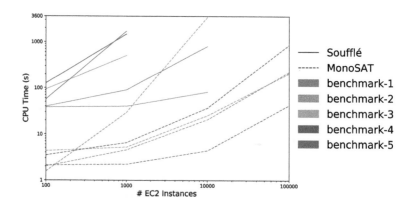

Fig. 4. Comparison of runtime in seconds for the different solver backends. Each benchmark uses a different color, *e.g.* SOUFFLÉ on benchmark-1 is a solid blue line, and MONOSAT on benchmark-1 is a dashed blue line. In these experiments, SOUFFLÉ recompiles each query before solving it, which adds ≈ 45 s to the runtime of each SOUFFLÉ query. In practice this cost can be amortized by caching compiled queries. (Color figure online)

Automating PCI Compliance Auditing. Many AWS services are built using other AWS services, *e.g.* AWS Lambda is built using AWS EC2 and the various AWS networking features. Thus within AWS we are using TIROS to prove the correctness of our own internal requirements. As an example, we use TIROS to partially automate evidence generation for compliance audits of Payment Card Industry Data Security Standard (PCI DSS) [10]. TIROS is used across the many customer-facing AWS services that are built using AWS networking to establish controls supporting PCI DSS requirements 1.2, 1.3.1, 1.3.2, 1.3.4, and 1.3.7a.

Custom Application. AWS's Professional Services team works with some of the most security-obsessed customers to use advanced tools such as TIROS to achieve custom-tailored solutions. For example, as discussed in a public lecture [6], Bridgewater Associates worked with AWS Professional Services to build a TIROS-based solution which proves invariants of new AWS-based network designs before they are deployed in Bridgewater's AWS environment. Proof of these invariants assures the absence of possible data exfiltration paths that could be leveraged by an adversary.

5   Conclusion

We have described the first complete formalization of AWS networking semantics into logic. For customers of AWS services, TIROS provides deep insights into AWS networking. Via the incorporation of TIROS into the Amazon Inspector service, millions of AWS customers are able to automatically and continuously maintain their network-based security posture. They can now show compliance with security requirements at a scale that was impossible before. Internally within AWS, we are also able to automate some aspects of compliance evidence generation, which lowers our costs and increases our ability to quickly launch new features and services.

References

1. Al-Shaer, E., Marrero, W., El-Atawy, A., Elbadawi, K.: Network configuration in A box: towards end-to-end verification of network reachability and security. In: Proceedings of the 17th Annual IEEE International Conference on Network Protocols, 2009. ICNP 2009, Princeton, NJ, USA, 13–16 October 2009, pp. 123–132 (2009). https://doi.org/10.1109/ICNP.2009.5339690
2. Ball, T., et al.: VeriCon: towards verifying controller programs in software-defined networks. In: ACM SIGPLAN Conference on Programming Language Design and Implementation, PLDI 2014, Edinburgh, UK, 9–11 June 2014, pp. 282–293 (2014). https://doi.org/10.1145/2594291.2594317, http://doi.acm.org/10.1145/2594291.2594317
3. Bayless, S., Bayless, N., Hoos, H.H., Hu, A.J.: SAT modulo monotonic theories. In: Proceedings of AAAI, pp. 3702–3709 (2015)
4. Biere, A., Cimatti, A., Clarke, E., Zhu, Y.: Symbolic model checking without BDDs. In: Cleaveland, W.R. (ed.) TACAS 1999. LNCS, vol. 1579, pp. 193–207. Springer, Heidelberg (1999). https://doi.org/10.1007/3-540-49059-0_14
5. Bjørner, N., Jayaraman, K.: Checking cloud contracts in Microsoft azure. In: Natarajan, R., Barua, G., Patra, M.R. (eds.) ICDCIT 2015. LNCS, vol. 8956, pp. 21–32. Springer, Cham (2015). https://doi.org/10.1007/978-3-319-14977-6_2

6. Bridgewater Associates: Bridgewater's model-based verification of AWS security controls. AWS New York Summit (2018). https://www.youtube.com/watch?v=gJhV35-QBE8
7. Burch, J.R., Clarke, E.M., McMillan, K.L., Dill, D.L., Hwang, L.J.: Symbolic model checking: 1020 states and beyond. Inf. Comput. **98**(2), 142–170 (1992)
8. Canini, M., Venzano, D., Peresini, P., Kostic, D., Rexford, J.: A nice way to test openflow applications. In: Proceedings of the 9th USENIX Symposium on Networked Systems Design and Implementation (NSDI). No. EPFL-CONF-170618 (2012)
9. Clark, K.L.: Negation as failure. In: Gallaire, H., Minker, J. (eds.) Logic and Data Bases, pp. 293–322. Springer, Boston (1977). https://doi.org/10.1007/978-1-4684-3384-5_11
10. CSS Council. Payment Card Industry (PCI) Data Security Standard Requirements and Security Assessment Procedures Version 3.2.1. PCI Security Standards Council (2018)
11. Dodge, C., Quigg, S.: A simpler way to assess the network exposure of EC2 instances: AWS releases new network reachability assessments in amazon inspector. AWS Security Blog (2018). https://aws.amazon.com/blogs/security/amazon-inspector-assess-network-exposure-ec2-instances-aws-network-reachability-assessments/
12. El-Hassany, A., Tsankov, P., Vanbever, L., Vechev, M.: Network-wide configuration synthesis. In: Majumdar, R., Kunčak, V. (eds.) CAV 2017. LNCS, vol. 10427, pp. 261–281. Springer, Cham (2017). https://doi.org/10.1007/978-3-319-63390-9_14
13. Fogel, A., et al.: A general approach to network configuration analysis. In: Proceedings of the 12th USENIX Conference on Networked Systems Design and Implementation, NSDI 2015, pp. 469–483. USENIX Association, Berkeley (2015). http://dl.acm.org/citation.cfm?id=2789770.2789803
14. Hajiyev, E., Verbaere, M., de Moor, O.: *codeQuest*: scalable source code queries with datalog. In: Thomas, D. (ed.) ECOOP 2006. LNCS, vol. 4067, pp. 2–27. Springer, Heidelberg (2006). https://doi.org/10.1007/11785477_2
15. Hoder, K., Bjørner, N., de Moura, L.: μZ– an efficient engine for fixed points with constraints. In: Gopalakrishnan, G., Qadeer, S. (eds.) CAV 2011. LNCS, vol. 6806, pp. 457–462. Springer, Heidelberg (2011). https://doi.org/10.1007/978-3-642-22110-1_36. http://dl.acm.org/citation.cfm?id=2032305.2032341
16. Jayaraman, K., Bjørner, N., Outhred, G., Kaufman, C.: Automated analysis and debugging of network connectivity policies. In: Microsoft Research, pp. 1–11 (2014)
17. Jordan, H., Scholz, B., Subotić, P.: SOUFFLÉ: on synthesis of program analyzers. In: Chaudhuri, S., Farzan, A. (eds.) CAV 2016. LNCS, vol. 9780, pp. 422–430. Springer, Cham (2016). https://doi.org/10.1007/978-3-319-41540-6_23
18. Kazemian, P., Varghese, G., McKeown, N.: Header space analysis: static checking for networks. In: NSDI, vol. 12, pp. 113–126 (2012)
19. Khurshid, A., Zou, X., Zhou, W., Caesar, M., Godfrey, P.B.: Veriflow: verifying network-wide invariants in real time. In: Proceedings of the 10th USENIX Symposium on Networked Systems Design and Implementation, NSDI 2013, Lombard, IL, USA, 2–5 April 2013, pp. 15–27 (2013). https://www.usenix.org/conference/nsdi13/technical-sessions/presentation/khurshid
20. Kotelnikov, E., Kovács, L., Voronkov, A.: A FOOLish encoding of the next state relations of imperative programs. In: Galmiche, D., Schulz, S., Sebastiani, R. (eds.) IJCAR 2018. LNCS (LNAI), vol. 10900, pp. 405–421. Springer, Cham (2018). https://doi.org/10.1007/978-3-319-94205-6_27

21. Kotelnikov, E.: Checking network reachability properties by automated reasoning in first-order logic. In: Kotelnikov, E. (ed.) Automated Theorem Proving with Extensions of First-Order Logic, chap. 5, pp. 114–131. Chalmers University of Technology, Gothenburg (2018). https://research.chalmers.se/publication/504640/file/504640_Fulltext.pdf

22. Kotelnikov, E., Kovács, L., Reger, G., Voronkov, A.: The vampire and the FOOL. In: Proceedings of the 5th ACM SIGPLAN Conference on Certified Programs 2016, pp. 37–48 (2016). https://doi.org/10.1145/2854065.2854071, http://doi.acm.org/10.1145/2854065.2854071

23. Kovács, L., Voronkov, A.: First-order theorem proving and VAMPIRE. In: Sharygina, N., Veith, H. (eds.) CAV 2013. LNCS, vol. 8044, pp. 1–35. Springer, Heidelberg (2013). https://doi.org/10.1007/978-3-642-39799-8_1

24. Lopes, N.P., Bjørner, N., Godefroid, P., Jayaraman, K., Varghese, G.: Checking beliefs in dynamic networks. In: Proceedings of the 12th USENIX Conference on Networked Systems Design and Implementation, NSDI 2015, pp. 499–512. USENIX Association, Berkeley (2015). http://dl.acm.org/citation.cfm?id=2789770.2789805

25. Mai, H., Khurshid, A., Agarwal, R., Caesar, M., Godfrey, B., King, S.T.: Debugging the data plane with anteater. In: Proceedings of the ACM SIGCOMM 2011 Conference on Applications, Technologies, Architectures, and Protocols for Computer Communications, Toronto, ON, Canada, 15–19 August 2011, pp. 290–301 (2011). https://doi.org/10.1145/2018436.2018470, http://doi.acm.org/10.1145/2018436.2018470

26. McCune, W.: A Davis-Putnam program and its application to finite first-order model search: Quasigroup existence problems. Technical report, Argonne National Laboratory (1994)

27. Reger, G., Suda, M., Voronkov, A.: Finding finite models in multi-sorted first-order logic. In: Creignou, N., Le Berre, D. (eds.) SAT 2016. LNCS, vol. 9710, pp. 323–341. Springer, Cham (2016). https://doi.org/10.1007/978-3-319-40970-2_20

28. Subotić, P.: Logic defined static analysis. Ph.D. thesis, University College London (2018)

5

High-Level Abstractions for Simplifying Extended String Constraints in SMT

Andrew Reynolds[1], Andres Nötzli[2(✉)],
Clark Barrett[2], and Cesare Tinelli[1]

[1] Department of Computer Science,
The University of Iowa, Iowa City, USA
[2] Department of Computer Science,
Stanford University, Stanford, USA
noetzli@cs.stanford.edu

Abstract. Satisfiability Modulo Theories (SMT) solvers with support for the theory of strings have recently emerged as powerful tools for reasoning about string-manipulating programs. However, due to the complex semantics of *extended string functions*, it is challenging to develop scalable solvers for the string constraints produced by program analysis tools. We identify several classes of simplification techniques that are critical for the efficient processing of string constraints in SMT solvers. These techniques can reduce the size and complexity of input constraints by reasoning about arithmetic entailment, multisets, and string containment relationships over input terms. We provide experimental evidence that implementing them results in significant improvements over the performance of state-of-the-art SMT solvers for extended string constraints.

1 Introduction

Most programming languages support strings natively and a considerable number of programs perform some form of string manipulation. Automated reasoning about string-manipulating programs for verification and test case generation purposes is then highly relevant for these languages and programs. Applications to security, such as finding SQL injection and XSS vulnerabilities in web applications [16,18,23] or proving their absence, are of critical importance. String constraints have also been used to generate relational database tables from SQL queries for unit testing purposes [21]. These applications require modeling all of the string operations that appear in real programs. This is challenging since some of those operations are complex and often realized by iterative applications of simpler operations. Additionally, since strings in many programming languages have variable length, reasoning accurately about them cannot be done by a reduction to bounded types such as bit-vectors, and requires instead the development of solvers for *unbounded* strings. To make this type of reasoning more scalable, the use of dedicated theory solvers natively supporting common string operations has been proposed [5,9]. Some string solvers are fully integrated within

Satisfiability Modulo Theories (SMT) solvers [4,12]; some are built (externally) on top of such solvers [9,16,19]; and others are independent of SMT solvers [23].

A major challenge in developing solvers for unbounded string constraints is the complex semantics of *extended string functions* beyond the basic operations of string concatenation and equality. Extended functions include replace, which replaces a string in another string, and indexof, which returns the position of a string in another string. Another challenge is that constraints using extended functions are often combined with constraints over other theories, e.g. integer constraints over string lengths or applications of indexof, which requires the involvement of solvers for those theories. Current string solvers address these challenges by reducing constraints with extended string functions to typically more verbose constraints over basic functions. As with every reduction, some of the higher level structure of the problem may be lost, with negative repercussions on the performance and scalability.

To address this issue, we have developed new techniques that reason about constraints with extended string operators before they are reduced to simpler ones. This analysis of complex terms can often eliminate the need for expensive reductions. The techniques are based on reasoning about relationships over strings with high-level abstractions, such as their arithmetic relationships (e.g., reasoning about their length), their string containment relationships, and their relationships as multisets of characters. We have implemented these techniques in CVC4, an SMT solver with native support for string reasoning. An experimental evaluation with benchmarks from various applications shows that our new techniques allows CVC4 to significantly outperform other state-of-the-art solvers that target extended string constraints.

Our main contributions are:

- A novel procedure for proving entailments over arithmetic predicates built from the theory of strings and linear integer arithmetic.
- Extensions of this technique for showing containment relationships between strings.
- A novel simplification technique based on abstracting strings as multisets.
- Experimental evidence that the simplification techniques provide significant performance improvements over current state-of-the-art solvers.

In the remainder of this section, we discuss related work. In Sect. 2, we provide some background on the theory of strings and how solvers reduce extended functions. In Sects. 3, 4 and 5, we describe, respectively, our arithmetic-based, containment-based, and multiset-based simplification techniques. Section 6 describes our implementation of those techniques, and Sect. 7 presents our evaluation.

Related Work. Various approaches to solving constraints over extended string functions have been proposed. Saxena et al. [16] showed that constraints from the symbolic execution of JavaScript code contain a significant number of extended string functions, which underlines their importance. Their approach translates string constraints to bit-vector constraints, similar to other approaches based on bounded strings such as HAMPI [9]. Bjørner et al. [5] proposed native support for extended string operators in string solvers for scaling symbolic execution of .NET code. They reduce extended string functions to basic ones after getting bounds for string lengths from an integer solver. They also showed that constraints involving unbounded strings and **replace** are undecidable. PASS [11] reduces string constraints over extended functions to arrays. Z3-str and its successors [4, 24, 25] reduce extended string functions to basic functions eagerly during preprocessing. S3 [18] reduces recursive functions such as **replace** incrementally by splitting and unfolding. Its successor S3P [19] refines this reduction by pruning the resulting subproblems for better performance. cvc4 [3] reduces constraints with extended functions lazily and leverages context-dependent simplifications to simplify the reductions [15]. Trau [1] reduces certain extended functions, such as **replace**, to context-free membership constraints. Ostrich [7] implements a decision procedure for a subset of constraints that include extended string functions. The simplification techniques presented in this paper are agnostic to the underlying solving procedure, so they can be combined with all of these approaches.

2   Preliminaries

We work in the context of many-sorted first-order logic with equality and assume the reader is familiar with the notions of signature, term, literal, formula, and formal interpretation of formulas. We review a few relevant definitions in the following. A *theory* is a pair $T = (\Sigma, \mathbf{I})$ where Σ is a signature and $\mathbf{I}$ is a class of Σ-interpretations, the *models* of T. We assume Σ contains the equality predicate $\approx$, interpreted as the identity relation, and the predicates $\top$ (for true) and $\bot$ (for false). A Σ-formula φ is *satisfiable* (resp., *unsatisfiable*) in T if it is satisfied by some (resp., no) interpretation in $\mathbf{I}$. We write $\models_T \varphi$ to denote that the Σ-formula φ is T-*valid*, i.e., is satisfied in every model of T. Two Σ-terms t_1 and t_2 are *equivalent* in T if $\models_T t_1 \approx t_2$.

   We consider an extended theory T_S of strings and length equations, whose signature Σ_S is given in Fig. 1 and whose models differ only on how they interpret variables.[1] We assume a fixed finite alphabet $\mathcal{A}$ of characters which includes the digits $\{0, \ldots, 9\}$. The signature includes the sorts Bool, Int, and Str denoting the Booleans, the integers ($\mathbb{Z}$), and Kleene closure of $\mathcal{A}$ ($\mathcal{A}^*$), respectively. The top half of Fig. 1 includes the usual symbols of *linear* integer arithmetic, interpreted as expected, a *string literal* l for each word/string of $\mathcal{A}^*$, a variadic function symbol con, interpreted as word concatenation, and a function symbol len, interpreted as the word length function. We write ϵ for the empty word and abbreviate len(s) as $|s|$. We use words over the characters a, b, and c, as in abca, as concrete examples of string literals.

   We refer to the function symbols in the bottom half of the figure as *extended functions* and refer to terms containing them as *extended terms*. A *position* in

---

[1] Our implementation supports a larger set of symbols, but for brevity, we only show the subset of the symbols used throughout this paper.

n : Int for all $n \in \mathbb{N}$ $+$: Int $\times$ Int $\to$ Int $-$: Int $\to$ Int $\geqslant$: Int $\times$ Int $\to$ Bool
l : Str for all $l \in \mathcal{A}^*$ con : Str $\times \cdots \times$ Str $\to$ Str   len : Str $\to$ Int

substr : Str $\times$ Int $\times$ Int $\to$ Str	contains : Str $\times$ Str $\to$ Bool
indexof : Str $\times$ Str $\times$ Int $\to$ Int	replace : Str $\times$ Str $\times$ Str $\to$ Str
str.to.int : Str $\to$ Int	int.to.str : Int $\to$ Str

Fig. 1. Functions in signature Σ_S. Str and Int denote strings and integers respectively.

a string $l \in \mathcal{A}^*$ is a non-negative integer n smaller than the length of l that identifies the $(n+1)^{th}$ character of l—with 0 identifying the first character, 1 the second, and so on. For all models $\mathcal{I}$ of T_S, all $l, l_1, l_2 \in \mathcal{A}^*$, and $n, m \in \mathbb{Z}$, $\mathsf{substr}^{\mathcal{I}}(l, n, m)$ (the interpretation of substr in $\mathcal{I}$ applied to l, n, m) is the longest substring of l starting at position n with length at most m, or ϵ if n is an invalid position or m is not positive; $\mathsf{contains}^{\mathcal{I}}(l_1, l_2)$ is true if and only if l_2 is a substring of l_1, with ϵ being a substring of every string; $\mathsf{indexof}^{\mathcal{I}}(l_1, l_2, n)$ is the position of the first occurrence of l_2 in l_1 at or after position n, n if l_2 is empty and $0 \leqslant n \leqslant |l_1|$, and -1 if n is an invalid position, or if no such occurrence exists; $\mathsf{replace}^{\mathcal{I}}(l, l_1, l_2)$ is the result of replacing the first occurrence of l_1 in l by l_2, l if l does not contain l_1, or the result of prepending l_2 to l if l_1 is empty; $\mathsf{str.to.int}^{\mathcal{I}}(l)$ is the non-negative integer represented by l in decimal notation or -1 if the string contains non-digit characters; $\mathsf{int.to.str}^{\mathcal{I}}(n)$ is the result of converting n to the corresponding string in decimal notation if n is non-negative, or ϵ otherwise. We write $\mathsf{substr}(t, u)$ as shorthand for the term $\mathsf{substr}(t, u, |t|)$, i.e. the suffix of t starting at position u.

Note that the semantics for replace and indexof correspond to the semantics in the current draft of the SMT-LIB standard for the theory of strings [17]; they are slightly different from the ones described in previous work [4,15,20].

2.1 Solving Extended String Constraints (with Simplification)

Various efficient solvers have been designed for the satisfiability problem for quantifier-free T_S-constraints, including CVC4 [3], s3# [20] and Z3STR3 [4]. In this section, we give an overview of how these solvers process extended functions in practice.

Generally speaking, constraints involving extended functions are converted to basic ones through a series of reductions performed in an incremental fashion by the solver. Operators whose reduction requires universal quantification are dealt with by guessing upper bounds on the lengths of input strings or by lazily adding constraints that block models that do not satisfy extended string constraints.

Example 1. To determine the satisfiability of $\neg\mathsf{contains}(t, s)$, the application of contains is reduced to constraints that ensure that s is not a substring of t at any position. Assuming we have a fixed upper bound n on the length of t, the above constraint is equivalent to the finite conjunction $\mathsf{substr}(t, 0, |s|) \not\approx s \wedge \cdots \wedge \mathsf{substr}(t, n, |s|) \not\approx s$. Each application of substr is then eliminated by introducing an equality that constrains a fresh variable x_i to have the semantics of that substring. Thus, reducing the formula above results in

$$\bigwedge_{i=0}^{n} |t| \geq i + |s| \Rightarrow (x_i \not\approx s \wedge t \approx \mathsf{con}(x_i^{pre}, x_i, x_i^{post}) \wedge |x_i^{pre}| \approx i \wedge |x_i| \approx |s|)$$

where $x_i, x_i^{pre}, x_i^{post}$ are fresh string variables.[2] The above conjunction involves only string concatenation, string length, and equality, and thus can be handled by a string solver with support for word equations with length constraints.

The reduction in Example 1 introduces $5 \cdot n$ theory literals over basic string functions and $3 \cdot n$ string variables. A full reduction accounting for all corner cases of substr is even more complex and thus more expensive to process, even for small values of n. These performance challenges can be addressed by aggressive simplifications that *eliminate* extended functions using high-level reasoning, as shown in the next example.

Example 2. Consider an instance of the previous example where $s = \mathsf{con}(\mathsf{a}, x)$ and $t = \mathsf{con}(\mathsf{b}, \mathsf{substr}(x, 0, n))$. A full reduction of $\neg\mathsf{contains}(t, s)$ that eliminates all applications of substr, including those in t, introduces $5 \cdot n + 5$ new theory literals and $3 \cdot n + 3$ string variables. However, based on the semantics of contains it is easy to see that $\neg\mathsf{contains}(t, s)$ is T_{S}-valid: if t were to contain s, then s would have to occur in the portion of t after its first character b, since the first character of s is a. However, $\mathsf{con}(\mathsf{a}, x)$ cannot be contained in $\mathsf{substr}(x, 0, n)$, since the length of the former is at least $|x| + 1$, while the length of the latter is at most $|x|$. A solver which recognizes that $\neg\mathsf{contains}(t, s)$ can be simplified to $\top$ in this case can avoid the reduction altogether.

We advocate for aggressive simplification techniques to improve the performance of string solvers for extended functions. In the next sections, we describe several classes of such techniques that can be applied to inputs as a preprocessing step or during solving as part of a context-dependent solving strategy [15]. We present them as sets R of rewrite rules of the form $t \rightarrow_R s$, where s is a (simplified) term equivalent to t in T_{S}. We assume a deterministic application strategy for these rules, such that each term t rewrites to a unique *simplified form*, denoted by $t\downarrow$, which is irreducible by the rules. We split our simplifications into four categories, presented in Figs. 4, 6, 7 and 8.[3]

3   Arithmetic-Based String Simplification

To simplify string terms, it is useful to establish relationships between quantities such as the lengths of strings. For example, $\mathsf{contains}(t, s)$ can be simplified to $\bot$

---

[2] This formula is a simplified form of the general reduction. The general reduction also expresses that i is a valid position in t and that the third argument of substr is non-negative [15].

[3] Some specialized rules have been omitted for space reasons.

for a particular s and t if it can be inferred that $|s|$ is strictly greater than $|t|$. This section defines an inference system for such arithmetic relationships and the simplifications that it enables.

We are interested in proving the T_S-validity of formulas of the form $u \geqslant 0$, where u is a Σ_S-term of integer type. We describe an inference system as a set of rules for deriving judgments of the form $\vdash u \geqslant 0$ and a specific rule application strategy we have implemented. The inference system is *sound* in the sense that $\models_{T_S} u \geqslant 0$ whenever $\vdash u \geqslant 0$ is derivable in it. It is, however, *incomplete* as it may fail to derive $\vdash u \geqslant 0$ in some cases when $\models_{T_S} u \geqslant 0$. This incompleteness is by design, since proving the T_S-validity of inequalities is generally expensive due to the NP-hardness of linear integer arithmetic. Without loss of generality, we require that the term u be in a simplified form, where terms of the form $|l|$ with l a string literal of n characters are rewritten to n, terms of the form $|\mathsf{con}(t_1, \ldots, t_n)|$ are rewritten to $|t_1| + \cdots + |t_n|$, and like monomials in arithmetic terms are combined in the usual way (e.g., $2 \cdot |x| + |x|$ is rewritten to $3 \cdot |x|$).

Definition 1 (Polynomial Form). *An arithmetic term u is in polynomial form if $u = m_1 \cdot u_1 + \ldots m_n \cdot u_n + m$, where $m_1, \ldots, m_n$ are non-zero integer constants, m is an integer constant, and each $u_1, \ldots, u_n$ is a unique term and one of the following:*

1. *an integer variable,*
2. *an application of length to a string variable, e.g. $|x|$,*
3. *an application of length to an extended function, e.g. $|\mathsf{substr}(t, v, w)|$, or*
4. *an application of an extended function of integer type, e.g. $\mathsf{indexof}(t, s, v)$.*

Given u in polynomial form, our inference system uses a set of over- and under-approximations for showing that $u \geqslant 0$ holds in all models of T_S. We define two auxiliary rewrite systems, denoted $\rightarrow_O$ and $\rightarrow_U$. If u rewrites to v (in zero or more steps) in $\rightarrow_O$, written $u \rightarrow_O^* v$, we say that v is an *over-approximation* of u. We can prove in that case that $\models_{T_S} v \geqslant u$. Dually, if u rewrites to v in $\rightarrow_U$, written $u \rightarrow_U^* v$, we say that v is an *under-approximation* of u and can prove that $\models_{T_S} u \geqslant v$. Based on these definitions, the core of our inference system can be summarized by the single inference rule schema provided in Fig. 2 together with the conditional rewrite systems $\rightarrow_O$ and $\rightarrow_U$ which are defined inductively in terms of the inference system and each other.

A majority of the rewrite rules have side conditions requiring the derivability of certain judgments in the same inference system. To improve their readability we take some liberties with the notation and write $\vdash u_1 \geqslant u_2$, say, instead of $\vdash u_1 - u_2 \geqslant 0$. For example, $|\mathsf{substr}(t, v, w)|$ is under-approximated by w if it can be inferred that the interval from v to $v + w$ is a valid range of positions in string t, which is expressed by the side conditions $\vdash v \geqslant 0$ and $\vdash |t| \geqslant v + w$. Note that some arithmetic terms, such as $|\mathsf{substr}(t, v, w)|$, can be approximated in *multiple* ways—hence the need for a strategy for choosing the best approximation for arithmetic string terms, described later. The rules for polynomials are written modulo associativity of $+$ and state that a monomial $m \cdot v$ in them can be over- or under-approximated based on the sign of the coefficient m. For simplicity,

$$\frac{u \to_U^* n \quad n \geq 0}{\vdash u \geq 0} \quad \text{where}$$

$$|t| \to_U 0$$

$$|\mathsf{substr}(t, v, w)| \to_U \begin{cases} w & \text{if } \vdash v \geq 0 \text{ and } \vdash |t| \geq v + w \\ |t| - v & \text{if } \vdash v \geq 0 \text{ and } \vdash v + w \geq |t| \end{cases}$$

$$|\mathsf{replace}(t, s, r)| \to_U \begin{cases} |t| & \text{if } \vdash |r| \geq |s| \text{ or } \vdash |r| \geq |t| \\ |t| - |s| \end{cases}$$

$$|\mathsf{int.to.str}(v)| \to_U 1 \quad \text{if } \vdash v \geq 0$$

$$\mathsf{indexof}(t, s, v) \to_U -1$$

$$\mathsf{str.to.int}(t) \to_U -1$$

$$m \cdot v + u' \to_U m \cdot w + u' \text{ if } v \to_U w \text{ and } m > 0 \text{ or } v \to_O w \text{ and } m < 0$$

$$|\mathsf{substr}(t, v, w)| \to_O w \quad \text{if } \vdash w \geq 0$$

$$|\mathsf{substr}(t, v, w)| \to_O \begin{cases} |t| - v & \text{if } \vdash |t| \geq v \\ |t| \end{cases}$$

$$|\mathsf{replace}(t, s, r)| \to_O \begin{cases} |t| & \text{if } \vdash |s| \geq |r| \\ |t| + |r| \end{cases}$$

$$|\mathsf{int.to.str}(v)| \to_O \begin{cases} v & \text{if } \vdash v > 0 \\ v + 1 & \text{if } \vdash v \geq 0 \end{cases}$$

$$\mathsf{indexof}(t, s, v) \to_O \begin{cases} |t| - |s| & \text{if } \vdash |t| \geq |s| \\ |t| \end{cases}$$

$$m \cdot v + u' \to_O m \cdot w + u' \text{ if } v \to_O w \text{ and } m > 0 \text{ or } v \to_U w \text{ and } m < 0$$

Fig. 2. Rules for arithmetic entailment based on under- and over-approximations computed for arithmetic terms containing extended string operators. We write t, s, r to denote string terms, u, u', v, w to denote integer terms and m, n to denote integer constants.

we silently assume in the figure that basic arithmetic simplifications are applied after each rewrite step to put the right-hand side in polynomial form.

Example 3. Let u be $|\mathsf{replace}(x, \mathsf{aa}, \mathsf{b})|$. Because $\vdash |\mathsf{aa}| \geq |\mathsf{b}|$, the first case of the over-approximation rule for $\mathsf{replace}$ applies, and we get that $u \to_O |x|$. This reflects that the result of replacing the first occurrence, if any, of aa in x with b is no longer than x.

Example 4. Let u be the same as in the previous example and let v be $-1 \cdot u + 2 \cdot |x|$. Since $u \to_O |x|$ and the coefficient of u in v is negative, we have that $v \to_U -1 \cdot |x| + 2 \cdot |x|$, which simplifies to $|x|$; moreover, $|x| \to_U 0$. Thus, $v \to_U^* 0$ and so $\vdash v \geq 0$. In other words, we can use the approximations to show that u is at most $2 \cdot |x|$.

3.1 A Strategy for Approximation

The rewrite systems $\to_O$ and $\to_U$ allow for many possible derivations. Thus, it is important to devise a strategy that is efficient and succeeds often in practice. We use a greedy rule application strategy that favors rule applications leading to the cancellation of monomials. For example, consider the term $|x| - |\mathsf{substr}(y, 0, |x|)|$, and observe that the subtrahend can be over-approximated either by $|y|$ or by $|x|$. However, proving the T_S-validity of $|x| - |\mathsf{substr}(y, 0, |x|)| \geqslant 0$ with the former over-approximation is impossible since $|x| - |y| \geqslant 0$ does not hold in all models of T_S. In contrast, the latter approximation produces $|x| - |x| \geqslant 0$ which is trivially T_S-valid.

STR-ARITH-APPROX(u), where $u = u_x + u_\ell + u_s + m$ and:
- $u_x = m_1^y \cdot y_1 + \ldots + m_n^y \cdot y_n$,
- $u_\ell = m_1^\ell \cdot |x_1| + \ldots + m_p^\ell \cdot |x_p|$,
- $u_s = m_1^v \cdot v_1 + \ldots + m_q^v \cdot v_q$.

for variables $x_1, \ldots, x_p, y_1, \ldots, y_n$ and extended terms $v_1, \ldots v_q$:
1. If $q > 0$, choose a v_i and v_i^a that maximize the following criteria (in descending order), where $u' = (u[m_i^v \cdot v_i \mapsto m_i^v \cdot v_i^a])\!\downarrow$:
   (a) (Soundness) $v_i \rightarrow_U v_i^a$ if $m_i^v > 0$ and $v_i \rightarrow_O v_i^a$ if $m_i^v < 0$;
   (b) (Avoids new terms) Minimizes the size of $\mathsf{negcoeff}(u')\backslash\mathsf{negcoeff}(u)$;
   (c) (Cancels existing terms) Maximizes the size of $\mathsf{negcoeff}(u)\backslash\mathsf{negcoeff}(u')$.
   Return $u \rightarrow_U u'$.
2. If $p > 0$ and $m_j^\ell > 0$ for some j, return $u \rightarrow_U (u[m_j^\ell \cdot |x_j| \mapsto 0])\!\downarrow$.

Fig. 3. A greedy strategy for showing arithmetic entailments in the theory T_S. We write $\mathsf{negcoeff}(u)$ to denote the set of terms whose coefficient is negative in u.

Recall that, given an arithmetic inequality $u \geqslant 0$, our goal is to find a reduction $u \rightarrow_U^* n$ where n is a non-negative constant. Our strategy for choosing which rule of $\rightarrow_U$ to apply to u is given in Fig. 3. We decompose u into three parts: the portion u_x consisting of a sum of integer variables, the portion u_ℓ consisting of a sum of lengths of string variables, and the remaining portion u_s which is a sum of monomials involving extended terms $v_1, \ldots, v_q$ as defined in Definition 1.

Since there are multiple choices for how terms in u_s are approximated, the strategy focuses primarily on this portion. In particular, we apply an approximation for one of the terms v_i, under-approximating or over-approximating depending on the sign of its coefficient, and replace the monomial in t by its corresponding approximation. The choice of v_i and v_i^a is based on maximizing the likelihood that the overall derivation will produce a non-negative constant.

For a term u in polynomial form, let $\mathsf{negcoeff}(u)$ be a set of integer terms whose coefficient is negative in u, e.g. $\mathsf{negcoeff}(y_1 + -1 \cdot y_2) = \{y_2\}$. Terms in this set can be seen as *obligations* for proving entailments in our derivations since if $y_2 \in \mathsf{negcoeff}(u)$, it must be the case that our derivation applies a rule that introduces a term with a positive coefficient for y_2. In Fig. 3, we say that our choice of $v_i \rightarrow_U v_i^a$ *avoids new terms* if it does not have the effect of adding any new terms to $\mathsf{negcoeff}(u)$, and *cancels existing terms* if it has the effect of removing terms from this set. If the portion u_s is empty, we apply the rule $|x_j| \rightarrow_U 0$ if there exists a monomial $m_j^\ell \cdot |x_j|$ where m_j^ℓ is positive. This rule is applied with lowest priority because these monomials may help to cancel negative terms introduced by the other steps.

Step 1 depends on knowing the set of possible one-step approximations $v_i \rightarrow_U v_i^a$ and $v_i \rightarrow_O v_i^a$ for terms from u. These are determined using the rules of Fig. 2. Whenever applicable, we break ties between rewrites in Step 1 by considering a fixed arbitrary ordering over extended terms.

Example 5. Let u be $1 + |t_1| + |t_2| - |x_1|$, where t_1 is $\mathsf{substr}(x_2, 1, |x_2| + |x_4|)$ and t_2 is $\mathsf{replace}(x_1, x_2, x_3)$. Step 1 of STR-ARITH-APPROX considers the possible approximations $|t_1| \rightarrow_U |x_2| - 1$ and $|t_2| \rightarrow_U |x_1| - |x_2|$. Note that under-approximations are needed because the coefficients of $|t_1|$ and $|t_2|$ are positive. The first approximation is an instance of the third rule in Fig. 2, noting that both $\vdash 1 \geq 0$ and $\vdash 1 + |x_2| + |x_4| \geq |x_2|$ are derivable by a *basic* strategy that, wherever applicable, under-approximates string length terms as zero. Our strategy chooses the first approximation since it introduces no new negative coefficient terms, thus obtaining: $u \rightarrow_U |x_2| + |t_2| - |x_1|$. We now choose the approximation $|t_2| \rightarrow_U |x_1| - |x_2|$, noting that it introduces no new negative coefficient terms and cancels an existing one, $|x_1|$. After arithmetic simplification, we have derived $u \rightarrow_U^* 0$, and hence $\vdash u \geq 0$.

One can show that our strategy is sound, terminating, and deterministic. This means that applying STR-ARITH-APPROX to completion produces a unique rewrite chain of the form $t \rightarrow_U u_1 \rightarrow_U \ldots \rightarrow_U u_n$ for a finite n, where each step is an application of one of the rewrite rules from Fig. 2.

3.2   Simplification Rules with Arithmetic Side Conditions

We use the inference system from the previous section for simplifications of string terms with arithmetic side conditions. Figure 4 summarizes those simplifications.

The first rule rewrites a string equality to $\bot$ if one of the two sides can be inferred to be strictly longer than the other. In the second rule, if one side of an equality, $\mathsf{con}(s, r, q)$, is such that the sum of lengths of s and q alone can be shown to be greater than or equal to the length of the other side, then r must be empty. The third rule recognizes that string containment reduces to string

$$
\begin{aligned}
t \approx s &\rightarrow \bot && \text{if } \vdash |t| \geq |s| + 1 \\
t \approx \mathsf{con}(s, r, q) &\rightarrow t \approx \mathsf{con}(s, q) \wedge r \approx \epsilon && \text{if } \vdash |s| + |q| \geq |t| \\
\mathsf{contains}(t, s) &\rightarrow t \approx s && \text{if } \vdash |s| \geq |t| \\
\mathsf{substr}(t, v, w) &\rightarrow \epsilon && \text{if } \vdash 0 > v \vee v \geq |t| \vee 0 \geq w \\
\mathsf{substr}(\mathsf{con}(t, s), v, w) &\rightarrow \mathsf{substr}(s, v - |t|, w) && \text{if } \vdash v \geq |t| \\
\mathsf{substr}(\mathsf{con}(s, t), v, w) &\rightarrow \mathsf{substr}(s, v, w) && \text{if } \vdash |s| \geq v + w \\
\mathsf{substr}(\mathsf{con}(t, s), 0, w) &\rightarrow \mathsf{con}(t, \mathsf{substr}(s, 0, w - |t|)) && \text{if } \vdash w \geq |t| \\
\mathsf{indexof}(t, s, v) &\rightarrow \mathsf{ite}(\mathsf{substr}(t, v) \approx s, v, -1) && \text{if } \vdash v + |s| \geq |t|
\end{aligned}
$$

Fig. 4. String simplification rules. Letters t, s, r, q denote string terms; v, w denote integer terms.

equality when it can be inferred that string s is at least as long as the string t that must contain it. The next rule captures the fact that substring simplifies to the empty string if it can be inferred that its position v is not within bounds, or its length w is not positive. In the figure, we write that rule with a disjunctive side condition; this is a shorthand to denote that we can pick any disjunct and show that it holds assuming the negation of the other disjuncts. We can use those assumptions to perform substitutions to simplify the derivation. Concretely, to show $\vdash u_1 \geqslant u_2 \vee \ldots \vee u \not\approx u'$ it is sufficient to infer $\vdash (u_1 \geqslant u_2)[u \mapsto u']$. We demonstrate this with an example.

Example 6. Consider the term $\mathsf{substr}(t, |t| + w, w)$. Our rules may simplify this term to ϵ by inferring that its start position $(|t| + w)$ is not within the bounds of t if we assume that its size (w) is positive. In detail, assume that $w > 0$ (the negation of the last disjunct in the side condition of the fourth rule), which is equivalent to $w \approx |x| + 1$ where x is a fresh string variable and $|x|$ denotes an unknown non-negative quantity. It is sufficient to derive the formula obtained by replacing all occurrences of w by $|x| + 1$ in the disjunct $|t| + w \geqslant |t|$ to show that the start position of our term is out of bounds. After simplification, we obtain $|x| + 1 \geqslant 0$, which is trivial to derive.

The next two rules in Fig. 4 apply if we can infer respectively that the start position of the substring comes strictly after a prefix t or that the end position of the substring comes strictly before a suffix t of the first argument string. In either case, t can be dropped.

Example 7. Let t be $\mathsf{substr}(\mathsf{con}(x_1, \mathsf{replace}(x_2, x_3, x_4)), 0, w)$, where w is $|x_1| - |x_2|$. We have that $t \to \mathsf{substr}(x_1, 0, w)$, noting that $\vdash |x_1| \geqslant 0 + |x_1| - |x_2|$. In other words, only the first component x_1 of the string concatenation is relevant to the substring since its end point must occur before the end of x_1.

The final rule for substr shows that a prefix of a substring can be pulled upwards if the start position is zero and we can infer that the substring is guaranteed to include at least a prefix string t. Finally, if we can infer that the last position of s in t starting from position v is at or beyond the end of t, then the $\mathsf{indexof}$ term can be rewritten as an if-then-else (ite) term that checks whether s is a suffix of t.

4 Containment-Based String Simplification

This section provides an overview of simplifications that are based on reasoning about the containment relationship between strings. We describe an inference system for deriving when one string is definitely contained or not contained in another. Following the notation from the last section, we write $\vdash t \ni s$ to denote the judgment of our inference system, denoting that string t contains string s in all models of T_S. Conversely, we write $\vdash t \not\ni s$ to denote string t does not contain string s. We write $\vdash t \ni^p s$ (resp., $\vdash t \ni^s s$) to denote the judgment indicating that s must be a prefix (resp., suffix) of t.

$$\dfrac{l_1 \text{ contains } l_2}{\vdash \mathsf{con}(l_1, t) \ni l_2} \qquad \dfrac{\vdash s \ni r}{\vdash \mathsf{con}(t, s) \ni r} \qquad \dfrac{\vdash t \ni^s r \quad \vdash s \ni^p q}{\vdash \mathsf{con}(t, s) \ni \mathsf{con}(r, q)} \qquad \dfrac{}{\vdash t \ni \mathsf{substr}(t, v, w)}$$

$$\dfrac{l_1 \text{ does not contain } l_2}{\vdash l_1 \not\ni \mathsf{con}(l_2, t)} \qquad \dfrac{\vdash r \not\ni t}{\vdash r \not\ni \mathsf{con}(s, t)} \qquad \dfrac{\vdash l_1 \setminus l_2 \not\ni t}{\vdash l_1 \not\ni \mathsf{con}(l_2, t)}$$

$$\dfrac{l_2 \text{ is a prefix of } l_1}{\vdash \mathsf{con}(l_1, t) \ni^p l_2} \qquad \dfrac{\vdash s \ni^p r}{\vdash \mathsf{con}(t, s) \ni^p \mathsf{con}(t, r)} \qquad \dfrac{}{\vdash t \ni^p t} \qquad \dfrac{\vdash v \le 0}{\vdash t \ni^p \mathsf{substr}(t, v, w)}$$

$$\dfrac{l_2 \text{ is a suffix of } l_1}{\vdash \mathsf{con}(t, l_1) \ni^s l_2} \qquad \dfrac{\vdash s \ni^s r}{\vdash \mathsf{con}(s, t) \ni^s \mathsf{con}(r, t)} \qquad \dfrac{}{\vdash t \ni^s t} \qquad \dfrac{\vdash v + w \ge |t|}{\vdash t \ni^s \mathsf{substr}(t, v, w)}$$

Fig. 5. Inferences for string containment $\ni$, is-prefix $\ni^p$ and is-suffix $\ni^s$.

Rules for inferring judgments of these forms are given in Fig. 5. Like our rules for arithmetic, these rules are solely based on the syntactic structure of terms, so inferences in this system can be computed statically. Both the assumptions and conclusions of the rules assume associativity of string concatenation with identity element ϵ, that is, $\mathsf{con}(t, s)$ may refer to a term of the form $\mathsf{con}(\mathsf{con}(t_1, t_2), s) = \mathsf{con}(t_1, t_2, s)$ or alternatively to $\mathsf{con}(\epsilon, s) = s$. Most of the rules are straightforward. The inference system has special rules for substring terms $\mathsf{substr}(t, v, w)$, using arithmetic entailments from Sect. 3 to show prefix and suffix relationships with the base string t. For negative containment, the rules of the inference system together can show a (possibly non-constant) string cannot occur in a constant string by reasoning that its characters cannot appear in order in that string. We write $l_1 \setminus l_2$ to denote the empty string if l_1 does not contain l_2, or the result of removing the smallest prefix of l_1 that contains l_2 from l_1 otherwise.

Example 8. Let t be abcab and let s be $\mathsf{con}(\mathsf{b}, x, \mathsf{a}, y, \mathsf{c})$. String s is not contained in t for any value of x, y. We derive $\vdash t \not\ni s$ using two applications of the rightmost rule for negative containment in Fig. 5, noting abcab $\setminus$ b = cab, cab $\setminus$ a = b, and b does not contain c. In other words, the containment does not hold since the characters b, a and c cannot be found in order in the constant abcad.

4.1   Simplification Rules Based on String Containment

Figure 6 gives rules for simplifying extended function terms based on the aforementioned judgments pertaining to string containment. First, equalities can be rewritten to false and applications of **contains** can be rewritten to a constant based on the appropriate judgment of our inference system. Applications of **indexof** can be simplified to -1 if it can be shown that the second argument does not appear in the suffix of the first argument starting at the position given by the third argument. The next two rules reason about cases where the second argument s definitely occurs in the first argument starting from position v. In this case, if we additionally know that s occurs within (beyond) a prefix t of

$$
\begin{aligned}
t \approx s &\rightarrow \bot && \text{if } \vdash t \not\ni s \\
\mathsf{contains}(t, s) &\rightarrow \bot && \text{if } \vdash t \not\ni s \\
\mathsf{contains}(t, s) &\rightarrow \top && \text{if } \vdash t \ni s \\
\mathsf{indexof}(t, s, v) &\rightarrow -1 && \text{if } \vdash \mathsf{substr}(t, v) \not\ni s \\
\mathsf{indexof}(\mathsf{con}(t, r), s, v) &\rightarrow \mathsf{indexof}(t, s, v) && \text{if } \vdash \mathsf{substr}(t, v) \ni s \\
\mathsf{indexof}(\mathsf{con}(t, r), s, v) &\rightarrow \mathsf{indexof}(r, s, v - |t|) + |t| && \text{if } \vdash \mathsf{substr}(\mathsf{con}(t, r), v) \ni s \text{ and} \\
& && \quad \vdash v \geqslant |t| \\
\mathsf{indexof}(t, s, v) &\rightarrow v && \text{if } \vdash \mathsf{substr}(t, v) \ni^p s \text{ and } \vdash v < |t| \\
\mathsf{replace}(t, s, r) &\rightarrow t && \text{if } \vdash t \not\ni s \\
\mathsf{replace}(\mathsf{con}(t, q), s, r) &\rightarrow \mathsf{con}(\mathsf{replace}(t, s, r), q) && \text{if } \vdash t \ni s \\
\mathsf{replace}(t, s, r) &\rightarrow \mathsf{con}(r, \mathsf{substr}(t, |s|)) && \text{if } \vdash t \ni^p s
\end{aligned}
$$

Fig. 6. Simplification rules based on string containment.

the first argument, then the suffix r (prefix t) can be dropped, where the start position and the return value of the result are modified accordingly. If we know s is a prefix of the first argument at position v, then the result is v if indeed v is in the bounds of t. Notice that the latter condition is necessary to handle the case where s is the empty string. The three rules for replace are analogous. First, the replace rewrites to the first argument if we know it does not contain the second argument s. If we know s is definitely contained in a prefix of the first argument, then we can pull the remainder of that string upwards. Finally, if we know s is a prefix of the first argument, then we can replace that prefix with r while concatenating the remainder. We use the term $\mathsf{substr}(t, |s|)$ to denote the remainder after the replacement for the sake of brevity, although this term typically does not involve extended functions after simplification, e.g. $\mathsf{replace}(\mathsf{con}(x, y), x, z) \rightarrow \mathsf{con}(z, y)$ noting that $(\mathsf{substr}(\mathsf{con}(x, y), |x|)){\downarrow} = y$, or $\mathsf{replace}(\mathsf{ab}, \mathsf{a}, x) \rightarrow \mathsf{con}(x, \mathsf{b})$ noting that $(\mathsf{substr}(\mathsf{ab}, |\mathsf{a}|)){\downarrow} = \mathsf{b}$.

4.2 Simplifications Based on Equivalence of String Containment

We further refine our approach based on inferring when one containment is *equivalent* to another one. For example, $\mathsf{con}(\mathsf{a}, x)$ is contained in $\mathsf{con}(\mathsf{b}, y)$ if and only if $\mathsf{con}(\mathsf{a}, x)$ is contained in y alone. We introduce simplifications for such equivalences by reasoning about the maximal overlap between two strings.

We adapt and extend the notation given in previous work [15]. Given string literals l_1 and l_2, the *sufficient left overlap* of l_1 and l_2, written $l_1 \sqcup_l l_2$, is the largest suffix of l_1 that is a prefix of l_2 or has l_2 as a prefix. For example, we have $\mathsf{abc} \sqcup_l \mathsf{cd} = \mathsf{c}$, $\mathsf{abc} \sqcup_l \mathsf{b} = \mathsf{bc}$, and $\mathsf{abc} \sqcup_l \mathsf{ba} = \epsilon$. We extend this definition to arbitrary strings s such that $l_1 \sqcup_l s$ is equivalent to $l_1 \sqcup_l l_2$ for the largest constant prefix l_2 of s, where notice that l_2 is the empty string if s does not have a constant prefix. For example, we have $\mathsf{abc} \sqcup_l \mathsf{con}(\mathsf{cde}, y) = \mathsf{c}$, $\mathsf{abc} \sqcup_l \mathsf{con}(\mathsf{b}, y) = \mathsf{bc}$, and $\mathsf{abc} \sqcup_l \mathsf{con}(\mathsf{a}, y) = \mathsf{abc}$. We define the dual operator *sufficient right overlap*, written $l_1 \sqcup_r l_2$, which is the largest prefix of l_1 that is a suffix of l_2 or has l_2 as a suffix, e.g. $\mathsf{abc} \sqcup_r \mathsf{b} = \mathsf{ab}$, and extend this to arbitrary strings in an analogous way. The sufficient left (resp., right) overlap operator can be used to determine how much of a constant string prefix l_1 (resp., suffix) can be safely removed from a string without impacting whether it contains another string.

$$
\begin{aligned}
\mathsf{contains}(\mathsf{con}(t,l),s) &\to \mathsf{contains}(\mathsf{con}(t,l \sqcup_r s),s) \\
\mathsf{contains}(\mathsf{con}(l,t),s) &\to \mathsf{contains}(\mathsf{con}(l \sqcup_l s,t),s) \\
\mathsf{indexof}(\mathsf{con}(t,l),s,v) &\to \mathsf{indexof}(\mathsf{con}(t,l \sqcup_r s),s,v) \\
\mathsf{indexof}(\mathsf{con}(l,t),s,v) &\to \mathsf{indexof}(\mathsf{con}(l_2,t),s,v - |l_1|) \quad \text{if } l = l_1 \cdot l_2 \text{ and } l_2 = l \sqcup_l s \\
&\quad +|l_1| \qquad\qquad\qquad\qquad\qquad \vdash \mathsf{substr}(\mathsf{con}(l,t),v) \ni s \\
\mathsf{replace}(\mathsf{con}(t,l),s,r) &\to \mathsf{con}(\mathsf{replace}(\mathsf{con}(t,l_1),s,r),l_2) \text{ if } l = l_1 \cdot l_2 \text{ and } l_1 = l \sqcup_r s \\
\mathsf{replace}(\mathsf{con}(l,t),s,r) &\to \mathsf{con}(l_1,\mathsf{replace}(\mathsf{con}(l_2,t),s,r)) \text{ if } l = l_1 \cdot l_2 \text{ and } l_2 = l \sqcup_l s
\end{aligned}
$$

Fig. 7. Simplification rules based on equivalence of string containment. We write l, l_1, l_2 to denote string literals, v, w to denote integer terms and t, s to denote string terms.

The rules in Fig. 7 simplify extended terms by considering string overlaps. The first two rules drop parts of string literals from the suffix or prefix of their first arguments. The two rules for indexof are similar: a suffix of the first argument can be dropped if it does not contribute to whether it contains the second argument. A prefix of an indexof term can be dropped if it does not contribute to containment, but only in the case where we know the second argument is definitely contained in the first argument. This is to guard against the case where the entire indexof term returns -1. The rules for replace are similar to those for contains, except that the suffix (resp., prefix) of the first argument is pulled upwards instead of being dropped.

5 Multiset-Based String Simplification

Next, we introduce simplifications based on reasoning about strings as multisets, i.e. collections of unordered characters. Such reasoning is sufficient for showing that equalities like $\mathsf{con}(\mathsf{a}, x) \approx \mathsf{con}(x, \mathsf{b})$ are equivalent to $\bot$, since the left side of the equality contains exactly one more occurrence of character a than the right-hand side. Similar to arithmetic reasoning from Sect. 3, we use approximations when reasoning about strings as multisets. We define the *multiset abstraction* of t, written $\mathcal{M}_t$, as the multiset $\{t_1, \ldots, t_n\}$ where t is equivalent to $\mathsf{con}(t_1, \ldots, t_n)$ and all constants in this set are characters. For example, $\mathcal{M}_{\mathsf{con}(\mathsf{aba},x)} = \{\mathsf{a}, \mathsf{a}, \mathsf{b}, x\}$. We define a rewrite system $\to_O^{\mathcal{M}}$ over strings where a rewritten string over-approximates the original string in the following sense: if $t \to_O^{\mathcal{M}} s$, then for all models of T_{S} and any character c, the number of occurrences of c in the strings in $\mathcal{M}_s$ is greater than or equal to the number of occurrences in the strings in $\mathcal{M}_t$.

Figure 8 lists the rules for the rewrite system $\to_O^{\mathcal{M}}$ and the simplifications based on multiset reasoning. Given a predicate $\mathsf{contains}(t, s)$, if over-approximating t with respect to the rules of $\to_O^{\mathcal{M}}$ results in a string r, and it can be determined that s contains strictly more occurrences of some character

c than r, then it cannot be the case that s is contained in t. To establish this, we check whether the multiset difference of $\mathcal{M}_s$ and $\mathcal{M}_r$ contains c, and conversely the difference of $\mathcal{M}_r$ and $\mathcal{M}_s$ contains only character constants which are distinct from c. In the second rule, if one side of an equality can be determined to contain *only* a character c, then one occurrence of that character can be dropped from both sides of the equality, since the relative position of that character does not matter. The three rules for $\rightarrow_O^{\mathcal{M}}$ state that the multiset abstraction of a term of the form $\mathsf{substr}(t, v, w)$ can be over-approximated as the entire string t; a term $\mathsf{replace}(t, s, r)$ can be over-approximated as a string having both t and r; and over-approximation can be applied to the children of con terms.

$$\mathsf{contains}(t, s) \rightarrow \bot \qquad\qquad \begin{aligned} &\text{if } t \rightarrow_O^{\mathcal{M}} {}^* r, \\ &\quad \mathcal{M}_s \backslash \mathcal{M}_r = \{c, s_1, \ldots, s_n\} \text{ and} \\ &\quad \mathcal{M}_r \backslash \mathcal{M}_s = \{c_1, \ldots, c_m\} \end{aligned}$$

$$\mathsf{con}(t, c, s) \approx \mathsf{con}(q, c, r) \rightarrow \mathsf{con}(t, s) \approx \mathsf{con}(q, r) \text{ if } \begin{aligned} &\mathcal{M}_{\mathsf{con}(t,c,s)} \rightarrow_O^{\mathcal{M}} {}^* p \text{ and} \\ &\mathcal{M}_p = \{c, \ldots, c\} \end{aligned}$$

$$\mathsf{substr}(t, v, w) \rightarrow_O^{\mathcal{M}} t$$
$$\text{where } \mathsf{replace}(t, s, r) \rightarrow_O^{\mathcal{M}} \mathsf{con}(t, r)$$
$$\mathsf{con}(t, s, r) \rightarrow_O^{\mathcal{M}} \mathsf{con}(t, q, r) \text{ if } s \rightarrow_O^{\mathcal{M}} q$$

Fig. 8. Simplification rules based on multiset reasoning. We write $c, c_1, \ldots$ to denote characters, v, w to denote integer terms, and t, s, r, q, p to denote string terms.

Example 9. We have that $\mathsf{con}(\mathsf{aaa}, \mathsf{substr}(x, y_1, y_2)) \approx \mathsf{con}(x, \mathsf{b}) \rightarrow \bot$ by noting that $\mathsf{con}(\mathsf{aaa}, \mathsf{substr}(x, y_1, y_2)) \rightarrow_O^{\mathcal{M}} {}^* \mathsf{con}(\mathsf{aaa}, x)$, $\mathcal{M}_{\mathsf{con}(\mathsf{aaa},x)} = \{\mathsf{a}, \mathsf{a}, \mathsf{a}, x\}$ and $\mathcal{M}_{\mathsf{con}(x,\mathsf{b})} = \{\mathsf{b}, x\}$. The difference of the latter with the former is $\{\mathsf{b}\}$, and the former with the latter is $\{\mathsf{a}, \mathsf{a}, \mathsf{a}\}$. Thus, the right side of the equality contains at least one more occurrence of b than the left side; hence, the equality is equivalent to false.

6 Implementation

We implemented the above simplification rules and others in the DPLL-based SMT solver CVC4, which implements a theory solver for a basic fragment of word equations with length, several other theory solvers, and reduction techniques for extended string functions as described in Sect. 2.1. Our simplification rules are run in a *preprocessing* pass as well as an *inprocessing* pass during solving. For the latter, we use a context-dependent simplification strategy that infers when an extended string constraint, e.g., $\neg\mathsf{contains}(t, s)$, simplifies to $\bot$ based on other assertions, e.g., $s \approx \epsilon$. Our simplification techniques do not affect the core procedure for the theory of strings, nor the compatibility of the string solver with other theories. In total, our implementation is about 3,500 lines of C++ code. We cache the results of the simplifications and the approximation-based arithmetic entailments to amortize their costs.

Additional Simplification Rules. The simplification rules in this paper are a subset of the rules in the implementation. We omit other uncategorized rules for lack of space. Many of these apply to specific term patterns, such as cases where two nested applications of substr can be combined; cases where an application of replace can be eliminated by case splitting; and other cases like $con(t, t) \approx a \to \bot$. An example of such rules is $contains(replace(t, w_1, w_2), w_3) \to contains(t, w_3)$ if w_3 does not overlap with either w_1 or w_2, because the replace does not change whether t contains w_3 or not. Another class of rules only applies to strings of length one because they cannot span multiple components of a concatenations, e.g. $contains(con(t, s), c) \to contains(t, c) \vee contains(s, c)$ where c is a character. Finally, there are rewrites that benefit from multiple techniques presented in this paper. For example, we have a rewrite that splits string equations into multiple smaller equations if it can determine that prefixes must have the same length: $con(a, t, s) \approx con(t, b, r) \to con(a, t) \approx con(t, b) \wedge s \approx r \to \bot$.

Validating Simplification Rules. The correctness of our simplification techniques is critical to the soundness of the overall solver. Due to the sophistication and breadth of those techniques, it is challenging to formally verify our implementation. As a pragmatic alternative, we periodically test our implementation using a testing infrastructure we developed for this purpose. We found this to be critical in our development process. Our testing infrastructure allows the developer to specify a context-free grammar in the syntax-guided synthesis format [2]. We generate all terms t in this grammar up to a fixed size and test the equivalence of t and its simplified form $t\downarrow$ on a set of randomly generated points. The most recent run of this system on two grammars (one for extended string terms and another for string predicates) up to a term size of three, validated 319,867 simplifications of string terms and 188,428 simplifications of string predicates on 1,000 sample points. This run took 924 s for string terms and 971 s for the string predicates using the same hardware as in Sect. 7.

7 Evaluation

We evaluate the impact of each simplification technique as implemented in CVC4 on three benchmark sets that use extended string operators: CMU, a dataset obtained from symbolic execution of Python code [15]; TERMEQ, a benchmark set consisting of the verification of term equivalences over strings [14]; and SLOG, a benchmark set extracted from vulnerability testing of web applications [22]. The SLOG set uses the replace function extensively but does not contain other extended functions. We also evaluate the impact on APLAS, a set of handcrafted benchmarks involving looping word equations [10] (string equalities whose left and right sides have variables in common).

We compare CVC4 with z3 commit 9cb1a0f [8],[4] a state-of-the-art string solver. Additionally, we compare against OSTRICH on the SLOG benchmarks but not other sets because it does not support some functions such as contains and

---

[4] 9cb1a0f is newer than the current release 4.8.4 and includes several fixes for critical issues.

indexof. We omit a comparison with Z3STR3 4.8.4 because we found multiple issues in its latest release including wrong answers, which we have reported to the authors. We also omit a comparison with S3# due to differing semantics. We compare four configurations of CVC4: **all**, which enables all optimizations; **-arith**, which disables arithmetic-based simplification techniques (discussed in Sect. 3); **-contain**, which disables containment-based simplification techniques (discussed in Sect. 4); and **-msets**, which disables multiset-based simplification techniques (discussed in Sect. 5). Additionally, to test the applicability of our techniques to other solvers, we test the effect of our simplifications on z3 by using CVC4 to generate simplified benchmarks and then running z3 on those benchmarks. We generate a set of simplified benchmarks that are simplified with CVC4 with $(z3_f)$ and without $(z3_b)$ the simplification techniques presented in this paper.

Table 1. Number of solved problems per benchmark set. Best results are in **bold**. Gray cells indicate benchmark sets not supported by a solver. "R%" indicates the reduction of extended string functions during preprocessing. All benchmarks ran with a timeout of 600 s.

Set		all	-arith	-contain	-msets	z3	$z3_b$	$z3_f$	OSTRICH	R%
CMU	sat	**5703**	5535	**5703**	**5703**	2343	3923	3943		
	unsat	**65**	29	**65**	**65**	50	58	61		32%
	×	154	358	154	154	3529	1941	1918		
TERMEQ	sat	**10**	**10**	**10**	**10**	4	5	5		
	unsat	51	37	28	51	35	40	**60**		68%
	×	19	33	42	19	41	35	15		
SLOG	sat	1302	1302	1302	1302	1133	1225	1225	**1304**	
	unsat	**2082**	**2082**	**2082**	**2082**	2080	2080	2080	**2082**	27%
	×	7	7	7	7	178	86	86	5	
APLAS	sat	**135**	**135**	**135**	**135**	9	51	46		
	unsat	**292**	**292**	171	171	94	129	**292**		n/a
	×	159	159	280	280	483	406	248		
Total	sat	**7150**	6982	**7150**	**7150**	3489	5204	5219	1304	
	unsat	2490	2440	2346	2369	2259	2307	**2493**	2082	
	×	339	557	483	460	4231	2468	2267	5	

We ran all benchmarks on a cluster equipped with Intel E5-2637 v4 CPUs running Ubuntu 16.04 and dedicated one core, 8 GB RAM, and 600 s for each job. Table 1 summarizes the number of solved instances for each configuration and the baseline solvers grouped by benchmark sets. We remark that the average reduction of extended string functions (with all simplification techniques enabled) shown in column "R%" is significant on all benchmark sets. The scatter plots in Fig. 9 detail the effects of disabling each family of simplifications. They distinguish between satisfiable and unsatisfiable instances. To emphasize

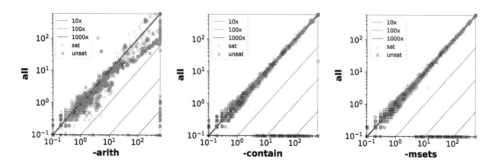

Fig. 9. Scatter plots showing the impact of disabling simplification techniques in CVC4 on both satisfiable and unsatisfiable benchmarks. All benchmarks ran with a timeout of 600 s.

non-trivial benchmarks, we omit the benchmarks that are solved in less than a second by all solvers.

The arithmetic-based simplification techniques have the most significant performance impact on the symbolic execution benchmarks CMU. The number of solved benchmarks is significantly lower when disabling those techniques. The scatter plot shows that for longer running satisfiable queries there is a large portion of the benchmarks that are solved up to an order of magnitude faster with the simplifications. These improvements in runtime on the CMU set are particularly compelling because they come from a symbolic execution application, which involves a large number of queries with a short timeout. The improvements are more pronounced for unsatisfiable benchmarks, where our results show that simplifications often give the solver the ability to derive a refutation in a matter of seconds, something that is infeasible with configurations without these techniques. The APLAS set contains no extended string operators and hence our arithmetic-based simplification techniques have little impact on this set.

In contrast, both containment and multiset-based rewrites have a high impact on the APLAS set, as **-contain** and **-msets** both solve 121 fewer benchmarks. Additionally, **-contain** has a high impact on the TERMEQ set, where the simplifications enable the best configuration to solve 61 out of 80 benchmarks. Since these techniques apply most frequently to looping word equations, they are less important for the CMU set, which does not have such equations. The containment-based and multiset-based techniques primarily help on unsatisfiable benchmarks, as shown in the scatter plots. On TERMEQ benchmarks, it tends to be easier to find counterexamples, i.e. to solve the satisfiable ones, so there is more to gain on unsatisfiable benchmarks.

On SLOG, OSTRICH solves two more instances than CVC4 but CVC4 is over 50 times faster on commonly solved instances while supporting a richer set of string operators. On all benchmark sets, CVC4 solves at least as many benchmarks as z3 and CVC4 has 12× fewer timeouts than z3. On the simplified benchmarks, z3 performs significantly better. On the CMU and the APLAS benchmarks, $z3_b$ outperforms z3 by a large margin. Additionally simplifying the benchmarks with the techniques presented in this paper improves performance further on most benchmark sets and allows $z3_f$ to solve the most unsatisfiable benchmarks overall. These results indicate that z3 could benefit from additional simplifications, and they underscore the importance of curating and publishing simplification techniques in order to improve the state-of-the-art.

8   Conclusion

We have presented a set of aggressive simplification techniques for reasoning about extended string constraints. Our results suggest that such techniques are key to advancing the state of the art in SMT string solving. Arithmetic-based simplifications lead to significant speedups in benchmarks from a symbolic execution application, while containment and multiset-based simplifications improve the performance on problems consisting of difficult term equivalences and looping word equations. Our approach is not limited to CVC4 and can be adapted to other solvers.

Given the encouraging results for each of the simplification techniques in our evaluation, we plan to extend them to other types of abstraction and make them context-aware. The latter extension involves taking into account other assertions when checking whether a side condition of a rule is fulfilled.

Acknowledgements. This work was partially supported by the National Science Foundation under award 1656926, the Defense Advanced Research Projects Agency under award FA8650-18-2-7854, and Amazon Web Services.

References

1. Abdulla, P.A., et al.: TRAU: SMT solver for string constraints. In: Bjørner, N., Gurfinkel, A. (eds.) 2018 Formal Methods in Computer Aided Design, FMCAD 2018, Austin, TX, USA, 30 October–2 November 2018, pp. 1–5. IEEE (2018)
2. Alur, R., et al.: Syntax-guided synthesis. In: Irlbeck, M., Peled, D.A., Pretschner, A. (eds.) Dependable Software Systems Engineering. NATO Sciencefor Peace and Security Series, D: Information and Communication Security, vol. 40, pp. 1–25. IOS Press (2015)
3. Barrett, C., et al.: CVC4. In: Gopalakrishnan, G., Qadeer, S. (eds.) CAV 2011. LNCS, vol. 6806, pp. 171–177. Springer, Heidelberg (2011). https://doi.org/10.1007/978-3-642-22110-1_14
4. Berzish, M., Ganesh, V., Zheng, Y.: Z3str3: a string solver with theory-aware heuristics. In: Stewart, D., Weissenbacher, G. (eds.) 2017 Formal Methods in Computer Aided Design, FMCAD 2017, Vienna, Austria, 2–6 October 2017, pp. 55–59. IEEE (2017)
5. Bjørner, N., Tillmann, N., Voronkov, A.: Path feasibility analysis for string-manipulating programs. In: Kowalewski, S., Philippou, A. (eds.) TACAS 2009. LNCS, vol. 5505, pp. 307–321. Springer, Heidelberg (2009). https://doi.org/10.1007/978-3-642-00768-2_27

6. Chaudhuri, S., Farzan, A. (eds.): Computer Aided Verification - 28th International Conference, CAV 2016, Toronto, ON, Canada, July 17-23, 2016, Proceedings, Part I. Lecture Notes in Computer Science, vol. 9779. Springer, Switzerland (2016). https://doi.org/10.1007/978-3-319-41528-4

7. Chen, T., Hague, M., Lin, A.W., Rümmer, P., Wu, Z.: Decision procedures for path feasibility of string-manipulating programs with complex operations. PACMPL **3**(POPL), 49:1–49:30 (2019)

8. de Moura, L., Bjørner, N.: Z3: an efficient SMT solver. In: Ramakrishnan, C.R., Rehof, J. (eds.) TACAS 2008. LNCS, vol. 4963, pp. 337–340. Springer, Heidelberg (2008). https://doi.org/10.1007/978-3-540-78800-3_24

9. Kiezun, A., Ganesh, V., Artzi, S., Guo, P.J., Hooimeijer, P., Ernst, M.D.: HAMPI: a solver for word equations over strings, regular expressions, and context-free grammars. ACM Trans. Softw. Eng. Methodol. **21**(4), 25:1–25:28 (2012)

10. Le, Q.L., He, M.: A decision procedure for string logic with quadratic equations, regular expressions and length constraints. In: Ryu, S. (ed.) APLAS 2018. LNCS, vol. 11275, pp. 350–372. Springer, Cham (2018). https://doi.org/10.1007/978-3-030-02768-1_19

11. Li, G., Ghosh, I.: PASS: string solving with parameterized array and interval automaton. In: Bertacco, V., Legay, A. (eds.) HVC 2013. LNCS, vol. 8244, pp. 15–31. Springer, Cham (2013). https://doi.org/10.1007/978-3-319-03077-7_2

12. Liang, T., Reynolds, A., Tinelli, C., Barrett, C., Deters, M.: A DPLL(T) theory solver for a theory of strings and regular expressions. In: Biere, A., Bloem, R. (eds.) CAV 2014. LNCS, vol. 8559, pp. 646–662. Springer, Cham (2014). https://doi.org/10.1007/978-3-319-08867-9_43

13. Majumdar, R., Kuncak, V. (eds.): Computer Aided Verification - 29th International Conference, CAV 2017, Heidelberg, Germany, July 24-28, 2017, Proceedings, Part II. Lecture Notes in Computer Science, vol. 10427. Springer, Heidelberg (2017). https://doi.org/10.1007/978-3-319-63387-9

14. Reynolds, A., et al.: Rewrites for SMT solvers using syntax-guided enumeration. SMT (2018)

15. Reynolds, A., Woo, M., Barrett, C., Brumley, D., Liang, T., Tinelli, C.: Scaling up DPLL(T) string solvers using context-dependent simplification. In: Majumdar and Kuncak [13], pp. 453–474

16. Saxena, P., Akhawe, D., Hanna, S., Mao, F., McCamant, S., Song, D.: A symbolic execution framework for Javascript. In: 31st IEEE Symposium on Security and Privacy, S&P 2010, 16–19 May 2010, Berleley/Oakland, California, USA, pp. 513–528. IEEE Computer Society (2010)

17. Tinelli, C., Barrett, C., Fontaine, P.: Unicode Strings (Draft 1.0) (2018). http://smtlib.cs.uiowa.edu/theories-UnicodeStrings.shtml

18. Trinh, M.T., Chu, D.H., Jaffar, J.: S3: a symbolic string solver for vulnerability detection in webapplications. In: Ahn, G., Yung, M., Li, N. (eds.) Proceedings of the 2014 ACM SIGSAC Conference on Computer and Communications Security, Scottsdale, AZ, USA, 3–7 November 2014, pp. 1232–1243. ACM (2014)

19. Trinh, M.T., Chu, D.H., Jaffar, J.: Progressive reasoning over recursively-defined strings. In: Chaudhuri and Farzan [6], pp. 218–240

20. Trinh, M.T., Chu, D.H., Jaffar, J.: Model counting for recursively-defined strings. In: Majumdar and Kuncak [13], pp. 399–418

21. Veanes, M., Tillmann, N., de Halleux, J.: Qex: symbolic SQL query explorer. In: Clarke, E.M., Voronkov, A. (eds.) LPAR 2010. LNCS (LNAI), vol. 6355, pp. 425–446. Springer, Heidelberg (2010). https://doi.org/10.1007/978-3-642-17511-4_24

22. Wang, H.E., Tsai, T.L., Lin, C.H., Yu, F., Jiang, J.H.R.: String analysis via automata manipulation with logic circuit representation. In: Chaudhuri and Farzan [6], pp. 241–260
23. Yu, F., Alkhalaf, M., Bultan, T.: STRANGER: an automata-based string analysis tool for PHP. In: Esparza, J., Majumdar, R. (eds.) TACAS 2010. LNCS, vol. 6015, pp. 154–157. Springer, Heidelberg (2010). https://doi.org/10.1007/978-3-642-12002-2_13
24. Zheng, Y.: Z3str2: an efficient solver for strings, regular expressions, and length constraints. Form. Methods Syst. Des. **50**(2–3), 249–288 (2017)
25. Zheng, Y., Zhang, X., Ganesh, V.: Z3-str: a z3-based string solver for web application analysis. In: Meyer, B., Baresi, L., Mezini, M. (eds.) Joint Meeting of the European Software Engineering Conference and the ACM SIGSOFT Symposium on the Foundations of Software Engineering, ESEC/FSE 2013, Saint Petersburg, Russian Federation, 18–26 August 2013, pp. 114–124. ACM (2013)

6

Icing: Supporting Fast-Math Style Optimizations in a Verified Compiler

Heiko Becker[1]([✉]), Eva Darulova[1], Magnus O. Myreen[2], and Zachary Tatlock[3]

[1] MPI-SWS, Saarland Informatics Campus (SIC), Saarbrücken, Germany
{hbecker,eva}@mpi-sws.org
[2] Chalmers University of Technology,
Gothenburg, Sweden
myreen@chalmers.se
[3] University of Washington, Seattle, USA
ztatlock@cs.washington.edu

Abstract. Verified compilers like CompCert and CakeML offer increasingly sophisticated optimizations. However, their deterministic source semantics and strict IEEE 754 compliance prevent the verification of "fast-math" style floating-point optimizations. Developers often selectively use these optimizations in mainstream compilers like GCC and LLVM to improve the performance of computations over noisy inputs or for heuristics by allowing the compiler to perform intuitive but IEEE 754-unsound rewrites.

We designed, formalized, implemented, and verified a compiler for Icing, a new language which supports selectively applying fast-math style optimizations in a verified compiler. Icing's semantics provides the first formalization of fast-math in a verified compiler. We show how the Icing compiler can be connected to the existing verified CakeML compiler and verify the end-to-end translation by a sequence of refinement proofs from Icing to the translated CakeML. We evaluated Icing by incorporating several of GCC's fast-math rewrites. While Icing targets CakeML's source language, the techniques we developed are general and could also be incorporated in lower-level intermediate representations.

Keywords: Compiler verification · Floating-point arithmetic · Optimization

1 Introduction

Verified compilers formally guarantee that compiled machine code behaves according to the specification given by the source program's semantics. This stringent requirement makes verifying "end-to-end" compilers for mainstream languages challenging, especially when proving sophisticated optimizations that developers rely on. Recent verified compilers like CakeML [38] for ML and

CompCert [24] for C have been steadily verifying more of these important optimizations [39–41]. While the gap between verified compilers and mainstream alternatives like GCC and LLVM has been shrinking, so-called "fast-math" floating-point optimizations remain absent in verified compilers.

Fast-math optimizations allow a compiler to perform rewrites that are often intuitive when interpreted as real-valued identities, but which may not preserve strict IEEE 754 floating-point behavior. Developers selectively enable fast-math optimizations when implementing heuristics, computations over noisy inputs, or error-robust applications like neural networks—typically at the granularity of individual source files. The IEEE 754-unsound rewrites used in fast-math optimizations allow compilers to perform strength reductions, reorder code to enable other optimizations, and remove some error checking [1,2]. Together these optimization can provide significant savings and are widely-used in performance-critical applications [12].

Unfortunately, strict IEEE 754 source semantics prevents proving fast-math optimizations correct in verified compilers like CakeML and CompCert. Simple strength-reducing rewrites like fusing the expression $x * y + z$ into a faster and locally-more-accurate fused multiply-add (`fma`) instruction cannot be included in such verified compilers today. This is because `fma` avoids an intermediate rounding and thus may not produce exactly the same bit-for-bit result as the unoptimized code. More sophisticated optimizations like vectorization and loop invariant code motion depend on reordering operations to make expressions available, but these cannot be verified since floating-point arithmetic is not associative. Even simple reductions like rewriting $x - x$ to 0 cannot be verified since the result can actually be `NaN` ("not a number") if x is `NaN`. Each of these cases represent rewrites that developers would often, in principle, be willing to apply manually to improve performance but which can be more conveniently handled by the compiler. Verified compilers' strict IEEE 754 source semantics similarly hinders composing their guarantees with recent tools designed to *improve accuracy* of a source program [14,16,32], as these tools change program behavior to reduce rounding error. In short, developers today are forced to choose between verified compilers and useful tools based on floating-point rewrites.

The crux of the mismatch between verified compilers and fast-math lies in the source semantics: verified compilers implement strict IEEE 754 semantics while developers are intuitively programming against a looser specification of floating-point closer to the reals. Developers currently indicate this perspective by passing compiler flags like `--ffast-math` for the parts of their code written against this looser semantics, enabling mainstream compilers to aggressively optimize those components. Ideally, verified compilers will eventually support such loosened semantics by providing an "approximate real" data type and let the developer specify error bounds under which the compiler could freely apply any optimization that stays within bounds. A good interface to tools for analyzing finite-precision computations [11,16] could even allow independently-established formal accuracy guarantees to be composed with compiler correctness.

As an initial step toward this goal, we present a pragmatic and flexible approach to supporting fast-math optimizations in verified compilers. Our approach follows the implicit design of existing mainstream compilers by providing two complementary features. First, our approach provides fine-grained control over which parts of a program the compiler may optimize under extended floating-point semantics. Second, our approach provides flexible extensions to the floating-point semantics specified by a set of high-level rewrites which can be specialized to different parts of a program. The result is a new nondeterministic source semantics which grants the compiler freedom to optimize floating-point code within clearly defined bounds.

Under such extended semantics, we verify a set of common fast-math optimizations with the simulation-based proof techniques already used in verified compilers like CakeML and CompCert, and integrate our approach with the existing compilation pipeline of the CakeML compiler. To enable these proofs, we provide various *local* lemmas that a developer can prove about their rewrites to ensure *global* correctness of the verified fast-math optimizer. Several challenges arise in the design of this decomposition including how to handle "duplicating rewrites" like distributivity that introduce multiple copies of a subexpression and how to connect context-dependent rewrites to other analyses (e.g., from accuracy-verification tools) via rewrite preconditions. Our approach thus provides a rigorous formalization of the intuitive fast-math semantics developers already use, provides an interface for dispatching proof obligations to formal numerical analysis tools via rewrite preconditions, and enables bringing fast-math optimizations to verified compilers.

In summary, the contributions of this paper are:

- We introduce an extensible, nondeterministic semantics for floating-point computations which allows for fast-math style compiler optimizations with flexible, yet fine-grained control in a language we call *Icing*.
- We implement three optimizers based on Icing: a baseline strict optimizer which provably preserves IEEE 754 semantics, a greedy optimizer, which applies any available optimization, and a conditional optimizer which applies an optimization whenever an (optimization-specific) precondition is satisfied. The code is available at https://gitlab.mpi-sws.org/AVA/Icing.
- We formalize Icing and verify our three different optimizers in HOL4.
- We connect Icing to CakeML via a translation from Icing to CakeML source and verify its correctness via a sequence of refinement proofs.

2   The Icing Language

In this section we define the Icing language and its semantics to support fast-math style optimizations in a verified compiler. Icing is a prototype language whose semantics is designed to be extensible and widely applicable instead of focusing on a particular implementation of fast-math optimizations. This allows us to provide a stable interface as the implementation of the compiler changes, as well as supporting different optimization choices in the semantics, depending on the compilation target.

2.1 Syntax

Icing's syntax is shown in Fig. 1. In addition to arithmetic, let-bindings and conditionals, Icing supports fma operators, lists ($[e_1 \ldots]$), projections ($e_1[n]$), and Map and Fold as primitives. Conditional guards consist of boolean constants (b), binary comparisons ($e_1 \square e_2$), and an isNaN predicate. isNaN e_1 checks whether e_1 is a so-called *Not-a-Number* (NaN) special value. Under the IEEE 754 standard, undefined operations (e.g., square root of a negative number) produce NaN results, and most operations propagate NaN results when passed a NaN argument. It is thus common to add checks for NaNs at the source or compiler level.

$$w: \text{64-bit floating-point word} \qquad x: \text{String} \qquad n \in \mathbb{N} \qquad b \in \{\text{True}, \text{False}\}$$

$$\diamond \in \{-, \text{sqrt}\} \qquad \circ \in \{+, -, *, /\} \qquad \square \in \{<, \leq, =\}$$

$$e_1, e_2, e_3 ::= w \mid x \mid [e_1, \ldots] \mid e_1[n] \mid \diamond e_1 \mid e_1 \circ e_2 \mid \text{fma}(e_1, e_2, e_3) \mid \text{opt} : (e_1) \mid$$
$$\text{let } x = e_1 \text{ in } e_2 \mid \text{if } c \text{ then } e_1 \text{ else } e_2 \mid \text{Map} (\lambda x.e_1) e_2 \mid \text{Fold} (\lambda x\, y.e_1) e_2\, e_3$$

$$c ::= b \mid \text{isNaN} e_1 \mid e_1 \square e_2 \mid \text{opt} : (c)$$

Fig. 1. Syntax of Icing expressions

We use the Map and Fold primitives to show that Icing can be used to express programs beyond arithmetic, while keeping the language simple. Language features like function definitions or general loops do not affect floating-point computations with respect to fast-math optimizations and are thus orthogonal.

The opt: scoping annotation implements one of the key features of Icing: floating-point semantics are relaxed only for expressions under an opt: scope. In this way, opt: provides fine-grained control both for expressions and conditional guards.

2.2 Optimizations as Rewrites

Fast-math optimizations are typically local and syntactic, i.e., peephole rewrites. In Icing, these optimizations are written as $s \to t$ to denote finding any subexpression matching pattern s and rewriting it to t, using the substitution from matching s to instantiate pattern variables in t as usual. The find and replace patterns of a rewrite are terms from the following pattern language which mirrors Icing syntax:

$$p_1, p_2, p_3 ::= w \mid b \mid x \mid \diamond p_1 \mid p_1 \circ p_2 \mid p_1 \square p_2 \mid \text{fma} (p_1, p_2, p_3) \mid \text{isNaN} p_1$$

Table 1 shows the set of rewrites currently supported in our development. While this set does not include all of GCC's fast-math optimizations, it does cover the three primary categories:

- performance and precision improving strength reduction which fuses $x * y + z$ into an fma instruction (Rewrite 1)

- reordering based on real-valued identities, here commutativity, and associativity of $+, *$, double negation and distributivity of $*$ (Rewrites 2–5)
- simplifying computation based on (assumed) real-valued behavior for computations by removing NaN error checks (Rewrite 6)

A key feature of Icing's design is that each rewrite can be guarded by a *rewrite precondition*. We distinguish *compiler rewrite preconditions* as those that must be true for the rewrite to be correct with respect to Icing semantics. Removing a NaN check, for example, can change the runtime behavior of a floating-point program: a previously crashing program may terminate or vice-versa. Thus a NaN-check can only removed if the value can never be a NaN.

In contrast, an *application rewrite precondition* guards a rewrite that can always be proven correct against the Icing semantics, but where a user may still want finer-grained control. By restricting the context where Icing may fire these rewrites, a user can establish end-to-end properties of their application, e.g., worst-case roundoff error. The crucial difference is that the compiler preconditions must be discharged before the rewrite can be proven correct against the Icing semantics, whereas the application precondition is an additional restriction limiting where the rewrite is applied for a specific application.

A key benefit of this design is that *rewrite preconditions can serve as an interface to external tools* to determine where optimizations may be conditionally applied. This feature enables Icing to address limitations that have prevented previous work from proving fast-math optimizations in verified compilers [5] since "The only way to exploit these [floating-point] simplifications while preserving semantics would be to apply them conditionally, based on the results of a static analysis (such as FP interval analysis) that can exclude the problematic cases." [5] In our setting, a static analysis tool can be used to establish an application rewrite precondition, while compiler rewrite preconditions can be discharged during (or potentially after) compilation via static analysis or manual proof.

This design choice essentially decouples the floating-point static analyzer from the general-purpose compiler. One motivation is that the compiler may perform hardware-specific rewrites, which source-code-based static analyzers would generally not be aware of. Furthermore, integrating end-to-end verification of these rewrites into a compiler would require it to always run a global static analysis. For this reason, we propose an interface which communicates only the necessary information.

Rewrites which duplicate matched subexpressions, e.g., distributing multiplication over addition, required careful design in Icing. Such rewrites can lead to unexpected results if different copies of the duplicated expression are optimized differently; this also complicates the Icing correctness proof. We show how preconditions additionally enabled us to address this challenge in Sect. 4.

Icing optimizes code by folding a list of rewrites over a program e:

```
rewrite ([],e) = e
rewrite ((s → t)::rws, e) =
  let e' = if (matches e s) then (app (s → t) e) else e in
  rewrite (rws, e')
```

For rewrite s→t at the head of `rws`, `rewrite (rws, e)` checks if s matches e, applies the rewrite if so, and recurses. Function `rewrite` is used in our optimizers in a bottom-up traversal of the AST. Icing users can specify which rewrites may be applied under each distinct `opt:` scope in their code or use a default set (shown in Table 1).

Table 1. Rewrites currently supported in Icing ($\circ \in \{+, *\}$)

	Name	Rewrite	Precondition
1	fma introduction	x * y + z → fma (x,y,z)	*application precond.*
2	∘ associative	(x ∘ y) ∘ z → x ∘ (y ∘ z)	*application precond.*
3	∘ commutative	x ∘ y → y ∘ x	*application precond.*
4	double negation	- (- x) → x	*x well-typed*
5	* distributive	x * (y + z) → (x * y) + (x * z)	*no control dependency on optimization result*
6	NaN check removal	isNaN x → false	*x is not a NaN*

2.3 Semantics of Icing

Next, we explain the semantics of Icing, highlighting two distinguishing features. First, values are represented as trees instead of simple floating-point words, thus delaying evaluation of arithmetic expressions. Secondly, rewrites in the semantics are applied nondeterministically, thus relaxing floating-point evaluation enough to prove fast-math optimizations.

We define the semantics of Icing programs in Fig. 2 as a big-step judgment of the form $(cfg, E, e) \rightarrow v$. cfg is a configuration carrying a list of rewrites $(s \rightarrow t)$ representing allowed optimizations, and a flag tracking whether optimizations are allowed in the current program fragment under an `opt:` scope (OptOk). E is the (runtime) execution environment mapping free variables to values and e an Icing expression. The value v is the result of evaluating e under E using optimizations from cfg.

The first key idea of Icing's semantics is that expressions are not evaluated to (64-bit) floating-point words immediately; the semantics rather evaluates them into *value trees* representing their computation result. As an example, if e_1 evaluates to value tree v_1 and e_2 to v_2, the semantics returns the value tree represented as $v_1 + v_2$ instead of the result of the floating-point addition of (flattened) v_1 and v_2. The syntax of value trees is:

$$c ::= b \mid \text{isNaN } v_1 \mid v_1 \,\square\, v_2 \mid \text{opt: } c$$
$$v_1, v_2, v_3 ::= w \mid \diamond v_1 \mid v_1 \circ v_2 \mid \text{fma}(v_1, v_2, v_3) \mid \text{opt: } v_1$$

$$\frac{}{(cfg,\ E,\ c) \to \mathrm{c}}\ \texttt{Const} \qquad \frac{}{(cfg,\ E,\ b) \to \mathrm{b}}\ \texttt{Bool}$$

$$\frac{\begin{array}{c}(cfg,\ E,\ e) \to v \\ (\diamond v,\ cfg)\ \mathsf{rewritesTo}\ r\end{array}}{(cfg,\ E,\ \diamond e) \to r}\ \texttt{Unary} \qquad \frac{E(x) = r}{(cfg,\ E,\ x) \to r}\ \texttt{Var}$$

$$\frac{\begin{array}{c}(cfg,\ E,\ e) \to vl \\ n < |vl| \\ vl[n] = r\end{array}}{(cfg,\ E,\ e[n]) \to r}\ \texttt{Ith} \qquad \frac{\begin{array}{c}(cfg,\ E,\ e_1) \to v_1 \\ (cfg,\ E,\ e_2) \to v_2 \\ (cfg,\ E,\ e_3) \to v_3 \\ (\texttt{fma}\ v_1\ v_2\ v_3,\ cfg)\ \mathsf{rewritesTo}\ r\end{array}}{(cfg,\ E,\ \texttt{fma}\ e_1\ e_2\ e_3) \to r}\ \texttt{fma}$$

$$\frac{\begin{array}{c}(cfg,\ E,\ e_1) \to v_1 \\ (cfg,\ E[x \mapsto v_1],\ e_2) \to v_2\end{array}}{(cfg,\ E,\ \texttt{let}\ x = e_1\ \texttt{in}\ e_2) \to v_2}\ \texttt{Let-bind} \qquad \frac{(cfg\ \mathsf{with}\ \mathsf{OptOk} := \mathsf{true},\ E,\ e) \to v}{(cfg,\ E,\ \texttt{Opt}:e) \to v}\ \texttt{Scope}$$

$$\frac{\begin{array}{c}(cfg,\ E,\ e_1) \to v_1 \\ (cfg,\ E,\ e_2) \to v_2 \\ (v_1 \circ v_2,\ cfg)\ \mathsf{rewritesTo}\ r\end{array}}{(cfg,\ E,\ e_1 \circ e_2) \to r}\ \texttt{Binary} \qquad \frac{\begin{array}{c}(cfg,\ E,\ c) \to cv \\ \mathsf{cTree2IEEE}\ cv = \mathrm{b} \\ (cfg,\ E,\ e_b) \to r\end{array}}{(cfg,\ E,\ \texttt{if}\ c\ \texttt{then}\ e_\mathrm{T}\ \texttt{else}\ e_\mathrm{F}) \to r}\ \texttt{If}$$

$$\frac{}{(cfg,\ E,\ \texttt{Map}\ (\lambda x.e)\ [])\to []}\ \texttt{Map []} \qquad \frac{(cfg,\ E,\ s) \to v}{(cfg,\ E,\ \texttt{Fold}\ (\lambda x\,y.e)\ s\ []) \to v}\ \texttt{Fold []}$$

$$\frac{\begin{array}{c}(cfg,\ E,\ e_1) \to v_1 \\ (cfg,\ E[x \mapsto v_1],\ e) \to v_\mathrm{res} \\ (cfg,\ E,\ \texttt{Map}\ (\lambda x.e)\ el) \to vl\end{array}}{(cfg,\ E,\ \texttt{Map}\ (\lambda x.e)\ (e_1 :: el)) \to v_\mathrm{res} :: vl}\ \texttt{Map cons}$$

$$\frac{\begin{array}{c}(cfg,\ E,\ e_1) \to v_1 \\ (cfg,\ E,\ \texttt{Fold}\ (\lambda x\,y.e)\ s\ el) \to v_\mathrm{res} \\ (cfg,\ E[x \mapsto v_1, y \mapsto v_\mathrm{res}],\ e) \to v_\mathrm{final}\end{array}}{(cfg,\ E,\ \texttt{Fold}\ (\lambda x\,y.e)\ s\ (e_1 :: el)) \to v_\mathrm{final}}\ \texttt{Fold cons}$$

$$\frac{\begin{array}{c}(cfg,\ E,\ e) \to v \\ (\texttt{isNaN}\ v,\ cfg)\ \mathsf{rewritesTo}\ r\end{array}}{(cfg,\ E,\ \texttt{isNaN}\ e) \to r}\ \texttt{isNaN} \qquad \frac{\begin{array}{c}(cfg,\ E,\ e_1) \to v_1 \\ (cfg,\ E,\ e_2) \to v_2 \\ (v_1\ \square\ v_2,\ cfg)\ \mathsf{rewritesTo}\ r\end{array}}{(cfg,\ E,\ e_1\ \square\ e_2) \to r}\ \texttt{Compare}$$

Fig. 2. Nondeterministic Icing semantics

```
let v1 = Map (λ x. opt:(x + 3.0)) vi in
let vsum = Fold (λ x y. opt:(x * x + y)) 0.0 v1 in sqrt vsum
```

Fig. 3. A simple Icing program

Constants are again defined as floating-point words and form the leaves of value trees (variables obtain a constant value from the execution environment E). On top of constants, value trees can represent the result of evaluating any floating-point operation Icing supports.

The second key idea of our semantics is that it nondeterministically applies rewrites from the configuration *cfg while evaluating* expression e instead of just returning its value tree. In the semantics, we model the nondeterministic choice of an optimization result for a particular value tree v with the relation `rewritesTo`, where (cfg, v) `rewritesTo` r if either the configuration *cfg* allows for optimizations to be applied, and value tree v can be rewritten into value tree r using rewrites from the configuration *cfg*; or the configuration does not allow for rewrites to be applied, and $v = r$. Rewriting on value trees reuses several definitions from Sect. 2.2. We add the nondeterminism on top of the existing functions by making the relation `rewritesTo` pick a subset of the rewrites from the configuration *cfg* which are applied to value tree v.

Icing's semantics allows optimizations to be applied for arithmetic and comparison operations. The rules `Unary`, `Binary`, `fma`, `isNaN`, and `Compare` first evaluate argument expressions into value trees. The final result is then nondeterministically chosen from the `rewritesTo` relation for the obtained value tree and the current configuration. Evaluation of `Map`, `Fold`, and let-bindings follows standard textbook evaluation semantics and does not apply optimizations.

Rule `Scope` models the fine-grained control over where optimizations are applied in the semantics. We store in the current configuration *cfg* that optimizations are allowed in the (sub-)expression e (`cfg with OptOk := true`).

Evaluation of a conditional (if c then e_T else e_F) first evaluates the conditional guard c to a value tree cv. Based on value tree cv the semantics picks a branch to continue evaluation in. This eager evaluation for conditionals (in contrast to delaying by leaving them in a value tree) is crucial to enable the later simulation proof to connect Icing to CakeML which also eagerly evaluates conditionals. As the value tree cv represents a delayed evaluation of a boolean value, we have to turn it into a boolean constant when selecting the branch to continue evaluation in. This is done using the functions `cTree2IEEE` and `tree2IEEE`. `cTree2IEEE` (v) computes the boolean value, and `tree2IEEE` (v) computes the floating-point word represented by the value tree v by applying IEEE 754 arithmetic operations and structural recursion.

Example. We illustrate Icing semantics and how optimizations are applied both in syntax and semantics with the example in Fig. 3. The example first translates the input list by 3.0 using a `Map`, and then computes the norm of the translated list with `Fold` and `sqrt`.

We want to apply $x + y \rightarrow y + x$ (commutativity of $+$) and fma-introduction $(x * y + z \rightarrow \mathtt{fma}(x, y, z))$ to our example program. Depending on their order the function `rewrite` will produce different results.

If we first apply commutativity of $+$, and then fma introduction, all $+$ operations in our example will be commuted, but no fma introduced as the fma introduction *syntactically* relies on the expression having the structure $x * y + z$ where x, y, z can be arbitrary. In contrast, if we use the opposite order of rewrites, the second line will be replaced by `let vsum = Fold (`λ`x y.fma(x,x,y)) 0.0 v1` and commutativity is only applied in the first line.

To illustrate how the semantics applies optimizations, we run the program on the 2D unit vector (`vi = [1.0,1.0]`) in a configuration that contains both rewrites. Consequently the `Map` application can produce `[1.0 + 3.0, 1.0 + 3.0]`, `[3.0 + 1.0, 1.0 + 3.0]`, ... Where the terms `1.0 + 3.0`, `3.0 + 1.0` correspond to the value trees representing the addition of `1.0` and `3.0`.

If we apply the `Fold` operation to this list, there are even more possible optimization results:

```
[(1.0 + 3.0) * (1.0 + 3.0) + (1.0 + 3.0) * (1.0 + 3.0)],
[(3.0 + 1.0) * (3.0 + 1.0) + (3.0 + 1.0) * (3.0 + 1.0)],
[fma ((3.0 + 1.0), (3.0 + 1.0), (3.0 + 1.0) * (3.0 + 1.0))],
[fma ((1.0 + 3.0), (1.0 + 3.0), (3.0 + 1.0) * (1.0 + 3.0))], ...
```

The first result is the result of evaluating the initial program without any rewrites, the second result corresponds to syntactically optimizing with commutativity of $+$ and then fma introduction, and the third corresponds to using the opposite order syntactically. The last two results can only be results of semantic optimizations as commutativity and fma introduction are applied to some intermediate results of `Map`, but not all. There is no syntactic application of commutativity and fma-introduction leading to such results.

3   Modelling Existing Compilers in Icing

Having defined the syntax and semantics of Icing, we next implement and prove correct functions which model the behavior of previous verified compilers, like CompCert or CakeML, and the behavior of unverified compilers, like GCC or Clang, respectively. For the former, we first define a translator of Icing expressions which preserves the IEEE 754 strict meaning of its input and does not allow for any further optimizations. Then we give a greedy optimizer that unconditionally optimizes expressions, as observed by GCC and Clang.

3.1   An IEEE 754 Preserving Translator

The Icing semantics nondeterministically applies optimizations if they are added to the configuration. However, when compiling safety-critical code or after applying some syntactic optimizations, one might want to preserve the strict IEEE 754 meaning of an expression.

To make sure that the behavior of an expression cannot be further changed and thus the expression exhibits strict IEEE 754 compliant behavior, we have implemented the function `compileIEEE754`, which essentially *disallows optimizations* by replacing all optimizable expressions `opt: e'` with non-optimizable expressions `e'`. Correctness of `compileIEEE754` shows that (a) no optimizations can be applied after the function has been applied, and (b) evaluation is deterministic. We have proven these properties as separate theorems.

3.2 A Greedy Optimizer

Next, we implement and prove correct an optimizer that mimics the (observed) behavior of GCC and Clang as closely as possible. The optimizer applies `fma` introduction, associativity and commutativity greedily. All these rewrites only have an application rewrite precondition which we instantiate to `True` to apply the rewrites unconstrained.

To give an intuition for greedy optimization, recall the example from Fig. 3. Greedy optimization does not consider whether applying an optimization is beneficial or not. If the optimization is allowed to be applied and it matches some subexpression of an optimizable expression, it is applied. Thus the order of optimizations matters. Applying the greedy optimizer with the rewrites `[associativity,fma-introduction, commutativity]` to the example, we get:

```
let v1 = Map (λ x. opt:(3.0 + x)) vi in
let vsum = Fold (λ x y. opt:(y + x * x)) 0.0 v1 in sqrt vsum
```

Only commutativity has been applied as associativity does not match and the possibility for an `fma`-introduction is ruled out by commutativity. If we reverse the list of optimizations we obtain:

```
let v1 = Map (λ x. opt:(3.0 + x)) vi in
let vsum = Fold (λ x y. opt:(fma (x,x,y))) 0.0 v1 in sqrt vsum
```

which we consider to be a more efficient version of the program from Fig. 3.

Greedy optimization is implemented in the function `optimizeGreedy (rws, e)` which applies the rewrites in `rws` in a bottom-up traversal to expression e. In combination with the greedy optimizer our fine-grained control (using `opt` annotations) allows the end-user to control *where* optimizations can be applied.

We have shown correctness of `optimizeGreedy` with respect to Icing semantics, i.e., we have shown that optimizing greedily gives the same result as applying the greedy rewrites in the semantics:[1]

Theorem 1. `optimizeGreedy` *is correct*
Let E be an environment, v a value tree and cfg a configuration.
If $(cfg, E, optimizeGreedy ([associativity, commutativity, fma-intro], e)) \rightarrow$
v then $(cfg\ with\ [associativity,\ commutativity, fma-intro], E, e) \rightarrow v$.

---

[1] As in many verified compilers, Icing's proofs closely follow the structure of optimizations. Achieving this required careful design and many iterations; we consider the simplicity of Icing's proofs to be a strength of this work.

Proving Theorem 1 without any additional lemmas is tedious as it requires showing correctness of a single optimization in the presence of other optimizations and dealing with the bottom-up traversal applying the optimization at the same time. Thus we reduce the proof of Theorem 1 to proving each rewrite separately and then chaining together these correctness proofs. Lemma 1 shows that applications of the function `rewrite` can be chained together in the semantics. This also means that adding, removing, or reordering optimizations simply requires changing the list of rewrites, thus making Icing easy to extend.

Lemma 1. *rewrite is compositional*
Let e be an expression, v a value tree, s → t a rewrite, and rws a set of rewrites. If the rewrite s → t can be correctly simulated in the semantics, and list rws can be correctly simulated in the semantics, then the list of rewrites (s → t) :: rws can be correctly simulated in the semantics.

4   A Conditional Optimizer

We have implemented an IEEE 754 optimizer which has the same behavior as CompCert and CakeML, and a greedy optimizer with the (observed) behavior of GCC and Clang. The fine-grained control of where optimizations are applied is essential for the usability of the greedy optimizer. However, in this section we explain that the control provided by the `opt` annotation is often not enough. We show how preconditions can be used to provide additional constraints on where rewrites can be applied, and sketch how preconditions serve as an interface between the compiler and external tools, which can and should discharge them.

We observe that in many cases, whether an optimization is acceptable or not can be captured with a precondition *on the optimization itself*, and not on every arithmetic operation separately. One example for such an optimization is removal of `NaN` checks as a check for a `NaN` should only be removed if the check never succeeds.

We argue that both application and compiler rewrite preconditions should be discharged by external tools. Many interesting preconditions for a rewrite depend on a global analysis. Running a global analysis as part of a compiler is infeasible, as maintaining separate analyses for each rewrite is not likely to scale. We thus propose to expose an *interface to external tools* in the form of preconditions.

We implement this idea in the *conditional optimizer* `optimizeCond` that supports three different applications of fast-math optimizations: applying optimizations `rws` unconstrained (`uncond rws`), applying optimizations if precondition `P` is true (`cond P rws`), and applying optimizations under the assumptions generation by function `A` which should be discharged externally (`assume A rws`). When applying `cond`, `optimizeCond` checks whether precondition `P` is true before optimizing, whereas for `assume` the propositions returned by `A` are assumed, and should then be discharged separately by a static analysis or a manual proof.

Correctness of `optimizeCond` relates syntactic optimizations to applying optimizations in the semantics. Similar to `optimizeGreedy`, we designed the proof modularly such that it suffices to prove correct each rewrite individually.

Our optimizer `optimizeCond` takes as arguments first a list of rewrite applications using `uncond`, `cond`, and `assume` then an expression e. If the list is empty, we have `optimizeCond ([], e) = e`. Otherwise the rewrite is applied in a bottom-up traversal to e and optimization continues recursively. For `uncond`, the rewrites are applied if they match; for `cond P rws` the precondition P is checked for the expression being optimized and the rewrites `rws` are applied if P is true; for `assume A rws`, the function A is evaluated on the expression being optimized. If execution of A fails, no optimization is applied. Otherwise, A returns a list of assumptions which are logged by the compiler and the rewrites are applied.

Using the interface provided by preconditions, one can prove external theorems showing additional properties of a compiler run using application rewrite preconditions, and external theorems showing how to discharge compiler rewrite preconditions with static analysis tools or a manual proof. We will call such external theorems *meta theorems*.

In the following we discuss two possible meta theorems, highlighting key steps required for implementing (and proving) them. A complete implementation consists of two connections: (1) from the compiler to rewrite preconditions and (2) from rewrite preconditions to external tools. We implement (1) independently of any particular tool. A complete implementation of (2) is out of scope of this paper; meta theorems generally depend on global analyses which are orthogonal to designing Icing, but several external tools already provide functionality that is a close match to our interface and we sketch possible connections below. We note that for these meta theorems, `optimizeCond` should track the context in which an assumption is made and use the context to express assumptions as *local* program properties. Our current `optimizeCond` implementation does not collect this contextual information yet, as this information at least partially depends on the particular meta theorems desired.

4.1 A Logging Compiler for NaN Special Value Checks

We show how a meta theorem can be used to discharge a compiler rewrite precondition on the example of removing a `NaN` check. Removing a `NaN` check, in general, can be unsound if the check could have succeeded. Inferring statically whether a value can be a `NaN` special value or not requires either a global static analysis, or a manual proof on all possible executions.

Preconditions are our interface to external tools. For `NaN` check removal, we implement a function `removeNaNcheck e` that returns the assumption that no NaN special value can be the result of evaluating the argument expression *e*. Function `removeNaNCheck` could then be used as part of an `assume` rule for `optimizeCond`. We prove a strengthened correctness theorem for `NaN` check removal, showing that if the assumption returned by `removeNaNcheck` is discharged externally (i.e. by the end-user or via static analysis), then we can simulate applying NaN check removal syntactically in Icing semantics *without additional sideconditions*.

The assumption from `removeNaNcheck` is additionally returned as the result of `optimizeCond` since it is faithfully assumed when optimizing. Such assumptions can be discharged by static analyzers like Verasco [22], or Gappa [17].

4.2 Proving Roundoff Error Improvement

Rewrites like associativity and distributivity change the results of floating-point programs. One way of capturing this behavior for a single expression is to compute the roundoff error, i.e. the difference between an idealized real-valued and a floating-point execution of the expression.

To compute an upper bound on the roundoff error, various formally verified tools have been implemented [3,17,30,37]. A possible meta theorem is thus to show that applying a particular list of optimizations does not increase the roundoff error of the optimized expression but only decreases or preserves it. The meta theorem for this example would show that (a) all the applied syntactic rewrites can be simulated in the semantics and (b) the worst-case roundoff error of the optimized expression is smaller or equal to the error of the input expression. Our development already proves (a) and we sketch the steps necessary to show (b) below.

We can leverage these roundoff error analysis tools as application preconditions in a `cond` rule, checking whether a rewrite should be applied or not in `optimizeCond`. For a particular expression `e`, an application precondition (`check (s→t, e)`) would return true if applying rewrite `s→t` does not increase the roundoff error of `e`.

Theorem 2. *check decreases roundoff error*
(cfg, E, optimizeCond (Cond (λe. check (s→t, e))) e) → v ⟹
(cfg with opts := cfg.opts ∪ {s → t}, E, e) → v ∧
error e ≤ error (optimizeCond (Cond (λe. check (s→t, e))) e)

Implementing `check (s→t, e)` requires computing a roundoff error for expression `e` and one for `e` rewritten with `s→t` and returning `True` if and only if the roundoff error has not increased by applying the rewrite. Proving the theorem would require giving a real-valued semantics for Icing, connecting Icing's semantics to the semantics of the roundoff error analysis tool, and a global range analysis on the Icing programs, which can be provided by Verasco or Gappa.

4.3 Supporting Distributivity in `optimizeCond`

The rewrites considered up to this point do not duplicate any subexpressions in the optimized output. In this section, we consider rewrites which do introduce additional occurrences of subexpressions, which we dub *duplicative rewrites*. Common duplicative rewrites are distributivity of $*$ with $+$ $(x * (y + x) \leftrightarrow x * y + x * z)$ and rewriting a single multiplication into multiple additions $(x * n \leftrightarrow \sum_{i=1}^{n} x)$. Here we consider distributivity as an example. A compiler might want to use this optimization to apply further strength reductions or `fma` introduction.

The main issue with duplicative rewrites is that they add new occurrences of a matched subexpression. Applying $(x * (y + z) \rightarrow x * y + x * z)$ to e1 * (2 + x) returns e1 * 2 + e1 * x. The values for the two occurrences of e1 may differ because of further optimizations applied to only one of it's occurrences.

Any correctness proof for such a duplicative rewrite must match up the two (potentially different) executions of e1 in the optimized expression (e1 * 2 + e1 * x) with the execution of e1 in the initial expression (e1 * (2 + x)). This can only be achieved by finding a common intermediate optimization (resp. evaluation) result shared by both subexpressions of e1 * 2 + e1 * x.

In general, existence of such an intermediate result can only be proven for expressions that do not depend on "eager" evaluation, i.e. which consists of let-bindings and arithmetic. We illustrate the problem using a conditional (if c then e1 else e2). In Icing semantics, the guard c is first evaluated to a value tree cv. Next, the semantics evaluates cv to a boolean value b using function cTree2IEEE. Computing b from cv loses the structural information of value tree cv by computing the results of previously delayed arithmetic operations. This loss of information means that rewrites that previously matched the structure of cv may no longer apply to b.

This is not a bug in the Icing semantics. On the contrary, our semantics makes this issue explicit, while in other compilers it can lead to unexpected behavior (e.g., in GCC's support for distributivity under fast-math). CakeML, for example, also eagerly evaluates conditionals and similarly loses structural information about optimizations that otherwise may have been applied. Having lazy conditionals in general would only "postpone" the issue until eager evaluation of the conditional expression for a loop is necessary.

An intuitive compiler precondition that enables proving duplicative rewrites is to forbid any control dependencies on the expression being optimized. However, this approach may be unsatisfactory as it disallows branching on the results of optimized expressions and requires a verified dependency analysis that must be rerun or incrementally updated after every rewrite, and thus could become a bottleneck for fast-math optimizers. Instead, in Icing we restrict duplicative rewrites to only fire when pattern variables are matched against program variables, e.g., pattern variables a, b, c only match against program variables x, y, z. This restriction to only matching let-bound variables is more scalable, as it can easily be checked syntactically, and allows us to loosen the restriction on control-flow dependence by simply let-binding subexpressions as needed.

5   Connecting to CakeML

We have shown how to apply optimizations in Icing and how to use it to preserve IEEE 754 semantics. Next, we describe how we connected Icing to an existing verified compiler by implementing a translation from Icing source to CakeML

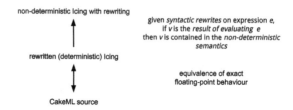

Fig. 4. Simulation diagram for Icing and the designed optimizers

source and showing an equivalence theorem.[2] The translation function toCML maps Icing syntax to CakeML syntax. We highlight the most interesting cases. The translations of Ith, Map, Fold relate an Icing execution to a predefined function from the CakeML standard library. We show separate theorems relating executions of list operations in Icing to CakeML closures of library functions. The predicate isNaN e is implemented as toCML e <> toCML e. The predicate is true in Icing semantics, if and only if e is a NaN special value. Recall that floating-point NaN values are incomparable (even to themselves) and thus we implement isNaN with an equality check.

To show that our translation function toCML correctly translates Icing programs into CakeML source, we proved a simulation between the two semantics, illustrated in Fig. 4. The top part consists of the correctness theorems we have shown for the optimizers, relating syntactic optimization to semantic rewriting. In the bottom part we relate a *deterministic* Icing execution which does not apply optimizations to CakeML source semantics and prove an equivalence. For the backward simulation between CakeML and Icing we require the Icing program to be well-typed which is independently checked.

6   Related Work

Verified Compilation of Floating-Point Programs. CompCert [25] uses a constructive formalization of IEEE 754 arithmetic [6] based on Flocq [7] which allows for verified constant propagation and strength reduction optimizations for divisions by powers of 2 and replacing $x \times 2$ by $x + x$. The situation is similar for CakeML [38] whose floating-point semantics is based on HOL's [19,20]. With Icing, we propose a semantics which allows important floating-point rewrites in a verified compiler by allowing users to specify a larger set of possible behaviors for their source programs. The precondition mechanism serves as an interface to external tools. While Icing is implemented in HOL, our techniques are not specific to higher-order logic or the details of CakeML and we believe that an analog of our "verified fast-math" approach could easily be ported to CompCert.

The Alive framework [27] has been extended to verify floating-point peephole optimizations [29,31]. While these tools relax some exceptional (NaN) cases,

---

[2] We also extended the CakeML source semantics with an fma operation, as CakeML's compilation currently does not support mapping fma's to hardware instructions.

most optimizations still need to preserve "bit-for-bit" IEEE 754 behavior, which precludes valuable rewrites like the `fma` introductions Icing supports.

Optimization of Floating-Point Programs. 'Mixed-precision tuning' can increase performance by decreasing precision at the expense of accuracy, for instance from double to single floating-point precision. Current tools [11,13,16,35], ensure that a user-provided error bound is satisfied either through dynamic or static analysis. In this work, we consider only uniform 64-bit floating-point precision, but Icing's optimizations are equally applicable to other precisions. Optimizations such as mixed-precision tuning are, however, out of scope of a compiler setting, as they require error bound annotations for kernel functions.

Spiral [33] uses real-valued linear algebra identities for rewriting at the algorithmic level to choose a layout which provides the best performance for a particular platform, but due to operation reordering is not IEEE 754 semantics preserving. Herbie [32] optimizes for accuracy, and not for performance by applying rewrites which are mostly based on real-valued identities. The optimizations performed by Spiral and Herbie go beyond what traditional compilers perform, but they fit our view that it is sometimes beneficial to relax the strict IEEE 754 specification, and could be considered in an extended implementation of Icing. On the other hand, STOKE's floating-point superoptimizer [36] for x86 binaries does not preserve real-valued semantics, and only provides approximate correctness using dynamic analysis.

Analysis and Verification of Floating-Point Programs. Static analysis for bounding roundoff errors of finite-precision computations w.r.t. to a real-valued semantics [15,17,18,28,30,37] (some with formal certificates in Coq or HOL), are currently limited to short, mostly straight-line functions and require fine-grained domain annotations at the function level. Whole program accuracy can be formally verified w.r.t. to a real-valued implementation with substantial user interaction and expertise [34]. Verification of elementary function implementations has also recently been automated, but requires substantial compute resources [23].

On the other hand, static analyses aiming to verify the absence of runtime exceptions like division by zero [4,10,21,22] scale to realistic programs. We believe that such tools can be used to satisfy preconditions and thus Icing would serve as an interface between the compiler and such specialized verification techniques.

The KLEE symbolic execution engine [9] has support for floating-point programs [26] through an interface to Z3's floating-point theory [8]. This theory is also based on IEEE 754 and will thus not be able to verify the kind of optimizations that Icing supports.

7 Conclusion

We have proposed a novel semantics for IEEE 754-unsound floating-point compiler optimizations which allows them to be applied in a verified compiler setting and which captures the intuitive semantics developers often use today when reasoning about their floating-point code. Our semantics is nondeterministic in order to provide the compiler the freedom to apply optimizations where they are useful for a particular application and platform—but within clearly defined bounds. The semantics is flexible from the developer's perspective, as it provides fine-grained control over which optimizations are available and where in a program they can be applied. We have presented a formalization in HOL4, implemented three prototype optimizers, and connected them to the CakeML verified compiler frontend. For our most general optimizer, we have explained how it can be used to obtain meta-theorems for its results by exposing a well-defined interface in the form of preconditions. We believe that our semantics can be integrated fully with different verified compilers in the future, and bridge the gap between compiler optimizations and floating-point verification techniques.

References

1. LLVM language reference manual - fast-math flags (2019). https://llvm.org/docs/LangRef.html#fast-math-flags
2. Semantics of floating point math in GCC (2019). https://gcc.gnu.org/wiki/FloatingPointMath
3. Becker, H., Zyuzin, N., Monat, R., Darulova, E., Myreen, M.O., Fox, A.: A verified certificate checker for finite-precision error bounds in Coq and HOL4. In: 2018 Formal Methods in Computer Aided Design (FMCAD), pp. 1–10. IEEE (2018)
4. Blanchet, B., et al.: A static analyzer for large safety-critical software. In: PLDI (2003)
5. Boldo, S., Jourdan, J.H., Leroy, X., Melquiond, G.: A formally-verified c compiler supporting floating-point arithmetic. In: 2013 21st IEEE Symposium on Computer Arithmetic (ARITH), pp. 107–115. IEEE (2013)
6. Boldo, S., Jourdan, J.H., Leroy, X., Melquiond, G.: Verified compilation of floating-point computations. J. Autom. Reasoning **54**(2), 135–163 (2015)
7. Boldo, S., Melquiond, G.: Flocq: a unified library for proving floating-point algorithms in Coq. In: 19th IEEE International Symposium on Computer Arithmetic, ARITH, pp. 243–252 (2011). https://doi.org/10.1109/ARITH.2011.40
8. Brain, M., Tinelli, C., Ruemmer, P., Wahl, T.: An automatable formal semantics for IEEE-754 floating-point arithmetic. Technical report (2015). http://smt-lib.org/papers/BTRW15.pdf
9. Cadar, C., Dunbar, D., Engler, D.: KLEE: unassisted and automatic generation of high-coverage tests for complex systems programs. In: OSDI (2008)
10. Chen, L., Miné, A., Cousot, P.: A sound floating-point polyhedra abstract domain. In: Ramalingam, G. (ed.) APLAS 2008. LNCS, vol. 5356, pp. 3–18. Springer, Heidelberg (2008). https://doi.org/10.1007/978-3-540-89330-1_2
11. Chiang, W.F., Baranowski, M., Briggs, I., Solovyev, A., Gopalakrishnan, G., Rakamarić, Z.: Rigorous floating-point mixed-precision tuning. In: Symposium on Principles of Programming Languages (POPL), pp. 300–315. ACM (2017)
12. Corden, M., Kreitzer, D.: Consistency of floating-point results using the Intel compiler. Technical report, Intel Corporation (2010)
13. Damouche, N., Martel, M.: Mixed precision tuning with salsa. In: PECCS, pp. 185–194. SciTePress (2018)

14. Damouche, N., Martel, M., Chapoutot, A.: Intra-procedural optimization of the numerical accuracy of programs. In: Núñez, M., Güdemann, M. (eds.) FMICS 2015. LNCS, vol. 9128, pp. 31–46. Springer, Cham (2015). https://doi.org/10.1007/978-3-319-19458-5_3

15. Darulova, E., Izycheva, A., Nasir, F., Ritter, F., Becker, H., Bastian, R.: Daisy - framework for analysis and optimization of numerical programs (tool paper). In: Beyer, D., Huisman, M. (eds.) TACAS 2018. LNCS, vol. 10805, pp. 270–287. Springer, Cham (2018). https://doi.org/10.1007/978-3-319-89960-2_15

16. Darulova, E., Sharma, S., Horn, E.: Sound mixed-precision optimization with rewriting. In: ICCPS (2018)

17. De Dinechin, F., Lauter, C.Q., Melquiond, G.: Assisted verification of elementary functions using Gappa. In: ACM Symposium on Applied Computing, pp. 1318–1322. ACM (2006)

18. Goubault, E., Putot, S.: Static analysis of finite precision computations. In: Jhala, R., Schmidt, D. (eds.) VMCAI 2011. LNCS, vol. 6538, pp. 232–247. Springer, Heidelberg (2011). https://doi.org/10.1007/978-3-642-18275-4_17

19. Harrison, J.: Floating point verification in HOL. In: Thomas Schubert, E., Windley, P.J., Alves-Foss, J. (eds.) TPHOLs 1995. LNCS, vol. 971, pp. 186–199. Springer, Heidelberg (1995). https://doi.org/10.1007/3-540-60275-5_65

20. Harrison, J.: Floating-point verification. In: Fitzgerald, J., Hayes, I.J., Tarlecki, A. (eds.) FM 2005. LNCS, vol. 3582, pp. 529–532. Springer, Heidelberg (2005). https://doi.org/10.1007/11526841_35

21. Jeannet, B., Miné, A.: APRON: a library of numerical abstract domains for static analysis. In: Bouajjani, A., Maler, O. (eds.) CAV 2009. LNCS, vol. 5643, pp. 661–667. Springer, Heidelberg (2009). https://doi.org/10.1007/978-3-642-02658-4_52

22. Jourdan, J.H.: Verasco: a formally verified C static analyzer. Ph.D. thesis, Université Paris Diderot (Paris 7), May 2016

23. Lee, W., Sharma, R., Aiken, A.: On automatically proving the correctness of math.h implementations. In: POPL (2018)

24. Leroy, X.: Formal certification of a compiler back-end, or: programming a compiler with a proof assistant. In: 33rd ACM Symposium on Principles of Programming Languages, pp. 42–54. ACM Press (2006)

25. Leroy, X.: A formally verified compiler back-end. J. Autom. Reasoning **43**(4), 363–446 (2009). http://xavierleroy.org/publi/compcert-backend.pdf

26. Liew, D., Schemmel, D., Cadar, C., Donaldson, A.F., Zähl, R., Wehrle, K.: Floating-point symbolic execution: a case study in n-version programming. In: Proceedings of the 32nd IEEE/ACM International Conference on Automated Software Engineering. IEEE Press (2017)

27. Lopes, N.P., Menendez, D., Nagarakatte, S., Regehr, J.: Provably correct peephole optimizations with alive. In: PLDI (2015)

28. Magron, V., Constantinides, G., Donaldson, A.: Certified roundoff error bounds using semidefinite programming. ACM Trans. Math. Softw. **43**(4), 1–34 (2017)

29. Menendez, D., Nagarakatte, S., Gupta, A.: Alive-FP: automated verification of floating point based peephole optimizations in LLVM. In: Rival, X. (ed.) SAS 2016. LNCS, vol. 9837, pp. 317–337. Springer, Heidelberg (2016). https://doi.org/10.1007/978-3-662-53413-7_16

30. Moscato, M., Titolo, L., Dutle, A., Muñoz, C.A.: Automatic estimation of verified floating-point round-off errors via static analysis. In: Tonetta, S., Schoitsch, E., Bitsch, F. (eds.) SAFECOMP 2017. LNCS, vol. 10488, pp. 213–229. Springer, Cham (2017). https://doi.org/10.1007/978-3-319-66266-4_14

31. Nötzli, A., Brown, F.: LifeJacket: verifying precise floating-point optimizations in LLVM. In: Proceedings of the 5th ACM SIGPLAN International Workshop on State of the Art in Program Analysis, pp. 24–29. ACM (2016)
32. Panchekha, P., Sanchez-Stern, A., Wilcox, J.R., Tatlock, Z.: Automatically improving accuracy for floating point expressions. In: Conference on Programming Language Design and Implementation (PLDI) (2015)
33. Püschel, M., et al.: SPIRAL - a generator for platform-adapted libraries of signal processing alogorithms. IJHPCA $18(1)$, 21–45 (2004)
34. Ramananandro, T., Mountcastle, P., Meister, B., Lethin, R.: A unified Coq framework for verifying C programs with floating-point computations. In: Certified Programs and Proofs (CPP) (2016)
35. Rubio-González, C., et al.: Precimonious: tuning assistant for floating-point precision. In: SC (2013)
36. Schkufza, E., Sharma, R., Aiken, A.: Stochastic optimization of floating-point programs with tunable precision. In: PLDI (2014)
37. Solovyev, A., Jacobsen, C., Rakamarić, Z., Gopalakrishnan, G.: Rigorous estimation of floating-point round-off errors with Symbolic Taylor Expansions. In: Bjørner, N., de Boer, F. (eds.) FM 2015. LNCS, vol. 9109, pp. 532–550. Springer, Cham (2015). https://doi.org/10.1007/978-3-319-19249-9_33
38. Tan, Y.K., Myreen, M.O., Kumar, R., Fox, A., Owens, S., Norrish, M.: The verified CakeML compiler backend. J. Funct. Program. 29 (2019)
39. Tristan, J.B., Leroy, X.: Formal verification of translation validators: a case study on instruction scheduling optimizations. In: Proceedings of the 35th ACM Symposium on Principles of Programming Languages (POPL 2008), pp. 17–27. ACM Press, January 2008
40. Tristan, J.B., Leroy, X.: Verified validation of lazy code motion. In: Proceedings of the 2009 ACM SIGPLAN Conference on Programming Language Design and Implementation (PLDI 2009), pp. 316–326 (2009)
41. Tristan, J.B., Leroy, X.: A simple, verified validator for software pipelining. In: Proceedings of the 37th ACM Symposium on Principles of Programming Languages (POPL 2010), pp. 83–92. ACM Press (2010)

7

SecCSL: Security Concurrent Separation Logic

Gidon Ernst[1]([⊠]) and Toby Murray[2]

[1] LMU Munich, Munich, Germany
gidon.ernst@lmu.de
[2] University of Melbourne, Melbourne, Australia
toby.murray@unimelb.edu.au

Abstract. We present SecCSL, a concurrent separation logic for proving expressive, data-dependent information flow security properties of low-level programs. SecCSL is considerably more expressive, while being simpler, than recent compositional information flow logics that cannot reason about pointers, arrays etc. To capture security concerns, SecCSL adopts a relational semantics for its assertions. At the same time it inherits the structure of traditional concurrent separation logics; thus SecCSL reasoning can be automated via symbolic execution. We demonstrate this by implementing SecC, an automatic verifier for a subset of the C programming language, which we apply to a range of benchmarks.

1 Introduction

Software verification successes abound, whether via interactive proof or via automatic program verifiers. While the former has yielded individual, deeply verified software artifacts [21, 24, 25] primarily by *researchers*, the latter appears to be having a growing impact on *industrial* software engineering [11, 36, 39].

At the same time, recent work has heralded major advancements in program logics for reasoning about secure *information flow* [23, 33, 34]—i.e. whether programs properly protect their secrets—yielding the first general program logics and proofs of information flow security for non-trivial concurrent programs [34]. Yet so far, such logics have remained confined to interactive proof assistants, making them practically inaccessible to industrial developers.

This is not especially surprising. The COVERN logic [34], for example, pays for its generality with regard to expressive security policies, in terms of complexity. Worse, these logics reason only over very simple toy programming languages, which even lack support for pointers, arrays, and structures. Their complexity, we argue, hinders proof automation and makes scaling up these logics to real-world languages impractical. How, therefore, can we leverage the power of existing automatic deductive verification approaches for security proofs?

In this paper we present *Security Concurrent Separation Logic* (SecCSL), which achieves an unprecedented combination of simplicity, power, and ease of automation by capturing core concepts such as data-dependent variable sensitivity [27,31,50], and shared invariants on sensitive memory [34] in the familiar style of Concurrent Separation Logic (CSL) [38], as exemplified in Sect. 2.

Prior work [14,20] has noted the promise of separation logic for reasoning about information flow yet, to date, that promise remains unrealised. Indeed, the only two prior encodings of information flow concepts into separation logics which we are aware of have overlooked crucial features like concurrency [14], and lack the ability to separately specify the sensitivity of *values* and memory *locations* as we explain in Sect. 2. The logic in [20] lacks soundness arguments altogether while [14] fail to satisfy basic properties needed for automation (see the discussion following Proposition 1).

Designing a logic with the right combination of features, with the right semantics, is therefore non-trivial. To manage this, SecCSL assertions have a *relational* interpretation [6,49] over a standard heap model (Sect. 3). This allows one to canonically encode information flow concepts while maintaining the approach and structure of traditional CSL proofs. To do so we adapt existing proof techniques for the soundness of CSL [46] into a compositional information flow security property (Sect. 4) that, like SecCSL itself, is simple and powerful. We have mechanized the soundness of SecCSL in Isabelle/HOL [37].

To demonstrate SecCSL's ease of use and capacity for automation, we implemented the prototype tool SecC (Sect. 5). We target C because it dominates low-level security-critical code. SecC automates SecCSL reasoning via symbolic execution, in the style of contemporary Separation Logic program verifiers like VeriFast [22], Viper [30], and Infer [10]. SecC correctly analyzes well-known benchmark problems (collected in [17]) within a few milliseconds; and we verify a variant of the CDDC case study [5] from the Covern project. Our Isabelle theories, the open source prototype tool SecC, and examples are available online at https://covern.org/secc [18].

2   An Overview of SecCSL

2.1   Specifying Information Flow Control in SecCSL

Consider the program in Fig. 1. It maintains a global pointer rec to a shared record, protected by the lock mutex. The is_classified field of the record identifies the confidentiality of the record's data: when is_classified is true, the value stored in the data field is confidential, and otherwise it is safe to release publicly. The left thread outputs the data in the record whenever it is public by writing to the (memory mapped) output device register pointer OUTPUT_REG (here also protected by mutex). The right thread updates the record, ensuring its content is not confidential, here by clearing its data.

Suppose assigning a value d to the OUTPUT_REG register causes d to be outputted to a publicly-visible location. Reasoning, then, that the example is secure requires capturing that (1) the data field of the record pointed to by rec is confidential precisely when the record's is_classified field says it is, and (2) data

```
/* globals shared between the two threads */
struct record { bool is_classified; int data; };
struct record * rec = /* ... initialisation omitted ... */;
volatile int * const OUTPUT_REG = /* memory-mapped IO device register */;
```

```
/* thread 1: output the record */    ║  /* thread 2: edit the record */
while(true) {                         ║  lock(mutex);
    lock(mutex);                      ║  /* clear the record */
    if (!rec->is_classified)         ║  rec->is_classified = FALSE;
        *OUTPUT_REG = rec->data;     ║  rec->data = 0;
    unlock(mutex); }                 ║  unlock(mutex);
```

Fig. 1. Example of concurrent information flow.

sink `OUTPUT_REG` should never have confidential data written to it. Therefore the example only ever writes non-confidential data into `OUTPUT_REG`.

Condition (1) specifies the sensitivity of a data *value* in memory, whereas condition (2) specifies the sensitivity of the data that a memory *location* (i.e. data sink) is permitted to hold. Prior security separation logics [14, 20] reason only about value-sensitivity condition (1) but, as we explain below, both are needed. Like those prior logics, in SECCSL one specifies the sensitivity of the value denoted by an expression e via a security *label* ℓ: the assertion $e :: \ell$ means that the sensitivity of the value denoted by expression e is at most ℓ. Security labels are drawn from a lattice with top element `high` (denoting the most confidential information), bottom element `low` (denoting public information), and ordered via $\sqsubseteq$: $\ell \sqsubseteq \ell'$ means that information labelled with ℓ' is at least as sensitive as that labelled by ℓ. Using this style of assertion, in conjunction with standard separation logic connectives (explained below), condition (1) can be specified as:

$$\exists c\, d.\; \mathtt{rec} \mapsto (c, d) \wedge c :: \mathtt{low} \wedge d :: (c\;?\;\mathtt{high}\;:\;\mathtt{low}) \tag{1}$$

Separation logic's points-to predicate $e \mapsto e'$ means the memory location denoted by expression e holds the value denoted by e'. Thus (1) can be read as saying that the `rec` pointer points to a pair of values (c, d). The first c (the value of the `is_classified` field) is public. The sensitivity of the second d (the value of the `data` field) is given by the value of the first c: it is `high` when c is true and is `low` otherwise. SECCSL integrates such reasoning about *value-dependent* sensitivity [27, 31, 50] neatly with functional properties of low-level data structures, which we think is more natural and straightforward than the approach of [34, 35] that keeps the two concerns separate.

Value-sensitivity assertion $e :: \ell$ is a judgement on the maximum sensitivity of the data *source(s)* from which e has been derived. Location-sensitivity assertions, on the other hand, are used to specify security policies on data *sinks* like `OUTPUT_REG`. These assertions augment the separation logic points-to predicate with a security label ℓ, and are used to specify which parts of the memory are observable to the attacker (and so must never contain sensitive information): $e \overset{\ell}{\mapsto} e'$ means that the value denoted by the expression e' is present in memory at the location denoted by e, and additionally that at all times the sensitivity of the value stored in that locations is never allowed to exceed ℓ. Thus in SECCSL, $e \mapsto e'$ abbreviates $e \overset{\text{high}}{\mapsto} e'$. In Fig. 1, that OUTPUT_REG is publicly-observable can be specified as:

$$\exists v. \; \texttt{OUTPUT\_REG} \overset{\text{low}}{\longmapsto} v \tag{2}$$

2.2 Reasoning in SECCSL

SECCSL judgements have the form:

$$\ell_A \vdash \{P\} \; c \; \{Q\} \tag{3}$$

Here ℓ_A is the *attacker security level*, c is the (concurrent) program command being executed, and P and Q are the program's pre- resp. postcondition. Judgement (3) means that if the program c begins in a state satisfying its precondition P then, when it terminates, the final state will satisfy its postcondition Q. Analogously to [44] the program is guaranteed to be memory safe. We defer a description of ℓ_A and the implied security property to Sect. 2.3.

As with traditional CSLs, SECCSL is geared towards reasoning over shared-memory programs that use lock-based synchronisation. Each lock l has an associated invariant inv(l), which is simply a predicate, like P or Q in (3), that describes the shared memory that the lock protects. In Fig. 1, where the lock mutex protects the shared pointer rec and OUTPUT_REG, the associated invariant inv(mutex) is simply the conjunction of (1) and (2).

$$(\exists c \; d. \; \texttt{rec} \mapsto (c,d) \wedge c :: \texttt{low} \wedge d :: (c \; ? \; \texttt{high} : \texttt{low})) \star (\exists v. \; \texttt{OUTPUT\_REG} \overset{\text{low}}{\longmapsto} v) \tag{4}$$

Separating conjunction $P \star Q$ asserts that the assertions P and Q both hold and, additionally, that the memory locations referenced by P and Q respectively do not overlap. Thus SECCSL invariants, like SECCSL assertions, describe together both functional properties (e.g. rec is a valid pointer) and security concerns (e.g. the OUTPUT_REG location is publicly visible) of the shared state.

When acquiring a lock one gets to assume that the lock's invariant holds [38]. Subsequently, when releasing the lock one must prove that the invariant has been re-established. For example, when reasoning about the code of the left-thread in Fig. 1, upon acquiring the mutex, SECCSL adds formula (4) to the intermediate assertion, which allows proving that the loop body is secure. When reasoning about the right thread, one must prove that the invariant has been re-established when it releases the mutex. This is the reason e.g. that the right thread must clear the data field after setting is_classified to false.

Reasoning in SECCSL proceeds forward over the program text according to the rules in Fig. 4. When execution forks, as in Fig. 1, one reasons over each thread individually. For Fig. 1, SECCSL requires proving that the guard of the if-condition is low, i.e. that the program is not branching on a secret (rule IF in Fig. 4), which would correspond to a timing channel, see Sect. 2.3 below. This follows from the part $c ::$ low of invariant (4). Secondly, after the write to OUTPUT_REG, SECCSL requires that the expression that is being written to the location OUTPUT_REG has sensitivity low (rule STORE in Fig. 4). This follows from $d :: (c$? high : low) in the invariant, which simplifies to $d ::$ high given the guard $c \equiv$ true of the if-statement. Finally, when the right thread releases mutex, invariant (4) holds for the updated contents of rec (rule UNLOCK in Fig. 4).

2.3 Security Intuition and Informal Security Property

But what does security mean in SECCSL? Indeed, the SECCSL a judgement $\ell_A \vdash \{P\} \; c \; \{Q\}$ additionally implies that the program c does not leak any sensitive information during its execution to potential attackers.

The attacker security level ℓ_A in (3) represents an upper bound on the parts of the program's memory that a potential, passive attacker is assumed to be able to observe before, during, and after the program's execution. Intuitively this encompasses all memory locations whose sensitivity is $\sqsubseteq \ell_A$. Which memory locations have sensitivity $\sqsubseteq \ell_A$ is defined by the *location-sensitivity* assertions in the precondition P and the lock invariants: A memory location loc is visible to the ℓ_A attacker iff P or a lock invariant contains some $e \overset{e_l}{\longmapsto} e'$ and in the program's initial state e evaluates to loc and e_l evaluates to some label ℓ such that $\ell \sqsubseteq \ell_A$ (see Fig. 3).

Which data is sensitive and should not be leaked to the ℓ_A attacker is defined by the *value-sensitivity* assertions in P and the lock invariants: an expression e is sensitive when P or a lock invariant contains some $e :: e_l$ and in the program's initial state e_l evaluates to some ℓ with $\ell \not\sqsubseteq \ell_A$. Security, then, requires that in all intermediate states of the program's execution no sensitive data (as defined by value-sensitivity assertions) can be inferred via the attacker-observable memory (as defined by location-sensitivity assertions).

SECCSL proves a *compositional* security property that formalises this intuition (see Definition 3). Since the property needs to be compositional with regards to concurrent execution, the resulting security property is *timing sensitive*, meaning that not only must the program never reveal sensitive data into attacker-observable memory locations but the times at which it updates these memory locations cannot depend on sensitive data. It is well-known that timing-insensitive security properties are not compositional under standard scheduling models [34,48]. For this reason SECCSL forbids programs from branching on sensitive values. We believe that this restriction could in principle be relaxed in the future via established techniques [28,29].

SECCSL's top-level soundness (Sect. 4) formalises the above intuitive definition of security in the style of traditional *noninterference* [19] that compares two program executions with respect to the observations that can be made by an attacker. SECCSL adopts a *relational* interpretation for the assertions P and Q, and the lock invariants, in which they are evaluated against pairs of execution states. This relational semantics directly expresses the comparison needed for noninterference. As a result, most of the complexities related to SECCSL's soundness are confined to the semantic level, whereas the calculus retains its similarity to standard separation logic and hence its simplicity.

Under this relational semantics (see Fig. 2 in Sect. 3), when a pair of states satisfies an assertion P, it implies that the two states agree on the values of all non-sensitive expressions as defined by P (Lemma 1). Noninterference is then stated as Theorem 2: Program c with precondition P is secure against the ℓ_A-attacker if, whenever executed twice from two initial states jointly satisfying P and the lock invariants (and so agreeing on the values of all data assumed to be initially observable to the ℓ_A attacker), in all intermediate pairs of states arrived at after running each execution for the same number of steps, the resulting states again agree at that initially ℓ_A-visible memory. This definition is timing sensitive as it compares executions that have the same number of steps.

3   The Logic SECCSL

3.1   Assertions

Pure expressions e that do not depend on the heap are composed of variables x, function applications, equations, and conditional expressions. Pure relational formulas ρ comprise boolean expressions ϕ, value sensitivity $e :: e_l$, and relational implication $\Rightarrow$ (wlog. covering relational $\neg$, $\wedge$, $\vee$). We assume a standard first-order many sorted typing discipline (not elaborated).

$$e ::= x \mid f(e_1, \ldots, e_n) \mid e_1 = e_2 \mid \phi \; ? \; e_1 : e_2 \qquad \rho ::= \phi \mid e :: e_l \mid \rho_1 \Rightarrow \rho_2$$

We postulate that the logical signature contains a sort Label, corresponding to the security lattice, with constants low, high: Label and a binary predicate symbol $\sqsubseteq$: Label $\times$ Label $\rightarrow$ Bool, whose interpretation satisfies the lattice axioms.

SECCSL's assertions P, Q may additionally refer to the heap and thus include the empty heap description, labelled points-to predicates (heap location sensitivity assertions), assertions guarded by (pure) conditionals, ordinary overlapping conjunction as well as separating conjunction, and existential quantification.

$$P ::= \rho \mid \mathsf{emp} \mid e_p \xrightarrow{e_l} e_v \mid (\phi \; ? \; P : Q) \mid P \wedge Q \mid P \star Q \mid \exists \, x. \; P$$

Disjunction, negation, and implication are excluded because they cause issues for describing the set of ℓ-visible heap location to the ℓ-attacker, similarly to the problem of defining heap footprints for non-precise assertions [26,40,41]. These connectives can still occur between pure and relational expressions.

The standard expression semantics $[\![e]\!]_s$ evaluates e over a store s, which assigns values to variables x as $s(x)$. The interpretation $f^{\mathcal{A}}$ of a function symbol f is a function, given statically by a logical structure $\mathcal{A}$. Specifically, $\sqsubseteq^{\mathcal{A}}$ is the semantic ordering of the security lattice. We write $s \models \phi$ if $[\![\phi]\!]_s = true$.

The relational semantics of assertions, written $(s, h), (s', h') \models_\ell P$, is defined in Fig. 2 over two states (s, h) and (s', h') each consisting of a store and a heap. The semantics is defined against the attacker security level ℓ (called ℓ_A in Sect. 2.3). Stores s and s' are related via $e :: e_l$. We require the expression e_l denoting the sensitivity to coincide on s and s' and whenever $[\![e_l]\!]_s \sqsubseteq^A \ell$ holds, e must evaluate to the same value both states, (7). Heaps are related by $(s, h), (s', h') \models_\ell e_p \xmapsto{e_l} e_v$, which similarly ensures that the two heap fragments are identical $h = h'$ when e_l says so, (9). Conditional assertions $\phi ? P : Q$ evaluate to P when ϕ holds (relationally), and to Q otherwise. The separating conjunction splits both heaps independently, (12). Similarly, the existential quantifier picks two values v and v', (13). Whether parts of the split resp. these two values actually agree will depend on other assertions made.

Using the abbreviation $s, h \models e_p \mapsto e_v \iff h = \{[\![e_p]\!]_s \mapsto [\![e_v]\!]_s\}$

$$(s, h), (s', h') \models_\ell \mathsf{emp} \iff h = h' = \varnothing \tag{5}$$

$$(s, h), (s', h') \models_\ell \phi \iff s \models \phi \text{ and } s' \models \phi \tag{6}$$

$$(s, h), (s', h') \models_\ell e :: e_l \tag{7}$$
$$\iff [\![e_l]\!]_s = [\![e_l]\!]_{s'} \text{ and } \left([\![e_l]\!]_s \sqsubseteq^A \ell \implies [\![e]\!]_s = [\![e]\!]_{s'}\right)$$

$$(s, h), (s', h') \models_\ell \rho_1 \Rightarrow \rho_2 \tag{8}$$
$$\iff (s, h), (s', h') \models_\ell \rho_1 \text{ implies } (s, h), (s', h') \models_\ell \rho_2$$

$$(s, h), (s', h') \models_\ell e_p \xmapsto{e_l} e_v \tag{9}$$
$$\iff s, h \models e_p \mapsto e_v \text{ and } s', h' \models e_p \mapsto e_v \text{ and } (s, h), (s', h') \models e_p :: e_l \wedge e_v :: e_l$$

$$(s, h), (s', h') \models_\ell (\phi ? P : Q) \tag{10}$$
$$\iff \begin{cases} (s, h), (s', h') \models_\ell P, & \text{if } s \models \phi \text{ and } s' \models \phi \\ (s, h), (s', h') \models_\ell Q, & \text{otherwise} \end{cases}$$

$$(s, h), (s', h') \models_\ell P \wedge Q \tag{11}$$
$$\iff (s, h), (s', h') \models_\ell P \text{ and } (s, h), (s', h') \models_\ell Q$$

$$(s, h), (s', h') \models_\ell P \star Q \tag{12}$$
$$\iff \text{there are disjoint sub-heaps } h_1, h_2 \text{ and } h_1', h_2'$$
$$\text{with } h = h_1 \uplus h_2 \text{ and } h' = h_1' \uplus h_2'$$
$$\text{such that } (s, h_1), (s', h_1') \models_\ell P_1 \text{ and } (s, h_2), (s', h_2') \models_\ell P_2$$

$$(s, h), (s', h') \models_\ell \exists x. P \tag{13}$$
$$\iff \text{there are values } v, v' \text{ such that } (s(x := v), h), (s'(x := v'), h') \models P$$

Fig. 2. Relational semantics of assertions.

To capture strong security properties, we require a declarative specification of which heap locations are considered visible to the ℓ-attacker, when assertion P

$$\text{lows}_\ell(\rho, s) = \emptyset, \qquad \text{notably lows}_\ell(e :: e_l, s) = \emptyset$$

$$\text{lows}_\ell(P \star Q, s) = \text{lows}_\ell(P \wedge Q, s) = \text{lows}_\ell(P, s) \cup \text{lows}_\ell(Q, s)$$

$$\text{lows}_\ell(e_p \xrightarrow{e_l} e_v, s) = \begin{cases} \{\llbracket e_p \rrbracket_s\}, & \llbracket e_l \rrbracket_s \sqsubseteq^A \ell \\ \emptyset, & \text{otherwise} \end{cases}$$

$$\text{lows}_\ell(\phi \ ? \ P : Q, s) = \begin{cases} \text{lows}_\ell(P, s), & s \models \phi \\ \text{lows}_\ell(Q, s), & \text{otherwise} \end{cases}$$

$$\text{lows}_\ell(\exists \ x. \ P, s) = \begin{cases} \text{lows}_\ell(P, s), & \forall \ v. \ \text{lows}_\ell(P, s) = \text{lows}_\ell(P, s(x \mapsto v)) \\ \emptyset, & \text{otherwise} \end{cases}$$

Fig. 3. Low locations of an assertion.

holds in some (initial) state (see Sect. 2.3). We define this set in Fig. 3, denoted $\text{lows}_\ell(P, s)$ for initial store s. Note that, by design, the definition does not give a useful result for an existential like $\exists p \ v. \ p \xrightarrow{\text{low}} v$. This mirrors the usual difficulty of defining footprints for non-precise separation logic assertions [26,40,41]. This restriction is not an issue in practice, as location sensitivity assertions $e_p \xrightarrow{e_l} e_v$ are intended to describe the static regions of memory (data sinks) visible to the attacker, for which existential quantification over variables free in e_p or e_l is not necessary. A generalization to all precise predicates should be possible.

3.2 Entailments

Although implications between spatial formulas is not part of the assertion language, entailments $P \overset{\ell}{\Longrightarrow} Q$ between assertions still play a role in SecCSL's Hoare style consequence rule (Conseq in Fig. 4). We discuss entailment now as it sheds useful light on some consequences of SecCSL's relational semantics.

Definition 1 (Secure Entailment). *$P \overset{\ell}{\Longrightarrow} Q$ holds iff*

- *$(s, h), (s', h') \models_\ell P$ implies $(s, h), (s', h') \models_\ell Q$ for all s, h and s', h', and*
- *$\text{lows}_\ell(P, s) \subseteq \text{lows}_\ell(Q, s)$ for all s*

The security level ℓ is used not just in the evaluation of the assertions but also to preserve the ℓ-attacker visible locations of P in Q. This reflects the intuition that P is stronger than Q, and so Q should make fewer assumptions than P on the limitations of an attacker's observational powers.

Proposition 1.

$$e = e' \wedge e_l = e_l' \wedge e :: e_l \overset{\ell}{\Longrightarrow} e' :: e_l' \tag{14}$$

$$e :: e_l \wedge e_l \sqsubseteq e_l' \wedge e_l' :: \ell \overset{\ell}{\Longrightarrow} e :: e_l' \tag{15}$$

$$e_l :: \ell \overset{\ell}{\Longrightarrow} c :: e_l \qquad \textit{for a constant } c \tag{16}$$

$$e_1 :: e_l \wedge \cdots \wedge e_n :: e_l \overset{\ell}{\Longrightarrow} f(e_1, \ldots, e_n) :: e_l \qquad \textit{for } n > 0 \tag{17}$$

$$e_p \overset{e_l}{\longmapsto} e_v \wedge e_l \sqsubseteq \ell \overset{\ell}{\Longrightarrow} e_p \overset{e_l}{\longmapsto} e_v \wedge e_p :: e_l \wedge e_v :: e_l \tag{18}$$

$$\big(\forall\ s.\ \mathrm{lows}_\ell(P, s) = \mathrm{lows}_\ell(Q, s)\big)\ \textit{implies}\ \phi \wedge (\phi\ ?\ P : Q) \overset{\ell}{\Longrightarrow} P \tag{19}$$

$$P \overset{\ell}{\Longrightarrow} P'\ \textit{and}\ Q \overset{\ell}{\Longrightarrow} Q'\ \textit{implies}\ P \star Q \overset{\ell}{\Longrightarrow} P' \star Q' \tag{20}$$

Entailment (14) in Proposition 1 shows that sensitivity of values is compatible with equality. This property fails in the security separation logic of [14], where labels are part of the semantics of expressions but are not compared by equality. The second property (15) captures the intuition that less-sensitive data can always be used in contexts where more-sensitive data might be expected (but not vice-versa). Recall that e_l' here is an expression. The additional condition $e_l' :: \ell$ guarantees that this expression denotes a meaningful security level, i.e. evaluates identically in both states (cf. (7)). (abusing notation to let the semantic ℓ stand for some expression that denotes it). Property (16) encodes that constants do not depend on any state; again the security level expression e_l must be meaningful, but trivially $c :: \ell$ when ℓ is constant, too. Value sensitivity is congruent with function application (17). This is not surprising, as functions map arguments equal in both states to equal results. Yet, as with (14) above, this property fails in [14] where security labels are attached to values. Note that the reverse entailment is false (e.g. for the constant function $\lambda x.c$).

Via (18), when $e_p \overset{e_l}{\longmapsto} e_v$ it follows that both the location e_p and the value e_v adhere to the level e_l, cf. (9). Note that the antecedent $e_p \overset{e_l}{\longmapsto} e_v$ is repeated in the consequent to ensure that the set of ℓ-attacker visible locations is preserved. Conditional assertions can be resolved when the test is definite, provided that P and Q describe the same set of public locations, (19) and symmetrically for $\neg\phi$. Finally, separating conjunction is monotone wrt. entailment (20).

3.3 Proof System

We consider a canonical concurrent programming language with shared heap locations protected by locks but without shared variables. Commands c comprise assignments to local variables, heap access (load and store),[1] sequential programming constructs, as well as parallel composition and locking. We assume

---

[1] Volatile memory locations can be treated analogously to locks by introducing an additional assertion characterizing that part of the heap, that is implicitly available to atomic commands. This feature is realized in the Isabelle theories [18] but omitted here in the interests of brevity.

a static collection of valid lock identifiers l, each of which has an assertion as its associated invariant $\text{inv}(l)$, characterizing the protected portion of the heap. We describe the program semantics in Sect. 4 as part of the soundness proof.

$$c ::= \; x := e \mid x := [e_v] \mid [e_p] := e_v \mid \text{lock } l \mid \text{unlock } l$$
$$c_1; c_2 \mid c_1 \parallel c_2 \mid \text{if } b \text{ then } c_1 \text{ else } c_2 \mid \text{while } b \text{ do } c$$

The SECCSL proof rules are shown in Fig. 4. They extend the standard rules of concurrent separation logic [38] (CSL) by additional side-conditions that amount to information flow checks $e :: \_$ as part of the respective preconditions. Similarly to [46], without loss of generality we require that assignments (rules ASG, LOAD) are always to distinct variables, to avoid renaming in the assertions. In the postcondition of LOAD, $x :: e_l$ can be derived by CONSEQ for (18). Storing to a heap location through an e_l-sensitive location $e_p \xrightarrow{e_l} e_v$ (rule STORE) requires that the value e_v written to that location admits the corresponding security level e_l of the location e_p. Note that due to monotonicity (15) the security level does not have to match exactly. The rules for locking are standard [12]. To preclude information leaks through timing channels, the execution can branch on non-secret values only. This manifests in side conditions $b :: \ell$ for the respective branching condition b where, recall, ℓ is the attacker security level (IF, WHILE). Logical SPLIT picks those two cases where $\llbracket \phi \rrbracket_s = \llbracket \phi \rrbracket_{s'}$, ruling out the other two by $\phi :: \ell$. The consequence rule (CONSEQ) uses entailment relative to ℓ (Definition 1). Rule PAR has the usual proviso that the variables modified in one thread cannot interfere with those relied on by the other and its pre-/postcondition.

4 Security Definition and Soundness

The soundness theorem for SECCSL guarantees that if some triple $\ell \vdash \{P\} \, c \, \{Q\}$ is derived using the rules of Fig. 4, then: all executions of c started in a state satisfying precondition P are memory *safe*, partially *correct* with respect to postcondition Q, and moreover *secure* with respect to the sensitivity of values as denoted by P and Q and at all times respect the sensitivity of locations as denoted by P (see Sect. 2.3). Proof outlines are relegated to Appendix B. All results have been mechanised in Isabelle/HOL [37] and are available at [18].

The top-level security property of SECCSL is a noninterference condition [19]. Noninterference as a security property specifies, roughly, that for any pair of executions that start in states that agree on the values of all attacker-observable inputs, then, from the attacker's point of view the resulting executions will be indistinguishable, i.e. all of the attacker visible observations will agree. In SECCSL, what is "attacker-observable" depends on the attacker level ℓ. The "inputs" are the expressions e, and the attacker-visible inputs are those expressions e whose sensitivity is given by $e :: \ell'$ judgements in the precondition P for which $\ell' \sqsubseteq \ell$. The attacker-visible observations are the contents of all memory locations in $\text{lows}_\ell(P, s)$, for initial store s and precondition P. Thus we define when two heaps are indistinguishable to the ℓ-attacker.

$$\frac{x \notin \mathrm{free}(e)}{\ell \vdash \{\mathrm{emp}\}\ x := e\ \{x = e\}}\ \mathrm{ASG}$$

$$\frac{x \notin \mathrm{free}(e_p, e_v, e_l)}{\ell \vdash \{e_p \xmapsto{e_l} e_v\}\ x := [e_p]\ \{x = e_v \wedge e_p \xmapsto{e_l} e_v\}}\ \mathrm{LOAD}$$

$$\frac{}{\ell \vdash \{e_v :: e_l \wedge e_p \xmapsto{e_l} \_\}\ [e_p] := e_v\ \{e_p \xmapsto{e_l} e_v\}}\ \mathrm{STORE}$$

$$\frac{}{\ell \vdash \{\mathrm{emp}\}\ \mathtt{lock}\ l\ \{\mathrm{inv}(l)\}}\ \mathrm{LOCK}$$

$$\frac{}{\ell \vdash \{\mathrm{inv}(l)\}\ \mathtt{unlock}\ l\ \{\mathrm{emp}\}}\ \mathrm{UNLOCK}$$

$$\frac{\ell \vdash \{b \wedge P\}\ c\ \{Q\} \quad \ell \vdash \{\neg b \wedge P\}\ c\ \{Q\}}{\ell \vdash \{b :: \ell \wedge P\}\ \mathtt{if}\ b\ \mathtt{then}\ c_1\ \mathtt{else}\ c_2\ \{Q\}}\ \mathrm{IF}$$

$$\frac{\ell \vdash \{\phi \wedge P\}\ c\ \{Q\} \quad \ell \vdash \{\neg\phi \wedge P\}\ c\ \{Q\}}{\ell \vdash \{\phi :: \ell \wedge P\}\ c\ \{Q\}}\ \mathrm{SPLIT}$$

$$\frac{\ell \vdash \{b \wedge b :: \ell \wedge P\}\ c\ \{b :: \ell \wedge P\}}{\ell \vdash \{b :: \ell \wedge P\}\ \mathtt{while}\ b\ \mathtt{do}\ c\ \{\neg b \wedge P\}}\ \mathrm{WHILE}$$

$$\frac{\ell \vdash \{P\}\ c_1\ \{R\} \quad \ell \vdash \{R\}\ c_2\ \{Q\}}{\ell \vdash \{P\}\ c_1; c_2\ \{Q\}}\ \mathrm{SEQ}$$

$$\frac{\mathrm{modified}(c) \cap \mathrm{free}(F) = \varnothing \quad \ell \vdash \{P\}\ c\ \{Q\}}{\ell \vdash \{P \star F\}\ c\ \{Q \star F\}}\ \mathrm{FRAME}$$

$$\frac{P \xRightarrow{\ell} P' \quad Q' \xRightarrow{\ell} Q \quad \ell \vdash \{P'\}\ c\ \{Q'\}}{\ell \vdash \{P\}\ c\ \{Q\}}\ \mathrm{CONSEQ}$$

$$\frac{\mathrm{modified}(c_i) \cap \mathrm{free}(c_j, P_j, Q_j) = \varnothing\ \text{for}\ i \neq j \quad \ell \vdash \{P_1\}\ c_1\ \{P_1\} \quad \ell \vdash \{P_2\}\ c_2\ \{P_2\}}{\ell \vdash \{P_1 \star P_2\}\ c_1 \parallel c_2\ \{Q_1 \star Q_2\}}\ \mathrm{PAR}$$

Fig. 4. Proof rules of SECCSL.

Definition 2 (ℓ Equivalence). *Two heaps coincide on a set of locations A, written $h \equiv_A h'$, iff for all $a \in A$. $a \in \mathrm{dom}\ (h) \cap \mathrm{dom}\ (h')$ and $h(a) = h'(a)$. Two heaps h and h' are ℓ-equivalent wrt. store s and assertion P, if $h \equiv_A h'$ for $A = \mathrm{lows}_\ell(P, s)$.*

Then, the ℓ-validity of an assertion P in the relational semantics witnesses ℓ-equivalence between the corresponding heaps.

Lemma 1. *If $(s, h), (s', h') \models_\ell P$, then $h \equiv_A h'$ for $A = \mathrm{lows}_\ell(P, s)$.*

Furthermore, if $(s, h), (s', h') \models_\ell P$, then $\mathrm{lows}_\ell(P, s) = \mathrm{lows}_\ell(P, s')$ since the security levels in labeled points-to predicates must coincide on s and s', cf. (9).

Semantics. Semantic configurations, denoted by k in the following, are one of three kinds: (**run** c, L, s, h) denotes a command c in a state s, h where L is a set of locks that are currently not held by any thread and can be acquired by c; (**stop** L, s, h) similarly denotes a final state s, h with residual locks L, and **abort** results from invalid heap access.

The single-step relation (**run** c, L, s, h) $\xrightarrow{\sigma}$ k takes running configurations to successors k with respect to a schedule σ that resolves the non-determinism of parallel composition. The schedule σ is a list of *actions*: the action $\langle \tau \rangle$ represents the execution of atomic commands and the evaluation of conditionals;

the actions $\langle 1 \rangle$ and $\langle 2 \rangle$ respectively denote the execution of the left- and right-hand sides of a parallel composition for a single step, and so define a deterministic scheduling discipline reminiscent of separation kernels [32]. For example, $(\mathbf{run}\ c_1\ \|\ c_2, L, s, h) \xrightarrow{\langle 1 \rangle \cdot \sigma} (\mathbf{run}\ c_1'\ \|\ c_2, L', s', h')$ if $(\mathbf{run}\ c_1, L, s, h) \xrightarrow{\sigma} (\mathbf{run}\ c_1', L', s', h')$. Configurations $(\mathbf{run}\ \mathtt{lock}\ l, L, s, h)$ can only be scheduled if $l \in L$ (symmetrically for $\mathtt{unlock}$)) and otherwise block without a possible step.

Executions $k_1 \xrightarrow{\sigma_1 \cdots \sigma_n}{}^* k_{n+1}$ chain several steps $k_i \xrightarrow{\sigma_i} k_{i+1}$ by accumulating the schedule. We are considering partial correctness only, thus the schedule is always finite and so are all executions. The rules for program steps are otherwise standard and can be found in Appendix A.

Compositional Security. To prove that SECCSL establishes its top-level non-interference condition, we first define a compositional security condition that provides the central characterization of security for a command c with respect to precondition P and postcondition Q. That central, compositional property we denote $\mathrm{secure}_\ell^n(P, c, Q)$ and formalize below in Definition 3. It ensures that the first n steps (or fewer if the program terminates before that) are safe and preserve ℓ-equivalence of the heap locations specified initially in P, but in a way that is compositional across multiple execution steps, across multiple threads of execution and across different parts of the heap. It is somewhat akin, although more precise than, prior characterizations based on *strong low bisimulation* [16,45].

Disregarding the case when c terminates before the n-th step for a moment, for a pair of initial states (s_1, h_1) and (s_1', h_1') and initial set of locks L_1, and a fixed schedule $\sigma = \sigma_1 \cdots \sigma_n$, $\mathrm{secure}_\ell^{n+1}(P_1, c_1, Q)$ requires that c performs a sequence of lockstep execution steps from each initial state

$$(\mathbf{run}\ c_i, L_i, s_i, h_i) \xrightarrow{\sigma_i} (\mathbf{run}\ c_{i+1}, L_{i+1}, s_{i+1}, h_{i+1}) \qquad \text{for } 1 \leq i \leq n$$

$$(\mathbf{run}\ c_i, L_i, s_i', h_i') \xrightarrow{\sigma_i} (\mathbf{run}\ c_{i+1}, L_{i+1}, s_{i+1}', h_{i+1}') \qquad (21)$$

These executions must agree on the intermediate commands c_i and locks L_i and the ith pair of states must satisfy an intermediate assertion of the following form:

$$(s_i, h_i), (s_i', h_i') \models_\ell P_i \star F \star \mathrm{invs}(L_i) \quad \text{where } \mathrm{invs}(L_i) = \bigstar_{l_i \in L_i} \mathrm{inv}(l_i) \quad (22)$$

Here P_i describes the part of the heap that command c_i is currently accessing. $\mathrm{invs}(L_i)$ is the set of lock invariants for the locks $l_i \in L_i$ not currently acquired. Its presence ensures that whenever a lock is acquired that the associated invariant can be assumed to hold. Finally F is an arbitrary *frame*, an assertion that does not mention variables updated by c_i. Its inclusion allows the security property to compose with respect to different parts of the heap.

Moreover, each $P_{i+1} \star \mathrm{invs}(L_{i+1})$ is required to preserve the sensitivity of all ℓ-visible heap locations of $P_i \star \mathrm{invs}(L_i)$, i.e. so that $\mathrm{lows}_\ell(P_i \star \mathrm{invs}(L_i), s_i) \subseteq \mathrm{lows}_\ell(P_{i+1} \star \mathrm{invs}(L_{i+1}), s_{i+1})$. If some intermediate step $m \leq n$ terminates, then $P_{m+1} = Q$, ensuring the postcondition holds when the executions terminate. Lastly, neither execution is allowed to reach an **abort** configuration.

If the initial state satisfies $P_1 \star F \star \mathrm{invs}(L_1)$ then (22) holds throughout the entire execution, and establishes the end-to-end property that any final state indeed satisfies the postcondition and that $\mathrm{lows}_\ell(P_1 \star \mathrm{invs}(L_1), s_1) \subseteq \mathrm{lows}_\ell(P_i \star \mathrm{invs}(L_i), s_i)$ with respect to the initially specified low locations.

The property $\mathrm{secure}_\ell^n(P, c, Q)$ is defined recursively to match the steps of the lockstep execution of the program.

Definition 3 (Security).

– $\mathrm{secure}_\ell^0(P_1, c_1, Q)$ *holds always.*
– $\mathrm{secure}_\ell^{n+1}(P_1, c_1, Q)$ *holds, iff for all pairs of states* (s_1, h_1), (s_1', h_1'), *frames* F, *and sets of locks* L_1, *such that* $(s_1, h_1), (s_1', h_1') \models_\ell P_1 \star F \star \mathrm{invs}(L_1)$, *and given two steps* $(\mathbf{run}\ c_1, L_1, s_1, h_1) \xrightarrow{\sigma} k$ *and* $(\mathbf{run}\ c_1, L_1, s_1', h_1') \xrightarrow{\sigma} k'$ *there exists an assertion* P_2 *and a pair of successor states with either of*
  • $k = (\mathbf{stop}\ L_2, s_2, h_2)$ *and* $k' = (\mathbf{stop}\ L_2, s_2', h_2')$ *and* $P_2 = Q$
  • $k = (\mathbf{run}\ c_2, L_2, s_2, h_2)$ *and* $k' = (\mathbf{run}\ c_2, L_2, s_2', h_2')$ *with* $\mathrm{secure}_\ell^n(P_2, c_2, Q)$
  such that $(s_2, h_2), (s_2', h_2') \models_\ell P_2 \star F \star \mathrm{invs}(L_2)$ *and* $\mathrm{lows}_\ell(P_1 \star \mathrm{invs}(L_1), s_1) \subseteq \mathrm{lows}_\ell(P_2 \star \mathrm{invs}(L_2), s_2)$ *in both cases.*

Two further side condition are imposed, ensuring all mutable shared state lies in the heap (cf. Sect. 3): c_1 doesn't modify variables occurring in $\mathrm{invs}(L_1)$ and F (which guarantees that both remain intact), and the free variables in P_2 can only mention those already present in P_1, c_1, or in any lock invariant (which guarantees that P_2 remains stable against concurrent assignments). Note that each step can pick a different frame F, as required for the soundness of rule PAR.

Lemma 2. $\ell \vdash \{P\}\ c\ \{Q\}$ *implies* $\mathrm{secure}_\ell^n(P, c, Q)$ *for every* $n \geq 0$.

Safety, Correctness and Noninterference. Execution safety and correctness with respect to pre- and postcondition follow straightforwardly from Lemma 2.

Corollary 1 (Safety). *Given initial states* $(s_1, h_1), (s_1', h_1') \models_\ell P \star \mathrm{invs}(L_1)$ *and two executions of a command* c *under the same schedule to resulting configurations* k *and* k' *respectively, then* $\ell \vdash \{P\}\ c\ \{Q\}$ *implies* $k \neq \mathbf{abort} \wedge k' \neq \mathbf{abort}$.

Theorem 1 (Correctness). *For initial states* $(s_1, h_1), (s_1', h_1') \models_\ell P \star \mathrm{invs}(L_1)$, *given two complete executions of a command* c *under the same schedule* σ

$$(\mathbf{run}\ c, L_1, s_1, h_1) \xrightarrow{\sigma *} (\mathbf{stop}\ L_2, s_2, h_2)$$

$$(\mathbf{run}\ c_i, L_i, s_i', h_i') \xrightarrow{\sigma *} (\mathbf{stop}\ L_2, s_2', h_2')$$

then $\ell \vdash \{P\}\ c\ \{Q\}$ *implies* $(s_2, h_2), (s_2', h_2') \models_\ell Q \star \mathrm{invs}(L_2)$.

The top-level noninterference property also follows from Lemma 2 via Lemma 1. For brevity, we state the noninterference property directly in the theorem:

Theorem 2 (Noninterference). *Given a command c, and initial states* $(s_1, h_1), (s'_1, h'_1) \models_\ell P \star \mathrm{invs}(L_1)$ *then* $\ell \vdash \{P\}\ c\ \{Q\}$ *implies* $h_i \equiv_A h'_i$*, where* $A = \mathrm{lows}_\ell(P \star \mathrm{invs}(L_1), s_1)$*, for all pairs of heaps* h_i *and* h'_i *arising from executing the same schedule from each initial state.*

5   SECC: Automating SECCSL

To demonstrate the ease by which SECCSL can be automated, we develop the prototype tool SECC, available at [18]. It implements the logic from Sect. 3 for a subset of C. SECC is currently used to explore reasoning about example programs with interesting security policies. Thus its engineering has focused on features related to security reasoning (e.g. deciding when conditions $e :: e_l$ are entailed) rather than reasoning about complex data structures.

Symbolic Execution. SECC automates SECCSL through symbolic execution, as pioneered for SL in [7]. Similarly to VeriFast's algorithm in [22], the verifier computes the strongest postcondition of a command c when executed in a symbolic state, yielding a set of possible final symbolic states. Each such state $\sigma = (\rho, s, \underline{P})$ maintains a path condition ρ of relational formulas (from procedure contracts, invariants, and the evaluation of conditionals) and a symbolic heap described by a list $\underline{P} = (P_1 \star \cdots \star P_n)$ of atomic spatial assertions (points-to and instances of defined predicates). The symbolic store s maps program variables to pure expressions, where $s(e)$ denotes substituting s into e. As an example, when $P_i = s(e_p) \mapsto v$ is part of the symbolic heap, a load $x := e_p$ in σ can be executed to yield the updated state $(\rho, s(x := v), \underline{P})$ where x is mapped to v.

To find the P_i we match the left-hand sides of points-to predicates. Similarly, matching is used during checking of entailments $\rho_1 \wedge \underline{P} \overset{\ell}{\implies} \exists\ \underline{x}.\ \rho_2 \wedge Q$, where the conclusion is normalized to prenex form. The entailment is reduced to a non-spatial problem by incrementally computing a substitution τ for the existentials $\underline{x}$, removing pairs $P_i = \tau(Q_j)$ in the process, as justified by (20) (see also "subtraction rules" in [7, Sec. 4]).

Finally, the remaining relational problem $\rho_1 \Rightarrow \rho_2$ without spatial connectives can be encoded into first-order [17], by duplicating the pure formulas in terms of fresh variables to represent the second state, and by the syntactic equivalent of (7). The resulting verification condition is discharged with Z3 [15]. This translation is semantically complete. For example, consider Fig. 4 from Prabawa et al. [43]. It has a conditional `if(b == b)` ..., whose check $(b = b) :: \mathrm{low}$, translated to $(b = b) = (b' = b')$ by SECC, holds independently of b's sensitivity.

Features. In addition to the logic from Sect. 3, SECC supports procedure modular verification with pre-/postconditions as usual; and it supports user-defined spatial predicates. While some issues of the C source language are not addressed (yet), such as integer overflow, those that impact directly on information flow security are taken into account. Specifically, the shortcut semantics of boolean operators `&&`, `||`, and ternary `_ ? _ : _` count as branching points and as such the left hand side resp. the test must not depend on sensitive data, similarly to the conditions of `if` statements and `while` loops.

A direct benefit of the integration of security levels into the assertion language is that it becomes possible to specify the sensitivity of data passed to library and operating system functions. For example, the execution time of `malloc(len)` would depend on the value of `len`, which can thus be required to satisfy `len :: low` by annotating its function header with an appropriate precondition, using SECC's `requires` annotation. Likewise, SECC can reason about limited forms of declassification, in which external functions are trusted to safely release otherwise sensitive data, by giving them appropriate pre-/postconditions. For example, a password hashing library function prototype might be annotated with a postcondition asserting its result is `low`, via SECC's `ensures` annotation.

Examples and Case Study. SECC proves Fig. 1 secure, and correctly flags buggy variants as insecure, e.g., where the test in thread 1 is reversed, or when thread 2 does not clear the `data` field upon setting the `is_classified` to `FALSE`. SECC also correctly analyzes those 7 examples from [17] that are supported by the logic and tool (each in ~10 ms). All examples are available at [18].

To compare SECC and SECCSL against the recent COVERN logic [34], we took a non-trivial example program that Murray et al. verified in COVERN, manually translated it to C, and verified it automatically using SECC. The original program[2], written in COVERN's tiny While language embedded in Isabelle/HOL, models the software functionality of a simplified implementation of the Cross Domain Desktop Compositor (CDDC) [5]. The CDDC is a device that facilitates interactions with multiple PCs, each of which runs applications at differing sensitivity, from a single keyboard, mouse and display. Its multi-threaded software handles routing of keyboard input to the appropriate PC and switching between the PCs via mouse gestures. Verifying the C translation required adding SECCSL annotations for procedure pre-/postconditions and loop invariants. The C translation including those annotations is ~250 lines in length. The present, unoptimised, implementation of SECC verifies the resulting artifact in ~5 s. In contrast, the COVERN proof of this example requires ~600 lines of Isabelle/HOL definitions/specification, plus ~550 lines of Isabelle proof script.

6   Related Work

There has been much work targeting type systems and program logics for concurrent information flow. Karbyshev et al. [23] provide an excellent overview. Here we concentrate on work whose ideas are most closely related to SECCSL.

Costanzo and Shao [14] propose a sequential separation logic for reasoning about information flow. Unlike SECCSL, theirs does not distinguish value and location sensitivity. Their separation logic assertions have a fairly standard (non-relational) semantics, at the price of having a *security-aware* language semantics

---

[2] https://bitbucket.org/covern/covern/src/master/examples/cddc/Example_CDDC_ WhileLockLanguage.thy.

that propagates security labels attached to values in the store and heap. As mentioned in Sect. 3.2, this has the unfortunate side-effect of breaking intuitive properties about sensitivity assertions. We conjecture that the absence of such properties would make their logic harder to automate than SECCSL, which SECC demonstrates is feasible. SECCSL avoids the aforementioned drawbacks by adopting a relational assertion semantics.

Gruetter and Murray [20] propose a security separation logic in Coq [8] for Verifiable C, the C subset of the Verified Software Toolchain [2,3]. However they provide no soundness proof for its rules and its feasibility to automate is unclear.

Two recent compositional logics for concurrent information flow are the COV-ERN logic [34] and the type and effect system of Karbyshev et al. [23]. Both borrow ideas from separation logic. However, unlike SECCSL, neither is defined for languages with pointers, arrays etc.

Like SECCSL, COVERN proves a timing-sensitive security property. Location sensitivity is defined statically by value-dependent predicates, and value sensitivity is tracked by a dependent security typing context Γ [35], relative to a Hoare logic predicate P over the entire shared memory. In COVERN locks carry non-relational invariants. In contrast, SECCSL unifies these elements together into separation logic assertions with a relational semantics. Doing so leads to a much simpler logic, amenable to automation, while supporting pointers, etc.

On the other hand, Karbyshev et al. [23] prove a timing-*insensitive* security property, but rely on primitives to interact with the scheduler to prevent leaks via scheduling decisions. Unlike SECCSL, which assumes a deterministic scheduling discipline, Karbyshev et al. support a wider class of scheduling policies. Their system tracks resource ownership and transfer between threads at synchronisation points, similar to CSLs. Their resources include *labelled scheduler resources* that account for scheduler interaction, including when scheduling decisions become tainted by secret data—something that cannot occur in SECCSL's deterministic scheduling model.

Prior logics for sequential languages, e.g. [1,4], have also adopted separation logic ideas to reason locally about memory, combining them with relational assertions similar to SECCSL's $e :: e_l$ assertions. For instance, the agreement assertions $A(e)$ of [4] coincide with SECCSL's $e ::$ low. Unlike SECCSL, some of these logics support languages with explicit declassification actions [4].

Self-composition is another technique to exploit existing verification infrastructure for proofs of general hyperproperties [13], including but not limited to non-interference. Eilers et al. [17] present such an approach for Viper, which supports an assertion language similar to that of separation logic. It does not support public heap locations (which are information sources and sinks at the same time) albeit sinks can be modeled via preconditions of procedures. A similar approach is implemented in Frama-C [9]. Both of [9,17] do not support concurrency, and it remains unclear how self-composition could avoid an exponential blow-up from concurrent interleaving, which SECCSL avoids.

The soundness proof for SECCSL follows the general structure of Vafeiadis' [46] for CSL, which is also mechanised in Isabelle/HOL. There is, however, a technical difference: His analog of Definition 3, a recursive predicate called $\mathrm{safe}_n(c, s, h, Q)$, refers to a semantic initial state s, h whereas we propagate a syntactic assertion (22) only. Our formulation has the benefit that some of the technical reasoning in the soundness proof is easier to automate. Its drawback is the need to impose technical side-conditions on the free variables of the frame F and the intermediate assertions P_i.

7 Conclusion

We presented SecCSL, a concurrent separation logic for proving expressive data-dependent information flow properties of programs. SecCSL is considerably simpler, yet handles features like pointers, arrays etc., which are out of scope for contemporary logics. It inherits the structure of traditional concurrent separation logics, and so like those logics can be automated via symbolic execution [10, 22,30]. To demonstrate this, we implemented SecC, an automatic verifier for expressive information flow security for a subset of the C language.

Separation logic has proved to be a remarkably powerful vehicle for reasoning about programs, weak memory concurrency [47], program synthesis [42], and many other domains. With SecCSL, we hope that in future the same possibilities might be opened to verified information flow security.

Acknowledgement. We thank the anonymous reviewers for their careful and detailed comments that helped significantly to clarify the discussion of finer points.

This research was sponsored by the Department of the Navy, Office of Naval Research, under award #N62909-18-1-2049. Any opinions, findings, and conclusions or recommendations expressed in this material are those of the author(s) and do not necessarily reflect the views of the Office of Naval Research.

A Command Semantics

Symmetric parallel rules in which c_2 is scheduled under the action $\langle 2 \rangle$ omitted.

$$\frac{s' = s(x \mapsto [\![e]\!]_s)}{(\mathbf{run}\ x := e, L, s, h) \xrightarrow{\langle \tau \rangle} (\mathbf{stop}\ L, s', h)} \qquad \frac{[\![e]\!]_s \notin \mathrm{dom}\ (h)}{(\mathbf{run}\ x := [e], L, s, h) \xrightarrow{\langle \tau \rangle} \mathbf{abort}}$$

$$\frac{[\![e]\!]_s \in \mathrm{dom}\ (h) \qquad s' = s(x \mapsto h([\![e]\!]_s))}{(\mathbf{run}\ x := [e], L, s, h) \xrightarrow{\langle \tau \rangle} (\mathbf{stop}\ L, s', h)} \qquad \frac{[\![e_1]\!]_s \notin \mathrm{dom}\ (h)}{(\mathbf{run}\ [e_1] := e_2, L, s, h) \xrightarrow{\langle \tau \rangle} \mathbf{abort}}$$

$$\frac{[\![e_1]\!]_s \in \mathrm{dom}\ (h) \qquad h' = h([\![e_1]\!]_s \mapsto [\![e_2]\!]_s)}{(\mathbf{run}\ [e_1] := e_2, L, s, h) \xrightarrow{\langle \tau \rangle} (\mathbf{stop}\ L, s, h')}$$

$$\frac{l \in L \qquad L' = L \setminus \{l\}}{(\mathbf{run}\ \mathsf{lock}\ l, L, s, h) \xrightarrow{\langle \tau \rangle} (\mathbf{stop}\ L', s, h)}$$

$$\frac{l \notin L \qquad L' = L \cup \{l\}}{(\mathbf{run}\ \mathtt{unlock}\ l, L, s, h) \xrightarrow{\langle \tau \rangle} (\mathbf{stop}\ L', s, h)} \qquad \frac{(\mathbf{run}\ c_1, L, s, h) \xrightarrow{\sigma} \mathbf{abort}}{(\mathbf{run}\ c_1; c_2, L, s, h) \xrightarrow{\sigma} \mathbf{abort}}$$

$$\frac{(\mathbf{run}\ c_1, L, s, h) \xrightarrow{\sigma} \mathbf{abort}}{(\mathbf{run}\ c_1 \parallel c_2, L, s, h) \xrightarrow{\langle 1 \rangle \cdot \sigma} \mathbf{abort}} \qquad \frac{(\mathbf{run}\ c_1, L, s, h) \xrightarrow{\sigma} (\mathbf{stop}\ L', s', h')}{(\mathbf{run}\ c_1; c_2, L, s, h) \xrightarrow{\sigma} (\mathbf{run}\ c_2, L', s', h')}$$

$$\frac{(\mathbf{run}\ c_1, L, s, h) \xrightarrow{\sigma} (\mathbf{run}\ c_1', L', s', h')}{(\mathbf{run}\ c_1; c_2, L, s, h) \xrightarrow{\sigma} (\mathbf{run}\ c_1'; c_2, L', s', h')}$$

$$\frac{(\mathbf{run}\ c_1, L, s, h) \xrightarrow{\sigma} (\mathbf{stop}\ L', s', h')}{(\mathbf{run}\ c_1 \parallel c_2, L, s, h) \xrightarrow{\langle 1 \rangle \cdot \sigma} (\mathbf{run}\ c_2, L', s', h')}$$

$$\frac{(\mathbf{run}\ c_1, L, s, h) \xrightarrow{\sigma} (\mathbf{run}\ c_1', L', s', h')}{(\mathbf{run}\ c_1 \parallel c_2, L, s, h) \xrightarrow{\langle 1 \rangle \cdot \sigma} (\mathbf{run}\ c_1' \parallel c_2, L', s', h')}$$

$$\frac{\text{if } s \models b \text{ then } c' = c_1 \text{ else } c' = c_2}{(\mathbf{run}\ \mathtt{if}\ b\ \mathtt{then}\ c_1\ \mathtt{else}\ c_2, L, s, h) \xrightarrow{\langle \tau \rangle} (\mathbf{run}\ c', L, s, h)}$$

$$\frac{s \not\models b}{(\mathbf{run}\ \mathtt{while}\ b\ \mathtt{do}\ c, L, s, h) \xrightarrow{\langle \tau \rangle} (\mathbf{stop}\ L, s, h)}$$

$$\frac{s \models b}{(\mathbf{run}\ \underbrace{\mathtt{while}\ b\ \mathtt{do}\ c}_{\omega}, L, s, h) \xrightarrow{\langle \tau \rangle} (\mathbf{run}\ (c; \omega), L, s, h)}$$

$$k \xrightarrow{\langle \rangle}{}^{*} k \qquad\qquad \frac{k \xrightarrow{\sigma_1} k' \qquad k' \xrightarrow{\sigma_2}{}^{*} k''}{k \xrightarrow{\sigma_1 \cdot \sigma_2}{}^{*} k''}$$

B Proofs

Proof of Lemma 1

If $(s, h), (s', h') \models_\ell P$, then $h \overset{A}{\equiv} h'$ for $A = \mathrm{lows}_\ell(P, s)$.

Proof. By induction on the structure of P, noting that $\mathrm{lows}_\ell(\_, s)$ contains locations of the corresponding sub-heap only. □

Proof of Lemma 2

$\ell \vdash \{P\}\ c\ \{Q\}$ implies $\text{secure}_\ell^n(P, c, Q)$ for every $n \geq 0$.

Proof (Outline). By induction on the derivation of the validity of the judgement. Noting that $n = 0$ is trivial, we may unfold the recursion of the security definition once to prove the base cases of assignment, load, store, and locking, which then follow from the respective side conditions of the proof rules.

For rules IF and WHILE, the side condition $b :: \ell$ guarantees that the test evaluates equivalently in the two states and thus execution proceeds with the same remainder program.

Except for IF, all remaining rules need a second induction on n to stepwise match security of the premise to security of the conclusion (e.g. over the steps of the first command in a sequential composition $c_1; c_2$).

The rule FRAME instantiates the frame F with the same assertion in each step, whereas PAR uses the frame F to preserve the current precondition P_2 of c_2 over steps of c_1 and vice-versa. $\qquad\square$

Proof of Corollary 1

Given a command c and initial states $(s_1, h_1), (s_1', h_1') \models_\ell P \star \text{invs}(L_1)$ and two executions under the same schedule to resulting configurations k and k' respectively, then $\ell \vdash \{P\}\ c\ \{Q\}$ implies $k \neq \textbf{abort} \land k' \neq \textbf{abort}$.

Proof. By induction on the number of steps n of the executions from $\text{secure}_\ell^n(P, c, Q)$ via Lemma 2. $\qquad\square$

Proof of Theorem 1

Given a command c and initial states $(s_1, h_1), (s_1', h_1') \models_\ell P \star \text{invs}(L_1)$ and two complete executions under the same schedule σ

$$(\textbf{run}\ c, L_1, s_1, h_1) \xrightarrow{\sigma}{}^* (\textbf{stop}\ L_2, s_2, h_2)$$

$$(\textbf{run}\ c_i, L_i, s_i', h_i') \xrightarrow{\sigma}{}^* (\textbf{stop}\ L_2, s_2', h_2')$$

then $\ell \vdash \{P\}\ c\ \{Q\}$ implies $(s_2, h_2), (s_2', h_2') \models_\ell Q \star \text{invs}(L_2)$.

Proof. By induction on the number of steps n of the executions from $\text{secure}_\ell^n(P, c, Q)$ via Lemma 2. $\qquad\square$

Proof of Theorem 2

Given a command c, and initial states $(s_1, h_1), (s_1', h_1') \models_\ell P \star \text{invs}(L_1)$ then $\ell \vdash \{P\}\ c\ \{Q\}$ implies $h_i \stackrel{A}{\equiv} h_i'$, where $A = \text{lows}_\ell(P, s_1)$, for all pairs of heaps h_i and h_i' arising from executing the same schedule from each initial state.

Proof. By induction on the number of steps i up to that state from $\text{secure}_\ell^i(P, c, Q)$ via Lemma 2 we have $\text{lows}_\ell(P \star \text{invs}(L_1), s_1) \subseteq \text{lows}_\ell(P_i \star \text{invs}(L_1), s_i)$ transitively over the prefix, where P_i and s_i are from the i-th state. The theorem then follows from Lemma 1 in Sect. 3.1. $\qquad\square$

References

1. Amtoft, T., Bandhakavi, S., Banerjee, A.: A logic for information flow in object-oriented programs. In: Proceedings of Principles of Programming Languages (POPL), pp. 91–102. ACM (2006)
2. Appel, A.W., et al.: Program Logics for Certified Compilers. Cambridge University Press, New York (2014)
3. Appel, A.W., et al.: The Verified Software Toolchain (2017). https://github.com/PrincetonUniversity/VST
4. Banerjee, A., Naumann, D.A., Rosenberg, S.: Expressive declassification policies and modular static enforcement. In: Proceedings of Symposium on Security and Privacy (S&P), pp. 339–353. IEEE (2008)
5. Beaumont, M., McCarthy, J., Murray, T.: The cross domain desktop compositor: using hardware-based video compositing for a multi-level secure user interface. In: Annual Computer Security Applications Conference (ACSAC), pp. 533–545. ACM (2016)
6. Benton, N.: Simple relational correctness proofs for static analyses and program transformations. In: Proceedings of Principles of Programming Languages (POPL), pp. 14–25. ACM (2004)
7. Berdine, J., Calcagno, C., O'Hearn, P.W.: Symbolic execution with separation logic. In: Yi, K. (ed.) APLAS 2005. LNCS, vol. 3780, pp. 52–68. Springer, Heidelberg (2005). https://doi.org/10.1007/11575467_5
8. Bertot, Y., Castéran, P.: Interactive Theorem Proving and Program Development. Coq'Art: The Calculus of Inductive Constructions. Texts in Theoretical Computer Science. An EATCS Series. Springer, Heidelberg (2004). https://doi.org/10.1007/978-3-662-07964-5
9. Blatter, L., Kosmatov, N., Le Gall, P., Prevosto, V., Petiot, G.: Static and dynamic verification of relational properties on self-composed C code. In: Dubois, C., Wolff, B. (eds.) TAP 2018. LNCS, vol. 10889, pp. 44–62. Springer, Cham (2018). https://doi.org/10.1007/978-3-319-92994-1_3
10. Calcagno, C., Distefano, D.: Infer: an automatic program verifier for memory safety of C programs. In: Bobaru, M., Havelund, K., Holzmann, G.J., Joshi, R. (eds.) NFM 2011. LNCS, vol. 6617, pp. 459–465. Springer, Heidelberg (2011). https://doi.org/10.1007/978-3-642-20398-5_33
11. Calcagno, C., et al.: Moving fast with software verification. In: Havelund, K., Holzmann, G., Joshi, R. (eds.) NFM 2015. LNCS, vol. 9058, pp. 3–11. Springer, Cham (2015). https://doi.org/10.1007/978-3-319-17524-9_1
12. Chlipala, A.: Formal Reasoning About Programs (2016)
13. Clarkson, M.R., Schneider, F.B.: Hyperproperties. In: Proceedings of Computer Security Foundations Symposium (CSF), pp. 51–65 (2008)
14. Costanzo, D., Shao, Z.: A separation logic for enforcing declarative information flow control policies. In: Abadi, M., Kremer, S. (eds.) POST 2014. LNCS, vol. 8414, pp. 179–198. Springer, Heidelberg (2014). https://doi.org/10.1007/978-3-642-54792-8_10
15. de Moura, L., Bjørner, N.: Z3: an efficient SMT solver. In: Ramakrishnan, C.R., Rehof, J. (eds.) TACAS 2008. LNCS, vol. 4963, pp. 337–340. Springer, Heidelberg (2008). https://doi.org/10.1007/978-3-540-78800-3_24
16. Del Tedesco, F., Sands, D., Russo, A.: Fault-resilient non-interference. In: Proceedings of Computer Security Foundations Symposium (CSF), pp. 401–416. IEEE (2016)

17. Eilers, M., Müller, P., Hitz, S.: Modular product programs. In: Ahmed, A. (ed.) ESOP 2018. LNCS, vol. 10801, pp. 502–529. Springer, Cham (2018). https://doi.org/10.1007/978-3-319-89884-1_18

18. Ernst, G., Murray, T.: SecC tool description and Isabelle theories for SecCSL (2019). https://covern.org/secc

19. Goguen, J., Meseguer, J.: Security policies and security models. In: Proceedings of Symposium on Security and Privacy (S&P), Oakland, California, USA, pp. 11–20, April 1982

20. Gruetter, S., Murray, T.: Short paper: towards information flow reasoning about real-world C code. In: Proceedings of Workshop on Programming Languages and Analysis for Security (PLAS), pp. 43–48. ACM (2017)

21. Gu, R., et al.: CertiKOS: an extensible architecture for building certified concurrent OS kernels. In: Proceedings of USENIX Symposium on Operating Systems Design and Implementation (OSDI), November 2016

22. Jacobs, B., Smans, J., Philippaerts, P., Vogels, F., Penninckx, W., Piessens, F.: VeriFast: a powerful, sound, predictable, fast verifier for C and java. In: Bobaru, M., Havelund, K., Holzmann, G.J., Joshi, R. (eds.) NFM 2011. LNCS, vol. 6617, pp. 41–55. Springer, Heidelberg (2011). https://doi.org/10.1007/978-3-642-20398-5_4

23. Karbyshev, A., Svendsen, K., Askarov, A., Birkedal, L.: Compositional noninterference for concurrent programs via separation and framing. In: Bauer, L., Küsters, R. (eds.) POST 2018. LNCS, vol. 10804, pp. 53–78. Springer, Cham (2018). https://doi.org/10.1007/978-3-319-89722-6_3

24. Klein, G., et al.: Comprehensive formal verification of an OS microkernel. ACM Trans. Comput. Syst. **32**(1), 2:1–2:70 (2014)

25. Leroy, X.: Formal verification of a realistic compiler. Commun. ACM **52**(7), 107–115 (2009)

26. Löding, C., Madhusudan, P., Murali, A., Peña, L.: A first order logic with frames. http://madhu.cs.illinois.edu/FOFrameLogic.pdf

27. Lourenço, L., Caires, L.: Dependent information flow types. In: Proceedings of Principles of Programming Languages (POPL), Mumbai, India, pp. 317–328, January 2015

28. Mantel, H., Sands, D.: Controlled declassification based on intransitive noninterference. In: Chin, W.-N. (ed.) APLAS 2004. LNCS, vol. 3302, pp. 129–145. Springer, Heidelberg (2004). https://doi.org/10.1007/978-3-540-30477-7_9

29. Mantel, H., Sands, D., Sudbrock, H.: Assumptions and guarantees for compositional noninterference. In: Proceedings of Computer Security Foundations Symposium (CSF), Cernay-la-Ville, France, pp. 218–232, June 2011

30. Müller, P., Schwerhoff, M., Summers, A.J.: Viper: a verification infrastructure for permission-based reasoning. In: Jobstmann, B., Leino, K.R.M. (eds.) VMCAI 2016. LNCS, vol. 9583, pp. 41–62. Springer, Heidelberg (2016). https://doi.org/10.1007/978-3-662-49122-5_2

31. Murray, T.: Short paper: on high-assurance information-flow-secure programming languages. In: Proceedings of Workshop on Programming Languages and Analysis for Security (PLAS), pp. 43–48 (2015)

32. Murray, T., et al.: seL4: from general purpose to a proof of information flow enforcement. In: Proceedings of Symposium on Security and Privacy (S&P), San Francisco, CA, pp. 415–429, May 2013

33. Murray, T., Sabelfeld, A., Bauer, L.: Special issue on verified information flow security. J. Comput. Secur. **25**(4–5), 319–321 (2017)

34. Murray, T., Sison, R., Engelhardt, K.: COVERN: a logic for compositional verification of information flow control. In: Proceedings of European Symposium on Security and Privacy (EuroS&P), London, United Kingdom, April 2018
35. Murray, T., Sison, R., Pierzchalski, E., Rizkallah, C.: Compositional verification and refinement of concurrent value-dependent noninterference. In: Proceedings of Computer Security Foundations Symposium (CSF), pp. 417–431, June 2016
36. Newcombe, C., Rath, T., Zhang, F., Munteanu, B., Brooker, M., Deardeuff, M.: How Amazon web services uses formal methods. Commun. ACM **58**(4), 66–73 (2015)
37. Nipkow, T., Wenzel, M., Paulson, L.C. (eds.): Isabelle/HOL-A Proof Assistant for Higher-Order Logic. LNCS, vol. 2283. Springer, Heidelberg (2002). https://doi.org/10.1007/3-540-45949-9
38. O'Hearn, P.W.: Resources, concurrency and local reasoning. In: Gardner, P., Yoshida, N. (eds.) CONCUR 2004. LNCS, vol. 3170, pp. 49–67. Springer, Heidelberg (2004). https://doi.org/10.1007/978-3-540-28644-8_4
39. O'Hearn, P.W.: Continuous reasoning: scaling the impact of formal methods. In: Proceedings of Logic in Computer Science (LICS), pp. 13–25. ACM (2018)
40. O'Hearn, P.W., Yang, H., Reynolds, J.C.: Separation and information hiding. ACM Trans. Programm. Lang. Syst. (TOPLAS) **31**(3), 11 (2009)
41. Piskac, R., Wies, T., Zufferey, D.: Automating separation logic using SMT. In: Sharygina, N., Veith, H. (eds.) CAV 2013. LNCS, vol. 8044, pp. 773–789. Springer, Heidelberg (2013). https://doi.org/10.1007/978-3-642-39799-8_54
42. Polikarpova, N., Sergey, I.: Structuring the synthesis of heap-manipulating programs. Proc. ACM Program. Lang. **3**(POPL), 72 (2019)
43. Prabawa, A., Al Ameen, M.F., Lee, B., Chin, W.-N.: A logical system for modular information flow verification. Verification, Model Checking, and Abstract Interpretation. LNCS, vol. 10747, pp. 430–451. Springer, Cham (2018). https://doi.org/10.1007/978-3-319-73721-8_20
44. Reynolds, J.C.: Separation logic: a logic for shared mutable data structures. In: Proceedings of Logic in Computer Science (LICS), pp. 55–74. IEEE (2002)
45. Sabelfeld, A., Sands, D.: Probabilistic noninterference for multi-threaded programs. In: Proceedings of Computer Security Foundations Workshop (CSFW), pp. 200–214. IEEE (2000)
46. Vafeiadis, V.: Concurrent separation logic and operational semantics. In: Proceedings of Mathematical Foundations of Programming Semantics (MFPS), pp. 335–351 (2011)
47. Vafeiadis, V., Narayan, C.: Relaxed separation logic: a program logic for C11 concurrency. In: Proceedings of Object Oriented Programming Systems Languages & Applications (OOPSLA), pp. 867–884. ACM (2013)
48. Volpano, D., Smith, G.: Probabilistic noninterference in a concurrent language. J. Comput. Secur. **7**(2,3), 231–253 (1999)
49. Yang, H.: Relational separation logic. Theor. Comput. Sci. **375**(1–3), 308–334 (2007)
50. Zheng, L., Myers, A.C.: Dynamic security labels and static information flow control. Int. J. Inf. Secur. **6**(2–3), 67–84 (2007)

8

Gradual Consistency Checking

Rachid Zennou[1,2](✉), Ahmed Bouajjani[1], Constantin Enea[1],
and Mohammed Erradi[2]

[1] Université de Paris, IRIF, CNRS, 75013 Paris, France
rachid.zennou@gmail.com, {abou,cenea}@irif.fr
[2] ENSIAS, University Mohammed V, Rabat, Morocco
mohamed.erradi@gmail.com

Abstract. We address the problem of checking that computations of a shared memory implementation (with write and read operations) adheres to some given consistency model. It is known that checking conformance to Sequential Consistency (SC) for a given computation is NP-hard, and the same holds for checking Total Store Order (TSO) conformance. This poses a serious issue for the design of scalable verification or testing techniques for these important memory models. In this paper, we tackle this issue by providing an approach that avoids hitting systematically the worst-case complexity. The idea is to consider, as an intermediary step, the problem of checking weaker criteria that are as strong as possible while they are still checkable in polynomial time (in the size of the computation). The criteria we consider are new variations of causal consistency suitably defined for our purpose. The advantage of our approach is that in many cases (1) it can catch violations of SC/TSO early using these weaker criteria that are efficiently checkable, and (2) when a computation is causally consistent (according to our newly defined criteria), the work done for establishing this fact simplifies significantly the work required for checking SC/TSO conformance. We have implemented our algorithms and carried out several experiments on realistic cache-coherence protocols showing the efficiency of our approach.

1 Introduction

This paper addresses the problem of checking whether a given implementation of a shared memory offers the expected consistency guarantees to its clients which are concurrent programs composed of several threads running in parallel. Indeed, users of a memory need to see it as an abstract object allowing to perform concurrent reads and writes over a set of variables, which conform to some *memory model* defining the valid visible sequences of such operations. Various memory models can be considered in this context. Sequential Consistency (SC) [24] is the model where operations can be seen as atomic, executing according to some interleaving of the operations issued by the different threads, while preserving the order in which these operations were issued by each of the threads. This fundamental model offers strong consistency in the sense that for each write operation, when it is issued by a thread, it is immediately visible to all the other threads. Other weaker memory models are adopted in order to meet performance and/or availability requirements in concurrent/distributed systems. One of the most widely used models in this context is Total Store Order (TSO) [29]. In this model, writes can be delayed, which means that after a write is issued, it is not immediately visible to all threads (except for the thread that issued it), and it is committed later after some arbitrary delay. However, writes issued by the same thread are committed in the same order are they were issued, and when a write is committed it becomes visible to all the other threads simultaneously. TSO is implemented in hardware but also in a distributed context over a network [22].

Implementing shared memories that are both highly performant and correct with respect to a given memory model is an extremely hard and error prone task. Therefore, checking that a given implementation is indeed correct from this point of view is of paramount importance. In this paper we address the issue of checking that a given execution of a shared memory implementation is consistent, and we consider as consistency criteria the cases of SC and TSO.

Checking SC or TSO conformance is known to be NP-complete [18, 21]. This is due to the fact that in order to justify that the execution is consistent, one has to find a total order between the writes which explains the read operations happening along the computation. It can be proved that one cannot avoid enumerating all the possible total orders between writes, in the worst case. The situation is different for other weaker criteria such as Causal Consistency (CC) and its different variations, which have been shown to be checkable in polynomial time (in the the the size of the computation) [6]. In fact, CC imposes fewer constraints than SC/TSO on the order between writes, and the way it imposes these constraints is "deterministic", in the sense that they can be derived from the history of the execution by applying a least fixpoint computation (which can be encoded for instance, as a standard DATALOG program). All these complexity results hold under the assumption that each value is written at most once, which is without loss of generality for implementations which are data-independent [31], i.e., their behavior doesn't depend on the concrete values read or written in the program. Indeed, any buggy behavior of such implementations can be exposed in executions satisfying this assumption [1].

The intrinsic hardness of the problem of checking SC/TSO poses a crucial issue for the design of scalable verification or testing techniques for these important consistency models. Tackling this issue requires the development of practical approaches that can work well (with polynomial complexity) when the instance of the problem does not need to generate the worst case (exponential) complexity.

---

[1] All the CC variations become NP-complete without the assumption that each value is written at most once [6]. This holds for the variations of CC we introduce in this paper as well.

The purpose of this paper is to propose such an approach. The idea is to reduce the amount of "nondeterminism" in searching for the write orders in order to establish SC/TSO conformance. For that, our approach for SC is to consider a weaker consistency model called CCM (for Convergent Causal Memory), that is "as strong as possible" while being polynomial time checkable. In fact CCM is stronger than both causal memory [2,26] (CM) and causal convergence [7] (CCv), two other well-known variations of causal consistency. Then, if CCM is already violated by the given computation then we can conclude that the computation does not satisfy the stronger criterion SC. Here the hope is that in practice many computations violating SC can be caught already at this stage using a polynomial time check. Now, in the case that the computation does not violate CCM, we exploit the fact that establishing CCM already imposes a set of constraints on the order between writes. We show that these constraints form a partial order which *must* be a subset of any total write order that would witness for SC conformance. Therefore, at this point, it is enough to find an extension of this partial write order, and the hope is that in many practical cases, this set of constraints is already large enough, letting only a small number of pairs of writes to be ordered in order to check SC conformance. For the case of TSO, we proceed in the same way, but we consider a different intermediary polynomial time checkable criterion called *weak* CCM (wCCM). This is due to the fact that some causality constraints need to be relaxed in order to take into account the program order relaxations of TSO, that allow reads to overtake writes. The definitions of the new criteria CCM and wCCM we use in our approach are quite subtle. Ensuring that these criteria are "as strong as possible" by including all possible order constraints on pairs of writes that can be computed (in polynomial time) using a least fixpoint calculation, while still ensuring that they are weaker than SC/TSO, and proving this fact, is not trivial.

As a proof of concept, we implemented our approach for checking SC/TSO and applied it to executions extracted from realistic cache coherence protocols within the Gem5 simulator [5] in system emulation mode. This evaluation shows that our approach scales better than a direct encoding of the axioms defining SC and TSO [3] into boolean satisfiability. We also show that the partial order of writes imposed by the stronger criteria CCM and wCCM leaves only a small percentage of writes unordered (6.6% in average) in the case that the executions are valid, and most SC/TSO violations are also CCM/wCCM violations.

2 Sequential Consistency and TSO

We consider multi-threaded programs over a set of shared variables $\mathsf{Var} = \{x, y, \ldots\}$. Threads issue read and write operations. Assuming an unspecified set of values Val and a set of operation identifiers Old, we let

$$\mathsf{Op} = \{\mathsf{read}_i(x, v), \mathsf{write}_i(x, v) : i \in \mathsf{Old}, x \in \mathsf{Var}, v \in \mathsf{Val}\}$$

be the set of operations reading a value v or writing a value v to a variable x. We omit operation identifiers when they are not important. The set of read, resp., write, operations is denoted by $\mathbb{R}$, resp., $\mathbb{W}$. The set of read, resp., write, operations in a set of operations O is denoted by $\mathbb{R}(O)$, resp., $\mathbb{W}(O)$. The variable accessed by an operation o is denoted by var(o).

Consistency criteria like SC or TSO are formalized on an abstract view of an execution called *history*. A history includes a set of write or read operations ordered according to a (partial) *program order* po which order operations issued by the same thread. Most often, po is a union of sequences, each sequence containing all the operations issued by some thread. Then, we assume that the history includes a *write-read* relation which identifies the write operation writing the value returned by each read in the execution. Such a relation can be extracted easily from executions where each value is written at most once. Since shared-memory implementations (or cache coherence protocols) are data-independent [31] in practice, i.e., their behavior doesn't depend on the concrete values read or written in the program, any potential buggy behavior can be exposed in such executions.

Definition 1. *A history* $\langle O, \text{po}, \text{wr} \rangle$ *is a set of operations O along with a strict partial program order* po *and a write-read relation* wr $\subseteq \mathbb{W}(O) \times \mathbb{R}(O)$*, such that the inverse of* wr *is a total function and if* $(\textit{write}(x,v), \textit{read}(x',v')) \in$ wr*, then $x = x'$ and $v = v'$.*

We assume that every history includes a write operation writing the initial value of variable x, for each variable x. These write operations precede all other operations in po. We use $h, h_1, h_2, \ldots$ to range over histories.

We now define the SC and TSO memory models (we use the same definitions as in the formal framework developed by Alglave et al. [3]). Given a *history* $h = \langle O, \text{po}, \text{wr} \rangle$ and a variable x, a *store order on x* is a strict total order ww$_x$ on the write operations write_$(x, \_)$ in O. A *store order* is a union of store orders ww$_x$, one for each variable x used in h. A *history* $\langle O, \text{po}, \text{wr} \rangle$ is *sequentially consistent* (SC, for short) if there exists a *store order* ww such that po $\cup$ wr $\cup$ ww $\cup$ rw is acyclic. The *read-write* relation rw is defined by rw $=$ wr^{-1} $\circ$ ww (where $\circ$ denotes the standard relation composition).

The definition of TSO relies on three additional relations: (1) the ppo relation which excludes from the program order pairs formed of a write and respectively, a read operation, i.e., ppo $=$ po $\setminus (\mathbb{W}(O) \times \mathbb{R}(O))$, (2) the po-loc relation which is a restriction of po to operations accessing the same variable, i.e., po-loc $=$ po$\cap\{(o, o') \mid \text{var}(o) = \text{var}(o')\}$, and (3) the write-read external relation wr$_e$ which is a restriction of the write-read relation to pairs of operations in different threads (not related by program order), i.e., wr$_e$ $=$ wr$\cap\{(o, o') \mid (o, o') \notin$ po and $(o', o) \notin$ po$\}$. Then, we say that a history satisfies TSO if there exists a *store order* ww such that po-loc $\cup$ wr$_e$ $\cup$ ww $\cup$ rw and ppo $\cup$ wr$_e$ $\cup$ ww $\cup$ rw are both acyclic.

Notice that the formal definition of the TSO given above is equivalent to the formal operational model of TSO that consists in considering that each thread has a store buffer, and then, each write issued by a thread is first sent to its store buffer before being committed to the memory later in a nondeterministic way. To read a value on some variable x, a thread first checks if it there is still a write on x pending in its own buffer and in this case it takes the value of the last such as write, otherwise it fetches the value of x in the memory.

3   Checking Sequential Consistency

We define an algorithm for checking whether a history satisfies SC which enforces a polynomially-time checkable criterion weaker than SC, a variation of causal consistency, in order to construct a *partial* store order, i.e., one in which not all the writes on the same variable are ordered. This partial store order is then completed until it orders every two writes on the same variable using a standard backtracking enumeration. This approach is efficient when the number of writes that remain to be ordered using the backtracking enumeration is relatively small, a hypothesis confirmed by our experimental evaluation (see Sect. 5.).

The variation of causal consistency mentioned above, called *convergent causal memory* (CCM, for short), is stronger than existing variations [6] while still being polynomially-time checkable (and weaker than SC). Its definition uses several relations between read and write operations which are analogous or even exactly the same relations used to define those variations. Section 3.1 recalls the existing notions of causal consistency as they are defined in [6] (using the so called "bad-pattern" characterization introduced in that paper), Sect. 3.2 introduces CCM, while Sect. 3.3 presents our algorithm for checking SC.

3.1   Causal Consistency

The weakest variation of causal consistency, called *weak causal consistency* (CC, for short), requires that any two causally-dependent values are observed in the same order by all threads, where causally-dependent means that either those values were written by the same thread (i.e., the corresponding writes are ordered by po), or that one value was written by a thread after reading the other value, or any transitive composition of such dependencies. Values written concurrently by two threads can be observed in any order, and even-more, this order may change in time. A *history* $\langle O, \mathsf{po}, \mathsf{wr} \rangle$ satisfies CC if $\mathsf{po} \cup \mathsf{wr} \cup \mathsf{rw}[\mathsf{co}]$ is acyclic where $\mathsf{co} = (\mathsf{po} \cup \mathsf{wr})^+$ is called the *causal relation*. The *read-write* relation $\mathsf{rw}[\mathsf{co}]$ induced by the causal relation is defined by

$$(\mathsf{read}(x, v), \mathsf{write}(x, v')) \in \mathsf{rw}[\mathsf{co}] \text{ iff } (\mathsf{write}(x, v), \mathsf{write}(x, v')) \in \mathsf{co} \text{ and}$$
$$(\mathsf{write}(x, v), \mathsf{read}(x, v)) \in \mathsf{wr}, \text{ for some } \mathsf{write}(x, v)$$

The read-write relation $\mathsf{rw}[\mathsf{co}]$ is a variation of rw from the definition of SC/TSO where the store order ww is replaced by the projection of co on pairs of writes. In general, given a binary relation R on operations, R_{ww} denotes the projection of R on pairs of writes on the same variable. Then,

Definition 2. *The read-write relation* $\mathsf{rw}[R]$ *induced by a relation R is defined by* $\mathsf{rw}[R] = \mathsf{wr}^{-1} \circ R_{\mathsf{ww}}$.

Causal convergence (CCv, for short) is a strengthening of CC where concurrent values are required to be observed in the same order by all threads.

A *history* $\langle O, \mathsf{po}, \mathsf{wr} \rangle$ satisfies CCv if it satisfies CC and $\mathsf{po} \cup \mathsf{wr} \cup \mathsf{cf}$ is acyclic where the *conflict relation* cf is defined by

$$(\mathsf{write}(x,v), \mathsf{write}(x,v')) \in \mathsf{cf} \text{ iff } (\mathsf{write}(x,v), \mathsf{read}(x,v')) \in \mathsf{co} \text{ and}$$
$$(\mathsf{write}(x,v'), \mathsf{read}(x,v')) \in \mathsf{wr}, \text{ for some } \mathsf{read}(x,v')$$

The conflict relation relates two writes w_1 and w_2 when w_1 is causally related to a read taking its value from w_2. The definition of CCM, our new variation of causal consistency, relies on a generalization of the conflict relation where a different relation is used instead of co. Given a binary relation R on operations, R_{WR} denotes the projection of R on pairs of writes and reads on the same variable, respectively.

Definition 3. *The conflict relation* cf$[R]$ *induced by a relation R is defined by* cf$[R] = R_{\mathrm{WR}} \circ \mathsf{wr}^{-1}$.

t_0: t_1:
write$(x,1)$ write$(x,2)$
read$(x,2)$ read$(x,1)$

(a) CM but not CCv nor wCCM

t_0: t_1:
write$(z,1)$ write$(x,2)$
write$(x,1)$ read$(z,0)$
write$(y,1)$ read$(y,1)$
                            read$(x,2)$

(b) CCv, wCCM and TSO but not CM

t_0: t_1:
write$(x,1)$ write$(y,1)$
write$(x,2)$ write$(y,2)$
read$(y,1)$ read$(y,2)$
                            read$(x,1)$

t_0: t_1:
write$(x,1)$ write$(x,2)$
read$(y,0)$ read$(y,0)$
write$(y,1)$ write$(y,2)$
read$(x,1)$ read$(x,2)$

(c) CM and CCv but not CCM   (d) CCM but not SC

Fig. 1. Histories with two threads used to compare different consistency models. Operations of the same thread are aligned vertically.

Finally, *causal memory* (CM, for short) is a strengthening of CC where roughly, concurrent values are required to be observed in the same order by a thread during its entire execution. Differently from CCv, this order can differ from one thread to another. Although this intuitive description seems to imply that CM is weaker than CCv, the two models are actually incomparable. For instance, the history in Fig. 1a is allowed by CM, but not by CCv. It is not allowed by CCv because reading 1 from x in the first thread implies that it observed write$(x,1)$ after write$(x,2)$ while reading 2 from x in the second thread implies that it observed $\mathsf{write}(x,2)$ after $\mathsf{write}(x,1)$. While this is allowed by CM where different threads can observe concurrent writes in different orders, it is not allowed by CCv. Then, the history in Fig. 1b is CCv but not CM. It is not allowed by CM because reading the initial value 0 from z implies that $\mathsf{write}(x,1)$ is observed after $\mathsf{write}(x,2)$ while reading 2 from x implies that $\mathsf{write}(x,2)$ is observed after $\mathsf{write}(x,1)$ ($\mathsf{write}(x,1)$ must have been observed because the same thread reads 1 from y and the writes on x and y are causally related). However, under CCv, a thread simply reads the most recent value on each variable and the order in which these values are ordered using timestamps for instance is independent of the order in which variables are read in a thread, e.g., reading 0 from z doesn't imply that the timestamp of $\mathsf{write}(x,2)$ is smaller than the timestamp of $\mathsf{write}(x,1)$. This history is admitted by CCv assuming that the order in which $\mathsf{write}(x,1)$ and $\mathsf{write}(x,2)$ are observed is $\mathsf{write}(x,1)$ before $\mathsf{write}(x,2)$.

Let us give the formal definition of CM. Let h=$\langle O, \mathsf{po}, \mathsf{wr}\rangle$ be a history. For every operation o in h, let hb_o be the smallest transitive relation such that:

1. if two operations are causally related, and each one causally related to o, then they are related by hb_o, i.e., $(o_1, o_2) \in \mathsf{hb}_o$ if $(o_1, o_2) \in \mathsf{co}$, $(o_1, o) \in \mathsf{co}$, and $(o_2, o) \in \mathsf{co}^*$ (where co^* is the reflexive closure of co), and

2. two writes w_1 and w_2 are related by hb_o if w_1 is hb_o-related to a read taking its value from w_2, and that read is done by the same thread executing o and before o (this scenario is similar to the definition of the conflict relation above), i.e., $(\mathsf{write}(x,v), \mathsf{write}(x,v')) \in \mathsf{hb}_o$ if $(\mathsf{write}(x,v), \mathsf{read}(x,v')) \in \mathsf{hb}_o$, $(\mathsf{write}(x,v'), \mathsf{read}(x,v')) \in \mathsf{wr}$, and $(\mathsf{read}(x,v'), o) \in \mathsf{po}^*$, for some $\mathsf{read}(x,v')$.

A history $\langle O, \mathsf{po}, \mathsf{wr}\rangle$ satisfies CM if it satisfies CC and for each operation o in the history, the relation hb_o is acyclic.

Bouajjani et al. [6] show that the problem of checking whether a history satisfies CC, CCv, or CM is polynomial time. This result is a straightforward consequence of the above definitions, since the union of relations required to be acyclic can be computed in polynomial time from the relations po and wr which are fixed in a given history. In particular, the union of these relations can be computed by a DATALOG program.

3.2   Convergent Causal Memory

We define a new variation of causal consistency which builds on causal memory, but similar to causal convergence it enforces that all threads agree on an order in which to observe values written by concurrent (causally-unrelated) writes, and also, it uses a larger read-write relation. A history $\langle O, \mathsf{po}, \mathsf{wr}\rangle$ satisfies *convergent causal memory* (CCM, for short) if $\mathsf{po} \cup \mathsf{wr} \cup \mathsf{pww} \cup \mathsf{rw}[\mathsf{pww}]$ is acyclic, where the *partial store order* pww is defined by

$$\mathsf{pww} = (\mathsf{hb}_{\mathsf{WW}} \cup \mathsf{cf}[\mathsf{hb}])^+ \quad \text{with } \mathsf{hb} = \Big(\bigcup_{o \in O} \mathsf{hb}_o \Big)^+.$$

The partial store order pww contains the ordering constraints between writes in all relations hb_o used to defined causal memory, and also, the conflict relation induced by this set of constraints (a weaker version of conflict relation was used to define causal convergence).

As a first result, we show that all the variations of causal consistency in Sect. 3.1, i.e., CC, CCv and CM, are strictly weaker than CCM.

Lemma 1. *If a history satisfies CCM, then it satisfies CC, CCv and CM.*

Proof. Let $h = \langle O, \mathsf{po}, \mathsf{wr} \rangle$ be a history satisfying CCM. By the definition of hb, we have that $\mathsf{co}_{\mathsf{WW}} \subseteq \mathsf{hb}_{\mathsf{WW}}$. Indeed, any two writes o_1 and o_2 related by co are also related by hb_{o_2}, which by the definition of hb, implies that they are related by $\mathsf{hb}_{\mathsf{WW}}$. Then, by the definition of pww, we have that $\mathsf{hb}_{\mathsf{WW}} \subseteq \mathsf{pww}$. This implies that $\mathsf{rw}[\mathsf{co}] \subseteq \mathsf{rw}[\mathsf{pww}]$ (by definition, $\mathsf{rw}[\mathsf{co}] = \mathsf{rw}[\mathsf{co}_{\mathsf{WW}}]$). Therefore, the acyclicity of $\mathsf{po} \cup \mathsf{wr} \cup \mathsf{pww} \cup \mathsf{rw}[\mathsf{pww}]$ implies that its subset $(\mathsf{po} \cup \mathsf{wr} \cup \mathsf{rw}[\mathsf{co}]$ is also acyclic, which means that h satisfies CC. Also, it implies that $\mathsf{po} \cup \mathsf{wr} \cup \mathsf{cf}[\mathsf{hb}]$ is acyclic (the last term of the union is included in pww), which by $\mathsf{co} \subseteq \mathsf{hb}$, implies that $\mathsf{po} \cup \mathsf{wr} \cup \mathsf{cf}[\mathsf{co}]$ is acyclic, and thus, h satisfies CCv. The fact that h satisfies CM follows from the fact that h satisfies CC (since $\mathsf{po} \cup \mathsf{wr}$ is acyclic) and hb is acyclic ($\mathsf{hb}_{\mathsf{WW}}$ is included in pww and the rest of the dependencies in hb are included in $\mathsf{po} \cup \mathsf{wr}$). □

The reverse of the above lemma doesn't hold. Figure 1c shows a history which satisfies CM and CCv, but it is not CCM. To show that this history does not satisfy CCM we use the fact that pww relates any two writes which are ordered by program order. Then, we get that $\mathsf{read}(x, 1)$ and $\mathsf{write}(x, 2)$ are related by $\mathsf{rw}[\mathsf{pww}]$ (because $\mathsf{write}(x, 1)$ is related by write-read with $\mathsf{read}(x, 1)$), which further implies that $(\mathsf{read}(x, 1), \mathsf{read}(y, 1)) \in \mathsf{rw}[\mathsf{pww}] \circ \mathsf{po}$. Similarly, we have that $(\mathsf{read}(y, 1), \mathsf{read}(x, 1)) \in \mathsf{rw}[\mathsf{pww}] \circ \mathsf{po}$, which implies that $\mathsf{po} \cup \mathsf{wr} \cup \mathsf{pww} \cup \mathsf{rw}[\mathsf{pww}]$ is *not* acyclic, and therefore, the history does not satisfy CCM. The fact that this history satisfies CM and CCv follows easily from definitions.

Next, we show that CCM is weaker than SC, which will be important in our algorithm for checking whether a history satisfies SC.

Lemma 2. *If a history satisfies SC, then it satisfies CCM.*

Proof. Using the definition of CCM, Let $h = \langle O, \mathsf{po}, \mathsf{wr} \rangle$ be a history satisfying SC. Then, there exists a *store order* ww such that $\mathsf{po} \cup \mathsf{wr} \cup \mathsf{ww} \cup \mathsf{rw}[\mathsf{ww}]$ is acyclic. We show that the two relations $\mathsf{hb}_{\mathsf{WW}}$ and $\mathsf{cf}[\mathsf{hb}]$, whose union constitutes pww, are both included in ww. We first prove that $\mathsf{hb} \subseteq (\mathsf{po} \cup \mathsf{wr} \cup \mathsf{ww} \cup \mathsf{rw}[\mathsf{ww}])^+$ by structural induction on the definition of hb_o:

1. if $(o_1, o_2) \in \mathsf{co} = (\mathsf{po} \cup \mathsf{wr})^+$, then clearly, $(o_1, o_2) \in (\mathsf{po} \cup \mathsf{wr} \cup \mathsf{ww} \cup \mathsf{rw}[\mathsf{ww}])^+$,
2. if $(\mathsf{write}(x, v), \mathsf{read}(x, v')) \in (\mathsf{po} \cup \mathsf{wr} \cup \mathsf{ww} \cup \mathsf{rw}[\mathsf{ww}])^+$ and there is $\mathsf{read}(x, v')$ such that $(\mathsf{write}(x, v'), \mathsf{read}(x, v')) \in \mathsf{wr}$, then $(\mathsf{write}(x, v), \mathsf{write}(x, v')) \in \mathsf{ww}$. Otherwise, assuming by contradiction that $(\mathsf{write}(x, v'), \mathsf{write}(x, v)) \in \mathsf{ww}$, we get that $(\mathsf{read}(x, v'), \mathsf{write}(x, v)) \in \mathsf{rw}[\mathsf{ww}]$ (by the definition of $\mathsf{rw}[\mathsf{ww}]$ using the hypothesis $(\mathsf{write}(x, v'), \mathsf{read}(x, v')) \in \mathsf{wr}$). Note that the latter implies that $\mathsf{po} \cup \mathsf{wr} \cup \mathsf{ww} \cup \mathsf{rw}[\mathsf{ww}]$ is cyclic.

Since $hb \subseteq (po \cup wr \cup ww \cup rw[ww])^+$, we get that $hb_{ww} \subseteq ww$. Also, since $cf[(po \cup wr \cup ww \cup rw[ww])^+] \subseteq (po \cup wr \cup ww \cup rw[ww])^+$ (using a similar argument as in point (2) above), we get that $cf[hb] \subseteq (po \cup wr \cup ww \cup rw[ww])^+$.

Finally, since $pww \subseteq ww$, we get that $(po \cup wr \cup pww \cup rw[pww])^+ \subseteq (po \cup wr \cup ww \cup rw[ww])^+$, which implies that the acyclicity of the latter implies the acyclicity of the former. Therefore, h satisfies CCM.   □

The reverse of the above lemma doesn't hold. For instance, the history in Fig. 1d is not SC but it is CCM. This history admits a partial store order pww where the writes in different threads are not ordered.

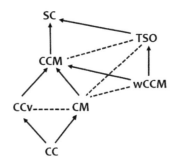

Fig. 2. Relationships between consistency models. Directed arrows denote the "weaker-than" relation while dashed lines connect incomparable models.

The left side of Fig. 2 (ignoring wCCM and TSO) summarizes the relationships between the consistency models presented in this section.

The partial store order pww can be computed in polynomial time (in the size of the input history). Indeed, the hb_o relations can be computed using a least fixpoint calculation that converges in at most a quadratic number of iterations and acyclicity can be decided in polynomial time. Therefore,

Theorem 1. *Checking whether a history satisfies CCM is polynomial time in the size of the history.*

3.3   An Algorithm for Checking Sequential Consistency

Algorithm 1 checks whether a given history satisfies sequential consistency. As a first step, it checks whether the given history satisfies CCM. If this is not the case, then, by Lemma 2, the history does not satisfy SC as well, and the algorithm returns *false*. Otherwise, it enumerates store orders which extend the partial store order pww, until finding one that witnesses for satisfaction of SC. The history is a violation to SC iff no such store order is found. The soundness of this last step is implied by the proof of Lemma 2, which shows that pww is included in any store order ww witnessing for SC satisfaction.

Theorem 2. *Algorithm 1 returns true iff the input history h satisfies SC.*

Input: A history $h = \langle O, \mathsf{po}, \mathsf{wr} \rangle$
Output: *true* iff h satisfies SC

1 **if** $\mathsf{po} \cup \mathsf{wr} \cup \mathsf{pww} \cup \mathsf{rw}[\mathsf{pww}]$ *is cyclic* **then**
2 | return *false*;
3 **end**
4 **foreach** $\mathsf{ww} \supset \mathsf{pww}$ **do**
5 | **if** $\mathsf{po} \cup \mathsf{wr} \cup \mathsf{ww} \cup \mathsf{rw}[\mathsf{ww}]$ *is acyclic* **then**
6 | | return *true*;
7 | **end**
8 **end**
9 **return** *false*;

Algorithm 1. Checking SC conformance.

4 Checking Conformance to the TSO Model

We consider now the problem of checking whether a history satisfies TSO. Following the approach developed above for SC, we define a polynomial time checkable criterion, based on a (different) variation of causal consistency that is suitable for the case of TSO. This allows to reduce the number of pairs of writes for which an order must be guessed in order to establish conformance to TSO.

The case of TSO requires the definition of a new intermediary consistency model because CCM is based on a causality order that includes the program order po which is relaxed in the context of TSO, compared to the SC model. Indeed, CCM is *not* weaker than TSO as shown by the history in Fig. 1b (note that this does not imply that other variations of causal consistency, CC and CCv, are also not weaker than TSO). This history satisfies TSO because, based on its operational model, the operation $\mathsf{write}(x, 2)$ of thread t_1 can be delayed (pending in the store buffer of t_1) until the end of the execution. Therefore, after executing $\mathsf{read}(z, 0)$, all the writes of thread t_0 are committed to the main memory so that thread t_1 can read 1 from y and 2 from x (it is obliged to read the value of x from its own store buffer). This history is not admitted by CCM because it is not admitted by the weaker causal consistency variation CM. Figure 3 shows a history admitted by CCM but not by TSO. Indeed, under TSO, both t_2 and t_3 should see the writes on x and y performed by t_0 and t_1, respectively, in the same order. This is not the case, because t_2 "observes" the write on x before the write on y (since it reads 0 from y) and t_3 "observes" the write on y before the write on x (since it reads 0 from x). This history is admitted by CCM because the two writes are causally independent and they concern different variables. We mention that TSO and CM are also incomparable. For instance, the history in Fig. 1a is allowed by CM, but not by TSO. The history in Fig. 1b is admitted by TSO, but not by CM.

Next, we define a weakening of CCM, called *weak convergent causal memory* (wCCM), which is also weaker than TSO. The model wCCM is based on causality relations induced by the relaxed program orders ppo and po-loc instead of po, and the external write-read relation instead of the full write-read relation.

t_0:
write$(x,1)$

t_1:
write$(y,1)$

t_2:
read$(x,1)$
read$(y,0)$

t_3:
read$(y,1)$
read$(x,0)$

Fig. 3. A history admitted by wCCM and CCM but not by TSO.

4.1 Weak Convergent Causal Memory

First, we define two causality relations relative to the partial program orders in the definition of TSO and the external write-read relation: For $\pi \in \{\text{ppo}, \text{po-loc}\}$, let $\text{co}^\pi = (\pi \cup \text{wr}_e)^+$. We also consider a notion of conflict that is defined in terms of the external write-read relation as follows: For a given relation R, let $\text{cf}_e[R] = R_{\text{WR}} \circ \text{wr}_e^{-1}$.

Then, given a history $\langle O, \text{po}, \text{wr} \rangle$, we define for each operation o two happens-before relations hb_o^{ppo} and $\text{hb}_o^{\text{po-loc}}$. The definition of these relations is similar to the one of hb_o (from causal memory), the differences being that po is replaced by ppo and po-loc respectively, co is replaced by co^{ppo} and $\text{co}^{\text{po-loc}}$ respectively, and wr is replaced by wr_e. Therefore, for $\pi \in \{\text{ppo}, \text{po-loc}\}$, hb_o^π is is the smallest transitive relation such that:

1. $(o_1, o_2) \in \text{hb}_o^\pi$ if $(o_1, o_2) \in \text{co}^\pi$, $(o_1, o) \in \text{co}^\pi$, and $(o_2, o) \in (\text{co}^\pi)^*$, and
2. $(\text{write}(x, v), \text{write}(x, v')) \in \text{hb}_o^\pi$ if $(\text{write}(x, v), \text{read}(x, v')) \in \text{hb}_o^\pi$, and $(\text{write}(x, v'), \text{read}(x, v')) \in \text{wr}$ and $(\text{read}(x, v'), o) \in \pi^*$, for some $\text{read}(x, v')$.

Let $\text{hb}^\pi = (\bigcup_{o \in O} \text{hb}_o^\pi)^+$, for $\pi \in \{\text{ppo}, \text{po-loc}\}$, and let $\text{whb} = (\text{hb}_o^{\text{ppo}} \cup \text{hb}_o^{\text{po-loc}})^+$. Then, the weak partial store order is defined as follows:

$$\text{wpww} = (\text{whb}_{\text{WW}} \cup \text{cf}_e[\text{hb}^{\text{po-loc}}] \cup \text{cf}_e[\text{hb}^{\text{ppo}}])^+$$

Then, we say that a history $\langle O, \text{po}, \text{wr} \rangle$ satisfies *weak convergent causal memory* (wCCM) if both relations:

$$\text{ppo} \cup \text{wr}_e \cup \text{wpww} \cup \text{rw}[\text{wpww}] \text{ and } \text{po-loc} \cup \text{wr}_e \cup \text{wpww} \cup \text{rw}[\text{wpww}]$$

are acyclic.

Lemma 3. *If a history satisfies TSO, then it satisfies wCCM.*

Proof. Let $h = \langle O, \text{po}, \text{wr} \rangle$ be a history satisfying TSO. Then, there exists a store order ww such that $\text{po-loc} \cup \text{wr}_e \cup \text{ww} \cup \text{rw}$ and $\text{ppo} \cup \text{wr}_e \cup \text{ww} \cup \text{rw}$ are both acyclic. The fact that

$$\text{hb}^{\text{po-loc}} \subseteq (\text{po-loc} \cup \text{wr}_e \cup \text{ww} \cup \text{rw})^+ \text{ and } \text{hb}^{\text{ppo}} \subseteq (\text{ppo} \cup \text{wr}_e \cup \text{ww} \cup \text{rw})^+$$

can be proved by structural induction like in the case of SC (the step of the proof showing that $\text{hb} \subseteq \text{po} \cup \text{wr} \cup \text{ww} \cup \text{rw}[\text{ww}]$). Then, since ww is a total order on writes on the same variable, we get that the projection of whb (the transitive closure of the union of $\text{hb}^{\text{po-loc}}$ and hb^{ppo}) on pairs of writes on the same variable is included in ww. Therefore, $\mathsf{whb_{ww}} \subseteq \mathsf{ww}$. Then, since $\mathsf{cf}_e[R^\pi] \subseteq R^\pi$ for each $R^\pi = (\pi \cup \mathsf{wr}_e \cup \mathsf{ww} \cup \mathsf{rw})^+$ with $\pi \in \{\mathsf{ppo}, \mathsf{po\text{-}loc}\}$ and since each $\mathsf{cf}_e[R^\pi]$ relates only writes on the same variable, we get that each $\mathsf{cf}_e[R^\pi]$ is included in ww. This implies that $\mathsf{wpww} \subseteq \mathsf{ww}$.

Finally, since $\mathsf{wpww} \subseteq \mathsf{ww}$, we get that $(\pi \cup \mathsf{wr} \cup \mathsf{wpww} \cup \mathsf{rw}[\mathsf{wpww}])^+ \subseteq (\pi \cup \mathsf{wr} \cup \mathsf{ww} \cup \mathsf{rw}[\mathsf{ww}])^+$, for each $\pi \in \{\mathsf{ppo}, \mathsf{po\text{-}loc}\}$. In each case, the acyclicity of the latter implies the acyclicity of the former. Therefore, h satisfies wCCM.

Input: A history $h = \langle O, \mathsf{po}, \mathsf{wr} \rangle$
Output: *true* iff h satisfies TSO

1   **if** $\mathsf{ppo} \cup \mathsf{wr}_e \cup \mathsf{wpww} \cup \mathsf{rw}[\mathsf{wpww}]$ *or* $\mathsf{po\text{-}loc} \cup \mathsf{wr}_e \cup \mathsf{pww} \cup \mathsf{rw}[\mathsf{wpww}]$ *is cyclic* **then**
2 | **return** *false*;
3   **end**
4   **foreach** $\mathsf{ww} \supset \mathsf{wpww}$ **do**
5 | **if** $\mathsf{ppo} \cup \mathsf{wr}_e \cup \mathsf{ww} \cup \mathsf{rw}[\mathsf{ww}]$ *and* $\mathsf{po\text{-}loc} \cup \mathsf{wr}_e \cup \mathsf{ww} \cup \mathsf{rw}[\mathsf{ww}]$ *are acyclic* **then**
6 | | **return** *true*;
7 | **end**
8   **end**
9   **return** *false*;

Algorithm 2. Checking TSO conformance.

The reverse of the above lemma does not hold. Indeed, it can be easily seen that wCCM is weaker than CCM (since wpww is included in pww) and the history in Fig. 3, which satisfies CCM but not TSO (as explained in the beginning of the section), is also an example of a history that satisfies wCCM but not TSO. Then, wCCM is incomparable to CM. For instance, the history in Fig. 1b is allowed by wCCM (since it is allowed by TSO as explained in the beginning of the section) but not by CM. Also, since CCM is stronger than CM, the history in Fig. 3 satisfies CM but not wCCM (since it does not satisfy TSO). These relationships are summarized in Fig. 2. Establishing the precise relation between CC/CCv and TSO is hard because they are defined using one, resp., two, acyclicity conditions. We believe that CC and CCv are weaker than TSO, but we don't have a formal proof.

Finally, it can be seen that, similarly to pww, the weak partial store order wpww can be computed in polynomial time, and therefore:

Theorem 3. *Checking whether a history satisfies wCCM is polynomial time in the size of the history.*

4.2 An Algorithm for Checking TSO Conformance

The algorithm for checking TSO conformance for a given history is given in Fig. 2. It starts by checking whether the history violates the weaker consistency model wCCM. If yes, it returns false. If not, it starts enumerating the orders between the writes that are not related by the weak partial store order wpww until it founds one that allows establishing TSO conformance and in this case it returns true. Otherwise it returns false.

Theorem 4. *Algorithm 2 returns true iff the input history h satisfies TSO.*

5 Experimental Evaluation

To demonstrate the practical value of the theory developed in the previous sections, we argue that our algorithms are efficient and scalable. We experiment with both SC and TSO algorithms, investigating their running time compared to a standard encoding of these models into boolean satisfiability on a benchmark obtained by running realistic cache coherence protocols within the Gem5 simulator [5] in system emulation mode.

Histories are generated with random clients of the following cache coherence protocols included in the Gem5 distribution: MI, MEOSI HAMMER, MESI TWO LEVEL, and MEOSI AMD Base. The randomization process is parametrized by the number of cpus (threads) and the total number of read-/write operations. We ensure that every value is written at most once.

We have compared two variations of our algorithms for checking SC/TSO with a standard encoding of SC/TSO into boolean satisfiability (named X-SAT where X is SC or TSO). The two variations differ in the way in which the partial store order pww dictated by CCM is completed to a total store order ww as required by SC/TSO: either using standard enumeration (named X-CCM+ENUM where X is SC or TSO) or using a SAT solver (named X-CCM+SAT where X is SC or TSO).

The computation of the partial store order pww is done using an encoding of its definition into a DATALOG program. The inductive definition of hb_o supports an easy translation to DATALOG rules, and the same holds for the union of two relations, or their composition. We used Clingo [19] to run DATALOG programs.

5.1 Checking SC

Figure 4 reports on the running time of the three algorithms while increasing the number of operations or cpus. All the histories considered in this experiment satisfy SC. This is intended because valid histories force our algorithms to enumerate extensions of the partial store order (SC violations may be detected while checking CCM). The graph on the left pictures the evolution of the running time when increasing the number of operations from 100 to 500, in increments of 100 (while using a constant number of 4 cpus). For each number of operations, we have considered 200 histories and computed the average running time. The graph on the right shows the running time when increasing the number of cpus from 2 to 6, in increments of 1. For x cpus, we have limited the number of operations to $50x$. As before for each number of cpus, we have considered 200 histories and computed

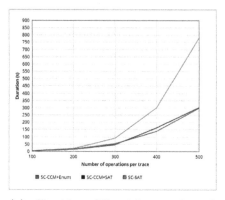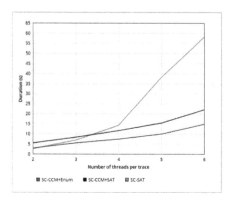

(a) Checking SC while varying the number of operations.

(b) Checking SC while varying the number of cpus.

Fig. 4. Checking SC for valid histories.

the average running time. As it can be observed, our algorithms scale much better than the SAT encoding and interestingly enough, the difference between an explicit enumeration of pww extensions and one using a SAT solver is not significant. Note that even small improvements on the average running time provide large speedups when taking into account the whole testing process, i.e., checking consistency for a possibly large number of (randomly-generated) executions. For instance, the work on McVerSi [13], which focuses on the complementary problem of finding clients that increase the probability of uncovering bugs, shows that exposing bugs in some realistic cache coherence implementations requires even 24 h of continuous testing.

Since the bottleneck in our algorithms is given by the enumeration of pww extensions, we have measured the percentage of pairs of writes that are *not* ordered by pww. Thus, we have considered a random sample of 200 histories (with 200 operations per history) and evaluated this percentage to be just 6.6%, which is surprisingly low. This explains the net gain in comparison to a SAT encoding of SC, since the number of pww extensions that need to be enumerated is quite low. As a side remark, using CCv instead of CCM in the algorithms above leads to a drastic increase in the number of unordered writes. For the same random sample of 200 histories, we conclude that using CCv instead of CCM leaves 57.75% of unordered writes in average which is considerably bigger than the percentage of unordered writes when using CCM.

We have also evaluated our algorithms on SC violations. These violations were generated by reordering statements from the MI implementation, e.g., swapping the order of the actions s_store_hit and p_profileHit in the transition transition(M, Store). As an optimization, our implementation checks gradually the weaker variations of causal consistency CC and CCv before checking CCM. This is to increase the chances of returning in the case of a violation (a violation to CC/CCv is also a violation to CCM and SC). We have considered 1000 histories with 100 to 400 operations and 2 to 8 cpus, equally distributed in function

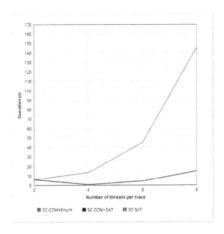

Fig. 5. Checking SC for invalid histories while increasing the number of cpus.

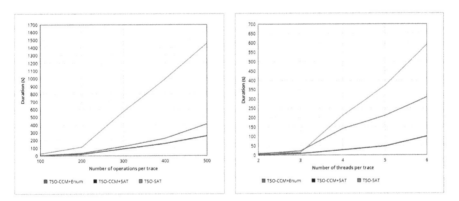

(a) Checking TSO while varying the number of operations.

(b) Checking TSO while varying the number of cpus.

Fig. 6. Checking TSO for valid histories.

of the number of cpus. Figure 5 reports on the evolution of the average running time. Since these histories happen to all be CCM violations, SC-CCM+ENUM and SC-CCM+SAT have the same running time. As an evaluation of our optimization, we have found that 50% of the histories invalidate weaker variations of causal consistency, CC or CCv.

5.2   Checking TSO

We have evaluated our TSO algorithms on the same set of histories used for SC in Fig. 4. Since these histories satisfy SC, they satisfy TSO as well. As in the case of SC, our algorithms scale better than the SAT encoding. However, differently from SC, the enumeration of **wpww** extensions using a SAT solver outperforms the explicit enumeration. Since this difference was more negligible in the case of SC, it seems that the SAT variation is generally better.

6   Related Work

While several static techniques have been developed to prove that a shared-memory implementation (or cache coherence protocol) satisfies SC [1, 4, 9–12, 17, 20, 23, 27, 28] few have addressed dynamic techniques such as testing and runtime verification (which scale to more realistic implementations). From the complexity standpoint, Gibbons and Korach [21] showed that checking whether a history is SC is NP-hard while Alur et al. [4] showed that checking SC for finite-state shared-memory implementations (over a bounded number of threads, variables, and values) is undecidable [4]. The fact that checking whether a history satisfies TSO is also NP-hard has been proved by Furbach et al. [18].

There are several works that addressed the testing problem for related criteria, e.g., linearizability. While SC requires that the operations in a history be explained by a linearization that is consistent with the program order, linearizability requires that such a linearization be also consistent with the real-time order between operations (linearizability is stronger than SC). The works in [25, 30] describe monitors for checking linearizability that construct linearizations of a given history incrementally, in an online fashion. This incremental construction cannot be adapted to SC since it strongly relies on the specificities of linearizability. Line-Up [8] performs systematic concurrency testing via schedule enumeration, and offline linearizability checking via linearization enumeration. The works in [15, 16] show that checking linearizability for some particular class of ADTs is polynomial time. Emmi and Enea [14] consider the problem of checking weak consistency criteria, but their approach focuses on specific relaxations in those criteria, falling back to an explicit enumeration of linearizations in the context of a criterion like SC or TSO. Bouajjani et al. [6] consider the problem of checking causal consistency. They formalize the different variations of causal consistency we consider in this work and show that the problem of checking whether a history satisfies one of these variations is polynomial time.

The complementary issue of test generation, i.e., finding clients that increase the probability of uncovering bugs in shared memory implementations, has been approached in the McVerSi framework [13]. Their methodology for checking a criterion like SC lies within the context of white-box testing, i.e., the user is required to annotate the shared memory implementation with events that define the store order in an execution. Our algorithms have the advantage that the implementation is treated as a black-box requiring less user intervention.

7   Conclusion

We have introduced an approach for checking the conformance of a computation to SC or to TSO, a problem known to be NP-hard. The idea is to avoid an explicit enumeration of the exponential number of possible total orders between writes in order to solve these problems. Our approach is to define weaker criteria that are as strong as possible but still polynomial time checkable. This is useful for (1) early detection of violations, and (2) reducing the number of pairs of writes for which an order must be found in order to check SC/TSO conformance. Morally, the approach consists in being able to capture an "as large as possible" partial order on writes that can be computed in polynomial time (using a least fixpoint calculation), and which is a subset of any total order witnessing SC/TSO conformance. Our experimental results show that this approach is indeed useful and performant: it allows to catch most of violations early using an efficient check, and it allows to compute a large kernel of write constraints that reduces significantly the number of pairs of writes that are left to be ordered in an enumerative way. Future work consists in exploring the application of this approach to other correctness criteria that are hard to check such a serializability in the context of transactional programs.

References

1. Abdulla, P.A., Haziza, F., Holík, L.: Parameterized verification through view abstraction. STTT **18**(5), 495–516 (2016). https://doi.org/10.1007/s10009-015-0406-x
2. Ahamad, M., Neiger, G., Burns, J.E., Kohli, P., Hutto, P.W.: Causal memory: definitions, implementation, and programming. Distrib. Comput. **9**(1), 37–49 (1995)
3. Alglave, J., Maranget, L., Tautschnig, M.: Herding cats: modelling, simulation, testing, and data mining for weak memory. ACM Trans. Program. Lang. Syst. **36**(2), 7:1–7:74 (2014). https://doi.org/10.1145/2627752
4. Alur, R., McMillan, K.L., Peled, D.A.: Model-checking of correctness conditions for concurrent objects. Inf. Comput. **160**(1–2), 167–188 (2000). https://doi.org/10.1006/inco.1999.2847
5. Binkert, N., et al.: The gem5 simulator. SIGARCH Comput. Archit. News **39**(2), 1–7 (2011). https://doi.org/10.1145/2024716.2024718
6. Bouajjani, A., Enea, C., Guerraoui, R., Hamza, J.: On verifying causal consistency. In: Castagna, G., Gordon, A.D. (eds.) Proceedings of the 44th ACM SIGPLAN Symposium on Principles of Programming Languages, POPL 2017, Paris, France, January 18–20, 2017, pp. 626–638. ACM (2017). http://dl.acm.org/citation.cfm?id=3009888
7. Burckhardt, S.: Principles of Eventual Consistency. Now publishers, Boston, October 2014
8. Burckhardt, S., Dern, C., Musuvathi, M., Tan, R.: Line-up: a complete and automatic linearizability checker. In: Zorn, B.G., Aiken, A. (eds.) Proceedings of the 2010 ACM SIGPLAN Conference on Programming Language Design and Implementation, PLDI 2010, Toronto, Ontario, Canada, 5–10 June 2010, pp. 330–340. ACM (2010). https://doi.org/10.1145/1806596.1806634
9. Clarke, E.M., et al.: Verification of the futurebus+ cache coherence protocol. In: Agnew, D., Claesen, L.J.M., Camposano, R. (eds.) Computer Hardware Description Languages and their Applications, Proceedings of the 11th IFIP WG10.2 International Conference on Computer Hardware Description Languages and their Applications - CHDL 1993, sponsored by IFIP WG10.2 and in cooperation with IEEE COMPSOC, Ottawa, Ontario, Canada, 26–28 April 1993. IFIP Transactions, vol. A-32, pp. 15–30. North-Holland (1993)

10. Delzanno, G.: Automatic verification of parameterized cache coherence protocols. In: Emerson, E.A., Sistla, A.P. (eds.) CAV 2000. LNCS, vol. 1855, pp. 53–68. Springer, Heidelberg (2000). https://doi.org/10.1007/10722167_8

11. Delzanno, G.: Constraint-based verification of parameterized cache coherence protocols. Formal Methods Syst. Des. **23**(3), 257–301 (2003)

12. Eiríksson, Á.T., McMillan, K.L.: Using formal verification/analysis methods on the critical path in system design: a case study. In: Wolper, P. (ed.) CAV 1995. LNCS, vol. 939, pp. 367–380. Springer, Heidelberg (1995). https://doi.org/10.1007/3-540-60045-0_63

13. Elver, M., Nagarajan, V.: Mcversi: a test generation framework for fast memory consistency verification in simulation. In: 2016 IEEE International Symposium on High Performance Computer Architecture, HPCA 2016, Barcelona, Spain, 12–16 March 2016, pp. 618–630. IEEE Computer Society (2016). https://doi.org/10.1109/HPCA.2016.7446099

14. Emmi, M., Enea, C.: Monitoring weak consistency. In: Chockler, H., Weissenbacher, G. (eds.) CAV 2018. LNCS, vol. 10981, pp. 487–506. Springer, Cham (2018). https://doi.org/10.1007/978-3-319-96145-3_26

15. Emmi, M., Enea, C.: Sound, complete, and tractable linearizability monitoring for concurrent collections. PACMPL **2**(POPL), 25:1–25:27 (2018). https://doi.org/10.1145/3158113

16. Emmi, M., Enea, C., Hamza, J.: Monitoring refinement via symbolic reasoning. In: Grove, D., Blackburn, S. (eds.) Proceedings of the 36th ACM SIGPLAN Conference on Programming Language Design and Implementation, Portland, OR, USA, 15–17 June, 2015, pp. 260–269. ACM (2015). https://doi.org/10.1145/2737924.2737983

17. Esparza, J., Finkel, A., Mayr, R.: On the verification of broadcast protocols. In: 14th Annual IEEE Symposium on Logic in Computer Science, Trento, Italy, 2–5 July 1999, pp. 352–359. IEEE Computer Society (1999). https://doi.org/10.1109/LICS.1999.782630

18. Furbach, F., Meyer, R., Schneider, K., Senftleben, M.: Memory-model-aware testing: a unified complexity analysis. ACM Trans. Embed. Comput. Syst. **14**(4), 63:1–63:25 (2015). https://doi.org/10.1145/2753761

19. Gebser, M., Kaminski, R., Kaufmann, B., Schaub, T.: Clingo = ASP + control: Preliminary report. CoRR abs/1405.3694 (2014). http://arxiv.org/abs/1405.3694

20. German, S.M., Sistla, A.P.: Reasoning about systems with many processes. J. ACM **39**(3), 675–735 (1992). https://doi.org/10.1145/146637.146681

21. Gibbons, P.B., Korach, E.: Testing shared memories. SIAM J. Comput. **26**(4), 1208–1244 (1997). https://doi.org/10.1137/S0097539794279614

22. Gotsman, A., Burckhardt, S.: Consistency models with global operation sequencing and their composition. In: Richa, A.W. (ed.) 31st International Symposium on Distributed Computing, DISC 2017, LIPIcs, 16–20 October 2017, Vienna, Austria, vol. 91, pp. 23:1–23:16. Schloss Dagstuhl - Leibniz-Zentrum fuer Informatik (2017). https://doi.org/10.4230/LIPIcs.DISC.2017.23

23. Ip, C.N., Dill, D.L.: Better verification through symmetry. Formal Methods Syst. Des. **9**(1/2), 41–75 (1996). https://doi.org/10.1007/BF00625968

24. Lamport, L.: How to make a multiprocessor computer that correctly executes multiprocess programs. IEEE Trans. Comput. **28**(9), 690–691 (1979). https://doi.org/10.1109/TC.1979.1675439

25. Lowe, G.: Testing for linearizability. Concurrency Comput. Pract. Experience 29(4) (2017). https://doi.org/10.1002/cpe.3928

26. Perrin, M., Mostefaoui, A., Jard, C.: Causal consistency: beyond memory. In: Proceedings of the 21st ACM SIGPLAN Symposium on Principles and Practice of Parallel Programming, PPoPP 2016, pp. 26:1–26:12. ACM, New York (2016)

27. Pong, F., Dubois, M.: A new approach for the verification of cache coherence protocols. IEEE Trans. Parallel Distrib. Syst. **6**(8), 773–787 (1995). https://doi.org/10.1109/71.406955

28. Qadeer, S.: Verifying sequential consistency on shared-memory multiprocessors by model checking. IEEE Trans. Parallel Distrib. Syst. **14**(8), 730–741 (2003). https://doi.org/10.1109/TPDS.2003.1225053

29. Sewell, P., Sarkar, S., Owens, S., Nardelli, F.Z., Myreen, M.O.: x86-tso: a rigorous and usable programmer's model for x86 multiprocessors. Commun. ACM **53**(7), 89–97 (2010). https://doi.org/10.1145/1785414.1785443

30. Wing, J.M., Gong, C.: Testing and verifying concurrent objects. J. Parallel Distrib. Comput. **17**(1–2), 164–182 (1993). https://doi.org/10.1006/jpdc.1993.1015

31. Wolper, P.: Expressing interesting properties of programs in propositional temporal logic. In: Conference Record of the Thirteenth Annual ACM Symposium on Principles of Programming Languages, St. Petersburg Beach, Florida, USA, January 1986, pp. 184–193. ACM Press (1986). https://doi.org/10.1145/512644.512661

9

Incremental Determinization
for Quantifier Elimination and Functional
Synthesis

Markus N. Rabe$^{(\boxtimes)}$

Google, Mountain View, CA, USA
mrabe@google.com

Abstract. Quantifier elimination and its cousin functional synthesis are fundamental problems in automated reasoning that could be used in many applications of formal methods. But, effective algorithms are still elusive. In this paper, we suggest a simple modification to a QBF algorithm to adapt it for quantifier elimination and functional synthesis. We demonstrate that the approach significantly outperforms previous algorithms for functional synthesis.

1 Introduction

Given a Boolean formula $\exists Y. \varphi$ with free variables X, *quantifier elimination* (also called *projection*) is the problem to find a formula $\psi \equiv \exists Y. \varphi$ that only contains variables X. Closely related, the *functional synthesis* problem is to find a function $f_y : 2^X \to \mathbb{B}$ for all $y \in Y$, such that $\varphi[Y \mapsto f_y(X)] \equiv \exists Y. \varphi$.

Quantifier elimination and functional synthesis are fundamental operations in automated reasoning, computer-aided design, and verification. Hence, progress in algorithms for these problems benefits a broad range of applications of formal methods. For example, typical algorithms for reactive synthesis reduce to computing the safe region of a safety game through repeated quantifier eliminations [1–3] or directly employ functional synthesis [4]. Until today, algorithms for quantifier elimination often involve (reduced ordered) Binary Decision Diagrams (BDDs) [5]. However, BDDs often grow exponentially for applications in verification, and extracting formulas (or strategies, etc.) from BDDs typically results in huge expressions. The search for alternatives resulted in CEGAR-style algorithms [6–10].

In this work, we take look at the closely related field of QBF solving. There pure CEGAR solving [11–13] on the CNF representation is not competitive anymore [14], and it has been augmented by preprocessing [15,16], circuit representations [17–21], and Incremental Determinization (ID) [22]. It may hence be fruitful to leverage some of the recent developments of QBF.

The contribution of this work is a simple modification of ID to enable quantifier elimination and functional synthesis. Incremental Determinization (ID) is an algorithm for solving quantified Boolean formulas of the shape $\forall X. \exists Y. \varphi$, where

φ is a propositional formula in conjunctive normal form (CNF), i.e. 2QBF. It follows a proof-theoretic approach, very similar to a SAT solver, alternating between building a model (i.e. Skolem functions for the existential variables Y) and a refutation proof [23]. This allows ID to provide a model (i.e. a Skolem function) when it determines that a formula is true, which sets it apart from other QBF algorithms.

The modification of ID to enable quantifier elimination for a given formula $\exists Y. \varphi$ is very simple: We run ID on the formula as if it was a quantified Boolean formula $\forall X. \exists Y. \varphi$, where X are the free variables, but add φ to the conflict check within ID. This suppresses the UNSAT result in the ID algorithm and it is hence forced to terminate with a model (that is, a function), which is guaranteed to satisfy the functional synthesis requirements. Quantifier elimination is then only a substitution away.

Our experimental evaluation shows that ID significantly outperforms previous algorithms for functional synthesis and quantifier elimination.

This paper is structured as follows: We review related work in Sect. 2 and introduce standard notation in Sect. 3. In Sect. 4 we first review the Incremental Determinization algorithm before introducing the change necessary to lift it to functional synthesis. The experimental evaluation is in Sect. 5. We summarize the current state of the tool CADET in Sect. 6 and conclude the paper in Sect. 7.

2   Related Work

Functional Synthesis. Early works on functional synthesis tried to exploit Craig interpolation, but did not scale well enough [24]. This was followed by first attempts to use CEGAR [6], which failed, however, to surpass the performance of BDDs [7]. More recent works revisited the use of BDDs, e.g. the tools SSyft [25] and RSynth [26,27]. This motivated the search for alternatives to BDDs [8–10]. At their core, these new algorithms all rely on counter-example guided abstraction refinement (CEGAR) [28], but they apply it in clever, compositional ways. However, they still inherit the well-known weaknesses of CEGAR (as, for example, discussed in the QBF literature): For the simple formula $\varphi = \bigwedge_{i<n} x_i \leftrightarrow y_i$, where $n = |X| = |Y|$ and $x_i \in X$ and $y_i \in Y$, CEGAR needs to browse through 2^n satisfying assignments just to recover that the function we were looking for is $f(x) = x$.

The Back-and-Forth algorithm explores stronger abstraction using MaxSAT solvers as a means to reduce the number of assignments that CEGAR needs to explore [8]. ParSyn attempts to combat the problem with parallel compute power and a compositional approach [9]. This compositional approach has later been refined using a wDNNF decomposition [10].

QBF Certification. Some solvers and preprocessors for QBF have the ability to not only provide a yes/no answer, but also produce a certificate (i.e. Skolem functions) for their result [13,22,29,30]. While most QBF approaches suffer heavy performance penalties when asked to provide a certificate, Incremental Determinization naturally computes Skolem functions that can be extracted easily from the final state [22].

3   Preliminaries

Boolean formulas over a finite set of variables $x \in X$ with domain $\mathbb{B} = \{0, 1\}$ are generated by the following grammar:

$$\varphi := \mathbf{0} \mid \mathbf{1} \mid x \mid \neg\varphi \mid (\varphi) \mid \varphi \vee \varphi \mid \varphi \wedge \varphi$$

Other logical operations, such as implication, XOR, and equality, are considered syntactic sugar with the usual definitions.

An *assignment* $\boldsymbol{x}$ to a set of variables X is a function $\boldsymbol{x} : X \to \mathbb{B}$ that maps each variable $x \in X$ to either $\mathbf{1}$ or $\mathbf{0}$. We denote the space of assignments to some set of variables X with 2^X.

Given formulas φ and φ', and a variable x, we denote the substitution of x by φ' in φ as $\varphi[x \to \varphi']$. We lift substitutions to sets of variables $\varphi[X \mapsto t_x]$ when t_x maps each $x \in X$ to a formula φ'.

A *literal* l is either a variable $x \in X$, or its negation $\neg x$. We use $\bar{l}$ to denote the literal that is the logical negation of l. A disjunction of literals $(l_1 \vee \ldots \vee l_n)$ is called a *clause* and their conjunction $(l_1 \wedge \ldots \wedge l_n)$ is called a *cube*. We denote the variable of a literal by $var(l)$ and lift the notion to clauses $var(l_1 \vee \cdots \vee l_n) = \{var(l_1), \ldots, var(l_n)\}$.

A formula is in *conjunctive normal form* (CNF), if it is a conjunction of clauses. Throughout this exposition, we assume that the input formula is given in CNF. (The output, however, can be a non-CNF formula.) It is trivial to lift the approach to general Boolean formulas: Given a Boolean formula φ over variables X, the Tseitin transformation provides us a formula ψ with $\varphi \equiv \exists Z.\psi$, where Z are fresh variables [31]. Note that eliminating a group of variables $X' \subseteq X$ in φ is then the same as eliminating $X' \cup Z$ in ψ.

Resolution is a well-known proof rule that allows us to merge two clauses as follows. Given two clauses $C_1 \vee v$ and $C_2 \vee \neg v$, we call $C_1 \otimes_v C_2 = C_1 \vee C_2$ their *resolvent* with pivot v. The resolution rule states that $C_1 \vee v$ and $C_2 \vee \neg v$ imply their resolvent. Resolution is *refutationally complete* for Boolean formulas in CNF, i.e. given a formula in CNF that is equivalent to false, we can derive the empty clause using only resolution.

4   Lifting Incremental Determinization

In the sequel, we formally define functional synthesis, review the working principle of Incremental Determinization for 2QBF, discuss how the solver state corresponds to functions, and then introduce the modification to Incremental Determinization to turn it into an algorithm for functional synthesis. The *functional synthesis* problem is to find a function $f_y : 2^X \to \mathbb{B}$ for all $y \in Y$, such that $\varphi[Y \mapsto f_y(X)] \equiv \exists Y. \varphi$. Functional synthesis is closely related to solving 2QBF: Given a true 2QBF problem $\forall X. \exists Y. \varphi$, any Skolem function that is a model for the formula is also a solution to the functional synthesis problem for variable sets X and Y. Only for false 2QBF there is a difference between the problems: if there is an assignment x to X for which there is no assignment to Y, the 2QBF cannot be proven with a Skolem function, but the functional synthesis problem still requires us to produce a function f. It is clear that for input x the f can produce any output. We will exploit this similarity between 2QBF and functional synthesis in the following to lift the Incremental Determinization algorithm to functional synthesis.

4.1 Working Principle of Incremental Determinization for 2QBF

ID was originally introduced as an algorithm for 2QBF, the fragment of quantified Boolean formulas with at most one quantifier alternation. Given a formula $\forall X. \exists Y. \varphi$, ID alternates between constructing a model (i.e. a Skolem function) to prove the formula correct, and constructing a Q-resolution proof to refute the formula [32]. During model construction, ID identifies which variables in Y have unique Skolem functions considering the current set of clauses. When all variables with unique Skolem functions are identified, ID greedily introduces additional clauses to reduce the space of possible Skolem functions, such that the remaining variables may get unique Skolem functions, too. Whenever the model construction ends up in a dead-end (=conflict), ID switches to constructing a refutation proof [32] and derives clauses using resolution. As soon as ID found a clause that prevents the model construction from trying the same partial model again, it switches back to the model search. Since there are only finitely many clauses and models, either the model construction or the refutation proof must eventually finish [22,23].

Example 1. We will use the following formula as a running example:

$$\forall x_1, x_2. \exists y_1, y_2, y_3. \; (x_1 \vee \neg y_1) \wedge (\neg x_1 \vee y_1) \wedge$$
$$(y_1 \vee \neg y_2) \wedge (\neg y_1 \vee \neg x_2 \vee y_2) \wedge$$
$$(\neg y_1 \vee y_3) \wedge (y_2 \vee \neg y_3) \wedge (x_2 \vee \neg y_3)$$

Looking at the first two clauses it is clear that y_1 is uniquely determined by x_1 and y_1's Skolem function must be $f_{y_1}(X) = x_1$. For this step, we intentionally ignore all clauses of y_1 that contain y_2 and y_3, as they do not yet have a Skolem function and we have to consider them as undefined. The other clauses containing y_1 will only become relevant when looking for Skolem functions for y_2 and y_3.

Variables y_2 and y_3 do not have *unique* Skolem functions in the formula above. ID would now greedily add a *decision clause*, such as $(x_2 \vee \neg y_2)$, to also make the Skolem function for y_2 unique. The added clause, plus clauses 3 and 4 in the formula define: $f_{y_2}(X) = f_{y_1}(X) \wedge x_2$.

This results in the situation that there is no Skolem function for y_3: For the assignment $x_1 \mapsto \mathbf{1}$, $x_2 \mapsto \mathbf{0}$, the functions for y_1 and y_2 assign $y_1 \mapsto \mathbf{1}$, $y_2 \mapsto \mathbf{0}$.

Then clauses 4 and 5 cannot be satisfied both by y_3, which means there is a conflict for this assignment to the universals. During conflict analysis, ID would now resolve clauses 5 and 6 to obtain clause $(\neg y_1 \vee y_2)$, and then backtrack to the point before introducing the decision clause. $\lhd$

4.2   Representation of Functions

What is particularly interesting about ID is its ability to produce Skolem functions when it has proven a formula correct. Other than previous QBF algorithms, these Skolem functions are produced without any overhead.

ID avoids costly representations of Skolem functions: It maintains a set $D \subseteq Y$ of variables that have a unique Skolem function, and its state includes a formula δ characterizing the input-output behavior of the Skolem functions for variables D. Formula δ satisfies $\forall X. \exists! D. \delta$, where $\exists! D$ means that there exists exactly one assignment to D. We can thus think of δ also as a function f_δ mapping X assignments to D assignments.

Example 2. Back to our running example. After identifying a unique Skolem function for y_1, formula δ consists exactly of the first two clauses of the formula, $(x_1 \vee \neg y_1) \wedge (\neg x_1 \vee y_1)$. After adding the decision clause and identifying a unique Skolem function for y_2, δ consists exactly of the first four clauses and the decision clause. $\lhd$

4.3   Conflict Checks in ID

The formulas representing functions have primarily one purpose: to check for the existence of *conflicts*. Whenever we attempt to grow the set D by a variable v, we need to check whether v has a unique Skolem function. This check consists of two parts; given an arbitrary universal assignment $\boldsymbol{x} \in 2^X$,

(1) is there *at most* one legal assignment to v, and
(2) is there *at least* one legal assignment to v?

To formally define this, let us consider the clauses $(d_1 \vee \cdots \vee d_n \vee l)$ in φ that contain a literal l of variable v and otherwise only contain literals d_i of variables in D and X. We call these the clauses with *unique consequence*, as they can be read as implications $(\neg d_1 \wedge \cdots \wedge \neg d_n \Rightarrow l)$, and we call $\neg d_1 \wedge \cdots \wedge \neg d_n$ the antecedent of that clause. Further, we define $\mathcal{A}_l$ as the disjunction over all antecedents of literal l. (Note that $\mathcal{A}_l$ depends on D and therefore changes as the state of the solver progresses.)

The two checks from above can now be defined as follows:

(1) $\exists X. \delta \wedge \neg \mathcal{A}_v \wedge \neg \mathcal{A}_{\neg v}$
(2) $\exists X. \delta \wedge \ \mathcal{A}_v \wedge \ \mathcal{A}_{\neg v}$

Checking for case (1) can be efficiently approximated [22], but checking for case (2) cannot easily be avoided. We thus query a SAT solver with $\delta \wedge \mathcal{A}_v \wedge \mathcal{A}_{\neg v}$ to perform a conflict check.

Example 3. We revisit the conflict described in Example 1. The starting point is the situation when $D = \{y_1, y_2\}$ and δ consists of the first four clauses of the formula as well as the decision clause $(x_2 \vee \neg y_2)$. The antecedents of y_3 are $\mathcal{A}_{y_3} = y_1$ and $\mathcal{A}_{\neg y_3} = \neg y_2 \vee \neg x_2$. It is easy to verify that the universal assignment $x_1 \mapsto \mathbf{1}, \ x_2 \mapsto \mathbf{0}, y_1 \mapsto \mathbf{1}, \ y_2 \mapsto \mathbf{0}$ satisfies the conflict criterion $\delta \wedge \mathcal{A}_v \wedge \mathcal{A}_{\neg v}$.   ◁

4.4 Functional Synthesis

Remember that in the case of functional synthesis for φ over sets of variables X and Y, we search for a function $f : 2^X \rightarrow 2^Y$ such that f produces a satisfying assignment whenever it can, but can produce anything when there is no assignment to Y satisfying the formula. In case there are satisfying assignments to Y for all X, we can simply run ID as if it was a QBF $\forall X. \exists. \varphi$ to obtain a Skolem function that also satisfies the functional synthesis criterion. In the other case, that there is an X for which there is no assignment to Y satisfying φ, ID for 2QBF would eventually detect a conflict that did not depend on a decision and return with UNSAT.

In order to lift ID to functional synthesis, we want to ignore universal assignments that have no satisfying assignment to Y. A simple way to suppress these conflicts is to add φ to the conflict check. In order for an assignment to X to remain a conflict, we must now additionally find an assignment to Y that demonstrates that the conflict could be prevented by a different decision.

All other parts of ID, including the extraction of functions, remain untouched. In particular, termination is still guaranteed, as the greedy model construction either results in a function for all variables in Y or in a conflict, upon which at least one model is excluded through resolution.

Example 4. For the conflict in our running example, the universal assignment $x_1 \mapsto \mathbf{1}, \ x_2 \mapsto \mathbf{0}$ is excluded in the modified conflict check. Consider the UNSAT core consisting of clauses 2, 5, and 7 for that universal assignment: propagate $y_1 \mapsto \mathbf{1}$ using clause 2; propagate $y_3 \mapsto \mathbf{1}$ using clause 5; and finally propagate $y_3 \mapsto \mathbf{0}$ using clause 7. So, instead of going into conflict analysis and backtracking, ID for functional synthesis concludes that it has found a function for all existential variables and terminates.

4.5 Quantifier Elimination

Given a formula $\exists Y. \varphi$ with free variables X, *quantifier elimination* is the problem to find a formula $\psi \equiv \exists Y. \varphi$ over variables X only. Hence, given a solution f to the functional synthesis problem for φ, we only have to substitute Y by f in φ to obtain the projected formula.

5 Experimental Evaluation

We implemented the modifications to ID in CADET,[1] a competitive 2QBF solver [22]. In this section, we compare CADET experimentally with existing

---

[1] CADET is available at https://github.com/MarkusRabe/cadet.

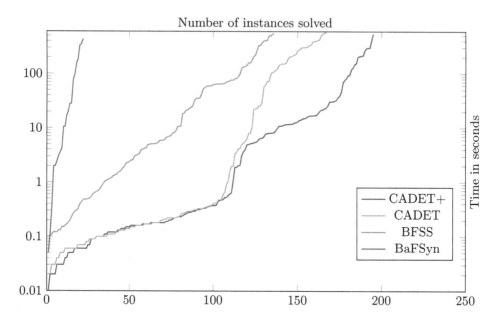

Fig. 1. Log-scale cactus plot comparing the performance over all instances.

algorithms for functional synthesis. Additionally, we implemented a certificate checker for functional synthesis and for quantifier elimination, to make sure that the computed functions are correct. The certificate checker only shares the code for AIGER circuits and the SAT solver (of which we have tried several), but is completely independent otherwise to reduce the chance of correlated bugs. The results of CADET have been checked with the proof checker; running times reported below are excluding the time to check the certificates.

So far, there is no standard benchmark for functional synthesis or quantifier elimination. Like previous works on functional synthesis, we resort to using the 2QBF benchmark from QBFEVAL'17 [14], and re-interpret them as functional synthesis problems. The 2QBF benchmark from QBFEVAL'17 is a collection of 384 formulas from various domains, mostly from software verification, program synthesis, and logical equivalences [33–36].

We compare CADET to the most recent tools on functional synthesis, BaF-Syn [8] and BFSS [10], the latter of which has been shown to consistently outperform the earlier, BDD-based tools SSyft [25] and RSynth [26,27]. We ran CADET in two configurations: with (CADET+) and without (CADET) its CEGAR module [23]. We present the results as a cactus plot, which is obtained by running each tool on all formulas, sorting the running times for each tool separately. A point x, y in this plot means that x formulas were solved in less than time y. Note that the time axis is in log-scale (Fig. 1).

CADET shows a clear edge in performance: it is one to two orders of magnitude faster than its strongest competitor, BFSS, and can solve significantly more formulas. But despite the clear performance advantage in this aggregate view, BaFSyn and BFSS can be faster for individual formulas or subfamilies of QBFEval, as shown in previous works [8,10].

6 The Current State of CADET

Originally designed as an experimentation platform, CADET has grown to become a performant and versatile tool for the synthesis of Boolean functions. It consistently wins awards at the annual QBFEVAL competitions, and is the only such tool able to prove all its results [14].

CADET reads specifications in the QDIMACS and the QAIGER formats, and now supports the synthesis of Boolean functions for 2QBF, functional synthesis, and quantifier elimination with the command line options -c [file], -f [file], and -e [file]. The functions computed by CADET are much smaller compared to those found by CEGAR-based algorithms [22], and in its default configuration, CADET double-checks its results before reporting them. This can be deactivated by the flag --dontverify.

It has also been integrated in py-aiger [37], a Python package for the convenient handling of circuits due to Marcell Vazquez-Chanlatte, which enables us to easily model and prototype new approaches. For example, we can write:

```
import aiger_analysis as aa
import aigerbv as bv
x = bv.atom(32, 'x')    # Create a 32 bit variable
y = bv.atom(32, 'y')
expr = (x != y)
result = aa.eliminate(expr, ['y'])
assert aa.is_equal(x, result)
```

CADET also has an experimental reinforcement learning interface that allows us to automatically learn decision heuristics with the help of graph neural networks. A recent effort shows that there is huge potential in learning better branching heuristics from scratch [38].

7 Conclusions

In this work, we extended ID with the ability to solve functional synthesis and quantifier elimination problems. The extension is very simple—we only need to add the clauses of the original formula to its conflict check. The resulting algorithm significantly outperforms previous algorithms for functional synthesis.

Acknowledgements. The author wants to thank to Shubham Goel, Shetal Shah, and Lucas Tabajara for insightful discussions and for their assistance with running their functional synthesis tools. In particular, I want to express my gratitude to Supratik Chakraborty for inspiring me to work on the topic in a discussion in the summer of 2016.

References

1. Ehlers, R.: Symbolic bounded synthesis. In: Touili, T., Cook, B., Jackson, P. (eds.) CAV 2010. LNCS, vol. 6174, pp. 365–379. Springer, Heidelberg (2010). https://doi.org/10.1007/978-3-642-14295-6_33
2. Brenguier, R., Pérez, G.A., Raskin, J., Sankur, O.: AbsSynthe: abstract synthesis from succinct safety specifications. In: Proceedings of SYNT, pp. 100–116 (2014)
3. Jacobs, S., et al.: The 4th reactive synthesis competition (syntcomp 2017): benchmarks, participants & results. arXiv preprint arXiv:1711.11439 (2017)
4. Zhu, S., Tabajara, L.M., Li, J., Pu, G., Vardi, M.Y.: Symbolic LTLf synthesis. In: Proceedings of IJCAI, IJCAI 2017, pp. 1362–1369. AAAI Press (2017)
5. Bryant, R.E.: Symbolic Boolean manipulation with ordered binary-decision diagrams. ACM Comput. Surv. **24**(3), 293–318 (1992)
6. Goldberg, E., Manolios, P.: Quantifier elimination by dependency sequents. Formal Methods Syst. Des. **45**(2), 111–143 (2014). https://doi.org/10.1007/s10703-014-0214-z
7. Goldberg, E., Manolios, P.: Quantifier elimination via clause redundancy. In: Formal Methods in Computer-Aided Design, pp. 85–92, October 2013
8. Chakraborty, S., Fried, D., Tabajara, L.M., Vardi, M.Y.: Functional synthesis via input-output separation. In: Proceedings of FMCAD, pp. 1–9. IEEE (2018)
9. Akshay, S., Chakraborty, S., John, A.K., Shah, S.: Towards parallel Boolean functional synthesis. In: Legay, A., Margaria, T. (eds.) TACAS 2017. LNCS, vol. 10205, pp. 337–353. Springer, Heidelberg (2017). https://doi.org/10.1007/978-3-662-54577-5_19
10. Akshay, S., Chakraborty, S., Goel, S., Kulal, S., Shah, S.: What's hard about boolean functional synthesis? In: Chockler, H., Weissenbacher, G. (eds.) CAV 2018. LNCS, vol. 10981, pp. 251–269. Springer, Cham (2018). https://doi.org/10.1007/978-3-319-96145-3_14
11. Janota, M., Klieber, W., Marques-Silva, J., Clarke, E.: Solving QBF with counterexample guided refinement. In: Cimatti, A., Sebastiani, R. (eds.) SAT 2012. LNCS, vol. 7317, pp. 114–128. Springer, Heidelberg (2012). https://doi.org/10.1007/978-3-642-31612-8_10
12. Janota, M., Marques-Silva, J.: Solving QBF by clause selection. In: Proceedings of IJCAI, pp. 325–331. AAAI Press (2015)
13. Rabe, M.N., Tentrup, L.: CAQE: a certifying QBF solver. In: Proceedings of FMCAD, pp. 136–143 (2015)
14. QBFEVAL: QBF solver evaluation portal. http://www.qbflib.org/index_eval.php. Accessed Jan 2018
15. Biere, A., Lonsing, F., Seidl, M.: Blocked clause elimination for QBF. In: Bjørner, N., Sofronie-Stokkermans, V. (eds.) CADE 2011. LNCS (LNAI), vol. 6803, pp. 101–115. Springer, Heidelberg (2011). https://doi.org/10.1007/978-3-642-22438-6_10
16. Wimmer, R., Reimer, S., Marin, P., Becker, B.: HQSpre – an effective preprocessor for QBF and DQBF. In: Legay, A., Margaria, T. (eds.) TACAS 2017. LNCS, vol. 10205, pp. 373–390. Springer, Heidelberg (2017). https://doi.org/10.1007/978-3-662-54577-5_21
17. Klieber, W., Sapra, S., Gao, S., Clarke, E.: A non-prenex, non-clausal QBF solver with game-state learning. In: Strichman, O., Szeider, S. (eds.) SAT 2010. LNCS, vol. 6175, pp. 128–142. Springer, Heidelberg (2010). https://doi.org/10.1007/978-3-642-14186-7_12

18. Jordan, C., Klieber, W., Seidl, M.: Non-CNF QBF solving with QCIR. In: AAAI Workshop: Beyond NP (2016)
19. Balabanov, V., Jiang, J.-H.R., Scholl, C., Mishchenko, A., Brayton, R.K.: 2QBF: challenges and solutions. In: Creignou, N., Le Berre, D. (eds.) SAT 2016. LNCS, vol. 9710, pp. 453–469. Springer, Cham (2016). https://doi.org/10.1007/978-3-319-40970-2_28
20. Tentrup, L.: Non-prenex QBF solving using abstraction. In: Creignou, N., Le Berre, D. (eds.) SAT 2016. LNCS, vol. 9710, pp. 393–401. Springer, Cham (2016). https://doi.org/10.1007/978-3-319-40970-2_24
21. Janota, M.: Circuit-based search space pruning in QBF. In: Beyersdorff, O., Wintersteiger, C.M. (eds.) SAT 2018. LNCS, vol. 10929, pp. 187–198. Springer, Cham (2018). https://doi.org/10.1007/978-3-319-94144-8_12
22. Rabe, M.N., Seshia, S.A.: Incremental determinization. In: Creignou, N., Le Berre, D. (eds.) SAT 2016. LNCS, vol. 9710, pp. 375–392. Springer, Cham (2016). https://doi.org/10.1007/978-3-319-40970-2_23
23. Rabe, M.N., Tentrup, L., Rasmussen, C., Seshia, S.A.: Understanding and extending incremental determinization for 2QBF. In: Chockler, H., Weissenbacher, G. (eds.) CAV 2018. LNCS, vol. 10982, pp. 256–274. Springer, Cham (2018). https://doi.org/10.1007/978-3-319-96142-2_17
24. Jiang, J.-H.R.: Quantifier elimination via functional composition. In: Bouajjani, A., Maler, O. (eds.) CAV 2009. LNCS, vol. 5643, pp. 383–397. Springer, Heidelberg (2009). https://doi.org/10.1007/978-3-642-02658-4_30
25. Zhu, S., Tabajara, L.M., Li, J., Pu, G., Vardi, M.Y.: A symbolic approach to safety LTL synthesis. In: Strichman, O., Tzoref-Brill, R. (eds.) Hardware and Software: Verification and Testing. LNCS, vol. 10629, pp. 147–162. Springer, Cham (2017). https://doi.org/10.1007/978-3-319-70389-3_10
26. Tabajara, L.M., Vardi, M.Y.: Factored Boolean functional synthesis. In: Proceedings of FMCAD, pp. 124–131. IEEE (2017)
27. Fried, D., Tabajara, L.M., Vardi, M.Y.: BDD-based Boolean functional synthesis. In: Chaudhuri, S., Farzan, A. (eds.) CAV 2016. LNCS, vol. 9780, pp. 402–421. Springer, Cham (2016). https://doi.org/10.1007/978-3-319-41540-6_22
28. Clarke, E., Grumberg, O., Jha, S., Lu, Y., Veith, H.: Counterexample-guided abstraction refinement. In: Emerson, E.A., Sistla, A.P. (eds.) CAV 2000. LNCS, vol. 1855, pp. 154–169. Springer, Heidelberg (2000). https://doi.org/10.1007/10722167_15
29. Lonsing, F., Biere, A.: DepQBF: a dependency-aware QBF solver. JSAT 7(2–3), 71–76 (2010)
30. Heule, M.J.H., Seidl, M., Biere, A.: A unified proof system for QBF preprocessing. In: Demri, S., Kapur, D., Weidenbach, C. (eds.) IJCAR 2014. LNCS (LNAI), vol. 8562, pp. 91–106. Springer, Cham (2014). https://doi.org/10.1007/978-3-319-08587-6_7
31. Tseitin, G.S.: On the complexity of derivation in propositional calculus. Stud. Constructive Math. Math. Log. 2(115–125), 10–13 (1968)
32. Buning, H., Karpinski, M., Flogel, A.: Resolution for quantified Boolean formulas. Inf. Comput. 117(1), 12–18 (1995)
33. Solar-Lezama, A., Rabbah, R.M., Bodík, R., Ebcioglu, K.: Programming by sketching for bit-streaming programs. In: Proceedings of PLDI, pp. 281–294 (2005)
34. Cook, B., Kroening, D., Rümmer, P., Wintersteiger, C.M.: Ranking function synthesis for bit-vector relations. In: Esparza, J., Majumdar, R. (eds.) TACAS 2010. LNCS, vol. 6015, pp. 236–250. Springer, Heidelberg (2010). https://doi.org/10.1007/978-3-642-12002-2_19

35. Wintersteiger, C.M., Hamadi, Y., De Moura, L.: Efficiently solving quantified bit-vector formulas. Proc. FMSD **42**(1), 3–23 (2013)
36. Jordan, C., Kaiser, L.: Experiments with reduction finding. In: Järvisalo, M., Van Gelder, A. (eds.) SAT 2013. LNCS, vol. 7962, pp. 192–207. Springer, Heidelberg (2013). https://doi.org/10.1007/978-3-642-39071-5_15
37. Vazquez-Chanlatte, M.: mvcisback/py-aiger, August 2018. https://doi.org/10.5281/zenodo.1326224
38. Lederman, G., Rabe, M.N., Lee, E.A., Seshia, S.A.: Learning heuristics for automated reasoning through deep reinforcement learning. arXiv preprint arXiv:1807.08058 (2018)

10

Alternating Automata Modulo First Order Theories

Radu Iosif[(⊠)] and Xiao Xu

CNRS, Verimag, Université de Grenoble Alpes, Grenoble, France
Radu.Iosif@univ-grenoble-alpes.fr, Xiao.Xu@univ-grenoble-alpes.fr

Abstract. We introduce first-order alternating automata, a generalization of boolean alternating automata, in which transition rules are described by multisorted first-order formulae, with states and internal variables given by uninterpreted predicate terms. The model is closed under union, intersection and complement, and its emptiness problem is undecidable, even for the simplest data theory of equality. To cope with the undecidability problem, we develop an abstraction refinement semi-algorithm based on lazy annotation of the symbolic execution paths with interpolants, obtained by applying (i) quantifier elimination with witness term generation and (ii) Lyndon interpolation in the quantifier-free theory of the data domain, with uninterpreted predicate symbols. This provides a method for checking inclusion of timed and finite-memory register automata, and emptiness of quantified predicate automata, previously used in the verification of parameterized concurrent programs, composed of replicated threads, with shared memory.

1 Introduction

Many results in automata theory rely on the finite alphabet hypothesis, which guarantees, in some cases, the existence of determinization, complementation and inclusion checking methods. However, this hypothesis prevents the use of automata as models of real-time systems or even simple programs, whose input and output are data values ranging over very large domains, typically viewed as infinite mathematical abstractions.

Traditional attempts to generalize classical Rabin-Scott automata to infinite alphabets, such as timed automata [1] and finite-memory automata [16] face the *complement closure* problem: there exist automata for which the complement language cannot be recognized by an automaton in the same class. This makes it impossible to encode a language inclusion problem $\mathcal{L}(A) \subseteq \mathcal{L}(B)$ as the emptiness of an automaton recognizing the language $\mathcal{L}(A) \cap \mathcal{L}^c(B)$, where $\mathcal{L}^c(B)$ denotes the complement of $\mathcal{L}(B)$.

Even for finite alphabets, complementation of finite-state automata faces inherent exponential blowup, due to nondeterminism. However, if we allow universal nondeterminism, in addition to the classical existential nondeterminism, complementation is possible is linear time. Having both existential and universal nondeterminism defines the *alternating automata* model [4]. A finite-alphabet alternating automaton is described by a set of transition rules $q \xrightarrow{a} \phi$, where q is a state, a is an input symbol and ϕ is a boolean formula, whose propositional variables denote successor states.

Our Contribution. We extend alternating automata to infinite data alphabets, by defining a model of computation in which all boolean operations, including complementation, can be done in linear time. The control states are given by k-ary predicate symbols $q(y_1, \ldots, y_k)$, the input consists of an event a from a finite alphabet and a tuple of data variables $x_1, \ldots, x_n$, ranging over an infinite domain, and transitions are of the form $q(y_1, \ldots, y_k) \xrightarrow{a(x_1, \ldots, x_n)} \phi(x_1, \ldots, x_n, y_1, \ldots, y_k)$, where ϕ is a formula in the first-order theory of the data domain. In this model, the arguments of a predicate atom $q(y_1, \ldots, y_k)$ represent the values of the *internal variables* associated with the state. Together with the input values $x_1, \ldots, x_n$, these values define the next configurations, but remain invisible in the input sequence.

The tight coupling of internal values and control states, by means of uninterpreted predicate symbols, allows for linear-time complementation just as in the case of classical propositional alternating automata. Complementation is, moreover, possible when the transition formulae contain first-order quantifiers, generating infinitely-branching execution trees. The price to be paid for this expressivity is that emptiness of first-order alternating automata is undecidable, even for the simplest data theory of equality [6].

The main contribution of this paper is an effective emptiness checking semi-algorithm for first-order alternating automata, in the spirit of the IMPACT lazy annotation procedure, originally developed for checking safety of nondeterministic integer programs [20, 21]. In a nutshell, a lazy annotation procedure unfolds an automaton A trying to find an execution that recognizes a word from $\mathcal{L}(A)$. If a path that reaches a final state does not correspond to a concrete run of the automaton, the positions on the path are labeled with interpolants from the proof of infeasibility, thus marking this path and all continuations as infeasible for future searches. Termination of lazy annotation procedures is not guaranteed, but having a suitable coverage relation between the nodes of the search tree may ensure convergence of many real-life examples. However, applying lazy annotation to first-order alternating automata faces two nontrivial problems:

1. Quantified transition rules make it hard, if not impossible, in general, to decide if a path is infeasible. This is mainly because adding uninterpreted predicate symbols to decidable first-order theories, such as Presburger arithmetic, results in undecidability [10]. To deal with this problem, we assume that the first-order data theory, without uninterpreted predicate symbols, has a quantifier elimination procedure, that instantiates quantifiers with effectively computable *witness terms*.

2. The interpolants that prove the infeasibility of a path are not *local*, as they may refer to input values encountered in the past. However, the future executions are oblivious to *when* these values have been seen in the past and depend only on the relation between the past and current values. We use this fact to define a labeling of nodes, visited by the lazy annotation procedure,

with conjunctions of existentially quantified interpolants combining predicate atoms with data constraints.

We use first-order alternating automata to develop practical semi-algorithms for a number of known undecidable problems, such as: inclusion of regular timed languages [1], inclusion of quasi-regular languages recognized by finite-memory automata [16] and emptiness of predicate automata, a subclass of first-order alternating automata used to verify parameterized concurrent programs [6,7].

Related Work. Recognizers for languages over infinite alphabets have found various applications, ranging from Unicode text recognition [5] to runtime program monitoring [2]. Extending finite automata to infinite alphabets has been considered in the context of *symbolic alternating finite automata* (s-AFA), whose transitions are labeled with guards taken from a decidable theory of the data domain [5]. As in our model, s-AFA are closed under union, intersection and complement and emptiness is decidable, due to the lack of registers. However, s-AFA are strictly less expressive than our model, because comparing data at different positions in the input word is not possible.

Constrained Horn clauses (CHC) are a branching computation model widespread in program verification [9]. The main difference between alternating and bottom-up branching computations is that, in an alternating model, all branches of the computation must synchronize on the same input word. With this in mind, it is possible to express emptiness of first-order alternating automata as the existence of solutions of a CHC over a higher-order theory of data, extended with algebraic data types (lists). The effectiveness of such an encoding depends on the effectiveness of interpolation and witness term generation for theories of algebraic data types [11].

The alternating automata model presented in this paper extends the alternating automata with variables ranging over infinite data considered in [14]. There all variables were required to be observable in the input. We overcome this restriction by allowing internal (invisible) variables. Another closely related work [13] considers an inclusion between an asynchronous product of automata $A_1 \times \ldots \times A_n$, extended with data variables, and a monitor automaton B. The semi-algorithm defined there was based on the assumption that all variables of the observer B must be declared in the automata $A_1, \ldots, A_n$ under check. This limitation can now be bypassed, since the inclusion problem can be encoded as emptiness of a first-order alternating automaton and, moreover, the emptiness checking semi-algorithm can handle invisible variables.

The work probably closest to ours concerns the model of *predicate automata* (PA) [6,7,17], used in the verification of parameterized concurrent programs with shared memory. In this model, the alphabet consists of pairs of program statements and thread identifiers and is considered infinite because the number of threads is unbounded. Since thread identifiers can only be compared for equality, the data theory in PA is the theory of equality. Even with this simplification, the emptiness problem is undecidable when either the predicates have arity greater than one [6] or use quantified transition rules [17]. Checking emptiness of quantifier-free PA is possible semi-algorithmically, by explicitly enumerating reachable configurations and checking coverage by looking for permutations of argument values. However, no semi-algorithm has been given for quantified PA. Dealing with quantified transition rules is one of our contributions.

1.1 Preliminaries

For two integers $0 \leq i \leq j$, we define $[i,j] \overset{\text{def}}{=} \{i,\dots,j\}$ and $[i] \overset{\text{def}}{=} [0,i]$. We consider two disjoint sorts $\mathbb{D}$ and $\mathbb{B}$, where $\mathbb{D}$ is an infinite domain and $\mathbb{B} = \{\top, \bot\}$ is the set of boolean values true ($\top$) and false ($\bot$), respectively. The $\mathbb{D}$ sort is equipped with countably many function symbols $f : \mathbb{D}^{\#(f)} \to \mathbb{D} \cup \mathbb{B}$, where $\#(f) \geq 0$ denotes the number of arguments (arity) of f. A *predicate* is a function symbol $p : \mathbb{D}^{\#(p)} \to \mathbb{B}$ that is, a $\#(p)$-ary relation.

We consider the interpretation of all function symbols $f : \mathbb{D}^{\#(f)} \to \mathbb{D}$ to be fixed by the interpretation of the $\mathbb{D}$ sort, for instance if $\mathbb{D}$ is the set of integers $\mathbb{Z}$, these are zero, the successor function and the arithmetic operations of addition and multiplication. We extend this convention to several predicates over $\mathbb{D}$, such as the inequality relation over $\mathbb{Z}$, and write Pred for the set of remaining *uninterpreted predicates*.

Let $\mathsf{Var} = \{x, y, z, \dots\}$ be a countably infinite set of variables, ranging over $\mathbb{D}$. Terms are either constants of sort $\mathbb{D}$, variables or function applications $f(t_1, \dots, t_{\#(f)})$, where $t_1, \dots, t_{\#(f)}$ are terms. The set of first-order formulae is defined by the syntax below:

$$\phi := t = s \mid p(t_1, \dots, t_{\#(p)}) \mid \neg\phi_1 \mid \phi_1 \wedge \phi_2 \mid \exists x \,.\, \phi_1$$

where $t, s, t_1, \dots, t_{\#(p)}$ denote terms and p is a predicate symbol. We write $\phi_1 \vee \phi_2$, $\phi_1 \to \phi_2$ and $\forall x \,.\, \phi_1$ for $\neg(\neg\phi_1 \wedge \neg\phi_2)$, $\neg\phi_1 \vee \phi_2$ and $\neg\exists x \,.\, \neg\phi_1$, respectively. $\mathrm{FV}(\phi)$ is the set of free variables in ϕ and the size $|\phi|$ of a formula ϕ is the number of symbols needed to write it down. A *sentence* is a formula ϕ with no free variables. A formula is *positive* if each uninterpreted predicate symbol occurs under an even number of negations and we denote by $\mathsf{Form}^+(Q, X)$ the set of positive formulae with predicates from the set $Q \subseteq \mathsf{Pred}$ and free variables from the set $X \subseteq \mathsf{Var}$. A formula is in *prenex form* if it is of the form $\varphi = Q_1 x_1 \dots Q_n x_n \,.\, \phi$, where ϕ has no quantifiers. In this case we call ϕ the *matrix* of φ. Every first-order formula can be written in prenex form, by renaming each quantified variable to a unique name and moving the quantifiers upfront.

An *interpretation* $\mathcal{I}$ maps each predicate symbol p into a set $p^{\mathcal{I}} \subseteq \mathbb{D}^{\#(p)}$, if $\#(p) > 0$, or into an element of $\mathbb{B}$ if $\#(p) = 0$. A *valuation* ν maps each variable x into an element of $\mathbb{D}$. Given a term t, we denote by t^{ν} the value obtained by replacing each variable x by the value $\nu(x)$ and evaluating each function application. For a formula ϕ, we define the forcing relation $\mathcal{I}, \nu \models \phi$ recursively on the structure of ϕ, as usual. For a formula ϕ and a valuation ν, we define $[\![\phi]\!]_{\nu} \overset{\text{def}}{=} \{\mathcal{I} \mid \mathcal{I}, \nu \models \phi\}$ and drop the ν subscript for sentences. A sentence ϕ is *satisfiable* if $[\![\phi]\!] \neq \emptyset$. An element of $[\![\phi]\!]$ is called a *model* of ϕ. A formula ϕ is *valid* if $\mathcal{I}, \nu \models \phi$ for every interpretation $\mathcal{I}$ and every valuation ν. We say that ϕ *entails* ψ, written $\phi \models \psi$ if and only if $[\![\phi]\!] \subseteq [\![\psi]\!]$.

Interpretations are partially ordered by the pointwise subset order, defined as $I_1 \subseteq I_2$ if and only if $p^{I_1} \subseteq p^{I_2}$ for each predicate symbol $p \in \mathsf{Pred}$. Given a formula ϕ and a valuation ν, we define $[\![\phi]\!]_\nu^\mu \stackrel{\text{def}}{=} \{I \mid I, \nu \models \phi,\ \forall I' \subseteq I\ .\ I', \nu \not\models \phi\}$ the set of minimal interpretations that, together with ν, form models of ϕ.

2   First Order Alternating Automata

Let Σ be a finite alphabet Σ of *input events*. Given a finite set of variables $X \subseteq \mathsf{Var}$, we denote by $X \mapsto \mathbb{D}$ the set of valuations of the variables X and $\Sigma[X] = \Sigma \times (X \mapsto \mathbb{D})$ be the possibly infinite set of *data symbols* (a, ν), where a is an input symbol and ν is a valuation. A *data word* (simply called word in the following) is a finite sequence $w = (a_1, \nu_1)(a_2, \nu_2) \ldots (a_n, \nu_n)$ of data symbols. Given a word w, we denote by $w_\Sigma \stackrel{\text{def}}{=} a_1 \ldots a_n$ its sequence of input events and by $w_\mathbb{D}$ the valuation associating each time-stamped variable $x^{(i)}$, where $x \in \mathsf{Var}$, the value $\nu_i(x)$, for all $i \in [1, n]$. We denote by ε the empty sequence, by Σ^* the set of finite input sequences and by $\Sigma[X]^*$ the set of finite data words over the variables X.

A *first-order alternating automaton* is a tuple $\mathcal{A} = \langle \Sigma, X, Q, \iota, F, \Delta \rangle$, where Σ is a finite set of input events, X is a finite set of input variables, Q is a finite set of predicates denoting control states, $\iota \in \mathsf{Form}^+(Q, \emptyset)$ is a sentence defining initial configurations, $F \subseteq Q$ is the set of predicates denoting final states and Δ is a set of *transition rules*. A transition rule is of the form $q(y_1, \ldots, y_{\#(q)}) \xrightarrow{a(X)} \psi$, where $q \in Q$ is a predicate, $a \in \Sigma$ is an input event and $\psi \in \mathsf{Form}^+(Q, X \cup \{y_1, \ldots, y_{\#(q)}\})$ is a positive formula, where $X \cap \{y_1, \ldots, y_{\#(q)}\} = \emptyset$. Without loss of generality, we consider, for each predicate $q \in Q$ and each input event $a \in \Sigma$, at most one such rule, as two or more rules can be joined using disjunction. The quantifiers occurring in the right-hand side formula of a transition rule are called *transition quantifiers*. The *size* of $\mathcal{A}$ is $|\mathcal{A}| \stackrel{\text{def}}{=} |\iota| + \sum \{|\psi| \mid q(\mathbf{y}) \xrightarrow{a(X)} \psi \in \Delta\}$.

The semantics of first-order alternating automata is analogous to the semantics of propositional alternating automata, with rules of the form $q \xrightarrow{a} \phi$, where q is a propositional variable and ϕ a positive boolean combination of propositional variables. For instance, $q_0 \xrightarrow{a} (q_1 \wedge q_2) \vee q_3$ means that the automaton can choose to transition in either both q_1 and q_2 or in q_3 alone. This leads to defining transitions as the *minimal models* of the right hand side of a rule[1]. The original definition of alternating automata [4] works around this problem and considers boolean valuations instead of formulae. In contrast, a finite description of a first-order alternating automaton cannot be given in terms of interpretations, as a first-order formula may have infinitely many models, corresponding to infinitely many initial or successor states occurring within an execution step.

Given an uninterpreted predicate symbol $q \in Q$ and data values $d_1, \ldots, d_{\#(q)} \in \mathbb{D}$, the tuple $(q, d_1, \ldots, d_{\#(q)})$ is called a *configuration*, sometimes written $q(d_1, \ldots, d_{\#(q)})$, when no confusion arises. A configuration is

---

[1] Both $\{q_1 \leftarrow \top, q_2 \leftarrow \top, q_3 \leftarrow \bot\}$ and $\{q_1 \leftarrow \bot, q_2 \leftarrow \bot, q_3 \leftarrow \top\}$ are minimal models, however $\{q_1 \leftarrow \top, q_2 \leftarrow \top, q_3 \leftarrow \top\}$ is a model but is not minimal.

final if $q \in F$. An interpretation $\mathcal{I}$ corresponds to a set of configurations $\mathsf{c}(\mathcal{I}) \stackrel{\text{def}}{=} \{(q, d_1, \ldots, d_{\#(q)}) \mid q \in Q, (d_1, \ldots, d_{\#(q)}) \in q^{\mathcal{I}}\}$, called a *cube*. This notation is lifted to sets of configurations in the usual way.

Definition 1. *Given a word* $w = (a_1, \nu_1) \ldots (a_n, \nu_n) \in \Sigma[X]^*$ *and a cube* c, *an* execution *of* $\mathcal{A} = \langle \Sigma, X, Q, \iota, F, \Delta \rangle$ *over* w, *starting with* c, *is a forest* $\mathcal{T} = \{T_1, T_2, \ldots\}$, *where each* T_i *is a tree labeled with configurations, such that:*

1. $c = \{T(\epsilon) \mid T \in \mathcal{T}\}$ *is the set of configurations labeling the roots of* $T_1, T_2, \ldots$ *and*
2. *if* $(q, d_1, \ldots, d_{\#(q)})$ *labels a node on the level* $j \in [n-1]$ *in* T_i, *then the labels of its children form a cube from* $\mathsf{c}(\llbracket \psi \rrbracket_{\eta}^{\mu})$, *where* $\eta = \nu_{j+1}[y_1 \leftarrow d_1, \ldots, y_{\#(q)} \leftarrow d_{\#(q)}]$ *and* $q(y_1, \ldots, y_{\#(q)}) \xrightarrow{a_{j+1}(X)} \psi \in \Delta$ *is a transition rule of* $\mathcal{A}$.

An execution $\mathcal{T}$ over w, starting with c, is *accepting* if and only if all paths in $\mathcal{T}$ have the same length and the frontier of each tree $T \in \mathcal{T}$ is labeled with final configurations. If $\mathcal{A}$ has an accepting execution over w starting with a cube $c \in \mathsf{c}(\llbracket \iota \rrbracket^{\mu})$, then $\mathcal{A}$ *accepts* w and let $\mathcal{L}(\mathcal{A})$ be the set of words accepted by $\mathcal{A}$. For example, consider the automaton $\mathcal{A} = \langle \{a\}, \{x\}, \{q_0, q_1, q_2, q_f\}, q_0(0), \{q_f\}, \Delta \rangle$, where Δ is the set: $q_0(y) \xrightarrow{a(x)} q_1(y+x) \wedge q_2(y-x)$, $q_1(y) \xrightarrow{a(x)} q_1(y+x) \vee (y > 0 \wedge q_f)$ and $q_2(y) \xrightarrow{a(x)} q_2(y-x) \vee (y > 0 \wedge q_f)$. A possible execution tree of this automaton is the following:

$$
\begin{array}{cccccc}
a, \{x \leftarrow 1\} & a, \{x \leftarrow 2\} & a, \{x \leftarrow 3\} & a, \{x \leftarrow 4\} & a, \{x \leftarrow 5\} \\
(q_1, 1) \longrightarrow & (q_1, 3) \longrightarrow & (q_1, 6) \longrightarrow & (q_1, 10) \longrightarrow & q_f \\
(q_0, 0) \\
(q_2, -1) \longrightarrow & (q_2, -3) \longrightarrow & (q_2, -6) \longrightarrow & (q_2, -10) \longrightarrow & (q_2, -15)
\end{array}
$$

The execution tree is not accepting, since its frontier is not labeled with final configurations everywhere. Incidentally, here we have $\mathcal{L}(\mathcal{A}) = \emptyset$, which is proved by our tool in $\sim 0.5\,\mathrm{s}$ on an average machine.

In the rest of this paper, we are concerned with the following problems:

1. *boolean closure*: given automata $\mathcal{A}_i = \langle \Sigma, X, Q_i, \iota_i, F_i, \Delta_i \rangle$, for $i = 1, 2$, do there exist automata $\mathcal{A}_{\cap}$, $\mathcal{A}_{\cup}$ and $\overline{\mathcal{A}_1}$ such that $L(\mathcal{A}_{\cap}) = L(\mathcal{A}_1) \cap L(\mathcal{A}_2)$, $L(\mathcal{A}_{\cup}) = L(\mathcal{A}_1) \cup L(\mathcal{A}_2)$ and $L(\overline{\mathcal{A}_1}) = \Sigma[X]^* \setminus L(\mathcal{A}_1)$?
2. *emptiness*: given an automaton $\mathcal{A}$, is $L(\mathcal{A}) = \emptyset$?

For technical reasons, we address the following problem next: given an automaton $\mathcal{A}$ and an input sequence $\alpha \in \Sigma^*$, does there exists a word $w \in \mathcal{L}(\mathcal{A})$ such that $w_{\Sigma} = \alpha$? By solving this problem first, we develop the machinery required to prove that first-order alternating automata are closed under complement and, further, set up the ground for developping a practical semi-algorithm for the emptiness problem.

2.1 Path Formulae

In the upcoming developments it is sometimes more convenient to work with logical formulae defining executions of automata, than with low-level execution forests. For this reason, we first introduce *path formulae* $\Theta(\alpha)$, which are formulae defining the executions of an automaton, over words that share a given sequence α of input events. Second, we restrict a path formula $\Theta(\alpha)$ to an *acceptance formula* $\Upsilon(\alpha)$, which defines only those executions that are accepting among $\Theta(\alpha)$. Consequently, the automaton accepts a word w such that $w_\Sigma = \alpha$ if and only if $\Upsilon(\alpha)$ is satisfiable.

Let $\mathcal{A} = \langle \Sigma, X, Q, \iota, F, \Delta \rangle$ be an automaton for the rest of this section. For any $i \in \mathbb{N}$, we denote by $Q^{(i)} = \{q^{(i)} \mid q \in Q\}$ and $X^{(i)} = \{x^{(i)} \mid x \in X\}$ the sets of time-stamped predicate symbols and variables, respectively. We also define $Q^{(\leq n)} \stackrel{\text{def}}{=} \{q^{(i)} \mid q \in Q, i \in [n]\}$ and $X^{(\leq n)} \stackrel{\text{def}}{=} \{x^{(i)} \mid x \in X, i \in [n]\}$. For a formula ψ and $i \in \mathbb{N}$, we define $\psi^{(i)} \stackrel{\text{def}}{=} \psi[X^{(i)}/X, Q^{(i)}/Q]$ the formula in which all input variables and state predicates (and only those symbols) are replaced by their time-stamped counterparts. Moreover, we write $q(\mathbf{y})$ for $q(y_1, \ldots, y_{\#(q)})$, when no confusion arises.

Given a sequence of input events $\alpha = a_1 \ldots a_n \in \Sigma^*$, the *path formula* of α is:

$$\Theta(\alpha) \stackrel{\text{def}}{=} \iota^{(0)} \wedge \bigwedge_{i=1}^{n} \bigwedge_{q(\mathbf{y}) \xrightarrow{a_i(X)} \psi \in \Delta} \forall y_1 \ldots \forall y_{\#(q)} \cdot q^{(i-1)}(\mathbf{y}) \to \psi^{(i)} \qquad (1)$$

The automaton $\mathcal{A}$, to which $\Theta(\alpha)$ refers, will always be clear from the context. To formalize the relation between the low-level configuration-based execution semantics and path formulae, consider a word $w = (a_1, \nu_1) \ldots (a_n, \nu_n) \in \Sigma[X]^*$. Any execution $\mathcal{T}$ of $\mathcal{A}$ over w has an associated interpretation $\mathcal{I}_\mathcal{T}$ of time-stamped predicates $Q^{(\leq n)}$:

$$\mathcal{I}_\mathcal{T}(q^{(i)}) \stackrel{\text{def}}{=} \{(d_1, \ldots, d_{\#(q)}) \mid (q, d_1, \ldots, d_{\#(q)}) \text{ labels a node on level } i \text{ in } \mathcal{T}\}, \ \forall q \in Q \ \forall i \in [n]$$

Lemma 1. *Given an automaton* $\mathcal{A} = \langle \Sigma, X, Q, \iota, F, \Delta \rangle$, *for any word* $w = (a_1, \nu_1) \ldots (a_n, \nu_n)$, *we have* $[\![\Theta(w_\Sigma)]\!]_{w_\mathbb{D}}^\mu = \{\mathcal{I}_\mathcal{T} \mid \mathcal{T} \text{ is an execution of } \mathcal{A} \text{ over } w\}$.

Next, we give a logical characterization of acceptance, relative to a given sequence of input events $\alpha \in \Sigma^*$. To this end, we constrain the path formula $\Theta(\alpha)$ by requiring that only final states of $\mathcal{A}$ occur on the last level of the execution. The result is the *acceptance formula* for α:

$$\Upsilon(\alpha) \stackrel{\text{def}}{=} \Theta(\alpha) \wedge \bigwedge_{q \in Q \setminus F} \forall y_1 \ldots \forall y_{\#(q)} \cdot q^{(n)}(\mathbf{y}) \to \bot \qquad (2)$$

The top-level universal quantifiers from a subformula $\forall y_1 \ldots \forall y_{\#(q)} \cdot q^{(i)}(\mathbf{y}) \to \psi$ of $\Upsilon(\alpha)$ will be referred to as *path quantifiers*, in the following. Notice that path quantifiers are distinct from the transition quantifiers that occur within a formula ψ of a transition rule $q(y_1, \ldots, y_{\#(q)}) \xrightarrow{a(X)} \psi$ of $\mathcal{A}$. The relation between the words accepted by $\mathcal{A}$ and the acceptance formula above, is formally captured by the following lemma:

Lemma 2. *Given an automaton* $\mathcal{A} = \langle \Sigma, X, Q, \iota, F, \Delta \rangle$, *for every word* $w \in \Sigma[X]^*$, *the following are equivalent: (1) there exists an interpretation* $\mathcal{I}$ *such that* $\mathcal{I}, w_\mathbb{D} \models \Upsilon(w_\Sigma)$ *and (2)* $w \in \mathcal{L}(\mathcal{A})$.

As an immediate consequence, one can decide whether $\mathcal{A}$ accepts some word w with a given input sequence $w_\Sigma = \alpha$, by checking whether $\Upsilon(\alpha)$ is satisfiable. However, unlike non-alternating infinite-state models of computation, such as counter automata (nondeterministic programs with integer variables), the satisfiability query for an acceptance (path) formula falls outside of known decidable theories, supported by standard SMT solvers. There are basically two reasons for this, namely (i) the presence of predicate symbols, and (ii) the non-trivial alternation of quantifiers. To understand this point, consider for example, the decidable theory of Presburger arithmetic [24]. Adding even only one monadic predicate symbol to it yields undecidability in the presence of non-trivial quantifier alternation [10]. On the other hand, the quantifier-free fragment of Presburger arithmetic extended with uninterpreted function symbols is decidable, by a Nelson-Oppen style congruence closure argument [22].

To tackle the problem of deciding satisfiability of $\Upsilon(\alpha)$ formulae, we start from the observation that their form is rather particular, which allows the elimination of path quantifiers and uninterpreted predicate symbols, by a couple of satisfiability-preserving transformations. The result of applying these transformations is a formula with no predicate symbols, whose only quantifiers are those introduced by the transition rules of the automaton. Next, in Sect. 3 we shall assume moreover that the first-order theory of the data sort $\mathbb{D}$ (without uninterpreted predicate symbols) has quantifier elimination, providing thus an effective decision procedure.

For the time being, let us formally define the elimination of transition quantifiers and predicate symbols. Let $\alpha = a_1 \dots a_n$ be a given sequence of input events and let α_i be the prefix $a_1 \dots a_i$ of α, for $i \in [n]$, where $\alpha_0 = \epsilon$. We consider the sequence of formulae $\widehat{\Theta}(\alpha_0), \dots, \widehat{\Theta}(\alpha_n)$ defined as $\widehat{\Theta}(\alpha_0) \stackrel{\text{def}}{=} \iota^{(0)}$ and, for all $i \in [1, n]$, let $\widehat{\Theta}(\alpha_i)$ be the conjunction of $\widehat{\Theta}(\alpha_{i-1})$ with all formulae $q^{(i-1)}(t_1, \dots, t_{\#(q)}) \to \psi^{(i)}[t_1/y_1, \dots, t_{\#(q)}/y_{\#(q)}]$, such that $q^{(i-1)}(t_1, \dots, t_{\#(q)})$ occurs in $\widehat{\Theta}(\alpha_{i-1})$, for some terms $t_1, \dots, t_{\#(q)}$. Next, we write $\widehat{\Upsilon}(\alpha)$ for the conjunction of $\widehat{\Theta}(\alpha_n)$ with all $q^{(n)}(t_1, \dots, t_{\#(q)}) \to \bot$, such that $q^{(n)}(t_1, \dots, t_{\#(q)})$ occurs in $\widehat{\Theta}(\alpha_n)$, for some $q \in Q \setminus F$. Note that $\widehat{\Upsilon}(\alpha)$ contains no path quantifiers, as required. On the other hand, the scope of the transition quantifiers in $\widehat{\Upsilon}(\alpha)$ exceeds the right-hand side formulae from the transition rules, as shown by the following example.

Example 1. Consider the automaton $\mathcal{A} = \langle \{a_1, a_2\}, \{x\}, \{q, q_f\}, \iota, \{q_f\}, \Delta \rangle$, where:

$$\iota = \exists z \, . \, z \geq 0 \wedge q(z)$$
$$\Delta = \{ q(y) \xrightarrow{a_1(x)} x \geq 0 \wedge \forall z \, . \, z \leq y \to q(x+z), \ q(y) \xrightarrow{a_2(x)} y < 0 \wedge q_f(x+y) \}$$

For the input event sequence $\alpha = a_1 a_2$, the acceptance formula is:

$$\begin{aligned}
\Upsilon(\alpha) = \exists z_1 \, . \, & z_1 \geq 0 \wedge q^{(0)}(z_1) \wedge \\
& \forall y \, . \, q^{(0)}(y) \to [x^{(1)} \geq 0 \wedge \forall z_2 \, . \, z_2 \geq y \to q^{(1)}(x^{(1)} + z_2)] \wedge \\
& \forall y \, . \, q^{(1)}(y) \to [y < 0 \wedge q_f^{(2)}(x^{(2)} + y)]
\end{aligned}$$

The result of eliminating the path quantifiers, in prenex normal form, is shown below:

$$\widehat{\Upsilon}(\alpha) = \exists z_1 \forall z_2 . z_1 \geq 0 \wedge q^{(0)}(z_1) \wedge$$
$$[q^{(0)}(z_1) \rightarrow x^{(1)} \geq 0 \wedge (z_2 \geq z_1 \rightarrow q^{(1)}(x^{(1)} + z_2))] \wedge$$
$$[q^{(1)}(x^{(1)} + z_2) \rightarrow x^{(1)} + z_2 < 0 \wedge q_f^{(2)}(x^{(2)} + x^{(1)} + z_2)]$$

Notice that the transition quantifiers $\exists z_1$ and $\forall z_2$ from $\Upsilon(\alpha)$ range now over $\widehat{\Upsilon}(\alpha)$. ∎

Lemma 3. *For any input event sequence $\alpha = a_1 \ldots a_n$ and each valuation $\nu :$ $X^{(\leq n)} \rightarrow \mathbb{D}$, the following hold, for every interpretation I: (1) if $I, \nu \models \Upsilon(\alpha)$ then $I, \nu \models \widehat{\Upsilon}(\alpha)$, and (2) if $I, \nu \models \widehat{\Upsilon}(\alpha)$ there exists an interpretation $J \subseteq I$ such that $J, \nu \models \Upsilon(\alpha)$.*

Further, we eliminate the predicate atoms from $\widehat{\Upsilon}(\alpha)$, by considering the sequence of formulae $\overline{\Theta}(\alpha_0) \stackrel{\text{def}}{=} \iota^{(0)}$ and $\overline{\Theta}(\alpha_i)$ is obtained by substituting each predicate atom $q^{(i-1)}(t_1, \ldots, t_{\#(q)})$ in $\overline{\Theta}(\alpha_{i-1})$ by $\psi^{(i)}[t_1/y_1, \ldots, t_{\#(q)}/y_{\#(q)}]$, where $q(\mathbf{y}) \xrightarrow{a_i(X)} \psi \in \Delta$, for all $i \in [1, n]$. We write $\overline{\Upsilon}(\alpha)$ for the formula obtained by replacing, in $\overline{\Theta}(\alpha)$, each occurrence of a predicate $q^{(n)}$, such that $q \in Q \setminus F$ (resp. $q \in F$), by $\bot$ (resp. $\top$).

Example 2 (Contd. from Example 1). The result of the elimination of predicate atoms from the acceptance formula in Example 1 is shown below:

$$\overline{\Upsilon}(\alpha) = \exists z_1 \forall z_2 . z_1 \geq 0 \wedge [x^{(1)} \geq 0 \wedge (z_2 \geq z_1 \rightarrow x^{(1)} + z_2 < 0)]$$

Since this formula is unsatisfiable, by Lemma 5 below, no word w with input event sequence $w_\Sigma = a_1 a_2$ is accepted by the automaton $\mathcal{A}$ from Example 1. ∎

At this point, we prove the formal relation between the satisfiability of the formulae $\widehat{\Upsilon}(\alpha)$ and $\overline{\Upsilon}(\alpha)$. Since there are no occurrences of predicates in $\overline{\Upsilon}(\alpha)$, for each valuation $\nu : X^{(\leq n)} \rightarrow \mathbb{D}$, there exists an interpretation I such that $I, \nu \models \overline{\Upsilon}(\alpha)$ if and only if $J, \nu \models \overline{\Upsilon}(\alpha)$, for every interpretation J. In this case we omit I and simply write $\nu \models \overline{\Upsilon}(\alpha)$.

Lemma 4. *For any input event sequence $\alpha = a_1 \ldots a_n$ and each valuation $\nu :$ $X^{(\leq n)} \rightarrow \mathbb{D}$, there exists a valuation I such that $I, \nu \models \widehat{\Upsilon}(\alpha)$ if and only if $\nu \models \overline{\Upsilon}(\alpha)$.*

Finally, we define the acceptance of a word with a given input event sequence by means of a quantifier-free formula in which no predicate atom occurs.

Lemma 5. *Given an automaton $\mathcal{A} = \langle \Sigma, X, Q, \iota, F, \Delta \rangle$, for every word $w \in \Sigma[X]^*$, we have $w_\mathbb{D} \models \overline{\Upsilon}(w_\Sigma)$ if and only if $w \in \mathcal{L}(\mathcal{A})$.*

2.2   Boolean Closure of First Order Alternating Automata

Given a positive formula ϕ, we define the *dual* formula $\phi^\sim$ recursively as follows:

$$(\phi_1 \vee \phi_2)^\sim \overset{\text{def}}{=} \phi_1{}^\sim \wedge \phi_2{}^\sim \qquad (\phi_1 \wedge \phi_2)^\sim \overset{\text{def}}{=} \phi_1{}^\sim \vee \phi_2{}^\sim \qquad (t = s)^\sim \overset{\text{def}}{=} t \neq s$$

$$(\exists x . \phi_1)^\sim \overset{\text{def}}{=} \forall x . \phi_1{}^\sim \qquad (\forall x . \phi_1)^\sim \overset{\text{def}}{=} \exists x . \phi_1{}^\sim \qquad (t \neq s)^\sim \overset{\text{def}}{=} t = s$$

$$q(x_1, \ldots, x_{\#(q)})^\sim \overset{\text{def}}{=} q(x_1, \ldots, x_{\#(q)})$$

The following theorem shows closure of automata under all boolean operations. Note that it is sufficient to show closure under intersection and negation because $\mathcal{L}(\mathcal{A}_1) \cup \mathcal{L}(\mathcal{A}_2)$ is the complement of the language $\mathcal{L}^c(\mathcal{A}_1) \cap \mathcal{L}^c(\mathcal{A}_2)$, for any two automata $\mathcal{A}_1$ and $\mathcal{A}_2$ with the same input event alphabet and set of input variables.

Theorem 1. *Given automata* $\mathcal{A}_i = \langle \Sigma, X, Q_i, \iota_i, F_i, \Delta_i \rangle$, *for* $i = 1, 2$, *such that* $Q_1 \cap Q_2 = \emptyset$, *the following hold:*

1. $\mathcal{L}(\mathcal{A}_\cap) = \mathcal{L}(\mathcal{A}_1) \cap \mathcal{L}(\mathcal{A}_2)$, *where* $\mathcal{A}_\cap = \langle \Sigma, X, Q_1 \cup Q_2, \iota_1 \wedge \iota_2, F_1 \cup F_2,$ $\Delta_1 \cup \Delta_2 \rangle$,
2. $\mathcal{L}(\overline{\mathcal{A}_i}) = \Sigma[X]^* \setminus \mathcal{L}(\mathcal{A}_i)$, *where* $\overline{\mathcal{A}_i} = \langle \Sigma, X, Q_i, \iota^\sim, Q_i \setminus F_i, \Delta_i^\sim \rangle$ *and* $\Delta_i^\sim = \{ q(\mathbf{y}) \xrightarrow{a(X)} \psi^\sim \mid q(\mathbf{y}) \xrightarrow{a(X)} \psi \in \Delta_i \}$, *for* $i = 1, 2$.

Moreover, $|\mathcal{A}_\cap| = O(|\mathcal{A}_1| + |\mathcal{A}_2|)$ *and* $|\overline{\mathcal{A}_i}| = O(|\mathcal{A}_i|)$, *for* $i = 1, 2$.

3   The Emptiness Problem

The emptiness problem is undecidable even for automata with predicates of arity two, whose transition rules use only equalities and disequalities, having no transition quantifiers [6]. Since even such simple classes of alternating automata have no general decision procedure for emptiness, we use an abstraction-refinement semi-algorithm based on *lazy annotation* [20,21]. In a nutshell, a lazy annotation procedure systematically explores the set of finite input event sequences searching for an accepting execution. For an input sequence, if the path formula is satisfiable, we compute a word in the language of the automaton, from the model of the path formula. Otherwise, i.e. the sequence is *spurious*, the search backtracks and each position in the sequence is annotated with an interpolant, thus marking the sequence as infeasible. The semi-algorithm uses moreover a coverage relation between sequences, ensuring that the continuations of already covered sequences are never explored. Sometimes this coverage relation provides a sound termination argument, in case when the automaton is empty.

For two input event sequences $\alpha, \beta \in \Sigma^*$, we say that α is a prefix of β, written $\alpha \preceq \beta$, if $\alpha = \beta\gamma$ for some sequence $\gamma \in \Sigma^*$. A set S of sequences is *prefix-closed* if for each $\alpha \in S$, if $\beta \preceq \alpha$ then $\beta \in S$, and *complete* if for each $\alpha \in S$, there exists $a \in \Sigma$ such that $\alpha a \in S$ if and only if $\alpha b \in S$ for all $b \in \Sigma$. A prefix-closed set is the backbone of a tree whose edges are labeled with input events. If the set is, moreover, complete, then every node of the tree has either zero successors, in which case it is called a *leaf*, or it has a successor edge labeled with a for each input event $a \in \Sigma$.

Definition 2. *An* unfolding *of an automaton* $\mathcal{A} = \langle \Sigma, X, Q, \iota, F, \Delta \rangle$ *is a finite partial mapping* $U : \Sigma^* \rightharpoonup_{fin} \mathsf{Form}^+(Q, \emptyset)$*, whose domain* $\mathrm{dom}(U)$ *is a finite prefix-closed complete set, such that* $U(\epsilon) = \iota$*, and for each sequence* $\alpha a \in \mathrm{dom}(U)$*, such that* $\alpha \in \Sigma^*$ *and* $a \in \Sigma$*:*

$$U(\alpha)^{(0)} \wedge \bigwedge\nolimits_{q(\mathbf{y}) \xrightarrow{a(X)} \psi} \forall y_1 \dots \forall y_{\#q} \cdot q^{(0)}(\mathbf{y}) \to \psi^{(1)} \models U(\alpha a)^{(1)}$$

A path α *is* safe *in* U *if and only if* $U(\alpha) \wedge \bigwedge_{q \in Q \setminus F} \forall y_1 \dots \forall y_{\#(q)} \cdot q(\mathbf{y}) \to \bot$ *is unsatisfiable. The unfolding* U *is* safe *if and only if every path in* $\mathrm{dom}(U)$ *is safe in* U*.*

Lazy annotation semi-algorithms [20, 21] build unfoldings of automata trying to discover counterexamples for emptiness. If the automaton $\mathcal{A}$ in question is non-empty, a systematic enumeration of the input event sequences[2] from Σ^* will suffice to discover a word $w \in \mathcal{L}(\mathcal{A})$, provided that the first-order theory of the data domain $\mathbb{D}$ is decidable (Lemma 2). However, if $\mathcal{L}(\mathcal{A}) = \emptyset$, the enumeration of input event sequences may, in principle, run forever. The typical way of fighting this divergence problem is to define a *coverage* relation between the nodes of the unfolding tree.

Definition 3. *Given an unfolding* U *of an automaton* $\mathcal{A} = \langle \Sigma, X, Q, \iota, F, \Delta \rangle$ *a node* $\alpha \in \mathrm{dom}(U)$ *is* covered *by another node* $\beta \in \mathrm{dom}(U)$*, denoted* $\alpha \sqsubseteq \beta$*, if and only if there exists a node* $\alpha' \preceq \alpha$ *such that* $U(\alpha') \models U(\beta)$*. Moreover,* U *is* closed *if and only if every leaf from* $\mathrm{dom}(U)$ *is covered by an uncovered node.*

A lazy annotation semi-algorithm will stop and report emptiness provided that it succeeds in building a closed and safe unfolding of the automaton. Notice that, by Definition 3, for any three nodes of an unfolding U, say $\alpha, \beta, \gamma \in \mathrm{dom}(U)$, if $\alpha \prec \beta$ and $\alpha \sqsubseteq \gamma$, then $\beta \sqsubseteq \gamma$ as well. As we show next (Theorem 2), there is no need to expand covered nodes, because, intuitively, there exists a word $w \in \mathcal{L}(\mathcal{A})$ such that $\alpha \preceq w_\Sigma$ and $\alpha \sqsubseteq \gamma$ only if there exists another word $u \in \mathcal{L}(\mathcal{A})$ such that $\gamma \preceq u_\Sigma$. Hence, exploring only those input event sequences that are continuations of γ (and ignoring those of α) suffices in order to find a counterexample for emptiness, if one exists.

An unfolding node $\alpha \in \mathrm{dom}(U)$ is said to be *spurious* if and only if $\Upsilon(\alpha)$ is unsatisfiable. In this case, we change (refine) the labels of (some of the) prefixes of α (and that of α), such that $U(\alpha)$ becomes $\bot$, thus indicating that there is no real execution of the automaton along that input event sequence. As a result of the change of labels, if a node $\gamma \preceq \alpha$ used to cover another node from $\mathrm{dom}(U)$, it might not cover it with the new label. Therefore, the coverage relation has to be recomputed after each refinement of the labeling. The semi-algorithm stops when (and if) a safe complete unfolding has been found.

Theorem 2. *If an automaton* $\mathcal{A}$ *has a nonempty safe closed unfolding then* $\mathcal{L}(A) = \emptyset$*.*

---

[2] For instance, using breadth-first search.

Algorithm 1. IMPACT-based Semi-algorithm for First Order Alternating Automata

---

input: a first order alternating automaton $\mathcal{A} = \langle \Sigma, X, Q, \iota, F, \Delta \rangle$

output: $\top$ if $L(\mathcal{A}) = \emptyset$, or word $w \in L(\mathcal{A})$, otherwise

data structures: WorkList and unfolding tree $\mathcal{U} = \langle N, E, \mathbf{r}, U, \lhd \rangle$, where:
- N is a set of nodes,
- $E \subseteq N \times \Sigma \times N$ is a set of edges labeled by input events,
- $U : N \rightarrow \mathsf{Form}^+(Q, \emptyset)$ is a labeling of nodes with positive sentences
- $\lhd \subseteq N \times N$ is a coverage relation,

initially WorkList $= \{\mathbf{r}\}$ and $N = E = U = \lhd = \emptyset$.

```
 1: while WorkList ≠ ∅ do
 2:     dequeue n from WorkList
 3:     N ← N ∪ {n}
 4:     let α(n) be a₁,…,aₖ
 5:     if T̄(α)(X⁽¹⁾,…,X⁽ᵏ⁾) is satisfiable then          ▷ counterexample is feasible
 6:         get model ν of T̄(α)(X⁽¹⁾,…,X⁽ᵏ⁾)
 7:         return w = (a₁,ν(X⁽¹⁾))…(aₖ,ν(X⁽ᵏ⁾))          ▷ w ∈ L(𝒜) by construction
 8:     else                                              ▷ spurious counterexample
 9:         let (I₀,…,Iₖ) be a GLI for α
10:         b ← ⊥
11:         for i = 0,…,k do
12:             if U(nᵢ) ⊭ Iᵢ then
13:                 Uncover ← {m ∈ N | (m,nᵢ) ∈ ⊲}
14:                 ⊲ ← ⊲ \ {(m,nᵢ) | m ∈ Uncover} ▷ uncover the nodes covered by nᵢ
15:                 for m ∈ Uncover such that m is a leaf of 𝒰 do
16:                     enqueue m into WorkList          ▷ reactivate uncovered leaves
17:                 U(nᵢ) ← U(nᵢ) ∧ Jᵢ          ▷ strenghten the label of nᵢ (Lemma 7)
18:                 if ¬b then
19:                     b ← Close(nᵢ)
20:     if n is not covered then
21:         for a ∈ Σ do                                  ▷ expand n
22:             let s be a fresh node and e = (n,a,s) be a new edge
23:             E ← E ∪ {e}
24:             U ← U ∪ {(s,⊤)}
25:             enqueue s into WorkList
26: return ⊤
27: function Close(x) returns 𝔹
28:     for y ∈ N such that α(y) ≺* α(x) do
29:         if U(x) ⊨ U(y) then
30:             ⊲ ← [⊲ \ {(p,q) ∈ ⊲ | q is x or a successor of x}] ∪ {(x,y)}
31:             return ⊤
32:     return ⊥
```

We describe the semi-algorithm used to check emptiness of first-order alternating automata. The execution of Algorithm 1 consists of three phases, corresponding to the CLOSE, REFINE and EXPAND of the original IMPACT procedure [20]. Let n be a node removed from the worklist at line 2 and let $\alpha(n)$ be the input sequence labeling the path from the root node to n. If $\overline{\varUpsilon}(\alpha(n))$ is satisfiable, the sequence $\alpha(n)$ is feasible, in which case a model of $\overline{\varUpsilon}(\alpha(n))$ is obtained and a word $w \in L(\mathcal{A})$ is returned. Otherwise, $\alpha(n)$ is an infeasible input sequence and the procedure enters the refinement phase (lines 9–19). The GLI for $\alpha(n)$ is used to strenghten the labels of all the ancestors of n, by conjoining the formulae of the interpolant, changed according to Lemma 7, to the existing labels.

In this process, the nodes on the path between $\mathbf{r}$ and n, including n, might become eligible for coverage, therefore we attempt to close each ancestor of n that is impacted by the refinement (line 19). Observe that, in this case the call to CLOSE must uncover each node which is covered by a successor of n (line 30 of the CLOSE function). This is required because, due to the over-approximation of the sets of reachable configurations, the covering relation is not transitive, as explained in [20]. If CLOSE adds a covering edge (n_i, m) to $\lhd$, it does not have to be called for the successors of n_i on this path, which is handled via the boolean flag b. Finally, if n is still uncovered (it has not been previously covered during the refinement phase) we expand n (lines 21–25) by creating a new node for each successor s via the input event $a \in \varSigma$ and inserting it into the worklist.

4   Interpolant Generation

Typically, when checking the unreachability of a set of program configurations, the interpolants used to annotate the unfolded control structure are assertions about the values of the program variables in a given control state, at a certain step of an execution [20]. Because we consider alternating computation trees (forests), we must distinguish between (i) locality of interpolants w.r.t. a given control state (control locality) and (ii) locality w.r.t. a given time stamp (time locality). In logical terms, *control-local* interpolants are formulae involving a single predicate symbol, whereas *time-local* interpolants involve only predicates $q^{(i)}$ and variables $x^{(i)}$, for a single $i \geq 0$. When considering alternating executions, control-local interpolants are not always enough to prove emptiness, because of the synchronization of several branches of the computation on the same input word. For this reason, the interpolants considered in this paper will never be control-local and we shall use the term *local* to denote time-local interpolants, with no free variables.

First, let us give the formal definition of the class of interpolants we shall work with. Given a formula ϕ, the *vocabulary* of ϕ, denoted $V(\phi)$ is the set of predicate symbols $q \in Q^{(i)}$ and variables $x \in X^{(i)}$, occurring in ϕ, for some $i \geq 0$. For a term t, its vocabulary $V(t)$ is the set of variables that occur in t. Observe that quantified variables and the interpreted function symbols of the data theory[3] do not belong to the vocabulary of a formula. By $P^+(\phi)$ $[P^-(\phi)]$ we denote the set of predicate symbols that occur in ϕ under an even [odd] number of negations.

---

[3] E.g., the arithmetic operators of addition and multiplication, when $\mathbb{D}$ is the set of integers.

Definition 4 ([19]). *Given formulae ϕ and ψ such that $\phi \wedge \psi$ is unsatisfiable, a* Lyndon interpolant *is a formula I such that $\phi \models I$, the formula $I \wedge \psi$ is unsatisfiable, $V(I) \subseteq V(\phi) \cap V(\psi)$, $P^+(I) \subseteq P^+(\phi) \cap P^+(\psi)$ and $P^-(I) \subseteq P^-(\phi) \cap P^-(\psi)$.*

In the rest of this section, fix an automaton $\mathcal{A} = \langle \Sigma, X, Q, \iota, F, \Delta \rangle$. The following definition generalizes interpolants from unsatisfiable conjunctions to input sequences:

Definition 5. *Given a sequence of input events $\alpha = a_1 \ldots a_n \in \Sigma^*$, a generalized Lyndon interpolant (GLI) is a sequence $(I_0, \ldots, I_n)$ of formulae such that, for all $k \in [n-1]$, the following hold: (1) $P^-(I_k) = \emptyset$, (2) $\iota^{(0)} \models I_0$, $I_k \wedge \left(\bigwedge_{q(\mathbf{y}) \xrightarrow{a_i(X)} \psi \in \Delta} \forall y_1 \ldots \forall y_{\#(q)} . q^{(k)}(\mathbf{y}) \rightarrow \psi^{(k+1)} \right) \models I_{k+1}$ and (3) $I_n \wedge \bigwedge_{q \in Q \backslash F} \forall y_1 \ldots \forall y_{\#(q)} . q(\mathbf{y}) \rightarrow \bot$ is unsatisfiable. Moreover, the GLI is local if and only if $V(I_k) \subseteq Q^{(k)}$, for all $k \in [n]$.*

The following proposition states the existence of local GLI for the theories in which Lyndon's Interpolation Theorem holds.

Proposition 1. *If there exists a Lyndon interpolant for any two formulae ϕ and ψ, in the first-order theory of data with uninterpreted predicate symbols, such that $\phi \wedge \psi$ is unsatisfiable, then any sequence of input events $\alpha = a_1 \ldots a_n \in \Sigma^*$, such that $\Upsilon(\alpha)$ is unsatisfiable, has a local GLI $(I_0, \ldots, I_n)$.*

A problematic point of the above proposition is that the existence of Lyndon interpolants (Definition 4) is proved in principle, but the proof is non-constructive. In other words, the proof of Proposition 1 does not yield an algorithm for computing GLIs, for the following reason. Building an interpolant for an unsatisfiable conjunction of formulae $\phi \wedge \psi$ is typically the job of the decision procedure that proves the unsatisfiability and, in general, there is no such procedure, when ϕ and ψ contain predicates and have non-trivial quantifier alternation. In this case, some provers use instantiation heuristics for the universal quantifiers that are sufficient for proving unsatisfiability, however these heuristics are not always suitable for interpolant generation. Consequently, from now on, we assume the existence of an effective Lyndon interpolation procedure only for decidable theories, such as the quantifier-free linear (integer) arithmetic with uninterpreted functions (UFLIA, UFLRA, etc.) [26].

This is where the predicate-free path formulae (defined in Sect. 2.1) come into play. Recall that, for a given event sequence α, the automaton $\mathcal{A}$ accepts a word w such that $w_\Sigma = \alpha$ if and only if $\overline{\Upsilon}(\alpha)$ is satisfiable (Lemma 5). Assuming further that the equality and interpreted predicates (e.g. inequalities for integers) atoms from the transition rules of $\mathcal{A}$ belong to a decidable first-order theory, such as Presburger arithmetic, Lemma 5 gives us an effective way of checking emptiness of $\mathcal{A}$, relative to a given event sequence. However, this method does not cope well with lazy annotation, because there is no way to extract, from the unsatisfiability proof of $\overline{\Upsilon}(\alpha)$, the interpolants needed to annotate α. This is because (I) the formula $\overline{\varUpsilon}(\alpha)$, obtained by repeated substitutions loses track of the steps of the execution, and (II) quantifiers that occur nested in $\overline{\varUpsilon}(\alpha)$ make it difficult to write $\overline{\varUpsilon}(\alpha)$ as an unsatisfiable quantifier-free conjunction of formulae from which interpolants are extracted (Definition 4).

The solution we adopt for the first issue (I) consists in partially recovering the time-stamped structure of the acceptance formula $\varUpsilon(\alpha)$ using the formula $\widehat{\varUpsilon}(\alpha)$, in which only transition quantifiers occur. The second issue (II) is solved under the additional assuption that the theory of the data domain $\mathbb{D}$ has *witness-producing quantifier elimination*. More precisely, we assume that, for each formula $\exists x . \phi(x)$, there exists an effectively computable term τ, in which x does not occur, such that $\exists x . \phi$ and $\phi[\tau/x]$ are equisatisfiable. These terms, called *witness terms* in the following, are actual definitions of the Skolem function symbols from the following folklore theorem:

Theorem 3 ([3]). *Given $Q_1 x_1 \ldots Q_n x_n . \phi$ a first-order sentence, where $Q_1, \ldots, Q_n \in \{\exists, \forall\}$ and ϕ is quantifier-free, let $\eta_i \stackrel{def}{=} f_i(y_1, \ldots, y_{k_i})$ if $Q_i = \forall$ and $\eta_i \stackrel{def}{=} x_i$ if $Q_i = \exists$, where f_i is a fresh function symbol and $\{y_1, \ldots, y_{k_i}\} = \{x_j \mid j < i, Q_j = \exists\}$. Then the entailment $Q_1 x_1 \ldots Q_n x_n . \phi \models \phi[\eta_1/x_1, \ldots, \eta_n/x_n]$ holds.*

Examples of witness-producing quantifier elimination procedures can be found in the literature for e.g. linear integer (real) arithmetic (LIA,LRA), Presburger arithmetic and boolean algebra of sets and Presburger cardinality constraints (BAPA) [18].

Under the assumption that witness terms can be effectively built, we describe the generation of a non-local GLI for a given input event sequence $\alpha = a_1 \ldots a_n$. First, we generate successively the acceptance formula $\varUpsilon(\alpha)$ and its equisatisfiable forms $\widehat{\varUpsilon}(\alpha) = Q_1 x_1 \ldots Q_m x_m . \widehat{\varPhi}$ and $\overline{\varUpsilon}(\alpha) = Q_1 x_1 \ldots Q_m x_m . \overline{\varPhi}$, both written in prenex form, with matrices $\widehat{\varPhi}$ and $\overline{\varPhi}$, respectively. Because we assumed that the first order theory of $\mathbb{D}$ has quantifier elimination, the satisfiability problem for $\overline{\varUpsilon}(\alpha)$ is decidable. If $\overline{\varUpsilon}(\alpha)$ is satisfiable, we build a counterexample for emptiness w such that $w_{\varSigma} = \alpha$ and $w_{\mathbb{D}}$ is a satisfying assignment for $\overline{\varUpsilon}(\alpha)$. Otherwise, $\overline{\varUpsilon}(\alpha)$ is unsatisfiable and there exist witness terms $\tau_{i_1} \ldots \tau_{i_\ell}$, where $\{i_1, \ldots, i_\ell\} = \{j \in [1, m] \mid Q_j = \forall\}$, such that $\overline{\varPhi}[\tau_{i_1}/x_{i_1}, \ldots, \tau_{i_\ell}/x_{i_\ell}]$ is unsatisfiable (Theorem 3). Then it turns out that the formula $\widehat{\varPhi}[\tau_{i_1}/x_{i_1}, \ldots, \tau_{i_\ell}/x_{i_\ell}]$, obtained analogously from the matrix of $\widehat{\varUpsilon}(\alpha)$, is unsatisfiable as well (Lemma 6 below). Because this latter formula is structured as a conjunction of formulae $\iota^{(0)} \wedge \phi_1 \ldots \wedge \phi_n \wedge \psi$, where $\mathrm{V}(\phi_k) \cap Q^{(\leq n)} \subseteq Q^{(k-1)} \cup Q^{(k)}$ and $\mathrm{V}(\psi) \cap Q^{(\leq n)} \subseteq Q^{(n)}$, it is now possible to use an existing interpolation procedure for the quantifier-free theory of $\mathbb{D}$, extended with uninterpreted function symbols, to compute a (not necessarily local) GLI $(I_0, \ldots, I_n)$ such that $\mathrm{V}(I_k) \cap Q^{(\leq n)} \subseteq Q^{(k)}$, for all $k \in [n]$.

Example 3 (Contd. from Examples 1 and 2). The formula $\overline{\varUpsilon}(\alpha)$ (Example 2) is unsatisfiable and let $\tau_2 \stackrel{def}{=} z_1$ be the witness term for the universally quantified variable z_2. Replacing z_2 with $\tau_2\,(z_1)$ in the matrix of $\widehat{\varUpsilon}(\alpha)$ (Example 1) yields the unsatisfiable conjunction below, obtained after trivial simplifications:

$$[z_1 \geq 0 \wedge q^{(0)}(z_1)] \wedge [q^{(0)}(z_1) \to x^{(1)} \geq 0 \wedge q^{(1)}(x^{(1)} + z_1)] \wedge$$
$$[q^{(1)}(x^{(1)} + z_1) \to x^{(1)} + z_1 < 0 \wedge q_f^{(2)}(x^{(2)} + x^{(1)} + z_1)]$$

A non-local GLI for the above conjunction is the sequence of formulae:

$$(q^{(0)}(z_1) \wedge z_1 \geq 0,\ x^{(1)} \geq 0 \wedge q^{(1)}(x^{(1)}+z_1) \wedge z_1 \geq 0,\ \bot) \qquad\blacksquare$$

We formalize and prove the correctness for the above construction of non-local GLI. A function $\xi : \mathbb{N} \to \mathbb{N}$ is *monotonic* iff for each $n < m$ we have $\xi(n) \leq \xi(m)$ and *finite-range* iff for each $n \in \mathbb{N}$ the set $\{m \mid \xi(m) = n\}$ is finite. If ξ is finite-range, we denote by $\xi_{\max}^{-1}(n) \in \mathbb{N}$ the maximal value m such that $\xi(m) = n$.

Lemma 6. *Given a non-empty input event sequence $\alpha = a_1 \ldots a_n \in \Sigma^*$, such that $\varUpsilon(\alpha)$ is unsatisfiable, let $Q_1 x_1 \ldots Q_m x_m . \widehat{\varPhi}$ be a prenex form of $\widehat{\varUpsilon}(\alpha)$ and let $\xi : [1, m] \to [n]$ be a monotonic finite-range function mapping each transition quantifier to the minimal index from the sequence $\widehat{\varTheta}(\alpha_0), \ldots, \widehat{\varTheta}(\alpha_n)$ where it occurs. Then one can effectively build:*

1. *witness terms $\tau_{i_1}, \ldots, \tau_{i_\ell}$, where $\{i_1, \ldots, i_\ell\} = \{j \in [1, m] \mid Q_j = \forall\}$ and $\mathrm{V}(\tau_{i_j}) \subseteq X^{(\leq \xi(i_j))} \cup \{x_k \mid k < i_j, Q_k = \exists\}$, $\forall j \in [1, \ell]$ such that $\widehat{\varPhi}[\tau_{i_1}/x_{i_1}, \ldots, \tau_{i_\ell}/x_{i_\ell}]$ is unsatisfiable, and*
2. *a GLI $(I_0, \ldots, I_n)$ for α, such that $\mathrm{V}(I_k) \subseteq Q^{(k)} \cup X^{(\leq k)} \cup \{x_j \mid j < \xi_{\max}^{-1}(k), Q_j = \exists\}$, for all $k \in [n]$.*

Consequently, under two assumptions about the first-order theory of the data domain, namely (i) witness-producing quantifier elimination, and (ii) Lyndon interpolation for the quantifier-free fragment with uninterpreted functions, we developed a generic method that produces GLIs for unfeasible input event sequences. Moreover, each formula in the interpolant refers only to the current predicate symbols, the current and past input variables and the existentially quantified transition variables introduced at the previous steps. The remaining questions are how to use these GLIs to label the sequences in the unfolding of an automaton (Definition 2) and compute coverage (Definition 3) between nodes of the unfolding.

4.1   Unfolding with Non-local Interpolants

As required by Definition 2, the unfolding U of an automaton $\mathcal{A} = \langle \Sigma, X, Q, \iota, F, \Delta \rangle$ is labeled by formulae $U(\alpha) \in \mathsf{Form}^+(Q, \emptyset)$, with no free symbols, other than predicate symbols, such that the labeling is compatible with the transition relation of the automaton. Each newly expanded input sequence of $\mathcal{A}$ is initially labeled with $\top$ and the labels are refined using GLIs computed from proofs of spuriousness. The following lemma describes the refinement of the labeling of an input sequence by a non-local GLI:

Lemma 7. *Let U be an unfolding of an automaton $\mathcal{A} = \langle \Sigma, X, Q, \iota, F, \Delta \rangle$ such that $\alpha = a_1 \ldots a_n \in \mathrm{dom}(U)$ and $(I_0, \ldots, I_n)$ is a GLI for α. Then the mapping $U' : \mathrm{dom}(U) \to \mathsf{Form}^+(Q, \emptyset)$ is an unfolding of $\mathcal{A}$, where:*

- *$U'(\alpha_k) = U(\alpha_k) \wedge J_k$, for all $k \in [n]$, where J_k is the formula obtained from I_k by removing the time stamp of each predicate symbol $q^{(k)}$ and existentially quantifying each free variable, and*
- *$U'(\beta) = U(\beta)$ if $\beta \in \mathrm{dom}(U)$ and $\beta \not\preceq \alpha$,*

Moreover, α is safe in U'.

Observe that, by Lemma 6(2), the set of free variables of a GLI formula I_k consists of (i) variables $X^{(\leq k)}$ keeping track of data values seen in the input at some earlier moment in time, and (ii) variables that track past choices made within the transition rules. Basically, it is not important when exactly in the past a certain input has been read or when a choice has been made, because only the relation between the values of these and the current variables determines the future behavior of the automaton. Quantifying these variables existentially does the job of ignoring when exactly in the past these values have been seen. Moreover, the last point of Lemma 7 ensures that the refined path is safe in the new unfolding and will stay safe in all future refinements of this unfolding.

The last ingredient of the lazy annotation semi-algorithm based on unfoldings consist in the implementation of the coverage check, when the unfolding of an automaton is labeled with conjunctions of existentially quantified formulae with predicate symbols, obtained from interpolation. By Definition 3, checking whether a given node $\alpha \in \mathrm{dom}(U)$ is covered amounts to finding a prefix $\alpha' \preceq \alpha$ and a node $\beta \in \mathrm{dom}(U)$ such that $U(\alpha') \models U(\beta)$, or equivalently, the formula $U(\alpha') \wedge \neg U(\beta)$ is unsatisfiable. However, the latter formula, in prenex form, has quantifier prefix in the language $\exists^* \forall^*$ and, as previously mentioned, the satisfiability problem for such formulae becomes undecidable when the data theory subsumes Presburger arithmetic [10].

Nevertheless, if we require just a yes/no answer (i.e. not an interpolant) recently developed quantifier instantiation heuristics [25] perform rather well in answering a large number of queries in this class. Observe, moreover, that coverage does not need to rely on a complete decision procedure. If the prover fails in answering the above satisfiability query, then the semi-algorithm assumes that the node is not covered and continues exploring its successors. Failure to compute complete coverage may lead to divergence (non-termination) and ultimately, to failure to prove emptiness, but does not affect the soundness of the semi-algorithm (real counterexamples will still be found).

5 Experimental Results

We have implemented a version of the IMPACT semi-algorithm [20] in a prototype tool, avaliable online [8]. The tool is written in Java and uses the Z3 SMT solver [27], via the JavaSMT interface [15], for spuriousness and coverage

Table 1. Experiments with First Order Alternating Automata

Example	$|\mathcal{A}|$ (bytes)	Predicates	Variables	Transitions	$L(\mathcal{A}) = \emptyset$?	Nodes expanded	Nodes visited	Time (msec)
incdec.pa	499	3	1	12	No	21	17	779
localdec.pa	678	4	1	16	No	49	35	1814
ticket.pa	4250	13	1	73	No	229	91	9543
count_thread0.pa	9767	14	1	126	No	154	128	8553
count_thread1.pa	10925	15	1	135	No	766	692	76771
local0.pa	10595	13	1	117	No	73	27	1431
local1.pa	11385	14	1	126	No	1135	858	101042
array_rotation.ada	1834	8	7	7	Yes	9	8	1543
array_simple.ada	3440	9	5	8	Yes	11	10	6787
array_shift.ada	874	6	5	5	Yes	6	5	413
abp.ada	6909	16	14	28	No	52	47	4788
train.ada	1823	10	4	26	Yes	68	67	7319
hw1.ada	322	3	2	5	Solver error	/	/	/
hw2.ada	674	7	2	8	Yes	20	22	4974
rr-crossing.foada	1780	10	1	16	Yes	67	67	7574
train-simple1.foada	5421	13	1	61	Yes	43	44	2893
train-simple2.foada	10177	16	1	118	Yes	111	113	8386
train-simple3.foada	15961	19	1	193	Yes	196	200	15041
fischer-mutex2.foada	3000	11	2	23	Yes	23	23	808
fischer-mutex3.foada	4452	16	2	34	Yes	33	33	1154

queries and also for interpolant generation. Table 1 reports the size of the input automaton in bytes, the numbers of Predicates, Variables and Transitions, the result of emptiness check, the number of Expanded and Visited Nodes during the unfolding and the Time in miliseconds. The experiments were carried out on a MacOS x64 - 1.3 GHz Intel Core i5 - 8 GB 1867 MHz LPDDR3 machine.

The test cases shown in Table 1, come from several sources, namely predicate automata models (*.pa) [6,7] available online [23], timed automata inclusion problems (`abp.ada`, `train.ada`, `rr-crossing.foada`), array logic entailments (`array_rotation.ada`, `array_simple.ada`, `array_shift.ada`) and hardware circuit verification (`hw1.ada`, `hw2.ada`), initially considered in [13], with the restriction that local variables are made visible in the input. The `train-simpleN.foada` and `fischer-mutexN.foada` examples are parametric verification problems in which one checks inclusions of the form $\bigcap_{i=1}^{N} \mathcal{L}(A_i) \subseteq \mathcal{L}(B)$, where A_i is the i-th copy of the template automaton.

The advantage of using FOADA over the INCLUDER [12] tool from [13] is the possibility of having automata over infinite alphabets with local variables, whose values are not visible in the input. In particular, this is essential for checking inclusion of timed automata that use internal clocks to control the computation.

6   Conclusions

We present first-order alternating automata, a model of computation that generalizes classical boolean alternating automata to first-order theories. Due to their expressivity, first-order alternating automata are closed under union, intersection and complement. However the emptiness problem is undecidable even in the most simple case, of the quantifier-free theory of equality with uninterpreted predicate symbols. We deal with the emptiness problem by developping a practical semi-algorithm that always terminates, when the automaton is not empty. In case of emptiness, termination of the semi-algorithm occurs in most practical test cases, as shown by a number of experiments.

References

1. Alur, R., Dill, D.L.: A theory of timed automata. Theor. Comput. Sci. **126**(2), 183–235 (1994)
2. Barringer, H., Rydeheard, D., Havelund, K.: Rule systems for run-time monitoring: from EAGLE to RULER. In: Sokolsky, O., Taşıran, S. (eds.) RV 2007. LNCS, vol. 4839, pp. 111–125. Springer, Heidelberg (2007). https://doi.org/10.1007/978-3-540-77395-5_10
3. Börger, E., Grädel, E., Gurevich, Y.: The Classical Decision Problem: Perspectives in Mathematical Logic. Springer, Heidelberg (1997)
4. Chandra, A.K., Kozen, D.C., Stockmeyer, L.J.: Alternation. J. ACM **28**(1), 114–133 (1981)
5. D'Antoni, L., Kincaid, Z., Wang, F.: A symbolic decision procedure for symbolic alternating finite automata. Electron. Notes Theor. Comput. Sci. **336**, 79–99 (2018). The Thirty-third Conference on the Mathematical Foundations of Programming Semantics (MFPS XXXIII)

6. Farzan, A., Kincaid, Z., Podelski, A.: Proof spaces for unbounded parallelism. SIGPLAN Not. **50**(1), 407–420 (2015)
7. Farzan, A., Kincaid, Z., Podelski, A.: Proving liveness of parameterized programs. In: Proceedings of the 31st Annual ACM/IEEE Symposium on Logic in Computer Science, LICS 2016, pp. 185–196. ACM (2016)
8. First Order Alternating Data Automata (FOADA). https://github.com/cathiec/FOADA
9. Grebenshchikov, S., Lopes, N.P., Popeea, C., Rybalchenko, A.: Synthesizing software verifiers from proof rules. SIGPLAN Not. **47**(6), 405–416 (2012)
10. Halpern, J.Y.: Presburger arithmetic with unary predicates is π_1^1 complete. J. Symb. Log. **56**(2), 637–642 (1991)
11. Hojjat, H., Rümmer, P.: Deciding and interpolating algebraic data types by reduction. Technical report. CoRR abs/1801.02367 (2018). http://arxiv.org/abs/1801.02367
12. Includer. http://www.fit.vutbr.cz/research/groups/verifit/tools/includer/
13. Iosif, R., Rogalewicz, A., Vojnar, T.: Abstraction refinement and antichains for trace inclusion of infinite state systems. In: Chechik, M., Raskin, J.-F. (eds.) TACAS 2016. LNCS, vol. 9636, pp. 71–89. Springer, Heidelberg (2016). https://doi.org/10.1007/978-3-662-49674-9_5
14. Iosif, R., Xu, X.: Abstraction refinement for emptiness checking of alternating data automata. In: Beyer, D., Huisman, M. (eds.) TACAS 2018. LNCS, vol. 10806, pp. 93–111. Springer, Cham (2018). https://doi.org/10.1007/978-3-319-89963-3_6
15. JavaSMT. https://github.com/sosy-lab/java-smt
16. Kaminski, M., Francez, N.: Finite-memory automata. Theor. Comput. Sci. **134**(2), 329–363 (1994)
17. Kincaid, Z.: Parallel proofs for parallel programs. Ph.D. thesis, University of Toronto (2016)
18. Kuncak, V., Mayer, M., Piskac, R., Suter, P.: Software synthesis procedures. Commun. ACM **55**(2), 103–111 (2012)
19. Lyndon, R.C.: An interpolation theorem in the predicate calculus. Pacific J. Math. **9**(1), 129–142 (1959)
20. McMillan, K.L.: Lazy abstraction with interpolants. In: Ball, T., Jones, R.B. (eds.) CAV 2006. LNCS, vol. 4144, pp. 123–136. Springer, Heidelberg (2006). https://doi.org/10.1007/11817963_14
21. McMillan, K.L.: Lazy annotation revisited. In: Biere, A., Bloem, R. (eds.) CAV 2014. LNCS, vol. 8559, pp. 243–259. Springer, Cham (2014). https://doi.org/10.1007/978-3-319-08867-9_16
22. Nelson, G., Oppen, D.C.: Fast decision procedures based on congruence closure. J. ACM **27**(2), 356–364 (1980)
23. Predicate Automata. https://github.com/zkincaid/duet/tree/ark2/regression/predicateAutomata
24. Presburger, M.: Über die Vollstandigkeit eines gewissen Systems der Arithmetik. Comptes rendus du I Congrés des Pays Slaves, Warsaw (1929)
25. Reynolds, A., King, T., Kuncak, V.: Solving quantified linear arithmetic by counterexample-guided instantiation. Form. Methods Syst. Des. **51**(3), 500–532 (2017)
26. Rybalchenko, A., Sofronie-Stokkermans, V.: Constraint solving for interpolation. J. Symb. Comput. **45**(11), 1212–1233 (2010)
27. Z3 SMT Solver. https://rise4fun.com/z3

11

Numerically-Robust Inductive Proof Rules for Continuous Dynamical Systems

Sicun Gao[1], James Kapinski[2], Jyotirmoy Deshmukh[3], Nima Roohi[1(✉)],
Armando Solar-Lezama[4], Nikos Arechiga[5], and Soonho Kong[5]

[1] University of California, San Diego,
La Jolla, USA
{sicung,nroohi}@ucsd.edu
[2] Toyota R&D, Gardena, USA
jim.kapinski@toyota.com
[3] University of Southern California,
Los Angeles, USA
jyotirmoy.deshmukh@usc.edu
[4] Massachusetts Institute of Technology, Cambridge, USA
asolar@csail.mit.edu
[5] Toyota Research Institute, Cambridge, USA
{nikos.arechiga,soonho.kong}@tri.global

Abstract. We formulate numerically-robust inductive proof rules for
unbounded stability and safety properties of continuous dynamical systems. These induction rules robustify standard notions of Lyapunov functions and barrier certificates so that they can tolerate small numerical
errors. In this way, numerically-driven decision procedures can establish
a sound and relative-complete proof system for unbounded properties of
very general nonlinear systems. We demonstrate the effectiveness of the
proposed rules for rigorously verifying unbounded properties of various
nonlinear systems, including a challenging powertrain control model.

1 Introduction

Infinite-time stability and safety properties of continuous dynamical systems are
typically established via inductive arguments over continuous time. For instance,
proving stability of a dynamical system is similar to proving termination of a
program. A system is stable at the origin in the sense of Lyapunov, if one can
find a Lyapunov function (essentially a ranking function) that is everywhere positive except for reaching exactly zero at the origin, and never increases over time
along the direction of the system dynamics [11]. Likewise, proving unbounded
safety of a dynamical system requires one to find a barrier function (or differential invariant [19]) that separates the system's initial state from the unsafe
regions, and whenever the system states reach the barrier, the system dynamics always points towards the safe side of the barrier [21]. In both cases, once
a candidate certificate (Lyapunov or barrier functions) is proposed, the verification problem is reduced to checking the validity of a universally-quantified

first-order formula over real-valued variables. The standard approaches for the validation step use symbolic quantifier elimination [4] or Sum-of-Squares techniques [17,18,24]. However, these algorithms are either extremely expensive or numerically brittle. Most importantly, they can not handle systems with non-polynomial nonlinearity, and thus fall short of a general framework for verifying practical systems of significant complexity.

The standard approach of checking invariance conditions in program analysis is to use Satisfiability Modulo Theories (SMT) solvers [16]. However, to check the inductive conditions for nonlinear dynamical systems, one has to solve nonlinear SMT problems over real numbers, which are highly intractable or undecidable [23]. Recent work on numerically-driven decision procedures provides a promising direction to bypass this difficulty [5,6]. They have been used for many bounded-time verification and synthesis problems for highly nonlinear systems [12]. However, the fundamental challenge with using numerically-driven methods in inductive proofs is that numerical errors make it impossible to verify the induction steps in the standard sense. Take the Lyapunov analysis of stability properties as an example. A dynamical system is stable if there exists a function that vanishes *exactly* at the origin and its derivatives *strictly* decreases over time. Since *any* numerical error blurs the difference between strict and non-strict inequality, one can conclude that numerically-driven methods are not suitable for verifying these strict constraints. However, proving a system is stable within an arbitrarily tiny neighborhood around the origin is all we really need in practice. Thus, there is a discrepancy between what the standard theory requires and what is needed in practice, or what can be achieved computationally. To bridge this gap, we need to rethink about the fundamental definitions.

In this paper, we formulate new inductive proof rules for continuous dynamical systems for establishing robust notions of stability and safety. These proof rules are practically useful and computationally certifiable in a very general sense. For instance, for stability, we define the notion of ε-stability that requires the system to be stable within an ε-bounded distance from the origin, instead of exactly at the origin. When ε is small enough, ε-stable systems are practically indistinguishable from stable systems. We then define the notion of ε-Lyapunov functions that are sufficient for establishing ε-stability. We then rigorously prove that the ε-Lyapunov conditions are numerically stable and can be correctly determined by δ-complete decisions procedures for nonlinear real arithmetic [7]. In this way, we can rely on various numerically-driven SMT solvers to establish a sound and relative-complete proof systems for unbounded stability and safety properties of highly nonlinear dynamical systems. We believe these new definitions have eliminated the core difficulty for reasoning about infinite-time properties of nonlinear systems, and will pave the way for adapting a wide range of automated methods from program analysis to continuous and hybrid systems. In short, the paper makes the following contributions:

- We define ε-stability and ε-Lyapunov functions in Sect. 3. We prove that finding ε-Lyapunov functions is sufficient for establishing ε-stability.
- We define two types of robust proof rules for unbounded safety in Sect. 3, which we call Type 1 and Type 2 ε-barrier functions. The former relies on

strict contraction, and the latter relies on reachable-set computation to guarantee bounded escape.

- We prove that δ-complete decision procedures provide a sound and relative-complete proof system for the proposed numerically-robust induction rules, in both Sects. 3 and 4.

We demonstrate the effectiveness of the proposed methods on various nonlinear systems in Sect. 5. Section 2 covers the basic definitions and Sect. 6 concludes the paper.

Related Work. Several lines of work have proposed relaxed and practical notions to capture the spirit of the stability requirements. Early work from the 1960s introduced practical stability, which defined bounds on system behaviors over finite time horizons [2,14,26,27]. These methods can show whether a system leaves a safe set or enters a goal set over a finite time horizon based on Lyapunov-like functions. Stability defined in this sense is equivalent to estimating the reachable set over a finite time horizon. Thus, the shortcoming is that it may not capture the desired behavior of the system over unbounded time. Similarly, notions of boundedness and ultimate boundedness specify limits on the system behaviors [11]. Boundedness specifies whether the system remains within a given bounded region. Ultimate boundedness specifies that the system eventually returns to the given bounded region. These properties can be established based on Lyapunov-like conditions. Related notions have been generalized to switched systems [29,30]. Also, the related notion of region stability defines systems that eventually enter and remain within a specified set [20]. We present stability concepts that unify and extend the above notions. A related relaxation of the traditional notions of stability includes *almost* Lyapunov functions [15], which allow the strict stability conditions to be neglected in a region near the equilibrium point. The challenge of applying this technique in practice is that the size and shape of the neglected region are not specified a priori, so a constructive technique for specifying a stability region is not straightforward. Our work is related to efforts to construct and check robust barrier certificates using Lyapunov-like functions to ensure that controllers satisfy safety constraints [28]. This work provides a framework in which to specify analytic constraints on controller behaviors. By contrast, our work focuses on providing constraints that can be checked fully automatically. Our notion of ε-barrier functions is closely related to t-barrier certificates from [1], though we choose to focus on distance bounds from the barrier (ε) rather than time bounds that indicate how long it takes for behaviors to re-enter the barrier once it has left (t).

2 Background

2.1 Dynamical Systems

Throughout the paper, we use the following definition of an n-dimensional autonomous dynamical system:

$$\frac{\mathrm{d}x(t)}{\mathrm{d}t} = f(x(t)),\ x(0) \in \mathsf{init} \text{ and } \forall t \in \mathbb{R}_{\geq 0}, x(t) \in D, \tag{1}$$

where an open set $D \subseteq \mathbb{R}^n$ is the state space, init $\subseteq D$ is a set of initial states, and $f : D \to \mathbb{R}^n$ is a vector field specified by Lipschitz-continuous functions on each dimension. For notational simplicity, *all variable and function symbols can represent vectors.* When vectors are used in logic formulas, they represent conjunctions of the formulas for each dimension. For instance, when $x = (x_1, \ldots, x_n)$, we write $x = 0$ to denote the formula $x_1 = 0 \wedge \cdots \wedge x_n = 0$. For any system defined by (1), we write its solution function as

$$F : D \times \mathbb{R}_{\geq 0} \to \mathbb{R}^n, \ F(x(0), t) = x(0) + \int_0^t f(x(s))\mathrm{d}s. \tag{2}$$

Note that F usually does not have an analytic form. However, since f is Lipschitz-continuous, F exists and is unique. We will often use Lie derivatives to measure the change of a scalar function along the flow defined by another vector field:

Definition 1 (Lie Derivative). *Let $f : D \to \mathbb{R}^n$ define a vector field. Write the ith component of f as f_i. Let $V : D \to \mathbb{R}$ be a differentiable scalar function. The Lie derivative of V over f is defined as $\nabla_f V(x) = \sum_{i=1}^{n} \frac{\partial V}{\partial x_i} f_i$.*

2.2 First-Order Language over the Reals $\mathcal{L}_{\mathbb{R}_\mathcal{F}}$

We will make extensive use of first-order formulas over real numbers with Type 2 computable functions [25] to express and infer properties of nonlinear dynamical systems. Definition 2 introduces the syntax of these formulas.

Definition 2 (Syntax of $\mathcal{L}_{\mathbb{R}_\mathcal{F}}$). *Let $\mathcal{F}$ be the class of all Type 2 computable functions over real numbers. We define:*

$$t ::= x_i \mid f(t(x)), \ where \ f \in \mathcal{F}, \ possibly \ constant;$$
$$\varphi ::= \top \mid \bot \mid t(x) > 0 \mid t(x) \geq 0 \mid \varphi \wedge \varphi \mid \varphi \vee \varphi \mid \exists x_i \varphi \mid \forall x_i \varphi.$$

We regard $\neg\varphi$ as an operation that is defined inductively as usual. For instance, $\neg(t > 0)$ is defined as $-t \geq 0$, and $\neg(\exists x_i \varphi)$ is defined as $\forall x_i \neg\varphi$. For any $\mathcal{L}_{\mathbb{R}_\mathcal{F}}$ terms u and v, variable x, and $\mathcal{L}_{\mathbb{R}_\mathcal{F}}$ predicate φ, we write $\exists^{[u,v]} x \varphi$ and $\forall^{[u,v]} x \varphi$ to denote $\exists x(u \leq x \wedge x \leq v \wedge \varphi)$ and $\forall x((u \leq x \wedge x \leq v) \to \varphi)$, respectively, which applies to open intervals too. Next, Definition 3 introduces syntactic perturbation of formulas in $\mathcal{L}_{\mathbb{R}_\mathcal{F}}$.

Definition 3 (δ-Strengthening and Robust Formulas [7]). *Let $\delta \in \mathbb{Q}^+$ be arbitrary. Let φ be an arbitrary $\mathcal{L}_{\mathbb{R}_\mathcal{F}}$ formula. The δ-strengthening of φ, denoted by $\varphi^{+\delta}$, is obtained from φ by replacing every atomic predicate of the form $t(x) > 0$ and $t(x) \geq 0$ with $t(x) - \delta > 0$ and $t(x) - \delta \geq 0$, respectively. We say φ is δ-robust iff $\varphi^{+\delta} \leftrightarrow \varphi$.*

Definition 4 (δ-Complete Decision Procedures [7]). *Let S be a class of $\mathcal{L}_{\mathbb{R}_\mathcal{F}}$-sentences. We say a decision procedure is δ-complete over S iff for any $\varphi \in S$, the procedure correctly returns one of the following answers:*

– true : φ *is true.*
– δ-false : $\varphi^{+\delta}$ *is false.*

When the two cases overlap, either decision can be returned.

It follows that if φ is δ-robust, then a δ-complete decision procedure can correctly determine the truth value of φ.

3 Robust Proofs for Stability

We first focus on stability. We will define the notion of ε-stability, as a relaxation of the standard Lyapunov stability, and then define ε-Lyapunov functions, which are sufficient for proving ε-stability in a robust way.

3.1 Stability and Lyapunov Functions

Conventionally, ε and δ are used to best highlight the connection with ε-δ conditions for continuity. We will mostly reserve the use of ε for defining conditions that are robust under ε-bounded numerical errors. Thus, we replace ε by τ in the standard definitions to avoid confusion.

Definition 5 (Stability). *We say the system in (1) is stable at the origin in the sense of Lyapunov, iff for any τ-ball neighborhood of the origin, there exists a δ-ball around the origin, such that, if the system starts within the δ-ball then it never escapes the τ-ball. We capture the definition by the following $\mathcal{L}_{\mathbb{R}_{\mathcal{F}}}$-formula:*

$$\mathsf{Stable}(f) \equiv_{df} \forall^{(0,\infty)}\tau \exists^{(0,\infty)}\delta \forall^D x_0 \forall^{[0,\infty)}t\Big(\|x_0\| < \delta \rightarrow \|F(x_0,t)\| < \tau\Big)$$

Definition 6 (Lyapunov Function). *Consider a dynamical system given in the form of (1), and let $V : D \rightarrow \mathbb{R}$ be a differentiable function. We say V is a non-strict Lyapunov function for the system, iff the following predicate is true:*

$$\mathsf{LF}(f,V) \equiv_{df} (V(0)=0) \wedge (f(0)=0) \wedge \forall^{D\setminus\{0\}}x\Big(V(x) > 0 \wedge \nabla_f V(x) \leq 0\Big)$$

Proposition 1. *For any dynamical system defined by f, if there exists a Lyapunov function V, then the system is stable. Namely, $\mathsf{LF}(f,V) \rightarrow \mathsf{Stable}(f)$.*

3.2 Epsilon-Stability

The standard definitions of stability requires a system to stabilize within arbitrarily small neighborhoods around the origin. However, very small neighborhoods are practically indistinguishable from the origin. Thus, it is practically sufficient to prove that a system is stable within some sufficiently small neighborhood. We capture this intuition by making a minor change to the standard definition, by simply putting a lower bound ε on the τ parameter in Definition 5. As a result, the system is required to exhibit the same behavior as standard stable systems outside the ε-ball, but can behave arbitrarily within the ε-ball (for instance, oscillate around the origin). The formal definition is as follows:

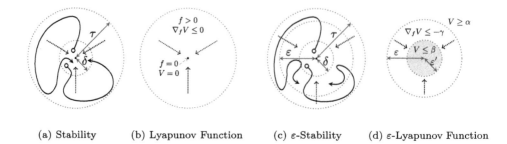

(a) Stability   (b) Lyapunov Function   (c) ε-Stability   (d) ε-Lyapunov Function

Fig. 1. Standard and ε-relaxed notions of stability and Lyapunov functions

Definition 7 (Epsilon-Stability). *Let $\varepsilon \in \mathbb{R}_+$ be arbitrary. We say a dynamical system in (1) is ε-stable at the origin in the sense of Lyapunov, iff it satisfies the following condition:*

$$\mathsf{Stable}_\varepsilon(f) \equiv_{df} \forall^{[\varepsilon,\infty)}\tau \exists^{(0,\infty)}\delta \forall^D x_0 \forall^{[0,\infty)} t \left(\|x_0\| < \delta \rightarrow \|F(x_0,t)\| < \tau \right)$$

In words, for any $\tau \geq \varepsilon$, there exists δ such that all trajectories that start within the δ-ball will stay within a τ-ball around the origin.

Note that the only difference with the standard definition is that τ is *bounded from below* by a positive ε instead of 0. The definition is depicted in Fig. 1c, which shows the difference with the standard notion in Fig. 1a. Since the only difference with the standard definition is the lower bound on the universally quantified τ, it is clear that ε-stability is strictly weaker than standard stability.

Proposition 2. *For any $\varepsilon \in \mathbb{R}_+$, $\mathsf{Stable}(f) \rightarrow \mathsf{Stable}_\varepsilon(f)$.*

Thus, any system that is stable in the standard definition is also ε-stable for any $\varepsilon \in \mathbb{R}_+$. On the other hand, one can always choose small enough ε such that an ε-stable system is practically indistinguishable from stable systems in the standard definition.

3.3   Epsilon-Lyapunov Function

We now define the corresponding notion of Lyapunov function that can be used for proving ε-stability. The robustness problem in the standard definition comes from the singularity of the origin. With the relaxed notion of stability, the system may oscillate within some ε-neighborhood of the origin. With the relaxation, we now have room for constructing a few nested neighborhoods that can trap the trajectories in a way that is robust under sufficiently small perturbations. To achieve this, we make use of balls of different sizes, as shown in the following definition. We write $\mathcal{B}_\varepsilon$ to denote open ε-balls around the origin.

Definition 8 (Epsilon-Lyapunov Functions). *Let $V : D \rightarrow \mathbb{R}$ be a differentiable scalar function defined for the system in (1), and let $\varepsilon \in \mathbb{R}_+$ be an arbitrary value. We say V is an ε-Lyapunov function for the system, iff it satisfies the following conditions:*

1. *Outside the ε-ball, there is some positive lower bound on the value of V. Namely, there exists $\alpha \in \mathbb{R}_+$ such that for any $x \in D \setminus \mathcal{B}_\varepsilon$, $V(x) \geq \alpha$.*
2. *Inside the ε-ball, there is a strictly smaller ε'-ball in which the value of V is bounded from above, to create a gap with its values outside the ε-ball. Formally, there exists $\varepsilon' \in (0, \varepsilon)$ and $\beta \in (0, \alpha)$ such that for all $x \in \mathcal{B}_{\varepsilon'}$, $V(x) \leq \beta$.*
3. *The Lie derivative of V is strictly negative outside of $\mathcal{B}_{\varepsilon'}$. Formally, there exists $\gamma \in \mathbb{R}_+$ such that for all $x \in D \setminus \mathcal{B}_{\varepsilon'}$, the Lie derivative of V along f satisfies $\nabla_f V(x) \leq -\gamma$.*

In sum, the three conditions can be expressed with the following $\mathcal{L}_{\mathbb{R}_\mathcal{F}}$-formula:

$$\mathsf{LF}_\varepsilon(f, V) \equiv_{df} \exists^{(0,\varepsilon)} \varepsilon' \exists^{(0,\infty)} \alpha \exists^{(0,\alpha)} \beta \exists^{(0,\infty)} \gamma$$
$$\forall^{D \setminus \mathcal{B}_\varepsilon} x \Big(V(x) \geq \alpha\Big) \wedge \forall^{\mathcal{B}_{\varepsilon'}} x \Big(V(x) \leq \beta\Big)$$
$$\wedge \forall^{D \setminus \mathcal{B}_{\varepsilon'}} x \Big(\nabla_f V(x) \leq -\gamma\Big)$$

It is important to note that ε', α, β, and γ, are not fixed constants, but existentially quantified variables. Thus the condition can hold true for infinitely many values of these parameters, which is critical to robustness. The only free variable in the formula is ε, used in $\mathcal{B}_\varepsilon$ and the bound for ε'. Note also that neither of $\mathsf{LF}_\varepsilon(f, V)$ and the standard definition $\mathsf{LF}(f, V)$ implies the other.

Remark 1. The logical structure of $\mathsf{LF}_\varepsilon(f, V)$ is seemingly more complex than the standard Lyapunov conditions in Definition 6 because of the extra existential quantification. In Theorem 3, we show that it does not add computational complexity in checking the conditions.

The key result is that the conditions for an ε-Lyapunov function are sufficient for establishing ε-stability.

Theorem 1. *If there exists an ε-Lyapunov function V for a dynamical system defined by f, then the system is ε-stable. Namely, $\mathsf{LF}_\varepsilon(f, V) \to \mathsf{Stable}_\varepsilon(f)$.*

Proof. Let $\tau \geq \varepsilon$ be arbitrary, and let $\alpha, \gamma \in \mathbb{R}_+$, $\beta \in (0, \alpha)$, and $\varepsilon' \in (0, \varepsilon)$ be as specified by the definition of $\mathsf{LF}_\varepsilon(f, V)$. Let $x_0 \in \mathcal{B}_{\varepsilon'}$ be an arbitrary point. For any $t \in \mathbb{R}_{\geq 0}$, let $x(t) := F(x_0, t)$ be the system state as defined in (2). We use contradiction to prove for any $t \in \mathbb{R}_+$, inequality $\|x(t)\| < \varepsilon \leq \tau$ holds. Since $\varepsilon' < \varepsilon$ and $F(x_0, .)$ is continuous, we know t_1 and t_2 with the following conditions exists ($\partial \mathcal{B}_{\varepsilon'}$ and $\partial \mathcal{B}_\varepsilon$ are boundaries of the corresponding balls):

$$0 \leq t_1 < t_2 \leq t, \quad x(t_1) \in \partial \mathcal{B}_{\varepsilon'}, \quad x(t_2) \in \partial \mathcal{B}_\varepsilon, \quad \forall^{(t_1, t_2)} t' \Big(x(t') \in \mathcal{B}_\varepsilon \setminus \mathcal{B}_{\varepsilon'}\Big)$$

We know $V(x(t_1)) \leq \beta < \alpha \leq V(x(t_2))$ and hence $V(x(t_1)) < V(x(t_2))$ are both true; however, this is in contradiction with the mean value theorem and the fact that $\mathcal{B}_\varepsilon \subset D$ and $\forall^{D \setminus \mathcal{B}_{\varepsilon'}} x \big(\nabla_f V(x) < -\gamma\big)$. $\quad \square$

Remark 2. Proof of Theorem 1 shows that once state of the system enters $\mathcal{B}_{\varepsilon'}$, it never leaves $\mathcal{B}_\varepsilon$. However, it would be still possible for the state to leave $\mathcal{B}_{\varepsilon'}$. One the other hand, since closure of $\mathcal{B}_\varepsilon \setminus \mathcal{B}_{\varepsilon'}$ is bounded, and for every x in this area, V is continuous at x and $\nabla_f V(x) \le -\gamma$, no trajectory can be trapped in the closure of $\mathcal{B}_\varepsilon \setminus \mathcal{B}_{\varepsilon'}$. Therefore, even though state of the system might leave $\mathcal{B}_{\varepsilon'}$, it will visit inside of this ball infinitely often.

Example 1. Consider the time-reversed Van der Pol system given by the following dynamics. Figure 3 shows the vector field of this system around the origin.

$$\begin{bmatrix} \dot{x}_1 \\ \dot{x}_2 \end{bmatrix} = \begin{bmatrix} -x_2 \\ (x_1^2 - 1)x_2 + x_1 \end{bmatrix}$$

A Lyapunov function $z^T P z$, where z^T is $[x_1, x_2, x_1^2, x_1 x_2, x_2^2, x_1^3, x_1^2 x_2,$ $x_1 x_2^2, x_2^3]$, and P is the 9×9 constant matrix given in [8], is a 6-degree polynomial that can be obtained using simulation-guided techniques from [10]. Using dReal [9] with $\delta := 10^{-25}$ and the Euclidean norm, we are able to prove that $z^T P z$ is a 10^{-12}-Lyapunov function. Table 1 lists the parameters used for this proof.

3.4   Automated Proofs with Delta-Decisions

We now prove that unlike the conventional conditions, the new inductive proof rules are numerically robust. It follows that δ-decision procedures provide a sound and relative-complete proof system for establishing the conditions in the following sense:

- (Soundness) A δ-complete decision procedure is always correct when it confirms the existence of an ε-Lyapunov function.
- (Relative Completeness) For a given ε-inductive certificate, there exists $\delta > 0$ such that a δ'-complete procedure is able to verify it, for any $0 < \delta' \le \delta$.

To prove these properties, the key fact is that the continuity of the functions in the induction conditions ensures that there is room for numerical errors in the conditions. Consequently, the formulas allow δ-perturbations in their parameters. This is captured by Lemma 1, and the proof is given in [8].

Lemma 1. *For any $\varepsilon \in \mathbb{R}_+$, there exists $\delta \in \mathbb{Q}_+$ such that* $\mathsf{LF}_\varepsilon(f, V)$ *is δ-robust.*

Note that if a formula ϕ is δ-robust then for every $\delta' \in (0, \delta)$, ϕ is δ'-robust as well. The soundness and relative-completeness then follow naturally.

Theorem 2 (Soundness). *If a δ-complete decision procedure confirms that* $\mathsf{LF}_\varepsilon(f, V)$ *is* true *then V is indeed an ε-Lyapunov function, and f is ε-stable.*

Proof. Using Definition 4, we know $\mathsf{LF}_\varepsilon(f, V)$, exactly as specified in Definition 8, is true. Therefore, V is ε-Lyapunov. Using Theorem 1, f is ε-stable.   □

Theorem 3 (Relative Completeness). *For any* $\varepsilon \in \mathbb{R}_+$, *if* $\mathsf{LF}_\varepsilon(f, V)$ *is true then there exists* $\delta \in \mathbb{Q}_+$ *such that any* δ-complete decision procedure must return that $\mathsf{LF}_\varepsilon(f, V)$ is *true*.

Proof. Fix an arbitrary $\varepsilon \in \mathbb{R}_+$ for which $\mathsf{LF}_\varepsilon(f, V)$ is true. Let $\phi := \mathsf{LF}_\varepsilon(f, V)$, and using Lemma 1, let $\delta \in \mathbb{Q}_+$ be such that ϕ is δ-robust. Since ϕ is true, we conclude $\phi^{+\delta}$ is true as well. Using Definition 4, no δ-complete decision procedure can return δ-false for ϕ. □

We remark that the quantifier alternation used in Definition 8 can be eliminated without extra search steps. It confirms that we only need to run SMT solving to handle the universally quantified subformula. The reason is that the α, β, and γ parameters can be found by estimating the range of $V(x)$ and $\nabla_f V(x)$ in the different neighborhoods. In fact, we can rewrite $\mathsf{LF}_\varepsilon(f, V)$ in the following way to eliminate the use of α, β, and γ:

$$\mathsf{LF}_\varepsilon(f, V) \leftrightarrow \exists^{(0,\varepsilon)} \varepsilon' \left(\sup_{x \in \mathcal{B}_{\varepsilon'}} V(x) < \inf_{x \in D \setminus \mathcal{B}_\varepsilon} V(x) \wedge \sup_{x \in D \setminus \mathcal{B}_{\varepsilon'}} \nabla_f V(x) < 0 \right)$$

Note that in this form the universal quantification is implicit in the sup and inf operators. In this way, the formula is existentially quantified on only ε', which can then be handled by binary search. This is an efficient way of checking the conditions in practice. We also remark that without this method, the original formulation with multiple parameters can be directly solved as $\exists\forall$-formulas as well using more expensive algorithms [13].

4   Robust Proofs for Safety

In this section, we define two types of ε-barrier functions that are robust to numerical perturbations.

Proving unbounded safety requires the use of barrier functions. The idea is that if one can find a barrier function that separates initial conditions from the set of unsafe states, such that no trajectories can cross the barrier from the safe to the unsafe side, then the system is safe. Here we use a formulation similar to the that of Prajna [21]. The standard conditions on barrier functions include constraints on the vector field of the system at the exact boundary of the barrier set, which introduces robustness problems. We show that it is possible to avoid these problems using two different formulations, which we call Type 1 and Type 2 ε-barrier functions. Type 1 ε-barrier functions strengthen the original definition and requires strict contraction of the barrier. Instead of only asking the system to be contractive exactly on the barrier's border, we force it to be contractive when reaching any state within a small distance from the border. Type 2 ε-barrier functions allow the system to escape the barrier for a controllable distance and a limited period of time. It should then return to the interior of the safe region. Type 1 ε-barriers can be seen as a subclass of Type 2 ε-barriers. The benefit for allowing bounded escape is that the shape of the barrier no longer needs to be an invariant set, which can be particularly helpful when the shape of the system invariants cannot be determined or expressed symbolically. The downside to Type 2 ε-barriers is that checking the corresponding conditions requires integration of the dynamics, which can be expensive but can still be handled by δ-complete decision procedures. The intuition behind the two definitions is shown in Fig. 2 and will be explained in detail in this section.

4.1 Safety and Barrier Functions

Before formally introducing robust safety and ε-barrier functions, we define the safety and barrier functions first. It is easy to see that the robustness problem with the barrier functions is similar to that of Lyapunov functions: if the boundary is exactly separating the safe and unsafe regions then the inductive conditions are not robust, since deviations in the variables by even a small amount from the barrier will make it impossible to complete the proof.

Definition 9 (Safety). *Let $B : D \to \mathbb{R}$ be a scalar function defined for the system in (1). We say $B \leq 0$ defines a safe (or forward invariant) set for the system, iff the following formula is true:*

$$\mathsf{Safe}(f, \mathsf{init}, B) \equiv_{df} \forall^D x_0 \forall^{[0,\infty)} t \Big(\mathsf{init}(x_0) \to B(F(x_0, t)) \leq 0 \Big).$$

Definition 10 (Barrier Function). *Let $B : X \to \mathbb{R}$ be a differentiable scalar function defined for the system in (1). We say B is a barrier function for the system, iff the following formula is true:*

$$\mathsf{Barrier}(f, \mathsf{init}, B) \equiv_{df} \forall^D x \Big(\big(\mathsf{init}(x) \to B(x) \leq 0 \big) \wedge \big(B(x) = 0 \to \nabla_f B(x) < 0 \big) \Big)$$

Proposition 3. $\mathsf{Barrier}(f, \mathsf{init}, B) \to \mathsf{Safe}(f, \mathsf{init}, B).$

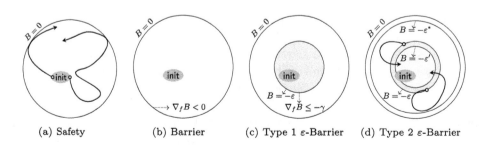

(a) Safety   (b) Barrier   (c) Type 1 ε-Barrier   (d) Type 2 ε-Barrier

Fig. 2. Type 1 and Type 2 ε-Barriers

4.2   Type 1: Strict Contraction

In the standard definition, the boundary of the barrier set is typically a manifold defined by equality, which is not numerically robust. To avoid this problem, we need the barrier boundary to be *belt-shaped* in the sense that there is a clear gap between the safe and unsafe regions. The idea is as shown in Fig. 2c: we need a second and stronger barrier defined by $B = -\varepsilon$ for some reasonable ε, so that the system is clearly separated from $B = 0$. The formal definition is as follows.

Definition 11 (ε-Barrier Certificates). *Let $\varepsilon \in \mathbb{R}_+$ be arbitrary. A differentiable scalar function $B : D \to \mathbb{R}$ is an ε-barrier function iff the following conditions are true:*

- *For all x, $\mathsf{init}(x)$ implies $B(x) \leq -\varepsilon$.*
- *There exists $\gamma \in \mathbb{R}_+$ such that for all x, $B(x) = -\varepsilon$ implies $\nabla_f B(x) \leq -\gamma$.*

Formally, the condition is defined as

$$\mathsf{Barrier}_\varepsilon(f, \mathsf{init}, B) \equiv_{df} \forall^D x \Big(\mathsf{init}(x) \to B(x) \leq -\varepsilon \Big)$$

$$\wedge \, \exists^{(0,\infty)} \gamma \forall^D x \Big(B(x) = -\varepsilon \to \nabla_f B(x) \leq -\gamma \Big)$$

It should be intuitively clear from the definition that the existence of ε-barrier functions is sufficient for establishing invariants and safety properties. The new requirement is that the system stays robustly within the barrier, by the area defined by $-\varepsilon \leq B(x) \leq 0$.

Theorem 4. *For any $\varepsilon \in \mathbb{R}_+$, $\mathsf{Barrier}_\varepsilon(f, \mathsf{init}, B) \to \mathsf{Safe}(f, \mathsf{init}, B)$.*

Proof. Assume $\mathsf{Barrier}_\varepsilon(f, \mathsf{init}, B)$ is true. It is easy to see $\mathsf{Barrier}(f, \mathsf{init}, B+\varepsilon)$, as specified in Definition 10, is also true. Therefore, using Proposition 3, we know $\mathsf{Safe}(f, \mathsf{init}, B + \epsilon)$ and hence $\mathsf{Safe}(f, \mathsf{init}, B)$ are both true. □

It is clear that there is room for numerically perturbing the size of the area and still obtaining a robust proof. The proof is similar to the one for Lemma 1 as shown in [8].

Theorem 5. *For any $\varepsilon \in \mathbb{R}_+$, there exists $\delta \in \mathbb{Q}_+$ such that $\mathsf{Barrier}_\varepsilon(f, \mathsf{init}, B)$ is a δ-robust formula.*

Example 2 (Type 1 ε-Barrier for timed-reversed Van der Pol). Consider the time-reversed Van der Pol system introduced in Example 1. We use the same example to demonstrate the effect of numerical errors in proving barrier certificates. The level sets of the Lyapunov functions in the stable region are barrier certificates; however, for the barriers that are very close to the limiting cycle, numerical sensitivity becomes a problem. In experiments, when $\varepsilon = 10^{-5}$ and $\delta = 10^{-4}$, we can verify that the level set $z^T P z = 90$, is a Type 1 ε-barrier. Table 2 lists parameters used in this proof. Figure 3 (Left) shows the direction field for the timed-reversed Van der Pol dynamics, the border of the set $z^T P z \leq 90$, which we prove is a type 1 ε-barrier, and the boundary of set $z^T P z \leq 110$, which is clearly not a barrier, since it is outside of the limit cycle.

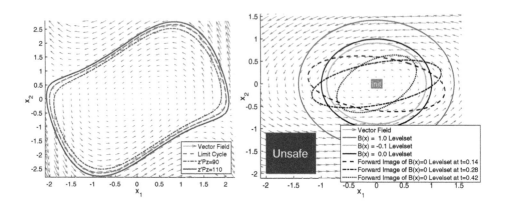

Fig. 3. (Left) Van der pol example (Right) Type 2 barrier example

The conditions for ε-Lyapunov and ε-barrier functions look very similar, but there is an important difference. In the case of Lyapunov functions, we do not evaluate the Lie derivative of the balls. Thus, the balls do not define barrier sets. On the other hand, the level sets of Lyapunov functions always define barriers.

Remark 3. The ε-barrier functions can also be used as a sufficient condition for ε-stability, if a barrier can be found within the ε-ball required in ε-stability.

Remark 4. A technical requirement for proving robustness of the ε-barrier conditions is that ¬init defines a simple set that can be over-approximated, such that for every $\varepsilon \in \mathbb{R}_+$, there is $\delta \in \mathbb{R}_+$ such that for any point that satisfies ¬init$^{+\delta}$ there is an ε-close point that satisfies ¬init. A sufficient condition for this restriction is that init be of the form $(\bigwedge_i a_i \leq x_i \leq b_i) \rightarrow \varphi(x)$, where $a_i, b_i \in \mathbb{Q}$ are arbitrary constants, and φ is a quantifier-free formula with only strict inequalities [22].

4.3   Type 2: Bounded Escape

We now introduce the second set of conditions for establishing ε-invariant sets. This set of conditions can be used only when the ε-variations are considered. This notion is inspired by the notion of k-step invariants [3] for discrete-time systems. The ε-margin that we allow at the boundary of the invariants allows us to exploit more techniques. Using reachable set computation, we can directly check if all states stay within the barrier set at each step. To ensure that the conditions are inductive and useful, we need to impose the following two requirements:

- (Contraction) Similar to the strengthening in barrier certificates, we require that the system does not *sit at the boundary*: the dynamics at the boundary should be contracting. The difference with Type 1 ε-barriers is that, this condition is not imposed through the vector field on the boundary. Instead, it is a reachability condition: after some amount of time, all states should return to the interior of an appropriate set.

– (Bounded Escape) Before reaching back to the invariant set, we allow the system to step outside the invariant, but only up to a bounded distance from the boundary.

The intuition is depicted in Fig. 2d. In the formal definition, we parameterize the conditions with the time for contraction and the maximum deviation from the invariant set, as follows.

Definition 12 (Type 2 Barrier Functions). *Let $T, \varepsilon \in \mathbb{R}_+$ be arbitrary. We say a continuous scalar function B defines a (T, ε)-elastic barrier function, iff the following conditions hold:*

1. *For any x, $\mathsf{init}(x)$ implies $B(x) \leq -\varepsilon$.*
2. *There exists $\varepsilon' > \varepsilon$ such that any state in $B(x) \leq -\varepsilon$ will enter $B(x) \leq -\varepsilon'$ after time T.*
3. *During time $[0, T]$, the system may step outside of $B(x) \leq -\varepsilon$ but there exists some $\varepsilon^* \in (0, \varepsilon]$ such that all states stay within $B(x) \leq -\varepsilon^*$.*

In all, we define the conditions with the following formula

$$\mathsf{Barrier}_{T,\varepsilon}(f, \mathsf{init}, B) \equiv_{df} \forall^D x \Big(\mathsf{init}(x) \to B(x) \leq -\varepsilon \Big)$$
$$\wedge\, \exists^{(0,\varepsilon]} \varepsilon^* \forall^D x \forall^{[0,T]} t \Big((B(x) = -\varepsilon) \to B(F(x,t)) \leq -\varepsilon^* \Big)$$
$$\wedge\, \exists^{(\varepsilon,\infty)} \varepsilon' \forall^D x \Big((B(x) = -\varepsilon) \to B(F(x,T)) \leq -\varepsilon' \Big)$$

Theorem 6, shows that conditions in Definition 12 ensure that the system never leaves the invariant $B \leq 0$. The key is the second condition: induction works because all states come back to the interior of the set defined by $B \leq -\varepsilon$. With the third condition only, we cannot perform induction because the set may keep growing.

Theorem 6. *For any $T, \varepsilon \in \mathbb{R}_+$, $\mathsf{Barrier}_{T,\varepsilon}(f, \mathsf{init}, B) \to \mathsf{Safe}(f, \mathsf{init}, B)$.*

Proof. For the purpose of contradiction, suppose starting from $x_0 \in \mathsf{init}$, the system is unsafe. Using continuity of the barrier B and the solution function F, let $t \in \mathbb{R}_{\geq 0}$ be a time at which $B(x(t)) = 0$, where $x(t)$ is by definition $F(x_0, t)$. By the 1st property in Definition 12, we know $B(x_0) \leq -\varepsilon < 0$. Using continuity of B and F, let $t' \in [0, t)$ be the supremum of all times at which $B(x(t')) = -\varepsilon$. By the 3rd property in Definition 12, we know $t - t' > T$, and by the 2nd property in Definition 12, we know $B(x(t' + T)) \leq -\varepsilon' < -\varepsilon$. Using continuity of B and F, we know there is a time $t'' \in (t' + T, t)$ at which $B(x(t'')) = -\varepsilon$. However, this is in contradiction with t' being the supremum. $\qquad\square$

Theorem 7. *For any $\varepsilon \in \mathbb{R}_+$, there exists $\delta \in \mathbb{Q}_+$ such that $\mathsf{Barrier}_{T,\varepsilon}(f, \mathsf{init}, B)$ is a δ-robust formula.*

Example 3. We use this example to show how Type 2 ε-barriers can be used to establish safety. Consider the following system.

$$\begin{bmatrix} \dot{x}_1 \\ \dot{x}_2 \end{bmatrix} = \begin{bmatrix} -0.1 & -10 \\ 4 & -2 \end{bmatrix} \begin{bmatrix} x_1 \\ x_2 \end{bmatrix}$$

Let init be the set $\{x \mid -0.1 \le x_1 \le 0.1, -0.1 \le x_2 \le 0.1\}$, and let U, the unsafe set, be the set $\{x \mid -2.0 \le x_1 \le -1.1, -2.0 \le x_2 \le -1.1\}$. The system is stable and safe with respect to the designated unsafe set. However, the safety cannot be shown using any invariant of the form $B(x) := x_1^2 + x_2^2 - c \le 0$, where $c \in \mathbb{Q}_+$ is a constant, in the standard definition. This is because the vector field on the boundary of such sets do not satisfy the inductive conditions. Nevertheless, we can show that for $c = 1$, $B(x)$ is a Type 2 ε-barrier. The dReal query verifies the conditions with $\varepsilon = 0.1$. Since $U(x) \to B(x) > \epsilon$ and init$(x) \to B(x) < -\varepsilon'$, we know that the system cannot reach any unsafe states. Figure 3 (Right), illustrates the example. The green set at the center represents init, and the red set represents unsafe set U. The $B(x) = 0$ level set is not invariant, as evidenced in the figure by the forward images at $t = 0.14$ and $t = 0.28$ leaving the set; however, as the dReal query proves, the reachable set over $0 \le t \le 10$ does not leave the $B(x) = 1.0$ level set and is completely contained in the $B(x) = -0.1$ level set by $t = 0.4$. Since $U(x) \to B(x) > 1.0$ and init$(x) \to B(x) < -0.1$, then the system cannot reach any state in U.

5   Experiments

In this section, we show examples of nonlinear systems that can be verified to be ε-stable or safe with ε-barriers.

Table 1. Results for the ε-Lyapunov functions. Each Lyapunov function is of the form $z^T P z$, where z is a vector of monomials over the state variables. We report the constant values satisfying the ε-Lyapunov conditions, and the time that verification of each example takes (in seconds).

Example	α	β	γ	ε	ε'	Time (s)
T.R. Van der Pol	2.10×10^{-23}	1.70×10^{-23}	10^{-25}	10^{-12}	5×10^{-13}	0.05
Norm. Pend.	7.07×10^{-23}	3.97×10^{-23}	10^{-50}	10^{-12}	5×10^{-13}	0.01
Moore-Greitzer	2.95×10^{-19}	2.55×10^{-19}	10^{-20}	10^{-10}	5×10^{-11}	0.04

Table 1 contains parameters we use to verify requirements of Definition 8 for ε-Lyapunov functions in our examples. Table 2 contains parameters we use to verify requirements of Definition 11 for Type 1 ε-barrier functions in our examples. The ε-Lyapunov functions in these examples are of the form $V(x) := z^T P z$, where z is a vector of products of the state variables and P is a constant

Table 2. Results for the ε-barrier functions. Each barrier function $B(x)$ is of the form $z^T P z - \ell$, where z is a vector of monomials over x. We indicate the highest degree of the monomials used in z, the size of the P, the level ℓ used for each barrier function, and the value of ε and γ used to the check $\nabla_f B(x) < -\gamma$.

Example	ℓ	ε	γ	degree (z)	Size of P	Time (s)
T.R. Van der Pol	90	10^{-5}	10^{-5}	3	9×9	6.47
Norm. Pend.	$[0.1, 10]$	10^{-2}	10^{-2}	1	2×2	0.08
Moore-Greitzer	$[1.0, 10]$	10^{-1}	10^{-1}	4	5×5	13.80
PTC	0.01	10^{-5}	10^{-5}	2	14×14	428.75

matrix obtained using simulation-guided techniques from [10]. All the P matrices are given in [8].

Time-Reversed Van der Pol. The time-reversed Van der Pol system has been used as an example in the previous sections. Figure 3 (Left) shows the direction field of this system around the origin. Using dReal with $\delta := 10^{-25}$, we are able to establish a 10^{-12}-Lyapunov function and a 10^{-5}-barrier function.

Normalized Pendulum. A standard pendulum system has continuous dynamics containing a transcendental function, which causes difficulty for many techniques. Here, we consider a normalized pendulum system with the following dynamics, in which x_1 and x_2 represent angular position and velocity, respectively. In our experiment, using $\delta = 10^{-50}$, we can prove that function $V := x^T P x$ is ε-Lyapunov, where $\varepsilon := 10^{-12}$.

$$\begin{bmatrix} \dot{x}_1 \\ \dot{x}_2 \end{bmatrix} = \begin{bmatrix} x_2 \\ -\sin(x_1) - x_2 \end{bmatrix} \tag{3}$$

Using $\delta := 0.01$, we are able to prove that for *any* value $\ell \in [0.1, 10]$, the function $B(x) := x^T P x - \ell$, with x being the system state, and P a constant matrix given in [8], is a Type 1 0.01-barrier function.

Moore-Greitzer Jet Engine. Next, we consider a simplified version of the Moore-Greitzer model for a jet engine. The system has the following dynamics, in which x_1 and x_2 are states related to mass flow and pressure rise.

$$\begin{bmatrix} \dot{x}_1 \\ \dot{x}_2 \end{bmatrix} = \begin{bmatrix} -x_2 - \frac{3}{2}x_1^2 - \frac{1}{2}x_1^3 \\ 3x_1 - x_2 \end{bmatrix} \tag{4}$$

In our experiment, using $\delta = 10^{-20}$ and $z := [x_1^2, x_1 x_2, x_2^2, x_1, x_2]^T$, we can prove that function $V := z^T P z$ is ε-Lyapunov, where $\varepsilon := 10^{-10}$.

Using dReal with $\delta := 0.1$, we are able to prove that for *any* value $\ell \in [1, 10]$, the function $B(x) := z^T P z - \ell$, with x being the system state, z being the vector of monomials defined in the previous section, and P a constant matrix given in [8], is a Type 1 0.1-barrier function.

Powertrain Control System. Next, we consider a closed-loop model of a powertrain control (PTC) system for an automotive application. The system dynamics consist of four state variables, two associated with a plant and two for a controller. The plant models fuel and air dynamics of an internal combustion engine and the controller is designed to regulate the air-fuel (A/F) ratio within a given range of an optimal value, referred as stoichiometric value. Two states related to the plant represent the manifold pressure, p, and the ratio between actual A/F ratio and stoichiometric value, r. The two associated with the controller are the estimated manifold pressure, p_{est}, and the internal state of the PI controller, i. The system is highly nonlinear, with the following dynamics

$$
\begin{aligned}
\dot{p} &= c_1 \left(2\hat{u}_1 \sqrt{\frac{p}{c_{11}} - \left(\frac{p}{c_{11}}\right)^2} - (c_3 + c_4 c_2 p + c_5 c_2 p^2 + c_6 c_2^2 p) \right) \\
\dot{r} &= 4 \left(\frac{c_3 + c_4 c_2 p + c_5 c_2 p^2 + c_6 c_2^2 p}{c_{13}(c_3 + c_4 c_2 p_{est} + c_5 c_2 p_{est}^2 + c_6 c_2^2 p_{est})(1 + i + c_{14}(r - c_{16}))} - r \right) \\
\dot{p}_{est} &= c_1 \left(2\hat{u}_1 \sqrt{\frac{p}{c_{11}} - \left(\frac{p}{c_{11}}\right)^2} - c_{13} \left(c_3 + c_4 c_2 p_{est} + c_5 c_2 p_{est}^2 + c_6 c_2^2 p_{est} \right) \right) \\
\dot{i} &= c_{15}(r - c_{16})
\end{aligned}
$$

which followed the detailed description of the model and the constant parameter values in [10]. We verified that there exists a function of the form $B(x) = z^T P z - 0.01$ (z consist of 14 monomials with a maximum degree of 2), where $\nabla_f B(x) < -\gamma$, when $B(x) = -\varepsilon$.

6   Conclusion

We formulated new inductive proof rules for stability and safety for dynamical systems. The rules are numerically robust, making them amenable to verification using automated reasoning tools such as those based on δ-decision procedures. We presented several examples demonstrating the value of the new approach, including safety verification tasks for highly nonlinear systems. The examples show that the framework can be used to prove stability and safety for examples that were out of reach for existing tools. The new framework relies on the ability to generate reasonable candidate Lyapunov functions, which are analogous to ranking functions from program analysis. Future work will include improved techniques for efficiently generating the ε-Lyapunov and ε-barrier functions and related theoretical questions.

Acknowledgement. Our work is supported by the United States Air Force and DARPA under Contract No. FA8750-18-C-0092, AFOSR No. FA9550-19-1-0041, and the National Science Foundation under NSF CNS No. 1830399. Any opinions, findings and conclusions or recommendations expressed in this material are those of the author(s) and do not necessarily reflect the views of the United States Air Force and DARPA.

References

1. Bak, S.: t-Barrier certificates: a continuous analogy to k-induction. In: IFAC Conference on Analysis and Design of Hybrid Systems (2018)
2. Bernfeld, S.R., Lakshmikantham, V.: Practical stability and Lyapunov functions. Tohoku Math. J. (2) **32**(4), 607–613 (1980)
3. Bobiti, R., Lazar, M.: A delta-sampling verification theorem for discrete-time, possibly discontinuous systems. In: HSCC (2015)
4. Collins, G.E.: Quantifier elimination for real closed fields by cylindrical algebraic decompostion. In: Brakhage, H. (ed.) GI-Fachtagung 1975. LNCS, vol. 33, pp. 134–183. Springer, Heidelberg (1975). https://doi.org/10.1007/3-540-07407-4_17
5. Fränzle, M., Herde, C., Teige, T., Ratschan, S., Schubert, T.: Efficient solving of large non-linear arithmetic constraint systems with complex boolean structure. JSAT **1**(3–4), 209–236 (2007)
6. Gao, S., Avigad, J., Clarke, E.: Delta-complete decision procedures for satisfiability over the reals. In: Proceedings of the Automated Reasoning - 6th International Joint Conference, IJCAR 2012, Manchester, UK, 26–29 June 2012, pp. 286–300 (2012)
7. Gao, S., Avigad, J., Clarke, E.M.: Delta-decidability over the reals. In: LICS, pp. 305–314. IEEE Computer Society (2012)
8. Gao, S., et al.: Numerically-robust inductive proof rules for continuous dynamical systems (extended version) (2019). https://dreal.github.io/CAV19/
9. Gao, S., Kong, S., Clarke, E.M.: dReal: an SMT solver for nonlinear theories over the reals. In: Bonacina, M.P. (ed.) CADE 2013. LNCS (LNAI), vol. 7898, pp. 208–214. Springer, Heidelberg (2013). https://doi.org/10.1007/978-3-642-38574-2_14
10. Kapinski, J., Deshmukh, J.V., Sankaranarayanan, S., Aréchiga, N.: Simulation-guided Lyapunov analysis for hybrid dynamical systems. In: Hybrid Systems: Computation and Control (2014)
11. Khalil, H.K.: Nonlinear Systems. Prentice Hall, Upper Saddle River (1996)
12. Kong, S., Gao, S., Chen, W., Clarke, E.: dReach: δ-reachability analysis for hybrid systems. In: Baier, C., Tinelli, C. (eds.) TACAS 2015. LNCS, vol. 9035, pp. 200–205. Springer, Heidelberg (2015). https://doi.org/10.1007/978-3-662-46681-0_15
13. Kong, S., Solar-Lezama, A., Gao, S.: Delta-decision procedures for exists-forall problems over the reals. In: Chockler, H., Weissenbacher, G. (eds.) CAV 2018. LNCS, vol. 10982, pp. 219–235. Springer, Cham (2018). https://doi.org/10.1007/978-3-319-96142-2_15
14. LaSalle, J.P., Lefschetz, S.: Stability by Liapunov's Direct Method: With Applications. Mathematics in Science and Engineering. Academic Press, New York (1961)
15. Liberzon, D., Ying, C., Zharnitsky, V.: On almost Lyapunov functions. In: 2014 IEEE 53rd Annual Conference on Decision and Control (CDC), pp. 3083–3088, December 2014
16. Monniaux, D.: A survey of satisfiability modulo theory. In: Gerdt, V.P., Koepf, W., Seiler, W.M., Vorozhtsov, E.V. (eds.) CASC 2016. LNCS, vol. 9890, pp. 401–425. Springer, Cham (2016). https://doi.org/10.1007/978-3-319-45641-6_26
17. Papachristodoulou, A., Prajna, S.: Analysis of non-polynomial systems using the sum of squares decomposition. In: Henrion, D., Garulli, A. (eds.) Positive Polynomials in Control. LNCIS, vol. 312, pp. 23–43. Springer, Heidelberg (2005). https://doi.org/10.1007/10997703_2
18. Parrilo, P.: Structured semidenite programs and semialgebraic geometry methods in robustness and optimization. Ph.D. thesis, August 2000

19. Platzer, A., Clarke, E.M.: Computing differential invariants of hybrid systems as fixedpoints. In: Gupta, A., Malik, S. (eds.) CAV 2008. LNCS, vol. 5123, pp. 176–189. Springer, Heidelberg (2008). https://doi.org/10.1007/978-3-540-70545-1_17

20. Podelski, A., Wagner, S.: Model checking of hybrid systems: from reachability towards stability. In: Hespanha, J.P., Tiwari, A. (eds.) HSCC 2006. LNCS, vol. 3927, pp. 507–521. Springer, Heidelberg (2006). https://doi.org/10.1007/11730637_38

21. Prajna, S.: Optimization-based methods for nonlinear and hybrid systems verification. Ph.D. thesis, California Institute of Technology, Pasadena, CA, USA (2005). AAI3185641

22. Roohi, N., Prabhakar, P., Viswanathan, M.: Relating syntactic and semantic perturbations of hybrid automata. In: CONCUR, pp. 26:1–26:16 (2018)

23. Tarski, A.: A Decision Method for Elementary Algebra and Geometry, 2nd edn. University of California Press, Berkeley (1951)

24. Topcu, U., Packard, A., Seiler, P.: Local stability analysis using simulations and sum-of-squares programming. Automatica 44, 2669–2675 (2008)

25. Weihrauch, K.: Computable Analysis: An Introduction, 1st edn. Springer, Heidelberg (2013)

26. Weiss, L., Infante, E.F.: On the stability of systems defined over a finite time interval. Proc. Nat. Acad. Sci. U.S.A. 54(1), 44 (1965)

27. Weiss, L., Infante, E.F.: Finite time stability under perturbing forces and on product spaces. IEEE Trans. Autom. Control 12(1), 54–59 (1967)

28. Xu, X., Tabuada, P., Grizzle, J.W., Ames, A.D.: Robustness of control barrier functions for safety critical control. IFAC-PapersOnLine 48(27), 54–61 (2015)

29. Zhai, G., Michel, A.N.: On practical stability of switched systems. In: Proceedings of the 41st IEEE Conference on Decision and Control, vol. 3, pp. 3488–3493, December 2002

30. Zhai, G., Michel, A.N.: Generalized practical stability analysis of discontinuous dynamical systems. In: Proceedings of the 42nd IEEE Conference on Decision and Control, vol. 2, pp. 1663–1668. IEEE (2003)

12

Efficient Verification of Network Fault Tolerance via Counterexample-Guided Refinement

Nick Giannarakis[1(✉)], Ryan Beckett[2],
Ratul Mahajan[3,4], and David Walker[1]

[1] Princeton University, Princeton, NJ 08544, USA
{ng8,dpw}@cs.princeton.edu
[2] Microsoft Research, Redmond, WA 98052, USA
ryan.beckett@microsoft.com

[3] University of Washington, Seattle, WA 98195, USA
ratul@cs.washington.edu
[4] Intentionet, Seattle, WA, USA

Abstract. We show how to verify that large data center networks satisfy key properties such as all-pairs reachability under a bounded number of faults. To scale the analysis, we develop algorithms that identify network symmetries and compute small abstract networks from large concrete ones. Using counter-example guided abstraction refinement, we successively refine the computed abstractions until the given property may be verified. The soundness of our approach relies on a novel notion of network approximation: routing paths in the concrete network are not precisely simulated by those in the abstract network but are guaranteed to be "at least as good." We implement our algorithms in a tool called Origami and use them to verify reachability under faults for standard data center topologies. We find that Origami computes abstract networks with 1–3 orders of magnitude fewer edges, which makes it possible to verify large networks that are out of reach of existing techniques.

1 Introduction

Most networks decide how to route packets from point A to B by executing one or more distributed routing protocols such as the Border Gateway Protocol (BGP) and Open Shortest Path First (OSPF). To achieve end-to-end policy objectives related to cost, load balancing, security, etc., network operators author configurations for each router. These configurations control various aspects of the route computation such as filtering and ranking route information received from neighbors, information injection from one protocol to another, and so on.

This flexibility, however, comes at a cost: Configuring individual routers to enforce the desired policies of the distributed system is complex and error-prone [15,21]. The problem of configuration is further compounded by three challenges. The first is network scale. Large networks such as those of cloud providers can consist of millions of lines of configuration spread across thousands of devices. The second is that operators must account for the interaction with external neighbors who may sent arbitrary routing messages. Finally one has to deal with *failures*. Hardware failures are common [14] and lead to a combinatorial explosion of different possible network behaviors.

To combat the complexity of distributed routing configurations, researchers have suggested a wide range of network verification [2,13,25] and simulation [11,12,23] techniques. These techniques are effective on small and medium-sized networks, but they cannot analyze data centers with 1000s of routers and all their possible failures. To enable scalable analyses, it seems necessary to exploit the symmetries that exist in most large real networks. Indeed, other researchers have exploited symmetries to scale verification in the past [3,22]. However, it has never been possible to account for failures, as they introduce asymmetries that change routing behaviors in unpredictable ways.

To address this challenge, we develop a new algorithm for verifying reachability in networks in the presence of faults, based on the idea of counterexample-guided abstraction refinement (CEGAR) [5]. The algorithm starts by factoring out symmetries using techniques developed in prior work [3] and then attempts verification of the abstract network using an SMT solver. If verification succeeds, we are done. However, if verification fails, we examine the counter-example to decide whether we have a true failure or we must refine the network further and attempt verification anew. By focusing on reachability, the refinement procedure can be accelerated by using efficient graph algorithms, such as min cut, to rule out invalid abstractions in the middle of the CEGAR loop.

We prove the correctness of our algorithm using a new theory of faulty networks that accounts for the impact of all combinations of k failures. Our key insight is that, while routes computed in the abstract network may not simulate those of the concrete network exactly, under the right conditions they are guaranteed to *approximate* them. The approximation relation between concrete and abstract networks suffices to verify key properties such as reachability.

We implemented our algorithms in a tool called Origami and measured their performance on common data center network topologies. We find that Origami computes abstract networks with 1–3 orders of magnitude fewer edges. This reduction speeds verification dramatically and enables verification of networks that are out of reach of current state-of-the-art tools [2].

2   Key Ideas

The goal of Origami is to speed up network verification in the presence of faults, and it does so by computing small, abstract networks with *similar* behavior to a given concrete network.

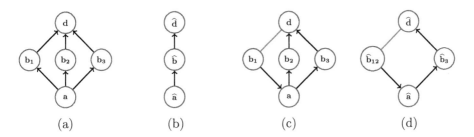

Fig. 1. All graph edges shown correspond to edges in the network topology, and we draw edges as directed to denote the direction of forwarding eventually determined for each node by the distributed routing protocols for a fixed destination d. In (a) nodes use shortest path routing to route to the destination d. (b) shows a compressed network that precisely captures the forwarding behavior of (a). (c) shows how forwarding is impacted by a link failure, shown as a red line. (d) shows a compressed network that is sound approximation of the original network for any single link failure. (Color figure online)

As a first approximation, one can view a network as a directed graph capturing the physical topology, and its routing solution as a subgraph where the remaining edges denote the forwarding decision at each node for some fixed destination. In the absence of faults, given a concrete and abstract network, one can define a natural notion of similarity as a graph homomorphism: assigning each concrete node a corresponding abstract node such that, for any solution to the routing problem, the concrete node forwards "in the same direction" as the corresponding abstract node. For example, the concrete network in Fig. 1a is related to its abstract counterpart in Fig. 1b according to the node colors.

Unfortunately, we run into two significant problems when defining abstractions in this manner in the presence of faults. First, the concrete nodes of Fig. 1a have at least 2 disjoint paths to the destination whereas abstract nodes of Fig. 1b have just one path to the destination, so the abstract network does not preserve the desired fault tolerance properties. Second, consider Fig. 1c, which illustrates how the routing decisions change when a failure occurs. Here, the nodes (b_1 in particular) no longer route "in the same direction" as the original network or its abstraction. Hence the invariant connecting concrete and abstract networks is violated.

Lossy Compression. To achieve compression given a bounded number of link failures, we relax the notion of similarity between concrete and abstract nodes: A node in the abstract network may merely *approximate* the behavior of concrete nodes. This makes it possible to compress nodes that, in the presence of failures, may route differently. In general, when we fail a single link in the abstract network, we are over-approximating the failures in the concrete network by failing multiple concrete links, possibly more than desired. Nevertheless, the paths taken in the concrete network can only deviate so much from the paths found in the abstract network:

Property 1. If a node has a route to the destination in the presence of k link failures then it has a route that is "at least as good" (as prescribed by the routing protocol) in the presence of k' link failures for $k' < k$.

This relation suffices to verify important network reliability properties, such as reachability, in the presence of faults. Just as importantly, it allows us to achieve effective network compression to scale verification.

Revisiting our example, consider the new abstract network of Fig. 1d. When the link between $\widehat{b}_{12}$ and $\widehat{d}$ has failed, $\widehat{b}_{12}$ still captures the behavior of b_1 precisely. However, b_2 has a better (in this case better means shorter) path to d. Despite this difference, if the operator's goal was to prove reachability to the destination under any single fault, then this abstract network suffices.

From Specification to Algorithm. It is not too difficult to find abstract networks that approximate a concrete network; the challenge is finding a valid abstract network that is *small enough* to make verification feasible and yet *large enough* to include sufficiently many paths to verify the given fault tolerance property. Rather than attempting to compute a single abstract network with the right properties all in one shot, we search the space of abstract networks using an algorithm based on *counter-example guided abstraction refinement* [5].

The CEGAR algorithm begins by computing the smallest possible valid abstract network. In the example above, this corresponds to the original compressed network in Fig. 1b, which faithfully approximates the original network when there are no link failures. However, if we try to verify reachability in the presence of a single fault, we will conclude that nodes $\widehat{b}$ and $\widehat{a}$ have no route to the destination when the link between $\widehat{b}$ and $\widehat{d}$ fails. The counterexample due to this failure could of course be spurious (and indeed it is). Fortunately, we can easily distinguish whether such a failure is due to lack of connectivity or an artifact of over-abstracting, by calculating the number of corresponding concrete failures. In this example a failure on the link $\langle \widehat{b}, \widehat{d} \rangle$ corresponds to 3 concrete failures. Since we are interested in verifying reachability for a single failure this cannot constitute an actual counterexample.

The next step is to *refine* our abstraction by splitting some of the abstract nodes. The idea is to use the counterexample from the previous iteration to split the abstract network in a way that avoids giving rise to the same spurious counterexample in the next iteration (Sect. 5). Doing so results in the somewhat larger network of Fig. 1d. A second verification pass over this larger network takes longer, but succeeds.

3   The Network Model

Though there are a wide variety of routing protocols in use today, they share a lot in common. Griffin *et al.* [16] showed that protocols like BGP and others solve instances of the *stable paths problem*, a generalization of the shortest paths problem, and Sobrinho [24] demonstrated their semantics and properties can be modelled using routing algebras. We extend these foundations by defining *stable paths problems with faults* (SPPFs), an extension of the classic Stable Paths Problem that admits the possibility of a bounded number of link failures. In later sections, we use this network model to develop generic network compression algorithms and reason about their correctness.

Stable Path Problems with Faults (SPPFs): An SPPF is an instance of the stable paths problem with faults. Informally, each instance defines the routing behavior of an operational network. The definition includes both the network topology as well as the routing policy. The policy specifies the way routing messages are transformed as they travel along links and through the user-configured import and export filters/transformers of the devices, and also how the preferred routes are chosen at a given device. In our formulation, each problem instance also incorporates a specification of the possible failures and their impact on the routing solutions.

Formally, an SPPF is a tuple with six components:

1. A graph $G = \langle V, E \rangle$ denoting the network topology.
2. A set of "attributes" (*i.e.*, routing messages) $A_\infty = A \cup \{\infty\}$ that may be exchanged between devices. The symbol ∞ represents the absence of a route.
3. A destination $d \in V$ and its initial route announcement $a_d \in A$. For simplicity, each SPPF has exactly one destination (d). (To model a network with many destinations, one would use a set of SPPFs.)
4. A partial order $\prec \subseteq A_\infty \times A_\infty$ ranks attributes. If $a \prec b$ then we say route a is preferred over route b. Any route $a \in A$ is preferred to no route ($a \prec \infty$).
5. A function $\mathsf{trans} : E \to A_\infty \to A_\infty$ that denotes how messages are processed across edges. This function models the route maps and filters that transform route announcements as they enter or leave routers.
6. A bound k on the maximum number of link failures that may occur.

Examples: By choosing an appropriate set of routing attributes, a preference relation and a transfer function, one can model the semantics of commonly used routing protocols. For instance, the Routing Information Protocol (RIP) is a simple shortest paths protocol. It can be modelled by an SPPF where (1) the set of attributes A is the set of integers between 0 and 15 (*i.e.*, the set of permitted path lengths), (2) the preference relation is integer inequality so shorter paths are preferred, and (3) the transfer function increments the received attribute by 1 or drops the route if it exceeds the maximum hop count of 15:

$$\mathsf{trans}(e, a) = \begin{cases} \infty & \text{if } a \geq 15 \\ a + 1 & \text{otherwise} \end{cases}$$

Going beyond simple shortest paths, BGP is a complex, policy-driven protocol that drives the Internet, and increasingly, data centers [18]. Operators often choose BGP due to its high expressiveness. We can model a version of BGP (simplified for presentation) using messages consisting of triples $(\mathrm{LP}, \mathrm{Comm}, \mathrm{Path})$

where LP is an integer-valued local preference, Comm is a set of community values (which are essentially string tags) and Path is a list of nodes, representing the path a routing message has traversed. The transfer function always adds the current device to the Path (or drops the message if a loop is detected) and will modify the LP and Comm components of the attribute according to the device configuration. For instance, one device may attach a community tag to a route and another device may filter or modify routes that have the tag attached. The protocol semantics dictates the preference relation (preferring routes with higher local preference first, and shorter paths second). A more complete BGP model is not fundamentally harder to model—it simply has additional attribute fields and more complex transfer and preference relations [20].

SPPF Solutions: In a network, routers will repeatedly exchange messages, applying their transfer functions to neighbor routes and selecting a current best route based on the preference relation, until the network reaches a fixpoint (stable state). Interestingly, Griffin *et al.* [16] showed that all routing solutions can be described via a set of local stability constraints. We exploit this insight to define a series of logical constraints that capture all possible routing behaviors in a setting that includes link failures. More specifically, we define a *solution* (*aka, stable state*) S of an SPPF to be a pair $\langle \mathcal{L}, \mathcal{F} \rangle$ of a labelling $\mathcal{L}$ and a failure scenario $\mathcal{F}$. The labelling $\mathcal{L}$ is an assignment of the final attributes to nodes in the network. If an attribute a is assigned to node v, we say that node has selected (or prefers) that attribute over other attributes available to it. The chosen route also determines packet forwarding. If a node X selects a route from neighbor Y, then X will forward packets to Y. The failure scenario $\mathcal{F}$ is an assignment of 0 (has not failed) or 1 (has failed) to each edge in the network.

A solution $S = \langle \mathcal{L}, F \rangle$ to an SPPF $= (G, A, a_{\mathrm{d}}, \prec, \mathsf{trans}, k)$ is a stable state satisfying the following conditions:

$$\mathcal{L}(u) = \begin{cases} a_{\mathrm{d}} & u = d \\ \infty & \mathsf{choices}_S(u) = \emptyset \\ min_{\prec}(\{a \mid (e, a) \in \mathsf{choices}_S(u)\}) & \mathsf{choices}_S(u) \neq \emptyset \end{cases}$$

$$\textbf{subject to } \sum_{e \in E} \mathcal{F}(e) \leq k$$

where the choices from the neighbors of node u are defined as:

$$\mathsf{choices}_S(u) = \{(e, a) \mid e = \langle u, v \rangle, \ a = \mathsf{trans}(e, \mathcal{L}(v)), \ a \neq \infty, \ \mathcal{F}(e) = 0\}$$

The constraints require that every node has selected the best attribute (according to its preference relation) amongst those available from its neighbors. The destination's label must always be the initial attribute a_d. For verification, this attribute (or parts of it) may be symbolic, which helps model potentially unknown routing announcements from peers outside our network. For other nodes u, the selected attribute a is the minimal attribute from the *choices* available to u. Intuitively, to find the choices available to u, we consider the attributes b chosen by neighbors v of u. Then, if the edge between v and u is not failed, we push b along that edge, modifying it according to the trans function. Finally, failure scenarios are constrained so that the sum of the failures is at most k.

4   Network Approximation Theory

Given a concrete SPPF and an abstract $\widehat{\text{SPPF}}$, a network abstraction is a pair of functions (f, h) that relate the two. The topology abstraction $f : V \rightarrow \widehat{V}$ maps each node in the concrete network to a node in the abstract network, while the attribute abstraction $h : A_\infty \rightarrow \widehat{A}_\infty$ maps a concrete attribute to an abstract attribute. The latter allows us to relate networks running protocols where nodes may appear in the attributes (*e.g.* as in the Path component of BGP).

The goal of Origami is to compute compact $\widehat{\text{SPPFs}}$ that may be used for verification. These compact $\widehat{\text{SPPFs}}$ must be closely related to their concrete counterparts. Otherwise, properties verified on the compact $\widehat{\text{SPPF}}$ will not be true of their concrete counterpart. Section 4.1 defines *label approximation*, which provides an intuitive, high-level, semantic relationship between abstract and concrete networks. We also explain some of the consequences of this definition and its limitations. Unfortunately, while this broad definition serves as an important theoretical objective, it is difficult to use directly in an efficient algorithm. Section 4.2 continues our development by explaining two *well-formedness* requirements of network policies that play a key role in establishing label approximation *indirectly*. Finally, Sect. 4.3 defines *effective SPPF approximation* for well-formed SPPFs. This definition is more conservative than label approximation, but has the advantage that it is easier to work with algorithmically and, moreover, it implies label approximation.

4.1   Label Approximation

Intuitively, we say the abstract $\widehat{\text{SPPF}}$ label-approximates the concrete SPPF when SPPF has at least as good a route at every node as $\widehat{\text{SPPF}}$ does.

Definition 1 (Label Approximation). *Consider any solutions $\mathcal{S}$ to SPPF and $\widehat{\mathcal{S}}$ to $\widehat{\text{SPPF}}$ and their respective labelling components $\mathcal{L}$ and $\widehat{\mathcal{L}}$. We say $\widehat{\text{SPPF}}$ label-approximates SPPF when $\forall u \in V.\ h(\mathcal{L}(u)) \preceq \widehat{\mathcal{L}}(f(u))$.*

If we can establish a label approximation relation between a concrete and an abstract network, we can typically verify a number of properties of the abstract network and be sure they hold of the concrete network. However, the details of exactly which properties we can verify depend on the specifics of the preference relation ($\prec$). For example, in an OSPF network, preference is determined by weighted path length. Therefore, if we know an abstract node has a path of weighted length n, we know that its concrete counterparts have paths of weighted length of at most n. More importantly, since "no route" is the worst route, we know that if a node has any route to the destination in the abstract network, so do its concrete counterparts.

Limitations. Some properties are beyond the scope of our tool (independent of the preference relation). For example, our model cannot reason about quantitative properties such as bandwidth, probability of congestion, or latency.

4.2 Well-Formed SPPFs

Not all SPPFs are well-behaved. For example, some never converge and others do not provide sensible models of any real network. To avoid dealing with such poorly-behaved models, we demand henceforth that all SPPFs are *well-formed*. Well-formedness entails that an SPPF is strictly monotonic and isotonic:

$$\forall a, e. \ \ a \neq \infty \Rightarrow a \prec \mathsf{trans}(e, a) \qquad\qquad strict \ monotonicity$$
$$\forall a, b, e. \ \ a \preceq b \Rightarrow \mathsf{trans}(e, a) \preceq \mathsf{trans}(e, b) \qquad\qquad isotonicity$$

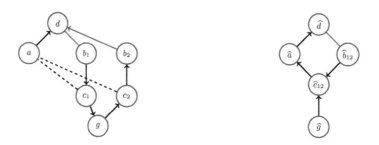

Fig. 2. Concrete network (left) and its corresponding abstraction (right). Nodes c_1, c_2 prefer to route through b_1 (resp. b_2), or g over a. Node b_1 (resp. b_2) drops routing messages that have traversed b_2 (resp. b_1). Red lines indicate a failed link. Dotted lines show a topologically available but unused link. A purple arrow show a route unusable by traffic from b_1. (Color figure online)

Monotonicity and isotonicity properties are often cited [7,8] as desirable properties of routing policies because they guarantee network convergence and prevent persistent oscillation. In practice too, prior studies have revealed that almost all real network configurations have these properties [13,19].

In our case, these properties help establish additional invariants that tie the routing behavior of concrete and abstract networks together. To gain some intuition as to why, consider the networks of Fig. 2. The concrete network on the left runs BGP with the routing policy that node c_1 (and c_2) prefers to route through node g instead of a, and that b_1 drops announcements coming from b_2. In this scenario, the similarly configured abstract node $\widehat{b}_{12}$ can reach the destination—it simply takes a route that happens to be less preferred by $\widehat{c}_{12}$ than it would if there had been no failure. However, in the concrete analogue, b_1, is *unable* to reach the destination because c_1 only sends it the route through b_2, which it cannot use. In this case, the concrete network has more topological paths than the abstract network, but, counterintuitively, due to the network's routing policy, this turns out to be a disadvantage. Hence having more paths does not necessarily make nodes more accessible. As a consequence, in general, abstract networks cannot soundly overapproximate the number of failures in a concrete network—an important property for the soundness of our theory.

The underlying issue here is that the networks of Fig. 2 are not isotonic: suppose $\mathcal{L}'(c_1)$ is the route from c_1 to the destination through node a, we have that $\mathcal{L}(c_1) \prec \mathcal{L}'(c_1)$ but since the transfer function over $\langle b_1, c_1 \rangle$ drops routes that have traversed node b_2, we have that $\mathsf{trans}(\langle b_1, c_1 \rangle, \mathcal{L}(c_1)) \not\prec \mathsf{trans}(\langle b_1, c_1 \rangle, \mathcal{L}'(c_1))$. Notice that $\mathcal{L}'(c_1)$ is essentially the route that the abstract network uses *i.e.* $h(\mathcal{L}'(c_1)) = \widehat{\mathcal{L}}(\hat{c}_{12})$, hence the formula above implies that $h(\mathcal{L}(b_1)) \not\prec \widehat{\mathcal{L}}(\hat{b}_{12})$ which violates the notion of label approximation. Fortunately, if a network is strictly monotonic and isotonic, such situations never arise. Moreover, we check these properties via an SMT solver using a local and efficient test.

4.3   Effective SPPF Approximation

We seek abstract networks that label-approximate given concrete networks. Unfortunately, to directly check that a particular abstract network label approximates a concrete network one must effectively compute their solutions. Doing so would defeat the entire purpose of abstraction, which seeks to analyze large concrete networks *without the expense of computing their solutions directly*.

In order to turn approximation into a useful computational tool, we define *effective approximation*, a set of simple conditions on the abstraction functions f and h that are *local* and can be checked efficiently. When true those conditions imply label approximation. Intuitively effective approximations impose three main restrictions on the abstraction functions:

1. The topology abstraction conforms to the ∀∃−abstraction condition; this requires that there is an abstract edge $(\hat{u}, \hat{v})$ iff for every concrete node u such that $f(u) = \hat{u}$ there is some node v such that $f(v) = \hat{v}$ and $(u, v) \in E$.
2. The abstraction preserves the rank of attributes *(rank-equivalence)*:

$$\forall a, b.\ a \prec b \iff h(a) \mathbin{\widehat{\precsim}} h(b)$$

3. The transfer function and the abstraction functions commute *(trans-equivalence)*:

$$\forall e, a.\ h(\mathsf{trans}(e, a)) = \widehat{\mathsf{trans}}(f(e), h(a))$$

We prove that when these conditions hold, we can approximate any solution of the concrete network with a solution of the abstract network.

Theorem 1. *Given a well-formed SPPF and its effective approximation $\widehat{\mathsf{SPPF}}$, for any solution $\mathcal{S} \in \mathsf{SPPF}$ there exists a solution $\hat{\mathcal{S}} \in \widehat{\mathsf{SPPF}}$, such that their labelling functions are label approximate.*

5   The Verification Procedure

The first step of verification is to compute a small abstract network that satisfies our SPPF *effective approximation* conditions. We do so by grouping network nodes and edges with equivalent policy and checking the forall-exists topological condition, using an algorithm reminiscent of earlier work [3]. Typically, however, this minimal abstraction will not contain enough paths to prove any fault-tolerance property. To identify a finer abstraction for which we can prove a fault-tolerance property we repeatedly:

1. Search the set of candidate refinements for the smallest *plausible* abstraction.
2. If the candidate abstraction satisfies the desired property, terminate the procedure. (We have successfully verified our concrete network.)
3. If not, examine whether the returned counterexample is an actual counterexample. We do so, by computing the number of concrete failures and check that it does not exceed the desired bound of link failures. (If so, we have found a property violation.)
4. If not, use the counterexample to *learn* how to expand the abstract network into a larger abstraction and repeat.

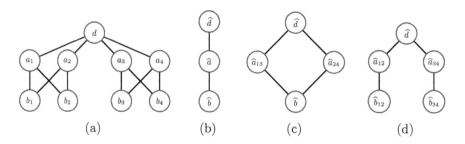

(a)   (b)   (c)   (d)

Fig. 3. Eight nodes in (a) are represented using two nodes in the abstract network (b). Pictures (c) and (d) show two possible ways to refine the abstract network (b).

Both the search for plausible candidates and the way we learn a new abstraction to continue the counterexample-guided loop are explained below.

5.1   Searching for Plausible Candidates

Though we might know an abstraction is not sufficient to verify a given fault tolerance property, there are many possible refinements. Consider, for example, Fig. 3(a) presents a simple concrete network that will tolerate a single link failure, and Fig. 3(b) presents an initial abstraction. The initial abstraction will not tolerate any link failure, so we must refine the network. To do so, we choose an abstract node to divide into two abstract nodes for the next iteration. We must also decide which concrete nodes correspond to each abstract node. For example, in Fig. 3(c), node $\hat{a}$ has been split into $\hat{a}_{13}$ and $\hat{a}_{24}$. The subscripts indicate the assignment of concrete nodes to abstract ones.

A significant complication is that once we have generated a new abstraction, we must check that it continues to satisfy the effective approximation conditions, and if not, we must do more work. Figure 3(c) satisfies those conditions, but if we were to split $\hat{a}$ into $\hat{a}_{12}$ and $\hat{a}_{34}$ rather than $\hat{a}_{13}$ and $\hat{a}_{24}$, the forall-exists condition would be violated—some of the concrete nodes associated with $\hat{b}$ are connected to the concrete nodes in $\hat{a}_{12}$ but not to the ones in $\hat{a}_{34}$ and vice versa. To repair the violation of the forall-exists condition, we need to split additional nodes. In this case, the $\hat{b}$ node, giving rise to diagram Fig. 3(d).

Overall, the process of splitting nodes and then recursively splitting further nodes to repair the forall-exists condition generates many possible candidate abstractions to consider. A key question is which candidate should we select to proceed with the abstraction refinement algorithm?

One consideration is size: A smaller abstraction avoids taxing the verifier, which is the ultimate goal. However, there are many small abstractions that we can quickly dismiss. Technically, we say an abstraction is *plausible* if all nodes of interest have at least $k + 1$ paths to the destination. Implausible abstractions cause nodes to become unreachable with k failures. To check whether an abstraction is plausible, we compute the *min-cut* of the graph. Figure 3(d) is an example of an implausible abstraction that arose after a poorly-chosen split of node $\hat{a}$. In this case, no node has 2 or more paths to the destination and hence they might not be able to reach the destination when there is a failure.

Clearly verification using an implausible abstraction will fail. Instead of considering such abstractions as candidates for running verification on, the refinement algorithm tries refining them further. A key decision the algorithm needs to make when refining an abstraction is *which abstract node to split*. For instance, the optimal refinement of Fig. 3(b) is Fig. 3(c). If we were to split node $\hat{b}$ instead of $\hat{a}$ we would end up with a sub-optimal (in terms of size) abstraction. Intuitively, splitting a node that lies on the min-cut and can reach the destination (e.g. $\hat{a}$) will increase the number of paths that its neighbors on the unreachable part of the min-cut (e.g. $\hat{b}$) can use to reach the destination.

To summarize, the search for new candidate abstractions involves (1) splitting nodes in the initial abstraction, (2) repairing the abstraction to ensure the forall-exists condition holds, (3) checking that the generated abstraction is *plausible*, and if not, (4) splitting additional nodes on the min cut. This iterative process will often generate many candidates. The *breadth* parameter of the search bounds the total number of plausible candidates we will generate in between verification efforts. Of all the plausible candidates generated, we choose the smallest one to verify using the SMT solver.

5.2 Learning from Counterexamples

Any nodes of an abstraction that have a min cut of less than $k+1$ definitely cannot tolerate k faults. If an abstraction is plausible, it satisfies a *necessary* condition for source-destination connectivity, but not a *sufficient* one—misconfigured routing policy can still cause nodes to be unreachable by modifying and/or subsequently dropping routing messages. For instance, the abstract network of Fig. 3c is plausible for one failure, but if $\widehat{b}$'s routing policy blocks routes of either $\widehat{a}_{13}$ or $\widehat{a}_{24}$ then the abstract network will not be 1-fault tolerant. Indeed, it is the complexity of routing policy that necessitates a heavy-weight verification procedure in the first place, rather than a simpler graph algorithm alone.

In a plausible abstraction, if the verifier computes a solution to the network that violates the desired fault-tolerance property, some node could not reach the destination because one or more of their paths to the destination could not be used to route traffic. We use the generated counterexample to learn edges that could not be used to route traffic due to the policy on them. To do so, we inspect the computed solution to find nodes $\widehat{u}$ that (1) lack a route to the destination (*i.e.* $\widehat{\mathcal{L}}(\widehat{u}) = \infty$), (2) have a neighbor $\widehat{v}$ that has a valid route to the destination, and (3) the link between $\widehat{u}$ and $\widehat{v}$ is not failed. These conditions imply the absence of a valid route to the destination not because link failures disabled all paths to the destination, but because the network policy dropped some routes. For example, in picture Fig. 3c, consider the case where $\widehat{b}$ does not advertise routes from $\widehat{a}_{13}$ and $\widehat{a}_{24}$; if the link between $\widehat{a}_{13}$ and $\widehat{d}$ fails, then $\widehat{a}_{13}$ has no route the destination and we learn that the edge $\langle \widehat{b}, \widehat{a}_{13} \rangle$ cannot be used. In fact, since $\widehat{a}_{13}$ and $\widehat{a}_{12}$ belonged to the same abstract group $\widehat{a}$ before we split them, their routing policies are equal modulo the abstraction function by trans-equivalence. Hence, we can infer that in a symmetric scenario, the link $\langle \widehat{b}, \widehat{a}_{24} \rangle$ will also be unusable.

Given a set of unuseable edges, learned from a counterexample, we restrict the min cut problems that define the plausible abstractions, by disallowing the use of those edges. Essentially, we enrich the refinement algorithm's topological based analysis (based on min-cut) with knowledge about the policy; the algorithm will have to generate abstractions that are plausible without using those edges. With those edges disabled, the refinement process continues as before.

6   Implementation

Origami uses the Batfish network analysis framework [12] to parse network configurations, and then translate them into a pure functional intermediate representation (IR) designed for network verification. This IR represents the structure of routing messages and the semantics of transfer and preference relations using standard functional data structures.

The translation generates a separate functional program for each destination subnet. In other words, if a network has 100 top-of-rack switches and each such switch announces the subnets for 30 adjacent hosts, then Origami generates 100 functional programs (*i.e.* problem instances). We separately apply our algorithms to each problem instance, converting the functional program to an SMT formula when necessary according to the algorithm described earlier. Since vendor routing configuration languages have limited expressive power (*e.g.*, no loops or recursion) the translation requires no user-provided invariants. We use Z3 [10] to determine satisfiability of the SMT problems. Solving the problems separately (and in parallel) provides a speedup over solving the routing problem for all destinations simultaneously: The individual problems are specialized to a particular destination. By doing so, opportunities for optimizations that reduce the problem size, such as dead code elimination, arise.

Optimizing Refinement: During the course of implementing Origami, we discovered a number of optimizations to the refinement phase.

- If the min-cut between the destination and a vertex u is less than or equal to the desired number of disjoint paths, then we do not need to compute another min-cut for the nodes in the unreachable portion of vertices T; we know nodes in T can be disconnected from the destination. This significantly reduces the number of min-cut computations.
- We stop exploring abstractions that are larger in size than the smallest plausible abstraction computed since the last invocation of the SMT solver.
- We bias our refinement process to explore the smallest abstractions first. When combined the previous optimization, this prunes our search space from some abstractions that were unnecessary large.

Minimizing Counterexamples: When the SMT solver returns a counterexample, it often uses the maximum number of failures. This is not surprising as maximizing failures simplifies the SMT problem. Unfortunately, it also confounds our analysis to determine whether a counterexample is real or spurious.

Topo	Con V/E	Fail	Abs V/E	Ratio	Abs Time	SMT Calls	SMT Time
FT20	500/8000	1	9/20	55.5/400	0.1	1	0.1
		3	40/192	12.5/41.67	1.0	2	7.6
		5	96/720	5.20/11.1	2.5	2	248
		10	59/440	8.48/18.18	0.9	-	-
FT40	2000/64000	1	12/28	166.7/2285.7	0.1	1	0.1
		3	45/220	44.4/290.9	33	2	12.3
		5	109/880	18.34/72.72	762.3	2	184.1
SP40	2000/64000	1	13/32	153.8/2000	0.2	1	0.1
		3	39/176	51.3/363.6	30.3	1	2
		5	79/522	25.3/122.6	372.2	1	22
FbFT	744/10880	1	20/66	37.2/164.8	0.1	3	1
		3	57/360	13.05/30.22	1	4	18.3
		5	93/684	8/15.9	408.9	-	-

Fig. 4. Compression results. **Topo:** the network topology. **Con V/E:** Number of nodes/edges of concrete network. **Fail:** Number of failures. **Abs V/E:** Number of nodes/edges of the best abstraction. **Ratio:** Compression ratio (nodes/edges). **Abs Time:** Time taken to find abstractions (sec.). **SMT Calls:** Number of calls to the SMT solver. **SMT Time:** Time taken by the SMT solver (sec.).

To mitigate the effect of this problem, we *could* ask the solver to minimize the returned counterexample, returning a counterexample that corresponds to the fewest concrete link failures. We could do so by providing the solver with additional constraints specifying the number of concrete links that correspond to each abstract link and then asking the solver to return a counterexample that minimizes this sum of concrete failures. Of course, doing so requires we solve a more expensive optimization problem. Instead, given an initial (possibly spurious counter-example), we simple ask the solver to find a new counterexample that (additionally) satisfies this constraint. If it succeeds, we have found a real counterexample. If it fails, we use it to refine our abstraction.

7   Evaluation

We evaluate Origami on a collection of synthetic data center networks that are using BGP to implement shortest-paths routing policies over common industrial datacenter topologies. Data centers are good fit for our algorithms as they can be very large but are highly symmetrical and designed for fault tolerance. Data center topologies (often called *fattree* topologies) are typically organized in layers, with each layer containing many routers. Each router in a layer is connected to a number of routers in the layer above (and below) it. The precise number of neighbors to which a router is connected, and the pattern of said connections, is part of the topology definition. We focus on two common topologies: fattree topologies used at Google (labelled FT20, FT40 and SP40 below) and a different fattree used at Facebook (labelled FB12). These are relatively large data center topologies ranging from 500 to 2000 nodes and 8000 to 64000 edges.

SP40 uses a pure shortest paths routing policy. For other experiments (FT20, FT40, FB12), we augment shortest paths with additional policy that selectively drops routing announcements, for example disabling "valley routing" in various places which allows up-down-up-down routes through the data centers instead of just up-down routes. The pure shortest paths policy represents a best-case scenario for our technology as it gives rise to perfect symmetry and makes our heuristics especially effective. By adding variations in routing policy, we provide a greater challenge for our tool.

Experiments were done on a Mac with a 4 GHz i7 CPU and 16 GB memory.

7.1   Compression Results

Figure 4 shows the level of compression achieved, along with the required time for compression and verification. In most cases, we achieve a high compression ratio especially in terms of links. This drastically reduces the possible failure combinations for the underlying verification process. The cases of 10 link failures on FT20 and 5 link failures on FbFT demonstrate another aspect of our algorithm. Both topologies cannot sustain that many link failures, *i.e.* some concrete nodes have less than 10 (resp. 5) neighbors. We can determine this as we refine the abstraction; there are (abstract) nodes that do not satisfy the min cut requirement and we cannot refine them further. This constitutes an actual counterexample and explains why the abstraction of FT20 for 10 link failures is smaller than the one for 5 link failures. Importantly, we did not use the SMT solver to find this counterexample. Likewise, we did not need to run a min cut on the much larger concrete topology. Intuitively, the rest of the network remained abstract, while the part that led to the counterexample became fully concrete.

7.2 Verification Performance

The verification time of Origami is dominated by abstraction time and SMT time, which can be seen in Fig. 4. In practice, there is also some time taken to parse and pre-process the configurations but it is negligible. The abstraction time is highly dependent on the size of the network and the abstraction search breadth used. In this case, the breadth was set to 25, a relatively high value.

While the verification time for a high number of link failures is not negligible, we found that verification without abstraction is essentially impossible. We used Minesweeper [2], the state-of-the-art SMT-based network verifier, to verify the same fault tolerance properties and it was unable to solve any of our queries. This is not surprising, as SMT-based verifiers do not scale to networks beyond the size of FT20 even without any link failures.

7.3 Refinement Effectiveness

We now evaluate the effectiveness of our search and refinement techniques.

Effectiveness of Search. To assess the effectiveness of the search procedure, we compute an initial abstraction of the FT20 network suitable for 5 link failures, using different values of the search breadth. On top of this, we additionally consider the impact of some of the heuristics described in Sect. 5. Figure 5 presents the size (the number of nodes are on the y axis and the number of edges on top of the bars) of the computed abstractions with respect to various values for the breadth of search and sets of heuristics:

– Heuristics off means that (almost) all heuristics are turned off. We still try to split nodes that are on the cut-set.

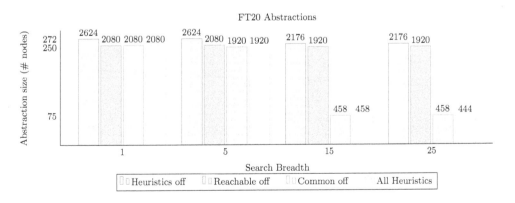

Fig. 5. The initial abstraction of FT20 for 5 link failures using different heuristics and search breadth. On top of the bars is the number of edges of each abstraction.

- Reachable off means that we do not bias towards splitting of nodes in the reachable portion of the cut-set.
- Common off means that we do not bias towards splitting reachable nodes that have the most connections to unreachable nodes.

The results of this experiment show that in order to achieve effective compression ratios we need to employ both smart heuristics and a wide search through the space of abstractions. It is possible that increasing the search breadth would make the heuristics redundant, however, in most cases this would make the refinement process exceed acceptable time limits.

Use of Counterexamples. We now assess how important it is to (1) use symmetries in policy to infer more information from counterexamples, and (2) minimize the counterexample provided by the solver.

We see in Fig. 6 that disabling them increases number of refinement iterations. While each of these refinements is performed quickly, the same cannot be guaranteed of the verification process that runs between them. Hence, it is important to keep refinement iterations as low as possible.

8   Related Work

Our approach to network fault-tolerance verification draws heavily from ideas in prior work exploiting symmetry and abstraction in model checking [4,6,17] and automatic abstraction refinement via CEGAR [1,5,9]. However, we apply these ideas to network routing, which introduces different challenges and opportunities. For example, our notion of abstraction ($\forall\exists-$abstraction) differs from the typical existential abstraction used in model checking [6]. In addition, we have to deal with network topological structure and asymmetries introduced by failures.

Bonsai [3] and Surgeries [22] both leverage abstraction to accelerate verification for routing protocols and packet forwarding respectively. Both tools compute a single abstract network that is bisimilar to the original concrete network. Alas, neither approach can be used to reason about properties when faults may occur.

Minesweeper [2] is a general approach to control plane verification based on a stable state encoding, which leverages an SMT solver in the back-end. It supports a wide range of routing protocols and properties, including fault tolerance properties. Our compression is complementary

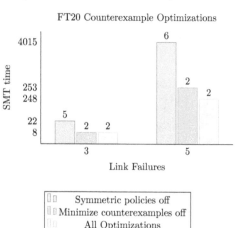

Fig. 6.   Effectiveness of minimizing counterexamples and of learning unused edges. On top of the bars is the number of SMT calls.

to such tools; it is used to alleviate the scaling problem that Minesweeper faces with large networks.

With respect to verification of fault tolerance, ARC [13] translates a limited class of routing policies to a weighted graph where fault-tolerance properties can be checked using graph algorithms. However, ARC only handles shortest path routing and cannot support stateful features such as BGP communities, or local preference, etc. While ARC applies graph algorithms on a statically-computed graph, we use graph algorithms as part of a refinement loop in conjunction with a general purpose solver.

9   Conclusions

We present a new theory of distributed routing protocols in the presence of bounded link failures, and we use the theory to develop algorithms for network compression and counterexample-guided verification of fault tolerance properties. In doing so, we observe that (1) even though abstract networks route differently from concrete ones in the presence of failures, the concrete routes wind up being "at least as good" as the abstract ones when networks satisfy reasonable well-formedness constraints, and (2) using efficient graph algorithms (min cut) in the middle of the CEGAR loop speeds the search for refinements.

We implemented our algorithms in a network verification tool called Origami. Evaluation of the tool on synthetic networks shows that our algorithms accelerate verification of fault tolerance properties significantly, making it possible to verify networks out of reach of other state-of-the-art tools.

References

1. Ball, T., Majumdar, R., Millstein, T.D., Rajamani, S.K.: Automatic predicate abstraction of C programs. In: Proceedings of the 2001 ACM SIGPLAN Conference on Programming Language Design and Implementation (PLDI), pp. 203–213 (2001)
2. Beckett, R., Gupta, A., Mahajan, R., Walker, D.: A general approach to network configuration verification. In: SIGCOMM, August 2017
3. Beckett, R., Gupta, A., Mahajan, R., Walker, D.: Control plane compression. In: Proceedings of the 2018 Conference of the ACM Special Interest Group on Data Communication, pp. 476–489. ACM (2018)
4. Clarke, E.M., Filkorn, T., Jha, S.: Exploiting symmetry in temporal logic model checking. In: Courcoubetis, C. (ed.) CAV 1993. LNCS, vol. 697, pp. 450–462. Springer, Heidelberg (1993). https://doi.org/10.1007/3-540-56922-7_37
5. Clarke, E., Grumberg, O., Jha, S., Lu, Y., Veith, H.: Counterexample-guided abstraction refinement. In: Emerson, E.A., Sistla, A.P. (eds.) CAV 2000. LNCS, vol. 1855, pp. 154–169. Springer, Heidelberg (2000). https://doi.org/10.1007/10722167_15
6. Clarke, E.M., Grumberg, O., Long, D.E.: Model checking and abstraction. ACM Trans. Program. Lang. Syst. **16**(5), 1512–1542 (1994)
7. Daggitt, M.L., Gurney, A.J.T., Griffin, T.G.: Asynchronous convergence of policy-rich distributed bellman-ford routing protocols. In: SIGCOMM, pp. 103–116 (2018)

8. Daggitt, M.L., Gurney, A.J., Griffin, T.G.: Asynchronous convergence of policy-rich distributed Bellman-Ford routing protocols. In: Proceedings of the 2018 Conference of the ACM Special Interest Group on Data Communication, pp. 103–116. ACM (2018)

9. Das, S., Dill, D.L.: Successive approximation of abstract transition relations. In: Proceedings of the 16th Annual IEEE Symposium on Logic in Computer Science, LICS 2001, p. 51 (2001)

10. de Moura, L., Bjørner, N.: Z3: an efficient SMT solver. In: Ramakrishnan, C.R., Rehof, J. (eds.) TACAS 2008. LNCS, vol. 4963, pp. 337–340. Springer, Heidelberg (2008). https://doi.org/10.1007/978-3-540-78800-3_24

11. Feamster, N., Rexford, J.: Network-wide prediction of BGP routes. IEEE/ACM Trans. Netw. **15**(2), 253–266 (2007)

12. Fogel, A., et al.: A general approach to network configuration analysis. In: NSDI (2015)

13. Gember-Jacobson, A., Viswanathan, R., Akella, A., Mahajan, R.: Fast control plane analysis using an abstract representation. In: SIGCOMM (2016)

14. Gill, P., Jain, N., Nagappan, N.: Understanding network failures in data centers: measurement, analysis, and implications. In: SIGCOMM (2011)

15. Godfrey, J.: The summer of network misconfigurations (2016). https://blog.algosec.com/2016/08/business-outages-caused-misconfigurations-headline-news-summer.html

16. Griffin, T.G., Shepherd, F.B., Wilfong, G.: The stable paths problem and interdomain routing. IEEE/ACM Trans. Netw. **10**(2), 232–243 (2002)

17. Kesten, Y., Pnueli, A.: Control and data abstraction: the cornerstones of practical formal verification. Softw. Tools Technol. Transf. **2**(4), 328–342 (2000)

18. Lapukhov, P., Premji, A., Mitchell, J.: Use of BGP for routing in large-scale data centers. Internet draft (2015)

19. Lopes, N.P., Rybalchenko, A.: Fast BGP simulation of large datacenters. In: Enea, C., Piskac, R. (eds.) VMCAI 2019. LNCS, vol. 11388, pp. 386–408. Springer, Cham (2019). https://doi.org/10.1007/978-3-030-11245-5_18

20. Lougheed, K.: A border gateway protocol (BGP). RFC 1163, RFC Editor (1989). http://www.rfc-editor.org/rfc/rfc1163.txt

21. Mahajan, R., Wetherall, D., Anderson, T.: Understanding BGP misconfiguration. In: SIGCOMM (2002)

22. Plotkin, G.D., Bjørner, N., Lopes, N.P., Rybalchenko, A., Varghese, G.: Scaling network verification using symmetry and surgery. In: POPL (2016)

23. Quoitin, B., Uhlig, S.: Modeling the routing of an autonomous system with C-BGP. Netw. Mag. Glob. Internetworking **19**(6), 12–19 (2005)

24. Sobrinho, J.A.L.: An algebraic theory of dynamic network routing. IEEE/ACM Trans. Netw. **13**(5), 1160–1173 (2005)

25. Weitz, K., Woos, D., Torlak, E., Ernst, M.D., Krishnamurthy, A., Tatlock, Z.: Formal semantics and automated verification for the border gateway protocol. In: NetPL (2016)

13

Loop Summarization with Rational Vector Addition Systems

Jake Silverman$^{(\boxtimes)}$ and Zachary Kincaid

Princeton University, Princeton, USA
{Jakers,ZKincaid}@CS.Princeton.edu

Abstract. This paper presents a technique for computing numerical loop summaries. The method synthesizes a rational vector addition system with resets ($\mathbb{Q}$-VASR) that simulates the action of an input loop, and then uses the reachability relation of that $\mathbb{Q}$-VASR to over-approximate the behavior of the loop. The key technical problem solved in this paper is to automatically synthesize a $\mathbb{Q}$-VASR that is a *best abstraction* of a given loop in the sense that (1) it simulates the loop and (2) it is simulated by any other $\mathbb{Q}$-VASR that simulates the loop. Since our loop summarization scheme is based on computing the *exact* reachability relation of a *best* abstraction of a loop, we can make theoretical guarantees about its behavior. Moreover, we show experimentally that the technique is precise and performant in practice.

1 Introduction

Modern software verification techniques employ a number of heuristics for reasoning about loops. While these heuristics are often effective, they are unpredictable. For example, an abstract interpreter may fail to find the most precise invariant expressible in the language of its abstract domain due to imprecise widening, or a software-model checker might fail to terminate because it generates interpolants that are insufficiently general. This paper presents a loop summarization technique that is capable of generating loop invariants in an expressive and decidable language and provides theoretical guarantees about invariant quality.

The key idea behind our technique is to leverage reachability results of vector addition systems (VAS) for invariant generation. Vector addition systems are a class of infinite-state transition systems with decidable reachability, classically used as a model of parallel systems [12]. We consider a variation of VAS, *rational VAS with resets* (*$\mathbb{Q}$-VASR*), wherein there is a finite number of rational-typed variables and a finite set of transitions that simultaneously update each variable in the system by either adding a constant value or (re)setting the variable to a constant value. Our interest in $\mathbb{Q}$-VASRs stems from the fact that there is (polytime) procedure to compute a linear arithmetic formula that represents a $\mathbb{Q}$-VASR's reachability relation [8].

Since the reachability relation of a $\mathbb{Q}$-VASR is computable, the dynamics of $\mathbb{Q}$-VASR can be analyzed without relying on heuristic techniques. However, there is a gap between $\mathbb{Q}$-VASR and the loops that we are interested in summarizing. The latter typically use a rich set of operations (memory manipulation, conditionals, non-constant increments, non-linear arithmetic, etc) and cannot be analyzed precisely. We bridge the gap with a procedure that, for any loop, synthesizes a $\mathbb{Q}$-VASR that simulates it. The reachability relation of the $\mathbb{Q}$-VASR can then be used to over-approximate the behavior of the loop. Moreover, we prove that if a loop is expressed in linear rational arithmetic (LRA), then our procedure synthesizes a *best* $\mathbb{Q}$-VASR abstraction, in the sense that it simulates any other $\mathbb{Q}$-VASR that simulates the loop. That is, imprecision in the analysis is due to inherent limitations of the $\mathbb{Q}$-VASR model, rather heuristic algorithmic choices.

One limitation of the model is that $\mathbb{Q}$-VASRs over-approximate multi-path loops by treating the choice between paths as non-deterministic. We show that $\mathbb{Q}$-VASRS, $\mathbb{Q}$-VASR extended with control states, can be used to improve our invariant generation scheme by encoding control flow information and inter-path control dependencies that are lost in the $\mathbb{Q}$-VASR abstraction. We give an algorithm for synthesizing a $\mathbb{Q}$-VASRS abstraction of a given loop, which (like our $\mathbb{Q}$-VASR abstraction algorithm) synthesizes *best* abstractions under certain assumptions.

Finally, we note that our analysis techniques extend to complex control structures (such as nested loops) by employing summarization compositionally (i.e., "bottom-up"). For example, our analysis summarizes a nested loop by first summarizing its inner loops, and then uses the summaries to analyze the outer loop. As a result of compositionality, our analysis can be applied to partial programs, is easy to parallelize, and has the potential to scale to large code bases.

The main contributions of the paper are as follows:

- We present a procedure to synthesize $\mathbb{Q}$-VASR abstractions of transition formulas. For transition formulas in linear rational arithmetic, the synthesized $\mathbb{Q}$-VASR abstraction is a *best* abstraction.
- We present a technique for improving the precision of our analysis by using $\mathbb{Q}$-VASR with states to capture loop control structure.
- We implement the proposed loop summarization techniques and show that their ability to verify user assertions is comparable to software model checkers, while at the same time providing theoretical guarantees of termination and invariant quality.

1.1 Outline

This section illustrates the high-level structure of our invariant generation scheme. The goal is to compute a *transition formula* that summarizes the behavior of a given program. A transition formula is a formula over a set of program variables Var along with primed copies Var$'$, representing the state of the program

```
procedure enqueue(elt):                    procedure enqueue():
  back := cons(elt,back)                     back_len := back_len + 1
  size := size + 1                           mem_ops := mem_ops + 1
                                             size := size + 1
procedure dequeue():                       procedure dequeue():
  if (front == nil) then                     if (front_len == 0) then
    // Reverse back, append to front           while (back_len != 0) do
    while (back != nil) do                       front_len := front_len + 1
      front := cons(head(back),front)            back_len := back_len - 1
      back := tail(back)                         mem_ops := mem_ops + 3
  result := head(front)                       size := size - 1
  front := tail(front)                       front_len := front_len - 1
  size := size - 1                           mem_ops := mem_ops + 2
  return result                            procedure harness():
                                             nb_ops := 0
        (a) Persistent queue                 while nondet() do
                                               nb_ops := nb_ops + 1
                                               if (size > 0 && nondet())
                                                 enqueue()
                                               else
                                                 dequeue()
```

(b) Integer model & harness

Fig. 1. A persistent queue and integer model. back_len and front_len models the lengths of the lists front and back; mem_ops counts the number of memory operations in the computation.

before and after executing a computation (respectively). For any given program P, a transition formula $\mathbf{TF}[P]$ can be computed by recursion on syntax:[1]

$$\mathbf{TF}[\mathrm{x} \; := \; e] \triangleq \mathrm{x}' = e \wedge \bigwedge_{\mathrm{y} \neq \mathrm{x} \in \mathsf{Var}} \mathrm{y}' = \mathrm{y}$$

$$\mathbf{TF}[\mathbf{if} \;\; c \;\; \mathbf{then} \;\; P_1 \;\; \mathbf{else} \;\; P_2] \triangleq (c \wedge \mathbf{TF}[P_1]) \vee (\neg c \wedge \mathbf{TF}[P_2])$$

$$\mathbf{TF}[P_1 ; P_2] \triangleq \exists X \in \mathbb{Z}.\mathbf{TF}[P_1][\mathsf{Var}' \mapsto X] \wedge \mathbf{TF}[P_2][\mathsf{Var} \mapsto X]$$

$$\mathbf{TF}[\mathbf{while} \;\; c \;\; \mathbf{do} \;\; P] \triangleq (c \wedge \mathbf{TF}[P])^* \wedge (\neg c[\mathsf{Var} \mapsto \mathsf{Var}'])$$

where $(-)^*$ is a function that computes an over-approximation of the transitive closure of a transition formula. The contribution of this paper is a method for computing this $(-)^*$ operation, which is based on first over-approximating the input transition formula by a $\mathbb{Q}$-VASR, and then computing the (exact) reachability relation of the $\mathbb{Q}$-VASR.

---

[1] This style of analysis can be extended from a simple block-structured language to one with control flow and recursive procedures using the framework of algebraic program analysis [13,23].

We illustrate the analysis on an integer model of a persistent queue data structure, pictured in Fig. 1. The example consists of two operations (enqueue and dequeue), as well as a test harness (harness) that non-deterministically executes enqueue and dequeue operations. The queue achieves $O(1)$ amortized memory operations (mem_ops) in enqueue and queue by implementing the queue as two lists, front and back (whose lengths are modeled as front_len and back_len, respectively): the sequence of elements in the queue is the front list followed by the reverse of the back list. We will show that the queue functions use $O(1)$ amortized memory operations by finding a summary for harness that implies a linear bound on mem_ops (the number of memory operations in the computation) in terms of nb_ops (the total number of enqueue/dequeue operations executed in some sequence of operations).

We analyze the queue compositionally, in "bottom-up" fashion (i.e., starting from deeply-nested code and working our way back up to a summary for harness). There are two loops of interest, one in dequeue and one in harness. Since the dequeue loop is nested inside the harness loop, dequeue is analyzed first. We start by computing a transition formula that represents one execution of the body of the dequeue loop:

$$Body_{\mathsf{deq}} = \mathtt{back\_len} > 0 \wedge \begin{pmatrix} \mathtt{front\_len}' = \mathtt{front\_len} + 1 \\ \wedge \, \mathtt{back\_len}' = \mathtt{back\_len} - 1 \\ \wedge \, \mathtt{mem\_ops}' = \mathtt{mem\_ops} + 3 \\ \wedge \, \mathtt{size}' = \mathtt{size} \end{pmatrix}$$

Observe that each variable in the loop is incremented by a constant value. As a result, the loop update can be captured faithfully by a vector addition system. In particular, we see that this loop body formula is simulated by the $\mathbb{Q}$-VASR V_{deq} (below), where the correspondence between the state-space of $Body_{\mathsf{deq}}$ and V_{deq} is given by the identity transformation (i.e., each dimension of V_{deq} simply represents one of the variables of $Body_{\mathsf{deq}}$).

$$\begin{bmatrix} w \\ x \\ y \\ z \end{bmatrix} = \begin{bmatrix} 1 & 0 & 0 & 0 \\ 0 & 1 & 0 & 0 \\ 0 & 0 & 1 & 0 \\ 0 & 0 & 0 & 1 \end{bmatrix} \begin{bmatrix} \mathtt{front\_len} \\ \mathtt{back\_len} \\ \mathtt{mem\_ops} \\ \mathtt{size} \end{bmatrix} ; \quad V_{\mathsf{deq}} = \left\{ \begin{bmatrix} w \\ x \\ y \\ z \end{bmatrix} \to \begin{bmatrix} w+1 \\ x-1 \\ y+3 \\ z \end{bmatrix} \right\}.$$

A formula representing the reachability relation of a vector addition system can be computed in polytime. For the case of V_{deq}, a formula representing k steps of the $\mathbb{Q}$-VASR is simply

$$w' = w + k \wedge x' = x - k \wedge y' = y + 3k \wedge z' = z. \tag{$\dagger$}$$

To capture information about the pre-condition of the loop, we can project the primed variables to obtain back_len > 0; similarly, for the post-condition, we can project the unprimed variables to obtain back_len' $\geq$ 0. Finally, combining ($\dagger$)

(translated back into the vocabulary of the program) and the pre/post-condition, we form the following approximation of the dequeue loop's behavior:

$$\exists k. k \geq 0 \wedge \begin{pmatrix} \texttt{front\_len}' = \texttt{front\_len} + k \\ \wedge \texttt{back\_len}' = \texttt{back\_len} - k \\ \wedge \texttt{mem\_ops}' = \texttt{mem\_ops} + 3k \\ \wedge \texttt{size}' = \texttt{size} \end{pmatrix} \wedge \left(k > 0 \Rightarrow \begin{pmatrix} \texttt{back\_len} > 0 \\ \wedge \texttt{back\_len}' \geq 0) \end{pmatrix} \right).$$

Using this summary for the dequeue loop, we proceed to compute a transition formula for the body of the harness loop (omitted for brevity). Just as with the dequeue loop, we analyze the harness loop by synthesizing a $\mathbb{Q}$-VASR that simulates it, V_{har} (below), where the correspondence between the state space of the harness loop and V_{har} is given by the transformation S_{har}:

$$\begin{bmatrix} v \\ w \\ x \\ y \\ z \end{bmatrix} = \underbrace{\begin{bmatrix} 0 & 0 & 0 & 1 & 0 \\ 0 & 1 & 0 & 0 & 0 \\ 0 & 3 & 1 & 0 & 0 \\ 1 & 1 & 0 & 0 & 0 \\ 0 & 0 & 0 & 0 & 1 \end{bmatrix}}_{S_{\text{har}}} \begin{bmatrix} \texttt{front\_len} \\ \texttt{back\_len} \\ \texttt{mem\_ops} \\ \texttt{size} \\ \texttt{nb\_ops} \end{bmatrix} ; i.e., \begin{pmatrix} \texttt{size} = v \\ \wedge \texttt{back\_len} = w \\ \wedge \texttt{mem\_ops} + 3\texttt{back\_len} = x \\ \wedge \texttt{back\_len} + \texttt{front\_len} = y \\ \wedge \texttt{nb\_ops} = z \end{pmatrix}.$$

$$V_{\text{har}} = \left\{ \underbrace{\begin{bmatrix} v \\ w \\ x \\ y \\ z \end{bmatrix} \rightarrow \begin{bmatrix} v+1 \\ w+1 \\ x+4 \\ y+1 \\ z+1 \end{bmatrix}}_{\text{enqueue}}, \underbrace{\begin{bmatrix} v \\ w \\ x \\ y \\ z \end{bmatrix} \rightarrow \begin{bmatrix} v-1 \\ w \\ x+2 \\ y-1 \\ z+1 \end{bmatrix}}_{\text{dequeue fast}}, \underbrace{\begin{bmatrix} v \\ w \\ x \\ y \\ z \end{bmatrix} \rightarrow \begin{bmatrix} v-1 \\ 0 \\ x+2 \\ y-1 \\ z+1 \end{bmatrix}}_{\text{dequeue slow}} \right\}$$

Unlike the dequeue loop, we do not get an exact characterization of the dynamics of each changed variable. In particular, in the slow dequeue path through the loop, the value of front_len, back_len, and mem_ops change by a variable amount. Since back_len is set to 0, its behavior can be captured by a reset. The dynamics of front_len and mem_ops cannot be captured by a $\mathbb{Q}$-VASR, but (using our dequeue summary) we can observe that the sum of front_len + back_len is decremented by 1, and the sum of mem_ops + 3back_len is incremented by 2.

We compute the following formula that captures the reachability relation of V_{har} (taking k_1 steps of enqueue, k_2 steps of dequeue fast, and k_3 steps of dequeue slow) under the inverse image of the state correspondence S_{har}:

$$\begin{pmatrix} \texttt{size}' = \texttt{size} + k_1 - k_2 - k_3 \\ \wedge ((k_3 = 0 \wedge \texttt{back\_len}' = \texttt{back\_len} + k_1) \vee (k_3 > 0 \wedge 0 \leq \texttt{back\_len}' \leq k_1)) \\ \wedge \texttt{mem\_ops}' + 3\texttt{back\_len}' = \texttt{mem\_ops} + 3\texttt{back\_len} + 4k_1 + 2k_2 + 2k_3 \\ \wedge \texttt{front\_len}' + \texttt{back\_len}' = \texttt{front\_len} + \texttt{back\_len} + k_1 - k_2 - k_3 \\ \wedge \texttt{nb\_ops}' = \texttt{nb\_ops} + k_1 + k_2 + k_3 \end{pmatrix}$$

From the above formula (along with pre/post-condition formulas), we obtain a summary for the harness loop (omitted for brevity). Using this summary we can prove (supposing that we start in a state where all variables are zero) that mem_ops is at most 4 times nb_ops (i.e., enqueue and dequeue use $O(1)$ amortized memory operations).

2   Background

The syntax of ∃LIRA, the existential fragment of linear integer/rational arithmetic, is given by the following grammar:

$$s, t \in \mathsf{Term} ::= c \mid x \mid s + t \mid c \cdot t$$
$$F, G \in \mathsf{Formula} ::= s < t \mid s = t \mid F \wedge G \mid F \vee G \mid \exists x \in \mathbb{Q}.F \mid \exists x \in \mathbb{Z}.F$$

where x is a (rational sorted) variable symbol and c is a rational constant. Observe that (without loss of generality) formulas are free of negation. ∃LRA (linear rational arithmetic) refers to the fragment of ∃LIRA that omits quantification over the integer sort.

A **transition system** is a pair $(S, \rightarrow)$ where S is a (potentially infinite) set of states and $\rightarrow \subseteq S \times S$ is a transition relation. For a transition relation $\rightarrow$, we use $\rightarrow^*$ to denote its reflexive, transitive closure.

A **transition formula** is a formula $F(\mathbf{x}, \mathbf{x}')$ whose free variables range over $\mathbf{x} = x_1, ..., x_n$ and $\mathbf{x}' = x'_1, ..., x'_n$ (we refer to the number n as the *dimension* of F); these variables designate the state before and after a transition. In the following, we assume that transition formulas are defined over ∃LIRA. For a transition formula $F(\mathbf{x}, \mathbf{x}')$ and vectors of terms $\mathbf{s}$ and $\mathbf{t}$, we use $F(\mathbf{s}, \mathbf{t})$ to denote the formula F with each x_i replaced by s_i and each x'_i replaced by t_i. A transition formula $F(\mathbf{x}, \mathbf{x}')$ defines a transition system $(S_F, \rightarrow_F)$, where the state space S_F is $\mathbb{Q}^n$ and which can transition $\mathbf{u} \rightarrow_F \mathbf{v}$ iff $F(\mathbf{u}, \mathbf{v})$ is valid.

For two rational vectors $\mathbf{a}$ and $\mathbf{b}$ of the same dimension d, we use $\mathbf{a} \cdot \mathbf{b}$ to denote the inner product $\mathbf{a} \cdot \mathbf{b} = \sum_{i=1}^d a_i b_i$ and $\mathbf{a} * \mathbf{b}$ to denote the pointwise (aka Hadamard) product $(\mathbf{a} * \mathbf{b})_i = a_i b_i$. For any natural number i, we use $\mathbf{e}_i$ to denote the standard basis vector in the ith direction (i.e., the vector consisting of all zeros except the ith entry, which is 1), where the dimension of $\mathbf{e}_i$ is understood from context. We use I_n to denote the $n \times n$ identity matrix.

Definition 1. *A **rational vector addition system with resets** (ℚ-VASR) of dimension d is a finite set $V \subseteq \{0, 1\}^d \times \mathbb{Q}^d$ of transformers. Each transformer $(\mathbf{r}, \mathbf{a}) \in V$ consists of a binary reset vector $\mathbf{r}$, and a rational addition vector $\mathbf{a}$, both of dimension d. V defines a transition system $(S_V, \rightarrow_V)$, where the state space S_V is $\mathbb{Q}^d$ and which can transition $\mathbf{u} \rightarrow_V \mathbf{v}$ iff $\mathbf{v} = \mathbf{r} * \mathbf{u} + \mathbf{a}$ for some $(\mathbf{r}, \mathbf{a}) \in V$.*

Definition 2. *A **rational vector addition system with resets and states** (ℚ-VASRS) of dimension d is a pair $\mathcal{V} = (Q, E)$, where Q is a finite set of control states, and $E \subseteq Q \times \{0, 1\}^d \times \mathbb{Q}^d \times Q$ is a finite set of edges labeled by (d-dimensional) transformers. $\mathcal{V}$ defines a transition system $(S_\mathcal{V}, \rightarrow_\mathcal{V})$, where the state space $S_\mathcal{V}$ is $Q \times \mathbb{Q}^n$ and which can transition $(q_1, \mathbf{u}) \rightarrow_\mathcal{V} (q_2, \mathbf{v})$ iff there is some edge $(q_1, (\mathbf{r}, \mathbf{a}), q_2) \in E$ such that $\mathbf{v} = \mathbf{r} * \mathbf{u} + \mathbf{a}$.*

Our invariant generation scheme is based on the following result, which is a simple consequence of the work of Haase and Halfon:

Theorem 1 ([8]). *There is a polytime algorithm which, given a d-dimensional* $\mathbb{Q}$*-VASRS* $\mathcal{V} = (Q, E)$*, computes an* $\exists LIRA$ *transition formula* $reach(\mathcal{V})$ *such that for all* $\mathbf{u}, \mathbf{v} \in \mathbb{Q}^d$*, we have* $(p, \mathbf{u}) \rightarrow_{\mathcal{V}}^{*} (q, \mathbf{v})$ *for some control states* $p, q \in Q$ *if and only if* $\mathbf{u} \rightarrow_{reach(\mathcal{V})} \mathbf{v}$.

Note that $\mathbb{Q}$-VASR can be realized as $\mathbb{Q}$-VASRS with a single control state, so this theorem also applies to $\mathbb{Q}$-VASR.

3   Approximating Loops with Vector Addition Systems

In this section, we describe a method for over-approximating the transitive closure of a transition formula using a $\mathbb{Q}$-VASR. This procedure immediately extends to computing summaries for programs (including programs with nested loops) using the method outlined in Sect. 1.1.

The core algorithmic problem that we answer in this section is: *given a transition formula, how can we synthesize a (best) abstraction of that formula's dynamics as a* $\mathbb{Q}$*-VASR?* We begin by formalizing the problem: in particular, we define what it means for a $\mathbb{Q}$-VASR to simulate a transition formula and what it means for an abstraction to be "best."

Definition 3. *Let* $A = (\mathbb{Q}^n, \rightarrow_A)$ *and* $B = (\mathbb{Q}^m, \rightarrow_B)$ *be transition systems operating over rational vector spaces. A **linear simulation** from A to B is a linear transformation* $S : \mathbb{Q}^{m \times n}$ *such that for all* $\mathbf{u}, \mathbf{v} \in \mathbb{Q}^n$ *for which* $\mathbf{u} \rightarrow_A \mathbf{v}$*, we have* $S\mathbf{u} \rightarrow_B S\mathbf{v}$*. We use* $A \Vdash_S B$ *to denote that S is a linear simulation from A to B.*

Suppose that $F(\mathbf{x}, \mathbf{x}')$ is an n-dimensional transition formula, V is a d-dimensional $\mathbb{Q}$-VASR, and $S : \mathbb{Q}^{d \times n}$ is linear transformation. The key property of simulations that underlies our loop summarization scheme is that if $F \Vdash_S V$, then $reach(V)(S\mathbf{x}, S\mathbf{x}')$ (i.e., the reachability relation of V under the inverse image of S) over-approximates the transitive closure of F. Finally, we observe that simulation $F \Vdash_S V$ can equivalently be defined by the validity of the entailment $F \models \gamma(S, V)$, where

$$\gamma(S, V) \triangleq \bigvee_{(\mathbf{r}, \mathbf{a}) \in V} S\mathbf{x}' = \mathbf{r} * S\mathbf{x} + \mathbf{a}$$

is a transition formula that represents the transitions that V simulates under transformation S.

Our task is to synthesize a linear transformation S and a $\mathbb{Q}$-VASR V such that $F \Vdash_S V$. We call a pair (S, V), consisting of a rational matrix $S \in \mathbb{Q}^{d \times n}$ and a d-dimensional $\mathbb{Q}$-VASR V, a $\mathbb{Q}$-**VASR abstraction**. We say that n is the *concrete dimension* of (S, V) and d is the *abstract dimension*. If $F \Vdash_S V$, then we say that (S, V) is a $\mathbb{Q}$-**VASR abstraction of** F. A transition formula may have many $\mathbb{Q}$-VASR abstractions; we are interested in computing a $\mathbb{Q}$-VASR abstraction (S, V) that results in the most precise over-approximation of the transitive closure of F. Towards this end, we define a preorder $\preceq$ on $\mathbb{Q}$-VASR abstractions, where $(S^1, V^1) \preceq (S^2, V^2)$ iff there exists a linear transformation $T \in \mathbb{Q}^{e \times d}$ such that $V^1 \Vdash_T V^2$ and $TS^1 = S^2$ (where d and e are the abstract dimensions of (S^1, V^1) and (S^2, V^2), respectively). Observe that if $(S^1, V^1) \preceq (S^2, V^2)$, then $reach(V^1)(S^1\mathbf{x}, S^1\mathbf{x}') \models reach(V^2)(S^2\mathbf{x}, S^2\mathbf{x}')$.

Thus, our problem can be stated as follows: given a transition formula F, synthesize a $\mathbb{Q}$-VASR abstraction (S, V) of F such that (S, V) is *best* in the sense that we have $(S, V) \preceq (\widetilde{S}, \widetilde{V})$ for any $\mathbb{Q}$-VASR abstraction $(\widetilde{S}, \widetilde{V})$ of F. A solution to this problem is given in Algorithm 1.

Algorithm 1. `abstract-VASR(F)`

---

    input : Transition formula F of dimension n
    output: $\mathbb{Q}$-VASR abstraction of F; Best $\mathbb{Q}$-VASR abstraction if F in $\exists$LRA
1 Skolemize existentials of F;
2 $(S, V) \leftarrow (I_n, \emptyset)$;   // $(I_n, \emptyset)$ `is least in` $\preceq$ `order`
3 $\Gamma \leftarrow F$;
4 **while** Γ *is satisfiable* **do**
5   Let M be a model of Γ;
6 $C \leftarrow$ cube of the DNF of F with $M \models C$;
7 $(S, V) \leftarrow (S, V) \sqcup \hat{\alpha}(C)$;
8 $\Gamma \leftarrow \Gamma \wedge \neg\gamma(S, V)$
9 **return** (S, V)

Algorithm 1 follows the familiar pattern of an AllSat-style loop. The algorithm takes as input a transition formula F. It maintains a $\mathbb{Q}$-VASR abstraction (S, V) and a formula Γ, whose models correspond to the transitions of F that are *not* simulated by (S, V). The idea is to build (S, V) iteratively by sampling transitions from Γ, augmenting (S, V) to simulate the sample transition, and then updating Γ accordingly. We initialize (S, V) to be $(I_n, \emptyset)$, the canonical least $\mathbb{Q}$-VASR abstraction in $\preceq$ order, and Γ to be F (i.e., $(I_n, \emptyset)$ does not simulate any transitions of F). Each loop iteration proceeds as follows. First, we sample a model M of Γ (i.e., a transition that is allowed by F but not simulated by (S, V)). We then generalize that transition to a set of transitions by using M to select a cube C of the DNF of F that contains M. Next, we use the procedure described in Sect. 3.1 to compute a $\mathbb{Q}$-VASR abstraction $\hat{\alpha}(C)$ that simulates the transitions of C. We then update the $\mathbb{Q}$-VASR abstraction (S, V) to be the least upper bound of (S, V) and $\hat{\alpha}(C)$ (w.r.t. $\preceq$ order) using the procedure described in Sect. 3.2 (line 7). Finally, we block any transition simulated by the least upper bound (including every transition in C) from being sampled again by conjoining $\neg\gamma(S, V)$ to Γ. The loop terminates when Γ is unsatisfiable, in which case we have that $F \Vdash_S V$. Theorem 2 gives the correctness statement for this algorithm.

Theorem 2. *Given a transition formula F, Algorithm 1 computes a simulation S and $\mathbb{Q}$-VASR V such that $F \Vdash_S V$. Moreover, if F is in $\exists LRA$, Algorithm 1 computes a* best *$\mathbb{Q}$-VASR abstraction of F.*

The proof of this theorem as well as the proofs to all subsequent theorems, lemmas, and propositions are in the extended version of this paper [20].

3.1 Abstracting Conjunctive Transition Formulas

This section shows how to compute a $\mathbb{Q}$-VASR abstraction for a consistent *conjunctive* formula. When the input formula is in $\exists LRA$, the computed $\mathbb{Q}$-VASR abstraction will be a best $\mathbb{Q}$-VASR abstraction of the input formula. The intuition is that, since $\exists LRA$ is a convex theory, a best $\mathbb{Q}$-VASR abstraction consists of a single transition. For $\exists LIRA$ formulas, our procedure produces a $\mathbb{Q}$-VASR abstract that is not guaranteed to be best, precisely because $\exists LIRA$ is not convex.

Let C be consistent, conjunctive transition formula. Observe that the set $Res_C \triangleq \{\langle \mathbf{s}, a \rangle : C \models \mathbf{s} \cdot \mathbf{x}' = a\}$, which represents linear combinations of variables that are *reset* across C, forms a vector space. Similarly, the set $Inc_C = \{\langle \mathbf{s}, a \rangle : C \models \mathbf{s} \cdot \mathbf{x}' = \mathbf{s} \cdot \mathbf{x} + a\}$, which represents linear combinations of variables that are *incremented* across C, forms a vector space. We compute bases for both Res_C and Inc_C, say $\{\langle \mathbf{s}_1, a_1 \rangle, ..., \langle \mathbf{s}_m, a_m \rangle\}$ and $\{\langle \mathbf{s}_{m+1}, a_{m+1} \rangle, ..., \langle \mathbf{s}_d, a_d \rangle\}$, respectively. We define $\hat{\alpha}(C)$ to be the $\mathbb{Q}$-VASR abstraction $\hat{\alpha}(C) \triangleq (S, \{(\mathbf{r}, \mathbf{a})\})$, where

$$
S \triangleq \begin{bmatrix} \mathbf{s}_1 \\ \vdots \\ \mathbf{s}_d \end{bmatrix} \quad \mathbf{r} \triangleq [\underbrace{0 \cdots 0}_{m \text{ times}} \overbrace{1 \cdots 1}^{(d-m) \text{ times}}] \quad \mathbf{a} \triangleq \begin{bmatrix} a_1 \\ \vdots \\ a_d \end{bmatrix}.
$$

Example 1. Let C be the formula $x' = x + y \wedge y' = 2y \wedge w' = w \wedge w = w + 1 \wedge z' = w$. The vector space of resets has basis $\{\langle [0\ 0\ -1\ 1], 0 \rangle\}$ (representing that $z - w$ is reset to 0). The vector space of increments has basis $\{\langle [1\ -1\ 0\ 0], 0 \rangle, \langle [0\ 0\ 1\ 0], 0 \rangle, \langle [0\ 0\ -1\ 1], 1 \rangle\}$ (representing that the difference $x - y$ does not change, the difference $z - w$ increases by 1, and the variable w does not change). A best abstraction of C is thus the four-dimensional $\mathbb{Q}$-VASR

$$
V = \left\{ \left(\begin{bmatrix} 0 \\ 1 \\ 1 \\ 1 \end{bmatrix}, \begin{bmatrix} 0 \\ 0 \\ 0 \\ 1 \end{bmatrix} \right) \right\}, S = \begin{bmatrix} 0 & 0 & -1 & 1 \\ 1 & -1 & 0 & 0 \\ 0 & 0 & 1 & 0 \\ 0 & 0 & -1 & 1 \end{bmatrix}.
$$

In particular, notice that since the term $z - w$ is both incremented and reset, it is represented by two different dimensions in $\hat{\alpha}(C)$.

Proposition 1. *For any consistent, conjunctive transition formula C, $\hat{\alpha}(C)$ is a $\mathbb{Q}$-VASR abstraction of C. If C is expressed in $\exists LRA$, then $\hat{\alpha}(C)$ is best.*

3.2 Computing Least Upper Bounds

This section shows how to compute least upper bounds w.r.t. the $\preceq$ order.

By definition of the $\preceq$ order, if (S, V) is an upper bound of (S^1, V^1) and (S^2, V^2), then there must exist matrices T^1 and T^2 such that $T^1 S^1 = S = T^2 S^2$, $V^1 \Vdash_{T^1} V$, and $V^2 \Vdash_{T^2} V$. As we shall see, if (S, V) is a *least* upper bound, then it is completely determined by the matrices T^1 and T^2. Thus, we shift our attention to computing simulation matrices T^1 and T^2 that induce a least upper bound.

In view of the desired equation $T^1 S^1 = S = T^2 S^2$, let us consider the constraint $T^1 S^1 = T^2 S^2$ on two *unknown* matrices T^1 and T^2. Clearly, we have $T^1 S^1 = T^2 S^2$ iff each (T^1_i, T^2_i) belongs to the set $\mathcal{T} \triangleq \{ (\mathbf{t}^1, \mathbf{t}^2) : \mathbf{t}^1 S^1 = \mathbf{t}^2 S^2 \}$. Observe that $\mathcal{T}$ is a vector space, so there is a *best* solution to the constraint $T^1 S^1 = T^2 S^2$: choose T^1 and T^2 so that the set of all row pairs (T^1_i, T^2_i) forms a basis for $\mathcal{T}$. In the following, we use *pushout*(S^1, S^2) to denote a function that computes such a *best* (T^1, T^2).

While *pushout* gives a *best* solution to the equation $T^1 S^1 = T^2 S^2$, it is not sufficient for the purpose of computing least upper bounds for $\mathbb{Q}$-VASR abstractions, because T^1 and T^2 may not respect the structure of the $\mathbb{Q}$-VASR V^1 and V^2 (i.e., there may be no $\mathbb{Q}$-VASR V such that $V^1 \Vdash_{T^1} V$ and $V^2 \Vdash_{T^2} V$). Thus, we must further constrain our problem by requiring that T^1 and T^2 are *coherent* with respect to V^1 and V^2 (respectively).

Definition 4. *Let V be a d-dimensional $\mathbb{Q}$-VASR. We say that $i, j \in \{1, ..., d\}$ are **coherent dimensions** of V if for all transitions $(\mathbf{r}, \mathbf{a}) \in V$ we have $r_i = r_j$ (i.e., every transition of V that resets i also resets j and vice versa). We denote that i and j are coherent dimensions of V by writing $i \equiv_V j$, and observe that $\equiv_V$ forms an equivalence relation on $\{1, ..., d\}$. We refer to the equivalence classes of $\equiv_V$ as the **coherence classes** of V.*

*A matrix $T \in \mathbb{Q}^{e \times d}$ **is coherent with respect to** V if and only if each of its rows have non-zero values only in the dimensions corresponding to a single coherence class of V.*

For any d-dimensional $\mathbb{Q}$-VASR V and coherence class $C = \{c_1, ..., c_k\}$ of V, define Π_C to be the $k \times d$ dimensional matrix whose rows are $\mathbf{e}_{c_1}, ..., \mathbf{e}_{c_k}$. Intuitively, Π_C is a projection onto the set of dimensions in C.

Coherence is a necessary and sufficient condition for linear simulations between $\mathbb{Q}$-VASR in a sense described in Lemmas 1 and 2.

Lemma 1. *Let V^1 and V^2 be $\mathbb{Q}$-VASR (of dimension d and e, respectively), and let $T \in \mathbb{Q}^{e \times d}$ be a matrix such that $V^1 \Vdash_T V^2$. Then T must be coherent with respect to V^1.*

Let V be a d-dimensional $\mathbb{Q}$-VASR and let $T \in \mathbb{Q}^{e \times d}$ be a matrix that is coherent with respect to V and has no zero rows. Then there is a (unique) e-dimensional $\mathbb{Q}$-VASR $image(V, T)$ such that its transition relation $\rightarrow_{image(V,T)}$

Algorithm 2. $(S^1, V^1) \sqcup (S^2, V^2)$

---

input : Normal $\mathbb{Q}$-VASR abstractions (S^1, V^1) and (S^2, V^2) of equal concrete dimension

output: Least upper bound (w.r.t. $\preceq$) of (S^1, V^2) and (S^1, V^2)

1   $S, T^1, T^2 \leftarrow$ empty matrices;

2   **foreach** *coherence class* C^1 *of* V^1 **do**

3   **foreach** *coherence class* C^2 *of* V^2 **do**

4         $(U^1, U^2) \leftarrow pushout(\Pi_{C^1} S^1, \Pi_{C^2} S^2)$;

5         $S \leftarrow \begin{bmatrix} S \\ U^1 \Pi_{C^1} S^1 \end{bmatrix}$; $T^1 \leftarrow \begin{bmatrix} T^1 \\ U^1 \Pi_{C^1} \end{bmatrix}$; $T^2 \leftarrow \begin{bmatrix} T^2 \\ U^2 \Pi_{C^2} \end{bmatrix}$;

6   $V \leftarrow image(V^1, T^1) \cup image(V^2, T^2)$;

7   **return** (S, V)

---

is equal to $\{(T\mathbf{u}, T\mathbf{v}) : \mathbf{u} \rightarrow_V \mathbf{v}\}$ (the image of V's transition relation under T). This $\mathbb{Q}$-VASR can be defined by:

$$image(V, T) \triangleq \{(T \boxtimes \mathbf{r}, T\mathbf{a}) : (\mathbf{r}, \mathbf{a}) \in V\}$$

where $T \boxtimes \mathbf{r}$ is the reset vector $\mathbf{r}$ translated along T (i.e., $(T \boxtimes \mathbf{r})_i = r_j$ where j is an arbitrary choice among dimensions for which T_{ij} is non-zero—at least one such j exists because the row T_i is non-zero by assumption, and the choice of j is arbitrary because all such j belong to the same coherence class by the assumption that T is coherent with respect to V).

Lemma 2. *Let V be a d-dimensional $\mathbb{Q}$-VASR and let $T \in \mathbb{Q}^{e \times d}$ be a matrix that is coherent with respect to V and has no zero rows. Then the transition relation of $image(V, T)$ is the image of V's transition relation under T (i.e., $\rightarrow_{image(V,T)}$ is equal to $\{(T\mathbf{u}, T\mathbf{v}) : \mathbf{u} \rightarrow_V \mathbf{v}\}$).*

Finally, prior to describing our least upper bound algorithm, we must define a technical condition that is both assumed and preserved by the procedure:

Definition 5. *A $\mathbb{Q}$-VASR abstraction (S, V) is **normal** if there is no non-zero vector $\mathbf{z}$ that is coherent with respect to V such that $\mathbf{z}S = 0$ (i.e., the rows of S that correspond to any coherence class of V are linearly independent).*

Intuitively, a $\mathbb{Q}$-VASR abstraction that is *not* normal contains information that is either inconsistent or redundant.

We now present a strategy for computing least upper bounds of $\mathbb{Q}$-VASR abstractions. Fix (normal) $\mathbb{Q}$-VASR abstractions (S^1, V^1) and (S^2, V^2). Lemmas 1 and 2 together show that a pair of matrices $\widetilde{T}^1$ and $\widetilde{T}^2$ induce an upper bound (not necessarily *least*) on (S^1, V^1) and (S^2, V^2) exactly when the following conditions hold: (1) $\widetilde{T}^1 S^1 = \widetilde{T}^2 S^2$, (2) $\widetilde{T}^1$ is coherent w.r.t. V^1, (3) $\widetilde{T}^2$ is coherent w.r.t. V^2, and (4) neither $\widetilde{T}^1$ nor $\widetilde{T}^2$ contain zero rows. The upper bound induced by $\widetilde{T}^1$ and $\widetilde{T}^2$ is given by

$$ub(\widetilde{T}^1, \widetilde{T}^2) \triangleq (\widetilde{T}^1 S^1, image(V^1, \widetilde{T}^1) \cup image(V^2, T^2)).$$

We now consider how to compute a *best* such $\widetilde{T}^1$ and $\widetilde{T}^2$. Observe that conditions (1), (2), and (3) hold exactly when for each row i, $(\widetilde{T}_i^1, \widetilde{T}_i^2)$ belongs to the set

$$\mathcal{T} \triangleq \{(\mathbf{t}^1, \mathbf{t}^2) : \mathbf{t}^1 S^1 = \mathbf{t}^2 S^2 \wedge \mathbf{t}^1 \text{ coherent w.r.t. } V^1 \wedge \mathbf{t}^1 \text{ coherent w.r.t. } V^2\}.$$

Since a row vector $\mathbf{t}^i$ is coherent w.r.t. V^i iff its non-zero positions belong to the same coherence class of V^i (equivalently, $\mathbf{t}^i = \mathbf{u}\Pi_{C^i}$ for some coherence class C^i and vector $\mathbf{u}$), we have $\mathcal{T} = \bigcup_{C^1, C^2} \mathcal{T}(C^1, C^2)$, where the union is over all coherence classes C^1 of V^1 and C^2 of V^2, and

$$\mathcal{T}(C^1, C^2) \triangleq \{(\mathbf{u}^1 \Pi_{C^1}, \mathbf{u}^2 \Pi_{C^2}) : \mathbf{u}^1 \Pi_{C^1} S^1 = \mathbf{u}^2 \Pi_{C^2} S^2\}.$$

Observe that each $\mathcal{T}(C^1, C^2)$ is a vector space, so we can compute a pair of matrices T^1 and T^2 such that the rows (T_i^1, T_i^2) collectively form a basis for each $\mathcal{T}(C^1, C^2)$. Since (S^1, V^1) and (S^2, V^2) are normal (by assumption), neither T^1 nor T^2 may contain zero rows (condition (4) is satisfied). Finally, we have that $ub(T^1, T^2)$ is the *least* upper bound of (S^1, V^1) and (S^2, V^2). Algorithm 2 is a straightforward realization of this strategy.

Proposition 2. *Let (S^1, V^1) and (S^2, V^2) be normal $\mathbb{Q}$-VASR abstractions of equal concrete dimension. Then the $\mathbb{Q}$-VASR abstraction (S, V) computed by Algorithm 2 is normal and is a least upper bound of (S^1, V^2) and (S^2, V^2).*

4   Control Flow and $\mathbb{Q}$-VASRS

In this section, we give a method for improving the precision of our loop summarization technique by using $\mathbb{Q}$-VASRS; that is, $\mathbb{Q}$-VASR extended with control states. While $\mathbb{Q}$-VASRs over-approximate control flow using non-determinism, $\mathbb{Q}$-VASRSs allow us to analyze phenomena such as oscillating and multi-phase loops.

We begin with an example that demonstrates the precision gained by $\mathbb{Q}$-VASRS. The loop in Fig. 2a oscillates between (1) incrementing variable i by 1 and (2) incrementing both variables i and x by 1. Suppose that we wish to prove

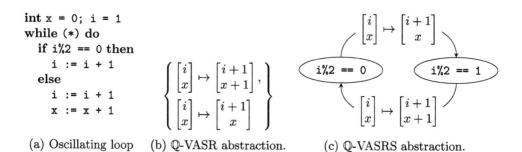

(a) Oscillating loop   (b) $\mathbb{Q}$-VASR abstraction.   (c) $\mathbb{Q}$-VASRS abstraction.

Fig. 2. An oscillating loop and its representation as a $\mathbb{Q}$-VASR and $\mathbb{Q}$-VASRS.

that, starting with the configuration $x = 0 \wedge i = 1$, the loop maintains the invariant that $2x \leq i$. The (best) $\mathbb{Q}$-VASR abstraction of the loop, pictured in Fig. 2b, over-approximates the control flow of the loop by treating the conditional branch in the loop as a non-deterministic branch. This over-approximation may violate the invariant $2x \leq i$ by repeatedly executing the path where both variables are incremented. On the other hand, the $\mathbb{Q}$-VASRS abstraction of the loop pictured in Fig. 2c captures the understanding that the loop must oscillate between the two paths. The loop summary obtained from the reachability relation of this $\mathbb{Q}$-VASRS is powerful enough to prove the invariant $2x \leq i$ holds (under the precondition $x = 0 \wedge i = 1$).

4.1 Technical Details

In the following, we give a method for over-approximating the transitive closure of a transition formula $F(\mathbf{x}, \mathbf{x}')$ using a $\mathbb{Q}$-VASRS. We start by defining *predicate* $\mathbb{Q}$-VASRS, a variation of $\mathbb{Q}$-VASRS with control states that correspond to disjoint state predicates (where the states intuitively belong to the transition formula F rather than the $\mathbb{Q}$-VASRS itself). We extend linear simulations and best abstractions to predicate $\mathbb{Q}$-VASRS, and give an algorithm for synthesizing best predicate $\mathbb{Q}$-VASRS abstractions (for a given set of predicates). Finally, we give an end-to-end algorithm for over-approximating the transitive closure of a transition formula.

Definition 6. *A **predicate** $\mathbb{Q}$-**VASRS** over $\mathbf{x}$ is a $\mathbb{Q}$-VASRS $\mathcal{V} = (P, E)$, such that each control state is a predicate over the variables $\mathbf{x}$ and the predicates in P are pairwise inconsistent (for all $p \neq q \in P$, $p \wedge q$ is unsatisfiable).*

We extend linear simulations to predicate $\mathbb{Q}$-VASRS as follows:

- Let $F(\mathbf{x}, \mathbf{x}')$ be an n-dimensional transition formula and let $\mathcal{V} = (P, E)$ be an m-dimensional $\mathbb{Q}$-VASRS over $\mathbf{x}$. We say that a linear transformation $S : \mathbb{Q}^{m \times n}$ is a linear simulation from F to $\mathcal{V}$ if for all $\mathbf{u}, \mathbf{v} \in \mathbb{Q}^n$ such that $\mathbf{u} \rightarrow_F \mathbf{v}$, (1) there is a (unique) $p \in P$ such that $p(\mathbf{u})$ is valid (2) there is a (unique) $q \in P$ such that $q(\mathbf{v})$ is valid, and (3) $(p, S\mathbf{u}) \rightarrow_{\mathcal{V}} (q, S\mathbf{v})$.
- Let $\mathcal{V}^1 = (P^1, E^1)$ and $\mathcal{V}^2 = (P^2, E^2)$ be predicate $\mathbb{Q}$-VASRSs over $\mathbf{x}$ (for some $\mathbf{x}$) of dimensions d and e, respectively. We say that a linear transformation $S : \mathbb{Q}^{e \times d}$ is a linear simulation from $\mathcal{V}^1$ to $\mathcal{V}^2$ if for all $p^1, q^1 \in P^1$ and for all $\mathbf{u}, \mathbf{v} \in \mathbb{Q}^d$ such that $(p^1, \mathbf{u}) \rightarrow_{\mathcal{V}^1} (q^1, \mathbf{v})$, there exists (unique) $p^2, q^2 \in P^2$ such that (1) $(p^2, S\mathbf{u}) \rightarrow_{\mathcal{V}^2} (q^2, S\mathbf{v})$, (2) $p^1 \models p^2$, and (3) $q^1 \models q^2$.

We define a $\mathbb{Q}$-VASRS abstraction over $\mathbf{x} = x_1, ..., x_n$ to be a pair $(S, \mathcal{V})$ consisting of a rational matrix $S \in \mathbb{Q}^{d \times n}$ and a predicate $\mathbb{Q}$-VASRS of dimension d over $\mathbf{x}$. We extend the simulation preorder $\preceq$ to $\mathbb{Q}$-VASRS abstractions in the natural way. Extending the definition of "best" abstractions requires more care, since we can always find a "better" $\mathbb{Q}$-VASRS abstraction (strictly smaller in $\preceq$ order) by using a finer set of predicates. However, if we consider only predicate

---

Algorithm 3. `abstract-VASRS`(F, P)

---

    input : Transition formula $F(\mathbf{x}, \mathbf{x}')$, set of pairwise-disjoint predicates P over
             $\mathbf{x}$ such that for all $\mathbf{u}, \mathbf{v}$ with $\mathbf{u} \rightarrow_F \mathbf{v}$, there exists $p, q \in P$ with $p(\mathbf{u})$
             and $q(\mathbf{v})$ both valid
    output: Best $\mathbb{Q}$-VASRS abstraction of F with control states P
1 For all $p, q \in P$, let $(S_{p,q}, V_{p,q}) \leftarrow$ `abstract-VASR`$(p(\mathbf{x}) \wedge F(\mathbf{x}, \mathbf{x}') \wedge q(\mathbf{x}'))$;
2 $(S, V) \leftarrow$ least upper bound of all $(S_{p,q}, V_{p,q})$;
3 For all $p, q \in P$, let $T_{p,q} \leftarrow$ the simulation matrix from $(S_{p,q}, V_{p,q})$ to (S, V);
4 $E = \{(p, \mathbf{r}, \mathbf{a}, q) : p, q \in P, (\mathbf{r}, \mathbf{a}) \in image(V_{p,q}, T_{p,q})\}$;
5 **return** $(S, (P, E))$

$\mathbb{Q}$-VASRS that share the same set of control states, then best abstractions do exist and can be computed using Algorithm 3.

Algorithm 3 works as follows: first, for each pair of formulas $p, q \in P$, compute a best $\mathbb{Q}$-VASR abstraction of the formula $p(\mathbf{x}) \wedge F(\mathbf{x}, \mathbf{x}') \wedge q(\mathbf{x}')$ and call it $(S_{p,q}, V_{p,q})$. $(S_{p,q}, V_{p,q})$ over-approximates the transitions of F that begin in a program state satisfying p and end in a program state satisfying q. Second, we compute the least upper bound of all $\mathbb{Q}$-VASR abstractions $(S_{p,q}, V_{p,q})$ to get a $\mathbb{Q}$-VASR abstraction (S, V) for F. As a side-effect of the least upper bound computation, we obtain a linear simulation $T_{p,q}$ from $(S_{p,q}, V_{p,q})$ to (S, V) for each p, q. A best $\mathbb{Q}$-VASRS abstraction of $F(\mathbf{x}, \mathbf{x}')$ with control states P has S as its simulation matrix and has the image of $V_{p,q}$ under $T_{p,q}$ as the edges from p to q.

Proposition 3. *Given an transition formula $F(\mathbf{x}, \mathbf{x}')$ and control states P over $\mathbf{x}$, Algorithm 3 computes the best predicate $\mathbb{Q}$-VASRS abstraction of F with control states P.*

We now describe `iter-VASRS` (Algorithm 4), which uses $\mathbb{Q}$-VASRS to over-approximate the transitive closure of transition formulas. Towards our goal of *predictable* program analysis, we desire the analysis to be *monotone* in the sense that if F and G are transition formulas such that F entails G, then `iter-VASRS`(F) entails `iter-VASRS`(G). A sufficient condition to guarantee monotonicity of the overall analysis is to require that the set of control states that we compute for F is at least as fine as the set of control states we compute for G. We can achieve this by making the set of control states P of input transition formula $F(\mathbf{x}, \mathbf{x}')$ equal to the set of connected regions of the topological closure of $\exists \mathbf{x}'.F$ (lines 1–4). Note that this set of predicates may fail the contract of `abstract-VASRS`: there may exist a transition $\mathbf{u} \rightarrow_F \mathbf{v}$ such that $\mathbf{v} \not\models \bigvee P$ (this occurs when there is a state of F with no outgoing transitions). As a result, $(S, \mathcal{V}) =$ `abstract-VASRS`(F, P) does not necessarily approximate F; however, it *does* over-approximate $F \wedge \bigvee P(\mathbf{x}')$. An over-approximation of the transitive closure of F can easily be obtained from $reach(\mathcal{V})(S\mathbf{x}, S\mathbf{x}')$ (the over-approximation of the transitive closure of $F \wedge \bigvee P(\mathbf{x}')$ obtained from the

$\mathbb{Q}$-VASRS abstraction $(S, \mathcal{V})$) by sequentially composing with the disjunction of F and the identity relation (line 6).

Algorithm 4. iter-VASRS(F)

---

    input : Transition formula $F(\mathbf{x}, \mathbf{x}')$
    output: Over-approximation of the transitive closure of F
1 $P \leftarrow$ topological closure of DNF of $\exists \mathbf{x}'.F$ (see [17]);
2 /* Compute connected regions   */
3 **while** $\exists p_1, p_2 \in P$ *with* $p_1 \wedge p_2$ *satisfiable* **do**
4    $\lfloor \; P \leftarrow (P \setminus \{p_1, p_2\}) \cup \{p_1 \vee p_2\}$
5 $(S, \mathcal{V}) \leftarrow$ abstract-VASRS(F, P);
6 **return** $reach(\mathcal{V})(S\mathbf{x}, S\mathbf{x}') \circ (\mathbf{x}' = \mathbf{x} \vee F)$

Precision Improvement. The `abstract-VASRS` algorithm uses predicates to infer the control structure of a $\mathbb{Q}$-VASRS, but after computing the $\mathbb{Q}$-VASRS abstraction, `iter-VASRS` makes no further use of the predicates (i.e., the predicates are irrelevant in the computation of $reach(\mathcal{V})$). Predicates can be used to improve `iter-VASRS` as follows: the reachability relation of a $\mathbb{Q}$-VASRS is expressed by a formula that uses auxiliary variables to represent the state at which the computation begins and ends [8]. These variables can be used to encode that the pre-state of the transitive closure must satisfy the predicate corresponding to the begin state and the post-state must satisfy the predicate corresponding to the end state. As an example, consider the Fig. 2 and suppose that we wish to prove the invariant $x \leq 2i$ under the pre-condition $i = 0 \wedge x = 0$. While this invariant holds, we cannot prove it because there is counter example if the computation begins at $i\%2 == 1$. By applying the above improvement, we can prove that the computation must begin at $i\%2 == 0$, and the invariant is verified.

5 Evaluation

The goals of our evaluation is the answer the following questions:

- Are $\mathbb{Q}$-VASR sufficiently expressive to be able to generate accurate loop summaries?
- Does the $\mathbb{Q}$-VASRS technique improve upon the precision of $\mathbb{Q}$-VASR?
- Are the $\mathbb{Q}$-VASR/$\mathbb{Q}$-VASRS loop summarization algorithms performant?

We implemented our loop summarization procedure and the compositional whole-program summarization technique described in Sect. 1.1. We ran on a suite of 165 benchmarks, drawn from the C4B [2] and HOLA [4] suites, as well as the safe, integer-only benchmarks in the loops category of SV-Comp 2019 [22]. We ran each benchmark with a time-out of 5 min, and recorded how many benchmarks were proved safe by our $\mathbb{Q}$-VASR-based technique and our $\mathbb{Q}$-VASRS-based technique. For context, we also compare with CRA [14] (a related loop summarization technique), as well as SeaHorn [7] and UltimateAutomizer [9] (state-of-the-art software model checkers). The results are shown in Fig. 3.

The number of assertions proved correct using Q-VASR is comparable to both SeaHorn and UltimateAutomizer, demonstrating that Q-VASR can indeed model interesting loop phenomena. Q-VASRS-based summarization significantly improves precision, proving the correctness of 93% of assertions in the svcomp suite, and more than any other tool in total. Note that the most precise tool for each suite is not strictly better than each of the other tools; in particular, there is only a single program in the HOLA suite that neither Q-VASRS nor CRA can prove safe.

CRA-based summarization is the most performant of all the compared techniques, followed by Q-VASR and Q-VASRS. SeaHorn and UltimateAutomizer employ abstraction-refinement loops, and so take significantly longer to run the test suite.

		Q-VASR		Q-VASRS		CRA		SeaHorn		UltAuto	
		#safe	time	#safe	time	#safe	time	#safe	time	#safe	time
C4B	35	21	37.9	**31**	35.4	27	**33.1**	23	2434.4	25	3881.6
HOLA	46	32	57.2	39	73.0	**40**	**56.0**	35	2115.0	36	2995.9
svcomp19-int	84	68	**86.9**	**78**	184.5	76	91.9	62	3038.0	64	6923.5

Fig. 3. Experimental results.

6   Related Work

Compositional Analysis. Our analysis follows the same high-level structure as compositional recurrence analysis (CRA) [5,14]. Our analysis differs from CRA in the way that it summarizes loops: we compute loop summaries by over-approximating loops with vector addition systems and computing reachability relations, whereas CRA computes loop summaries by extracting recurrence relations and computing closed forms. The advantage of our approach is that is that we can use Q-VASR to accurately model multi-path loops and can make theoretical guarantees about the precision of our analysis; the advantage of CRA is its ability to generate non-linear invariants.

Vector Addition Systems. Our invariant generation method draws upon Haase and Halfon's polytime procedure for computing the reachability relation of integer vector addition systems with states and resets [8]. Generalization from the integer case to the rational case is straightforward. Continuous Petri nets [3] are a related generalization of vector addition systems, where time is taken to be continuous (Q-VASR, in contrast, have rational state spaces but discrete time). Reachability for continuous Petri nets is computable polytime [6] and definable in ∃LRA [1].

Sinn et al. present a technique for resource bound analysis that is based on modeling programs by lossy vector addition system with states [21]. Sinn et al. model programs using vector addition systems with states over the natural numbers, which enables them to use termination bounds for VASS to compute upper bounds on resource usage. In contrast, we use VASS with resets over the rationals, which (in contrast to VASS over $\mathbb{N}$) have a $\exists$LIRA-definable reachability relation, enabling us to summarize loops. Moreover, Sinn et al.'s method for extracting VASS models of programs is heuristic, whereas our method gives precision guarantees.

Affine and Polynomial Programs. The problem of *polynomial* invariant generation has been investigated for various program models that generalize $\mathbb{Q}$-VASR, including solvable polynomial loops [19], (extended) P-solvable loops [11,15], and affine programs [10]. Like ours, these techniques are *predictable* in the sense that they can make theoretical guarantees about invariant quality. The kinds invariants that can be produced using these techniques (conjunctions of polynomial equations) is incomparable with those generated by the method presented in this paper ($\exists$LIRA formulas).

Symbolic Abstraction. The main contribution of this paper is a technique for synthesizing the best abstraction of a transition formula expressible in the language of $\mathbb{Q}$-VASR (with or without states). This is closely related to the *symbolic abstraction* problem, which computes the best abstraction of a formula within an abstract domain. The problem of computing best abstractions has been undertaken for finite-height abstract domains [18], template constraint matrices (including intervals and octagons) [16], and polyhedra [5,24]. Our best abstraction result differs in that (1) it is for a disjunctive domain and (2) the notion of "best" is based on simulation rather than the typical order-theoretic framework.

References

1. Blondin, M., Finkel, A., Haase, C., Haddad, S.: Approaching the coverability problem continuously. In: Chechik, M., Raskin, J.-F. (eds.) TACAS 2016. LNCS, vol. 9636, pp. 480–496. Springer, Heidelberg (2016). https://doi.org/10.1007/978-3-662-49674-9_28
2. Carbonneaux, Q., Hoffmann, J., Shao, Z.: Compositional certified resource bounds. In: PLDI (2015)
3. David, R., Alla, H.: Continuous Petri nets. In: Proceedings of 8th European Workshop on Applications and Theory Petri Nets, pp. 275–294 (1987)
4. Dillig, I., Dillig, T., Li, B., McMillan, K.: Inductive invariant generation via abductive inference. In: OOPSLA (2013)
5. Farzan, A., Kincaid, Z.: Compositional recurrence analysis. In: FMCAD (2015)
6. Fraca, E., Haddad, S.: Complexity analysis of continuous Petri nets. Fundam. Inf. **137**(1), 1–28 (2015)
7. Gurfinkel, A., Kahsai, T., Komuravelli, A., Navas, J.A.: The SeaHorn verification framework. In: Kroening, D., Păsăreanu, C.S. (eds.) CAV 2015. LNCS, vol. 9206, pp. 343–361. Springer, Cham (2015). https://doi.org/10.1007/978-3-319-21690-4_20

8. Haase, C., Halfon, S.: Integer vector addition systems with states. In: Ouaknine, J., Potapov, I., Worrell, J. (eds.) RP 2014. LNCS, vol. 8762, pp. 112–124. Springer, Cham (2014). https://doi.org/10.1007/978-3-319-11439-2_9

9. Heizmann, M., et al.: Ultimate automizer and the search for perfect interpolants. In: Beyer, D., Huisman, M. (eds.) TACAS 2018. LNCS, vol. 10806, pp. 447–451. Springer, Cham (2018). https://doi.org/10.1007/978-3-319-89963-3_30

10. Hrushovski, E., Ouaknine, J., Pouly, A., Worrell, J.: Polynomial invariants for affine programs. In: Logic in Computer Science, pp. 530–539 (2018)

11. Humenberger, A., Jaroschek, M., Kovács, L.: Invariant Generation for Multi-Path Loops with Polynomial Assignments. In: Verification, Model Checking, and Abstract Interpretation. LNCS, vol. 10747, pp. 226–246. Springer, Cham (2018). https://doi.org/10.1007/978-3-319-73721-8_11

12. Karp, R.M., Miller, R.E.: Parallel program schemata. J. Comput. Syst. Sci. **3**(2), 147–195 (1969)

13. Kincaid, Z., Breck, J., Forouhi Boroujeni, A., Reps, T.: Compositional recurrence analysis revisited. In: PLDI (2017)

14. Kincaid, Z., Cyphert, J., Breck, J., Reps, T.: Non-linear reasoning for invariant synthesis. PACMPL **2**(POPL), 1–33 (2018)

15. Kovács, L.: Reasoning algebraically about P-solvable loops. In: Ramakrishnan, C.R., Rehof, J. (eds.) TACAS 2008. LNCS, vol. 4963, pp. 249–264. Springer, Heidelberg (2008). https://doi.org/10.1007/978-3-540-78800-3_18

16. Li, Y., Albarghouthi, A., Kincaid, Z., Gurfinkel, A., Chechik, M.: Symbolic optimization with SMT solvers. In: POPL, pp. 607–618 (2014)

17. Monniaux, D.: A quantifier elimination algorithm for linear real arithmetic. In: Cervesato, I., Veith, H., Voronkov, A. (eds.) LPAR 2008. LNCS (LNAI), vol. 5330, pp. 243–257. Springer, Heidelberg (2008). https://doi.org/10.1007/978-3-540-89439-1_18

18. Reps, T., Sagiv, M., Yorsh, G.: Symbolic implementation of the best transformer. In: Steffen, B., Levi, G. (eds.) VMCAI 2004. LNCS, vol. 2937, pp. 252–266. Springer, Heidelberg (2004). https://doi.org/10.1007/978-3-540-24622-0_21

19. Rodríguez-Carbonell, E., Kapur, D.: Automatic generation of polynomial loop invariants: algebraic foundations. In: ISSAC, pp. 266–273 (2004)

20. Silverman, J., Kincaid, Z.: Loop summarization with rational vector addition systems (extended version). arXiv e-prints. arXiv:1905.06495, May 2019

21. Sinn, M., Zuleger, F., Veith, H.: A simple and scalable static analysis for bound analysis and amortized complexity analysis. In: Biere, A., Bloem, R. (eds.) CAV 2014. LNCS, vol. 8559, pp. 745–761. Springer, Cham (2014). https://doi.org/10.1007/978-3-319-08867-9_50

22. 8th International Competition on Software Verification (SV-COMP 2019) (2019). https://sv-comp.sosy-lab.org/2019/

23. Tarjan, R.E.: A unified approach to path problems. J. ACM **28**(3), 577–593 (1981)

24. Thakur, A., Reps, T.: A method for symbolic computation of abstract operations. In: Madhusudan, P., Seshia, S.A. (eds.) CAV 2012. LNCS, vol. 7358, pp. 174–192. Springer, Heidelberg (2012). https://doi.org/10.1007/978-3-642-31424-7_17

14

Formal Verification of Quantum Algorithms Using Quantum Hoare Logic

Junyi Liu[1,2], Bohua Zhan[1,2(✉)], Shuling Wang[1(✉)], Shenggang Ying[1], Tao Liu[1], Yangjia Li[1], Mingsheng Ying[1,3,4], and Naijun Zhan[1,2]

[1] State Key Laboratory of Computer Science, Institute of Software, Chinese Academy of Sciences, Beijing, China
{liujy,bzhan,wangsl,yingsg,liut,yangjia,znj}@ios.ac.cn
[2] University of Chinese Academy of Sciences, Beijing, China
[3] University of Technology Sydney, Sydney, Australia
[4] Tsinghua University, Beijing, China

Abstract. We formalize the theory of quantum Hoare logic (QHL) [TOPLAS 33(6),19], an extension of Hoare logic for reasoning about quantum programs. In particular, we formalize the syntax and semantics of quantum programs in Isabelle/HOL, write down the rules of quantum Hoare logic, and verify the soundness and completeness of the deduction system for partial correctness of quantum programs. As preliminary work, we formalize some necessary mathematical background in linear algebra, and define tensor products of vectors and matrices on quantum variables. As an application, we verify the correctness of Grover's search algorithm. To our best knowledge, this is the first time a Hoare logic for quantum programs is formalized in an interactive theorem prover, and used to verify the correctness of a nontrivial quantum algorithm.

1 Introduction

Due to the rapid progress of quantum technology in the recent years, it is predicted that practical quantum computers can be built within 10–15 years. Especially during the last 3 years, breakthroughs have been made in quantum hardware. Programmable superconductor quantum computers and trapped ion quantum computers have been built in universities and companies [1,3,4,6,23].

In another direction, intensive research on quantum programming has been conducted in the last decade [16,45,51,53], as surveyed in [27,52]. In particular, several quantum programming languages have been defined and their compilers have been implemented, including Quipper [31], Scaffold [35], QWire [47], Microsoft's LIQUi|⟩ [25] and Q# [57], IBM's OpenQASM [22], Google's Cirq [30], ProjectQ [56], Chisel-Q [40], Quil [55] and $Q\,|SI\rangle$ [39]. These research allow quantum programs to first run on an ideal simulator for testing, and then on physical devices [5]. For instance, many small quantum algorithms and protocols have already been programmed and run on IBM's simulators and quantum computers [1,2].

Clearly, simulators can only be used for testing. It shows the correctness of the program on one or a few inputs, not its correctness under all possible inputs. Various theories and tools have been developed to formally reason about quantum programs for all inputs on a fixed number of qubits. Equivalence checking [7,8], termination analysis [38], reachability analysis [64], and invariant generation [62] can be used to verify the correctness or termination of quantum programs. Unfortunately, the size of quantum programs on which these tools are applicable is quite limited. This is because all of these tools still perform calculations over the entire state space, which for quantum algorithms has size exponential in the number of qubits. For instance, even on the best supercomputers today, simulation of a quantum program is restricted to about 50–60 qubits. Most model-checking algorithms, which need to perform calculations on operators over the state space, are restricted to 25–30 qubits with the current computing resources.

Deductive program verification presents a way to solve this state space explosion problem. In deductive verification, we do not attempt to execute the program or explore its state space. Rather, we define the semantics of the program using precise mathematical language, and use mathematical reasoning to prove the correctness of the program. These proofs are checked on a computer (for example, in proof assistants such as Coq [15] or Isabelle [44]) to ensure a very high level of confidence.

To apply deductive reasoning to quantum programs, it is necessary to first define a precise semantics and proof system. There has already been a lot of work along these lines [9,20,21,61]. A recent result in this direction is *quantum Hoare logic* (QHL) [61]. It extends to sequential quantum programs the Floyd-Hoare-Naur inductive assertion method for reasoning about correctness of classical programs. QHL is proved to be (relatively) complete for both partial correctness and total correctness of quantum programs.

In this paper, we formalize the theory of quantum Hoare logic in Isabelle/HOL, and use it to verify a non-trivial quantum algorithm – Grover's search algorithm[1]. In more detail, the contributions of this paper are as follows.

1. We formally prove the main results of quantum Hoare logic in Isabelle/HOL. That is, we write down the syntax and semantics of quantum programs, specify the basic Hoare triples, and prove the soundness and completeness of the resulting deduction system (for partial correctness of quantum programs). To our best knowledge, this is the first formalization of a Hoare logic for quantum programs in an interactive theorem prover.
2. As an application of the above formalization, we verify the correctness of Grover's search algorithm. In particular, we prove that the algorithm always succeeds on the (infinite) class of inputs where the expected probability of success is 1.
3. As preparation for the above, we extend Isabelle/HOL's library for linear algebra. Based on existing work [13,58], we formalize many further results in linear algebra for complex matrices, in particular positivity and the Löwner

---

[1] Available online at https://www.isa-afp.org/entries/QHLProver.html.

order. Another significant part of our work is to define the tensor product of vectors and matrices, in a way that can be used to extend and combine operations on quantum variables in a consistent way. Finally, we implement algorithms to automatically prove identities in linear algebra to ease the formalization process.

The organization of the rest of the paper is as follows. Section 2 gives a brief introduction to quantum Hoare logic. Section 3 describes in detail our formalization of QHL in Isabelle/HOL. Section 4 describes the application to Grover's algorithm. Section 5 discusses automation techniques, and gives some idea about the cost of the formalization. Section 6 reviews some related work. Finally, we conclude in Sect. 7 with a discussion of future directions of work.

We expect theorem proving techniques will play a crucial role in formal reasoning about quantum computing, as they did for classical computing, and we hope this paper will be one of the first steps in its development.

2 Quantum Hoare Logic

In this section, we briefly recall the basic concepts and results of quantum Hoare logic (QHL). We only introduce the proof system for partial correctness, since the one for total correctness is not formalized in our work. In addition, we make two simplifications compared to the original work: we consider only variables with finite dimension, and we remove the initialization operation. The complete version of QHL can be found in [61].

In QHL, the number of quantum variables is pre-set before each run of the program. Each quantum variable q_i has dimension d_i. The (pure) state of the quantum variable takes value in a complex vector space of dimension d_i. The overall (pure) state takes value in the tensor product of the vector spaces for the variables, which has dimension $d = \prod d_i$. The mixed state for variable q_i (resp. overall) is given by a $d_i \times d_i$ (resp. $d \times d$) matrix satisfying certain conditions (making them *partial density operators*). The notation $\overline{q}$ is used to denote some finite sequence of distinct quantum variables (called a *quantum register*). We denote the vector space corresponding to $\overline{q}$ by $\mathcal{H}_{\overline{q}}$.

The syntax of quantum programs is given by the following grammar:

$$S ::= \textbf{skip} \mid \overline{q} := U\overline{q} \mid S_1; S_2 \mid \textbf{measure } M[\overline{q}] : \overline{S} \mid \textbf{while } M[\overline{q}] = 1 \textbf{ do } S$$

where

- In $\overline{q} := U\overline{q}$, U is a unitary operator on $\mathcal{H}_{\overline{q}}$, i.e., $U^\dagger U = UU^\dagger = \mathbb{I}$, where $U^\dagger$ is the conjugate transpose of U.
- In **measure** $M[\overline{q}] : \overline{S}$, $M = \{M_m\}$ is a quantum measurement on $\mathcal{H}_{\overline{q}}$, and $\overline{S} = \{S_m\}$ gives quantum programs that will be executed after each possible outcome of the measurement;
- In **while** $M[\overline{q}] = 1$ **do** S, $M = \{M_0, M_1\}$ is a yes-no measurement on $\overline{q}$.

Quantum programs can be regarded as quantum extensions of classical **while** programs. The **skip** statement does nothing, which is the same as in the classical case. The unitary transformation changes the state of $\overline{q}$ according to U. It is the counterpart to the assignment operation in classical programming languages. The sequential composition is similar to its classical counterpart. The measurement statement is the quantum generalisation of the classical case statement **if** $(\square m \cdot b_m \rightarrow S_m)$ **fi**. The loop statement is a quantum generalisation of the classical loop **while** b **do** S.

(Skip)	$\{P\}$ **skip** $\{P\}$
(UT)	$\{U^\dagger PU\}\, \overline{q} := U\overline{q}\, \{P\}$
(Seq)	$\dfrac{\{P\}\, S_1\, \{Q\} \qquad \{Q\}\, S_2\, \{R\}}{\{P\}\, S_1; S_2\, \{R\}}$
(Mea)	$\dfrac{\{P_m\}\, S_m\, \{Q\} \text{ for all } m}{\{\sum_m M_m{}^\dagger P_m M_m\}\ \textbf{measure } M[\overline{q}] :\ \overline{S}\, \{Q\}}$
(Loop)	$\dfrac{\{Q\}\, S\, \{M_0^\dagger P M_0 + M_1^\dagger Q M_1\}}{\{M_0^\dagger P M_0 + M_1^\dagger Q M_1\}\ \textbf{while } M[\overline{q}] = 1\ \textbf{do}\ S\, \{P\}}$
(Order)	$\dfrac{P \sqsubseteq P' \quad \{P'\}\, S\, \{Q'\} \quad Q' \sqsubseteq Q}{\{P\}\, S\, \{Q\}}$

Fig. 1. Proof system qPD for partial correctness

Formally, the denotational semantics for quantum programs is defined as a super-operator $[\![S]\!](\cdot)$, assigning to each quantum program S a mapping between partial density operators. As usual, the denotational semantics is defined by induction on the structure of the quantum program:

1. $[\![\textbf{skip}]\!](\rho) = \rho$.
2. $[\![\overline{q} := U\overline{q}]\!](\rho) = U\rho U^\dagger$.
3. $[\![S_1; S_2]\!](\rho) = [\![S_2]\!]([\![S_1]\!](\rho))$.
4. $[\![(\textbf{measure } M[\overline{q}] :\ \overline{S})]\!](\rho) = \sum_m [\![S_m]\!](M_m \rho M_m^\dagger)$.
5. $[\![(\textbf{while } M[\overline{q}] = 1\ \textbf{do}\ S)]\!](\rho) = \bigvee_{n=0}^{\infty} [\![(\textbf{while } M[\overline{q}] = 1\ \textbf{do}\ S)^n]\!](\rho)$, where $\bigvee$ stands for the least upper bound of partial density operators according to the Löwner partial order $\sqsubseteq$.

The correctness of a quantum program S is expressed by a quantum extension of the Hoare triple $\{P\}S\{Q\}$, where the precondition P and the postcondition Q are matrices satisfying certain conditions for *quantum predicates* [24]. The semantics for partial correctness is defined as follows:

$$\models_{par} \{P\}S\{Q\} \text{ iff } \mathrm{tr}(P\rho) \leq \mathrm{tr}(Q[\![S]\!](\rho)) + \mathrm{tr}(\rho) - \mathrm{tr}([\![S]\!](\rho))$$

for all partial density operators ρ. Here tr is the trace of a matrix. The semantics for total correctness is defined similarly:

$$\models_{tot} \{P\}S\{Q\} \text{ iff } \operatorname{tr}(P\rho) \leq \operatorname{tr}(Q[\![S]\!](\rho)).$$

We note that they become the same when the quantum program S is terminating, i.e. $\operatorname{tr}([\![S]\!](\rho)) = \operatorname{tr}(\rho)$ for all partial density operators ρ.

The proof system qPD for partial correctness of quantum programs is given in Fig. 1. The soundness and (relative) completeness of qPD is proved in [61]:

Theorem 1. *The proof system qPD is sound and (relative) complete for partial correctness of quantum programs.*

3   Formalization in Isabelle/HOL

In this section, we describe the formalization of quantum Hoare logic in Isabelle/HOL. Isabelle/HOL [44] is an interactive theorem prover based on higher-order logic. It provides a flexible language in which one can state and prove theorems in all areas of mathematics and computer science. The proofs are checked by the Isabelle kernel according to the rules of higher-order logic, providing a very high level of confidence in the proofs. A standard application of Isabelle/HOL is the formalization of program semantics and Hoare logic. See [43] for a description of the general technique, applied to a very simple classical programming language.

3.1   Preliminaries in Linear Algebra

Our work is based on the linear algebra library developed by Thiemann and Yamada in the AFP entry [58]. We also use some results on the construction of tensor products in another AFP entry by Bentkamp [13].

In these libraries, the type $'a$ *vec* of vectors with entries in type $'a$ is defined as pairs (n, f), where n is a natural number, and f is a function from natural numbers to $'a$, such that $f(i)$ is undefined when $i \geq n$. Likewise, the type $'a$ *mat* of matrices is defined as triples (nr, nc, f), where nr and nc are natural numbers, and f is a function from pairs of natural numbers to $'a$, such that $f(i, j)$ is undefined when $i \geq nr$ or $j \geq nc$. The terms *carrier_vec* n (resp. *carrier_mat* m n) represent the set of vectors of length n (resp. matrices of dimension $m \times n$). In our work, we focus almost exclusively on the case where $'a$ is the complex numbers. For this case, existing libraries already define concepts such as the adjoint of a matrix, and the (complex) inner product between two vectors. We further define concepts such as Hermitian and unitary matrices, and prove their basic properties.

A key result in linear algebra that is necessary for our work is the Schur decomposition theorem. It states that any complex $n \times n$ matrix A can be written in the form QUQ^{-1}, where Q is unitary and U is upper triangular. In particular, if A is normal (that is, if $AA^\dagger = A^\dagger A$), then A is diagonalizable. A version of the Schur decomposition theorem is formalized in [58], showing that any matrix is similar to an upper-triangular matrix U. However, it does not show that Q can be made unitary. We complete the proof of the full theorem, following the outline of the previous proof.

Next, we define the key concept of positive semi-definite matrices (called positive matrices from now on for simplicity). An $n \times n$ matrix A is positive if $v^\dagger A v \geq 0$ for any vector v. We formalize the basic theory of positive matrices, in particular showing that any positive matrix is Hermitian.

Density operators and partial density operators are then defined as follows:

definition *density_operator A* $\longleftrightarrow$ *positive A* $\wedge$ *trace A* $= 1$
definition *partial_density_operator A* $\longleftrightarrow$ *positive A* $\wedge$ *trace A* ≤ 1

Next, the Löwner partial order is defined as a partial order on the type *complex mat* as follows:

definition *lowner_le* (**infix** $\leq_L$ *65*) **where**
   $A \leq_L B \longleftrightarrow dim\_row\ A = dim\_row\ B \wedge dim\_col\ A = dim\_col\ B \wedge positive\ (B - A)$

A key result that we formalize states that under the Löwner partial order, any non-decreasing sequence of partial density operators has a least upper bound, which is the pointwise limit of the operators when written as $n \times n$ matrices. This is used to define the infinite sum of matrices, necessary for the semantics of the while loop.

3.2 Syntax and Semantics of Quantum Programs

We now begin with the definition of syntax and semantics of quantum programs. First, we describe how to model states of a quantum program. Recall that each quantum program operates on a fixed set of quantum variables q_i, where each q_i has dimension d_i. These information can be recorded in a locale [33] as follows:

locale *state_sig* $=$
  fixes *dims :: nat list*

The total dimension d is given by (here *prod_list* denotes the product of a list of natural numbers).

definition $d = prod\_list\ dims$

The (mixed) state of the system is given by a partial density operator with dimension $d \times d$. Hence, we declare

type_synonym *state* $=$ *complex mat*

definition *density_states :: state set* **where**
  $density\_states = \{\rho \in carrier\_mat\ d\ d.\ partial\_density\_operator\ \rho\}$

Next, we define the concept of quantum programs. They are declared as an inductively-defined datatype in Isabelle/HOL, following the grammar given in Sect. 2.

datatype *com =*
  SKIP
 | *Utrans (complex mat)*
 | *Seq com com (_;;/_ [60, 61] 60)*
 | *Measure nat (nat ⇒ complex mat) (com list)*
 | *While (nat ⇒ complex mat) com*

At this stage, we assume that all matrices involved operate on the global state (that is, all of the quantum variables). We will define commands that operate on a subset of quantum variables later. Measurement is defined over any finite number of matrices. Here *Measure n f C* is a measurement with n options, $f\,i$ for $i < n$ are the measurement matrices, and $C!\,i$ is the command to be executed when the measurement yields result i. Likewise, the first argument to *While* gives measurement matrices, where only the first two values are used.

Next, we define well-formedness and denotation of quantum programs. The predicate *well_com :: com ⇒ bool* expresses the well-formedness condition. For a quantum program to be well-formed, all matrices involved should have the right dimension, the argument to *Utrans* should be unitary, and the measurements for *Measure* and *While* should satisfy the condition $\sum_i M_i^\dagger M_i = \mathbb{I}_n$. Denotation is written as *denote :: com ⇒ state ⇒ state*, defined as in Sect. 2. Both *well_com* and *denote* is defined by induction over the structure of the program. The details are omitted here.

3.3   Hoare Triples

In this section, we define the concept of Hoare triples, and state what needs to be proved for soundness and completeness of the deduction system. First, the concept of quantum predicates is defined as follows:

definition *is_quantum_predicate P ⟷ P ∈ carrier_mat d d ∧ positive P ∧ P ≤_L 1_m d*

With this, we can give the semantic definition of Hoare triples for partial and total correctness. These definitions are intended for the case where P and Q are quantum predicates, and S is a well-formed program. They define what Hoare triples are *valid*.

definition *hoare_total_correct (⊨_t {(1_)}/ (_)/ {(1_)} 50)* **where**
  *⊨_t {P} S {Q} ⟷ (∀ρ∈density_states. trace (P * ρ) ≤ trace (Q * denote S ρ))*

definition *hoare_partial_correct (⊨_p {(1_)}/ (_)/ {(1_)} 50)* **where**
  ⊨_p {P} S {Q} ⟷ (∀ρ∈density_states.
    *trace (P * ρ) ≤ trace (Q * denote S ρ) + (trace ρ − trace (denote S ρ)))*

Next, we define what Hoare triples are *provable* in the *qPD* system. A Hoare triple for partial correctness is provable (written as $\vdash_p \{P\}\ S\ \{Q\}$) if it can be derived by combining the rules in Fig. 1. This condition can be defined in Isabelle/HOL as an inductive predicate. The definition largely parallels the formulae shown in the figure.

With these definitions, we can state and prove soundness and completeness of the Hoare rules for partial correctness. Note that the statement for completeness is very simple, seemingly without needing to state "relative to the theory of the field of complex numbers". This is because we are taking a shallow embedding for predicates, hence any valid statement on complex numbers, in particular positivity of matrices, is in principle available for use in the deduction system (for example, in the assumption to the **order** rule).

theorem *hoare_partial_sound:*
$\vdash_p \{P\} \, S \, \{Q\} \implies well\_com \, S \implies \models_p \{P\} \, S \, \{Q\}$

theorem *hoare_partial_complete:*
$\models_p \{P\} \, S \, \{Q\} \implies well\_com \, S \implies$
$is\_quantum\_predicate \, P \implies is\_quantum\_predicate \, Q \implies \vdash_p \{P\} \, S \, \{Q\}$

The soundness of the Hoare rules is proved by induction on the predicate $\vdash_p$, showing that each rule is sound with respect to $\models_p$. Completeness is proved using the concept of weakest-preconditions, following [61].

3.4   Partial States and Tensor Products

So far in our development, all quantum operations act on the entire global state. However, for the actual applications, we are more interested in operations that act on only a few of the quantum variables. For this, we need to define an *extension* operator, that takes a matrix on the quantum state for a subset of the variables, and extend it to a matrix on all of the variables. More generally, we need to define tensor products on vectors and matrices defined over disjoint sets of variables. These need to satisfy various consistency properties, in particular commutativity and associativity of the tensor product. Note that directly using the Kronecker product is not enough, as the matrix to be extended may act on any (possibly non-adjacent) subset of variables, and we need to distinguish between all possible cases.

Before presenting the definition, we first review some preliminaries. We make use of existing work in [13], in particular their encode and decode operations, and emulate their definitions of *matricize* and *dematricize* (used in [13] to convert between tensors represented as a list and matrices). Given a list of dimensions d_i, the encode and decode operations (named *digit_encode* and *digit_decode*) produce a correspondence between lists of indices a_i satisfying $a_i < d_i$ for each $i < n$, and a natural number less than $\prod_i d_i$. This works in a way similar to finding the binary representation of a number (in which case all "dimensions" are 2). List operation *nths xs S* constructs the subsequence of *xs* containing only the elements at indices in the set S.

The locale *partial_state* extends *state_sig*, adding *vars* for a subset of quantum variables. Our goal is to define the tensor product of two vectors or matrices over *vars* and its complement $-vars$, respectively.

locale *partial_state = state_sig +*
   fixes *vars :: nat set*

First, *dims1* and *dims2* are dimensions of variables *vars* and *-vars*:

definition *dims1 = nths dims vars*
definition *dims2 = nths dims (−vars)*

The operation *encode1* (resp. *encode2*) provides the map from the product of *dims* to the product of *dims1* (resp. *dims2*).

definition *encode1 i = digit_decode dims1 (nths (digit_encode dims i) vars)*
definition *encode2 i = digit_decode dims2 (nths (digit_encode dims i) (−vars))*

With this, tensor products on vectors and matrices are defined as follows (here *d* is the product of *dims*).

definition *tensor_vec :: 'a vec ⇒ 'a vec ⇒ 'a vec* **where**
   *tensor_vec v1 v2 = Matrix.vec d (λi. v1 $ encode1 i * v2 $ encode2 i)*

definition *tensor_mat :: 'a mat ⇒ 'a mat ⇒ 'a mat* **where**
   tensor_mat m1 m2 = Matrix.mat d d (λ(i,j).
     *m1 $$ (encode1 i, encode1 j) * m2 $$ (encode2 i, encode2 j))*

We prove the basic properties of *tensor_vec* and *tensor_mat*, including that they behave correctly with respect to identity, multiplication, adjoint, and trace.

   Extension of matrices is a special case of the tensor product, where the matrix on −*vars* is the identity (here *d2* is the product of *dim2*).

definition *mat_extension :: 'a mat ⇒ 'a mat* **where**
   mat_extension m = tensor_mat m (1_m d2)

With *mat_extension*, we can define "partial" versions of quantum program commands *Utrans*, *Measure* and *While*. They take a set of variables $\bar{q}$ as an extra parameter, and all matrices involved act on the vector space associated to $\bar{q}$. These commands are named *Utrans_P*, *Measure_P* and *While_P*. They are usually used in place of the global commands in actual applications.

   More generally, we can define the tensor product of vectors and matrices on any two subsets of quantum variables. For this, we define another locale:

locale *partial_state2 = state_sig +*
   fixes *vars1 :: nat set* **and** *vars2 :: nat set*
   assumes *disjoint: vars1 ∩ vars2 = {}*

To make use of *tensor_mat* to define tensor product in this more general setting, we need to find the relative position of variables *vars1* within *vars1* ∪ *vars2*. This is done using *ind_in_set*, which counts the position of *x* within *A*.

definition *ind_in_set A x = card {i. i ∈ A ∧ i < x}*
definition *vars1' = (ind_in_set (vars1 ∪ vars2)) ' vars1*

Finally, the more general tensor products are defined as follows (note since we are now outside the *partial_state* locale, we must use qualified names for *tensor_vec* and *tensor_mat*, and supply extra arguments for variables in the locale. Here *dims0 = nths dims (vars1 ∪ vars2)* is the total list of dimensions).

definition *ptensor_vec :: 'a vec ⇒ 'a vec ⇒ 'a vec* **where**
  ptensor_vec v1 v2 = partial_state.tensor_vec dims0 vars1' v1 v2

definition *ptensor_mat :: 'a mat ⇒ 'a mat ⇒ 'a mat* **where**
  ptensor_mat m1 m2 = partial_state.tensor_mat dims0 vars1' m1 m2

The partial extension *pmat_extension* is defined in a similar way as before.

definition *pmat_extension :: 'a mat ⇒ 'a mat* **where**
  pmat_extension m = ptensor_mat m (1_m d2)

The definitions *ptensor_vec* and *ptensor_mat* satisfy several key consistency properties. In particular, they satisfy associativity of tensor product. For matrices, this is expressed as follows:

theorem *ptensor_mat_assoc:*
  v1 ∩ v2 = {} ⟹
  (v1 ∪ v2) ∩ v3 = {} ⟹
  v1 ∪ v2 ∪ v3 ⊆ {0..<length dims} ⟹
  ptensor_mat dims (v1 ∪ v2) v3 (ptensor_mat dims v1 v2 m1 m2) m3 =
  ptensor_mat dims v1 (v2 ∪ v3) m1 (ptensor_mat dims v2 v3 m2 m3)

Together, these constructions and consistency properties provide a framework in which one can reason about arbitrary tensor product of vectors and matrices, defined on mutually disjoint sets of quantum variables.

3.5   Case Study: Products of Hadamard Matrices

In this section, we illustrate the above framework for tensor product of matrices with an application, to be used in the verification of Grover's algorithm in the next section.

In many quantum algorithms, we need to deal with the tensor product of an arbitrary number of Hadamard matrices. The Hadamard matrix (denoted *hadamard* in Isabelle) is given by:

$$H = \frac{1}{\sqrt{2}} \begin{bmatrix} 1 & 1 \\ 1 & -1 \end{bmatrix}$$

For example, in Grover's algorithm, we need to apply the Hadamard transform on each of the first n quantum variables, given by *vars1*. A single Hadamard transform on the i'th quantum variable, extended to a matrix acting on the first n quantum variables, is defined as follows:

definition *hadamard_on_i :: nat ⇒ complex mat* **where**
   hadamard_on_i i = pmat_extension dims {i} (vars1 − {i}) hadamard

The effect of consecutively applying the Hadamard transform on each of the first n quantum variables is equivalent to multiplying the quantum state by *exH_k (n − 1)*, where *exH_k* is defined as follows.

fun *exH_k :: nat ⇒ complex mat* **where**
   exH_k 0 = hadamard_on_i 0
 | *exH_k (Suc k) = exH_k k * hadamard_on_i (Suc k)*

Crucially, this matrix product of extensions of Hadamard matrices must equal the tensor product of Hadamard matrices. That is, with *H_k* defined as

fun *H_k :: nat ⇒ complex mat* **where**
   H_k 0 = hadamard
 | *H_k (Suc k) = ptensor_mat dims {0..<Suc k} {Suc k} (H_k k) hadamard*

we have the theorem

lemma *exH_eq_H: exH_k (n − 1) = H_k (n − 1)*

The proof of this result is by induction, requiring the use of associativity of tensor product stated above.

4   Verification of Grover's Algorithm

In this section, we describe our application of the above framework to the verification of Grover's quantum search algorithm [32]. Quantum search algorithms [18, 32] concern searching an unordered database for an item satisfying some given property. This property is usually specified by an oracle. In a database of N items, where M items satisfy the property, finding an item with the property requires on average $O(N/M)$ calls to the oracle for classical computers. Grover's algorithm reduces this complexity to $O(\sqrt{N/M})$.

The basic idea of Grover's algorithm is rotation. The algorithm starts from an initial state/vector. At every step, it rotates towards the target state/vector for a small angle. As summarised in [18, 19, 42], it can be mathematically described by the following equation [42, Eq. (6.12)]:

$$G^k |\psi_0\rangle = \cos(\frac{2k+1}{2}\theta) |\alpha\rangle + \sin(\frac{2k+1}{2}\theta) |\beta\rangle,$$

where G represents the operator at each step, $|\psi_0\rangle$ is the initial state, $\theta = 2\arccos\sqrt{(N − M)/N}$, $|\alpha\rangle$ is the bad state (for items not satisfying the property), and $|\beta\rangle$ is the good state (for items satisfying the property). Thus when θ is very small, i.e., $M \ll N$, it costs $O(\sqrt{N/M})$ rounds to reach a target state.

Originally, Grover's algorithm only resolves the case $M = 1$ [32]. It is immediately generalized to the case of known M with the same idea and the case of unknown M with some modifications [18]. After that, the idea is generalized to all invertible quantum processes [19].

The paper [61] uses Grover's algorithm as the main example illustrating quantum Hoare logic. We largely follow its approach in this paper. See also [42, Chapter 6] for a general introduction.

First, we setup a locale for the inputs to the search problem.

locale *grover_state* =
  fixes n :: *nat* **and** f :: *nat* $\Rightarrow$ *bool*
  assumes *n*: $n > 1$
    and *dimM*: *card* $\{i.\ i < (2::nat)\ \hat{}\ n \wedge f\ i\} > 0$
           card $\{i.\ i < (2::nat)\ \hat{}\ n \wedge f\ i\} < (2::nat)\ \hat{}\ n$

Here n is the number of qubits used to represent the items. That is, we assume $N = 2^n$ items in total. The oracle is represented by the function f, where only its values on inputs less than 2^n are used. The number of items satisfying the property is given by $M = card\ \{i.\ i < N \wedge f\ i\}$.

Next, we setup a locale for Grover's algorithm.

locale *grover_state_sig* = *grover_state* + *state_sig* +
  fixes R :: *nat* **and** K :: *nat*
  assumes *dims_def*: *dims* = *replicate n 2* @ [K]
  assumes *R*: $R = \pi\ /\ (2 * \theta) - 1\ /\ 2$
  assumes *K*: $K > R$

As in [61], we assume $R = \pi/2\theta - 1/2$ is an integer. This implies that the quantum algorithm succeeds with probability 1. This condition holds, for example, for all N, M where $N = 4M$. Since we did not formalize quantum states with infinite dimension, we replace the loop counter, which is infinite dimensional in [61], with a variable of dimension $K > R$. We also remove the control variable for the oracle used in [61]. Overall, our quantum state consists of n variables of dimension 2 for representing the items, and one variable of dimension K for the loop counter.

We now present the quantum program to be verified. First, the operation that performs the Hadamard transform on each of the first n variables is defined by induction as follows.

fun *hadamard_n* :: *nat* $\Rightarrow$ *com* **where**
  hadamard_n 0 = *SKIP*
  | *hadamard_n (Suc i)* = *hadamard_n i* ;; *Utrans (tensor_P (hadamard_on_i i) (1_m K))*

Here *tensor_P* denotes the tensor product of a matrix on the first n variables (of dimension $2^n \times 2^n$) and a matrix on the loop variable (of dimension $K \times K$). Executing this program is equivalent to multiplying the quantum state corresponding to the first n variables by $H^{\otimes n}$, as shown in Sect. 3.5.

The body of the loop is given by:

definition D :: *com* **where**
  D = *Utrans_P vars1 mat_O* ;;

> *hadamard_n n ;;*
> *Utrans_P vars1 mat_Ph ;;*
> *hadamard_n n ;;*
> *Utrans_P vars2 (mat_incr n)*

where each of the three matrices *mat_O*, *mat_Ph* and *mat_incr* can be defined directly.

definition *mat_O :: complex mat* **where**
   mat_O = mat N N (λ(i,j). if i = j then (if f i then 1 else −1) else 0)
definition *mat_Ph :: complex mat* **where**
   mat_Ph = mat N N (λ(i,j). if i = j then if i = 0 then 1 else −1 else 0)
definition *mat_incr :: nat ⇒ complex mat* **where**
   mat_incr n = mat n n (λ(i,j). if i = 0 then (if j = n − 1 then 1 else 0)
                         else (if i = j + 1 then 1 else 0))

Finally, the Grover's algorithm is as follows. Since we do not have initialization, we skip initialization to zero at the beginning and instead assume that the state begins in the zero state in the precondition.

definition *Grover :: com* **where**
   Grover = hadamard_n n ;;
          While_P vars2 M0 M1 D ;;
          Measure_P vars1 N testN (replicate N SKIP)

where the measurements for the while loop and at the end of the algorithm are:

definition *M0 = mat K K (λ(i,j). if i = j ∧ i ≥ R then 1 else 0)*
definition *M1 = mat K K (λ(i,j). if i = j ∧ i < R then 1 else 0)*
definition *testN k = mat N N (λ(i,j). if i = k ∧ j = k then 1 else 0)*

We can now state the final correctness result. Let *proj v* be the outer product $vv^{\dagger}$, and *proj_k k* be $|k\rangle\langle k|$, where $|k\rangle$ is the *k*'th basis vector on the vector space corresponding to the loop variable. Let *pre* and *post* be given as follows:

definition *pre = proj (vec N (λk. if k = 0 then 1 else 0))*
definition *post = mat N N (λ(i, j). if i = j ∧ f i then 1 else 0)*

Then, the (partial) correctness of Grover's algorithm is specified by the following Hoare triple.

theorem *grover_partial_correct:*
   $\models_p$ *{tensor_P pre (proj_k 0)}*
      Grover
      {tensor_P post (1_m K)}

We now briefly outline the proof strategy. Following the definition of *Grover*, the proof of the above Hoare triple is divided into three main parts, for the initialization by Hadamard matrices, for the while loop, and for the measurement at the end.

In each part, assertions are first inserted around commands according to the Hoare rules to form smaller Hoare triples. In particular, the precondition of the while loop part is exactly the invariant of the loop. Moreover, it has to be shown that these assertions satisfy the conditions for being quantum predicates, which involve computing their dimension, showing positiveness, and being bounded by the identity matrix under the Löwner order. Then, these Hoare triples are derived using our deduction system. Before combining them together, we have to show that the postcondition of each command is equal to the precondition of the later one. After that, the three main Hoare triples can be obtained by combining these smaller ones.

After the derivation of the three Hoare triples above, we prove the Löwner order between the postcondition of each triple and the precondition of the following triple. Afterwards, the triples can be combined into the Hoare triple below:

theorem *grover_partial_deduct:*
   $\vdash_p$ *{tensor_P pre (proj_k 0)}*
      Grover
      {tensor_P post (1_m K)}

Finally, the (partial) correctness of Grover's algorithm follows from the soundness of our deduction system.

5   Discussion

Compared to classical programs, reasoning about quantum programs is more difficult in every respect. Instead of discrete mathematics in the classical case, even the simplest reasoning about quantum programs involves complex numbers, unitary and positivity properties of matrices, and the tensor product. Hence, it is to be expected that formal verification of quantum Hoare logic and quantum algorithms will take much more effort. In this section, we describe some of the automation that we built to simplify the manual proof, and give some statistics concerning the amount of effort involved in the formalization.

5.1   Automatic Proof of Identities in Linear Algebra

During the formalization process, we make extensive use of ring properties of matrices. These include commutativity and associativity of addition, associativity of multiplication, and distributivity. Compared to the usual case of numbers, applying these rules for matrices is more difficult in Isabelle/HOL, since they involve extra conditions on dimensions of matrices. For example, the rule for commutativity of addition of matrices is stated as:

lemma *comm_add_mat:*
   $A \in carrier\_mat\ nr\ nc \implies B \in carrier\_mat\ nr\ nc \implies A + B = B + A$

These extra conditions make the rules difficult to apply for standard Isabelle automation. For our work, we implemented our own tactic handling these rules. In addition to the ring properties, we also frequently need to use the cyclic property of trace (e.g. $\text{tr}(ABC) = \text{tr}(BCA)$), as well as the properties of adjoint ($(AB)^\dagger = B^\dagger A^\dagger$ and $A^{\dagger\dagger} = A$). For simplicity, we restrict to identities involving only $n \times n$ matrices, where n is a parameter given to the tactic.

The tactic is designed to prove equality between two expressions. It works by computing the normal form of the expressions – using ring identities and identities for the adjoint to fully expand the expression into polynomial form. To handle the trace, the expression $\text{tr}(A_1 \cdots A_n)$ is normalized to put the A_i that is the largest according to Isabelle's internal term order last. All dimension assumptions are collected and reduced (for example, the assumption $A * B \in$ *carrier_mat n n* is reduced to $A \in$ *carrier_mat n n* and $B \in$ *carrier_mat n n*).

Overall, the resulting tactic is used 80 times in our proofs. Below, we list some of the more complicated equations resolved by the tactic. The tactic reduces the goal to dimensional constraints on the atomic matrices (e.g. $M \in$ *carrier_mat n n* and $P \in$ *carrier_mat n n* in the first case).

$$\text{tr}(MM^\dagger(PP^\dagger)) = \text{tr}((P^\dagger M)(P^\dagger M)^\dagger)$$
$$\text{tr}(M_0 A M_0^\dagger) + \text{tr}(M_1 A M_1^\dagger) = \text{tr}((M_0^\dagger M_0 + M_1^\dagger M_1)A)$$
$$H^\dagger(Ph^\dagger(H^\dagger Q_2 H)Ph)H = (HPhH)^\dagger Q_2(HPhH)$$

5.2 Statistics

Overall, the formalization consists of about 11,500 lines of Isabelle theories. An old version of the proof is developed on and off for two years. The current version is re-developed, using some ideas from the old version. The development of the new version took about 5 person months. Detailed breakdown of number of lines for different parts of the proof is given in the following table.

Description	Files	Number of lines
Preliminaries	*Complex_Matrix, Matrix_Limit, Gates*	4197
Semantics	*Quantum_Program*	1110
Hoare logic	*Quantum_Hoare*	1417
Tensor product	*Partial_State*	1664
Grover's algorithm	*Grover*	3184
Total		11572

In particular, with the verification framework in place, the proof of correctness for Grover's search algorithm takes just over 3000 lines. While this shows that it is realistic to use the current framework to verify more complicated algorithms such as Shor's algorithm, it is clear that more automation is needed to enable verification on a larger scale.

6   Related Work

The closest work to our research is Robert Rand's implementation of $\mathcal{Q}$wire in Coq [49,50]. $\mathcal{Q}$wire [47] is a language for describing *quantum circuits*. In this model, quantum algorithms are implemented by connecting together quantum gates, each with a fixed number of bit/qubit inputs and outputs. How the gates are connected is determined by a classical host language, allowing classical control of quantum computation. The work [49] defines the semantics of $\mathcal{Q}$wire in Coq, and uses it to verify quantum teleportation, Deutsch's algorithm, and an example on multiple coin flips to illustrate applicability to a family of circuits. In this framework, program verification proceeds directly from the semantics, without defining a Hoare logic. As in our work, it is necessary to solve the problem of how to define extensions of an operation on a few qubits to the global state. The approach taken in [49] is to use the usual Kronecker product, augmented either by the use of swaps between qubits, or by inserting identity matrices at strategic positions in the Kronecker product.

There are two main differences between [49] and our work. First, quantum algorithms are expressed using quantum circuits in [49], while we use quantum programs with while loops. Models based on quantum circuits have the advantage of being concrete, and indeed most of the earlier quantum algorithms can be expressed directly in terms of circuits. However, several new quantum algorithms can be more properly expressed by while loops, e.g. quantum walks with absorbing boundaries, quantum Bernoulli factory (for random number generation), HHL for systems of linear equations and qPCA (Principal Component Analysis). Second, we formalized a Hoare logic while [49] uses denotational semantics directly. As in verification of classical programs, Hoare logic encapsulates standard forms of argument for dealing with each program construct. Moreover, the rules for QHL is in weakest-precondition form, allowing the possibility of automated verification condition generation after specifying the loop invariants (although this is not used in the present paper).

Besides Rand's work, quite a few verification tools have been developed for quantum communication protocols. For example, Nagarajan and Gay [41] modeled the BB84 protocol [12] and verified its correctness. Ardeshir-Larijani et al. [7,8] presented a tool for verification of quantum protocols through equivalence checking. Existing tools, such as PRISM [37] and Coq, are employed to develop verification tools for quantum protocols [17,29]. Furthermore, an automatic tool called Quantum Model-Checker (QMC) is developed [28,46].

Recently, several specific techniques have been proposed to algorithmically check properties of quantum programs. In [63], the Sharir-Pnueli-Hart method for verifying probabilistic programs [54] has been generalised to quantum programs by exploiting the Schrödinger-Heisenberg duality between quantum states and observables. Termination analysis of nondeterministic and concurrent quantum programs [38] was carried out based on reachability analysis [64]. Invariants can be generated at some steps in quantum programs for debugging and verification of correctness [62]. But up to now no tools are available that implements these techniques. Another Hoare-style logic for quantum programs was proposed in [36], but without (relative) completeness.

Interactive theorem proving has made significant progress in the formal verification of classical programs and systems. Here, we focus on listing some tools designed for special kinds of systems. EasyCrypt [10,11] is an interactive framework for verifying the security of cryptographic constructs in the computational model. It is developed based on a probabilistic relational Hoare logic to support machine-checked construction and verification of game-based proofs. Recently, verification of hybrid systems via interactive theorem proving has also been studied. KeYmaera X [26] is a theorem prover implementing differential dynamic logic $(d\mathcal{L})$ [48], for the verification of hybrid programs. In [60], a prover has been implemented in Isabelle/HOL for reasoning about hybrid processes described using hybrid CSP [34].

Our work is based on existing formalization of matrices and tensors in Isabelle/HOL. In [59] (with corresponding AFP entry [58]), Thiemann et al. developed the matrix library that we use here. In [14] (with corresponding AFP entry [13]), Bentkamp et al. developed tensor analysis based on the above work, in an effort to formalize an expressivity result of deep learning algorithms.

7 Conclusion

We formalized quantum Hoare logic in Isabelle/HOL, and verified the soundness and completeness of the deduction system for partial correctness. Using this deduction system, we verified the correctness of Grover's search algorithm. This is, to our best knowledge, the first formalization of a Hoare logic for quantum programs in an interactive theorem prover.

This work is intended to be the first step of a larger project to construct a framework under which one can efficiently verify the correctness of complex quantum programs and systems. In this paper, our focus is on formalizing the mathematical machinery to specify the semantics of quantum programs, and prove the correctness of quantum Hoare logic. To verify more complicated programs efficiently, better automation is needed at every stage of the proof. We have already begun with some automation for proving identities in linear algebra. In the future, we plan to add to it automation facility for handling matrix computations, tensor products, positivity of matrices, etc., all linked together by a verification condition generator.

Another direction of future work is to formalize various extensions of quantum Hoare logic, to deal with classical control, recursion, concurrency, etc., with the eventual goal of being able to verify not only sequential programs, but also concurrent programs and communication systems.

Acknowledgements. This research is supported through grants by NSFC under grant No. 61625206, 61732001. Bohua Zhan is supported by CAS Pioneer Hundred Talents Program under grant No. Y9RC585036. Yangjia Li is supported by NSFC grant No. 61872342.

References

1. IBM Q devices and simulators. https://www.research.ibm.com/ibm-q/technology/devices/
2. IBM Q experience community. https://quantumexperience.ng.bluemix.net/qx/community?channel=papers&category=ibm
3. IonQ. https://ionq.co/resources
4. A preview of Bristlecone, Google's new quantum processor. https://ai.googleblog.com/2018/03/a-preview-of-bristlecone-googles-new.html
5. Qiskit Aer. https://qiskit.org/aer, https://medium.com/qiskit/qiskit-aer-d09d0fac7759
6. Unsupervised machine learning on Rigetti 19Q with Forest 1.2. https://medium.com/rigetti/unsupervised-machine-learning-on-rigetti-19q-with-forest-1-2-39021339699
7. Ardeshir-Larijani, E., Gay, S.J., Nagarajan, R.: Equivalence checking of quantum protocols. In: Piterman, N., Smolka, S.A. (eds.) TACAS 2013. LNCS, vol. 7795, pp. 478–492. Springer, Heidelberg (2013). https://doi.org/10.1007/978-3-642-36742-7_33
8. Ardeshir-Larijani, E., Gay, S.J., Nagarajan, R.: Verification of concurrent quantum protocols by equivalence checking. In: Ábrahám, E., Havelund, K. (eds.) TACAS 2014. LNCS, vol. 8413, pp. 500–514. Springer, Heidelberg (2014). https://doi.org/10.1007/978-3-642-54862-8_42
9. Baltag, A., Smets, S.: LQP: the dynamic logic of quantum information. Math. Struct. Comput. Sci. **16**(3), 491–525 (2006)
10. Barthe, G., Dupressoir, F., Grégoire, B., Kunz, C., Schmidt, B., Strub, P.-Y.: EasyCrypt: a tutorial. In: Aldini, A., Lopez, J., Martinelli, F. (eds.) FOSAD 2012-2013. LNCS, vol. 8604, pp. 146–166. Springer, Cham (2014). https://doi.org/10.1007/978-3-319-10082-1_6
11. Barthe, G., Grégoire, B., Heraud, S., Béguelin, S.Z.: Computer-aided security proofs for the working cryptographer. In: Rogaway, P. (ed.) CRYPTO 2011. LNCS, vol. 6841, pp. 71–90. Springer, Heidelberg (2011). https://doi.org/10.1007/978-3-642-22792-9_5
12. Bennett, C.H., Brassard, G.: Quantum cryptography: public key distribution and coin tossing. In: International Conference on Computers, Systems and Signal Processing, pp. 175–179. IEEE (1984)
13. Bentkamp, A.: Expressiveness of deep learning. Archive of Formal Proofs, Formal proof development, November 2016. http://isa-afp.org/entries/Deep_Learning.html
14. Bentkamp, A., Blanchette, J.C., Klakow, D.: A formal proof of the expressiveness of deep learning. In: Interactive Theorem Proving - 8th International Conference, ITP 2017, Brasília, Brazil, September 26–29, 2017, Proceedings, pp. 46–64 (2017). https://dblp.org/rec/bib/conf/itp/BentkampBK17
15. Bertot, Y., Castran, P.: Interactive Theorem Proving and Program Development: Coq'Art The Calculus of Inductive Constructions, 1st edn. Springer, Heidelberg (2010). https://doi.org/10.1007/978-3-662-07964-5
16. Bettelli, S., Calarco, T., Serafini, L.: Toward an architecture for quantum programming. Eur. Phys. J. D **25**, 181–200 (2003)
17. Boender, J., Kammüller, F., Nagarajan, R.: Formalization of quantum protocols using Coq. In: QPL 2015 (2015)

18. Boyer, M., Brassard, G., Høyer, P., Tapp, A.: Tight bounds on quantum searching. Fortschr. der Phys. Prog. Phys. **46**(4–5), 493–505 (1998)
19. Brassard, G., Hoyer, P., Mosca, M., Tapp, A.: Quantum amplitude amplification and estimation. Contemp. Math. **305**, 53–74 (2002)
20. Brunet, O., Jorrand, P.: Dynamic quantum logic for quantum programs. Int. J. Quantum Inf. **2**, 45–54 (2004)
21. Chadha, R., Mateus, P., Sernadas, A.: Reasoning about imperative quantum programs. Electron. Notes Theoret. Comput. Sci. **158**, 19–39 (2006)
22. Cross, A.W., Bishop, L.S., Smolin, J.A., Gambetta, J.M.: Open quantum assembly language. arXiv preprint arXiv:1707.03429 (2017)
23. Debnath, S., Linke, N.M., Figgatt, C., Landsman, K.A., Wright, K., Monroe, C.: Demonstration of a small programmable quantum computer with atomic qubits. Nature **536**(7614), 63–66 (2016)
24. D'Hondt, E., Panangaden, P.: Quantum weakest preconditions. Math. Struct. Comput. Sci. **16**, 429–451 (2006)
25. Wecker, D., Svore, K.: Liqui|⟩: a software design architecture and domain-specific language for quantum computing. (http://research.microsoft.com/en-us/projects/liquid/)
26. Fulton, N., Mitsch, S., Quesel, J.-D., Völp, M., Platzer, A.: KeYmaera X: an axiomatic tactical theorem prover for hybrid systems. In: Felty, A.P., Middeldorp, A. (eds.) CADE 2015. LNCS (LNAI), vol. 9195, pp. 527–538. Springer, Cham (2015). https://doi.org/10.1007/978-3-319-21401-6_36
27. Gay, S.: Quantum programming languages: survey and bibliography. Math. Struct. Comput. Sci. **16**, 581–600 (2006)
28. Gay, S.J., Nagarajan, R., Papanikolaou, N.: QMC: a model checker for quantum systems. In: Gupta, A., Malik, S. (eds.) CAV 2008. LNCS, vol. 5123, pp. 543–547. Springer, Heidelberg (2008). https://doi.org/10.1007/978-3-540-70545-1_51
29. Gay, S.J., Nagarajan, R., Papanikolaou, N.: Probabilistic model-checking of quantum protocols. In: DCM Proceedings of International Workshop on Developments in Computational Models, p. 504007. IEEE (2005). https://arxiv.org/abs/quant-ph/0504007
30. Google AI Quantum team. https://github.com/quantumlib/Cirq
31. Green, A.S., Lumsdaine, P.L., Ross, N.J., Selinger, P., Valiron, B.: Quipper: a scalable quantum programming language. In: Proceedings of the 34th ACM SIGPLAN Conference on Programming Language Design and Implementation, PLDI 2013, pp. 333–342. ACM, New York (2013)
32. Grover, L.K.: A fast quantum mechanical algorithm for database search. In: Proceedings of the Twenty-eighth Annual ACM Symposium on Theory of Computing, STOC 1996, pp. 212–219. ACM, New York (1996)
33. Haftmann, F., Wenzel, M.: Local theory specifications in isabelle/isar. In: Berardi, S., Damiani, F., de'Liguoro, U. (eds.) TYPES 2008. LNCS, vol. 5497, pp. 153–168. Springer, Heidelberg (2009). https://doi.org/10.1007/978-3-642-02444-3_10
34. He, J.: From CSP to hybrid systems. In: A Classical Mind, Essays in Honour of C.A.R. Hoare, pp. 171–189. Prentice Hall International (UK) Ltd. (1994)
35. JavadiAbhari, A., et al.: ScaffCC: scalable compilation and analysis of quantum programs. In: Parallel Computing, vol. 45, pp. 3–17 (2015)
36. Kakutani, Y.: A logic for formal verification of quantum programs. In: Datta, A. (ed.) ASIAN 2009. LNCS, vol. 5913, pp. 79–93. Springer, Heidelberg (2009). https://doi.org/10.1007/978-3-642-10622-4_7

37. Kwiatkowska, M., Norman, G., Parker, P.: Probabilistic symbolic model-checking with PRISM: a hybrid approach. Int. J. Softw. Tools Technol. Transf. **6**, 128–142 (2004)
38. Li, Y., Yu, N., Ying, M.: Termination of nondeterministic quantum programs. Acta Informatica **51**, 1–24 (2014)
39. Liu, S., et al.: $Q|SI\rangle$: a quantum programming environment. In: Jones, C., Wang, J., Zhan, N. (eds.) Symposium on Real-Time and Hybrid Systems. LNCS, vol. 11180, pp. 133–164. Springer, Cham (2018). https://doi.org/10.1007/978-3-030-01461-2_8
40. Liu, X., Kubiatowicz, J.: Chisel-Q: designing quantum circuits with a scala embedded language. In: 2013 IEEE 31st International Conference on Computer Design (ICCD), pp. 427–434. IEEE (2013)
41. Nagarajan, R., Gay, S.: Formal verification of quantum protocols (2002). arXiv: quant-ph/0203086
42. Nielsen, M.A., Chuang, I.L.: Quantum Computation and Quantum Information: 10th Anniversary Edition, 10th edn. Cambridge University Press, New York (2011)
43. Nipkow, T., Klein, G.: Concrete Semantics: With Isabelle/HOL. Springer, Cham (2014). https://doi.org/10.1007/978-3-319-10542-0
44. Nipkow, T., Wenzel, M., Paulson, L.C. (eds.): Isabelle/HOL: A Proof Assistant for Higher-Order Logic. LNCS, vol. 2283. Springer, Heidelberg (2002). https://doi.org/10.1007/3-540-45949-9
45. Ömer, B.: Structured quantum programming. Ph.D. thesis, Technical University of Vienna (2003)
46. Papanikolaou, N.: Model checking quantum protocols. Ph.D. thesis, Department of Computer Science, University of Warwick (2008)
47. Paykin, J., Rand, R., Zdancewic, S.: QWIRE: a core language for quantum circuits. In: Proceedings of 44th ACM Symposium on Principles of Programming Languages (POPL), pp. 846–858 (2017)
48. Platzer, A.: A complete uniform substitution calculus for differential dynamic logic. J. Autom. Reas. **59**(2), 219–265 (2017)
49. Rand, R.: Formally verified quantum programming. Ph.D. thesis, University of Pennsylvania (2018)
50. Robert Rand, J.P., Zdancewic, S.: QWIRE practice: formal verification of quantum circuits in coq. In: Quantum Physics and Logic (2017)
51. Sanders, J.W., Zuliani, P.: Quantum programming. In: Backhouse, R., Oliveira, J.N. (eds.) MPC 2000. LNCS, vol. 1837, pp. 80–99. Springer, Heidelberg (2000). https://doi.org/10.1007/10722010_6
52. Selinger, P.: A brief survey of quantum programming languages. In: Kameyama, Y., Stuckey, P.J. (eds.) FLOPS 2004. LNCS, vol. 2998, pp. 1–6. Springer, Heidelberg (2004). https://doi.org/10.1007/978-3-540-24754-8_1
53. Selinger, P.: Towards a quantum programming language. Math. Struct. Comput. Sci. **14**(4), 527–586 (2004)
54. Sharir, M., Pnueli, A., Hart, S.: Verification of probabilistic programs. SIAM J. Comput. **13**, 292–314 (1984)
55. Smith, R.S., Curtis, M.J., Zeng, W.J.: A practical quantum instruction set architecture. arXiv preprint arXiv:1608.03355 (2016)
56. Steiger, D.S., Häner, T., Troyer, M.: ProjectQ: an open source software framework for quantum computing. Quantum **2**, 49 (2018)
57. Svore, K., et al.: Q#: enabling scalable quantum computing and development with a high-level DSL. In: Proceedings of the Real World Domain Specific Languages Workshop 2018, pp. 7:1–7:10 (2018)

58. Thiemann, R., Yamada, A.: Matrices, Jordan normal forms, and spectral radius theory. Archive of Formal Proofs, Formal proof development, August 2015. http://isa-afp.org/entries/Jordan_Normal_Form.html

59. Thiemann, R., Yamada, A.: Formalizing Jordan normal forms in Isabelle/HOL. In: Proceedings of the 5th ACM SIGPLAN Conference on Certified Programs and Proofs, CPP 2016, pp. 88–99. ACM, New York (2016)

60. Wang, S., Zhan, N., Zou, L.: An improved HHL prover: an interactive theorem prover for hybrid systems. In: Butler, M., Conchon, S., Zaïdi, F. (eds.) ICFEM 2015. LNCS, vol. 9407, pp. 382–399. Springer, Cham (2015). https://doi.org/10.1007/978-3-319-25423-4_25

61. Ying, M.: Floyd-Hoare logic for quantum programs. ACM Trans. Programm. Lang. Syst. **33**(6), 19:1–19:49 (2011)

62. Ying, M., Ying, S., Wu, X.: Invariants of quantum programs: characterisations and generation. In: Proceedings of the 44th ACM SIGPLAN Symposium on Principles of Programming Languages, POPL 2017, pp. 818–832 (2017)

63. Ying, M., Yu, N., Feng, Y., Duan, R.: Verification of quantum programs. Sci. Comput. Programm. **78**, 1679–1700 (2013)

64. Ying, S., Feng, Y., Yu, N., Ying, M.: Reachability probabilities of quantum Markov chains. In: D'Argenio, P.R., Melgratti, H. (eds.) CONCUR 2013. LNCS, vol. 8052, pp. 334–348. Springer, Heidelberg (2013). https://doi.org/10.1007/978-3-642-40184-8_24

Permissions

The contributors of this book come from diverse backgrounds, making this book a truly international effort. This book will bring forth new frontiers with its revolutionizing research information and detailed analysis of the nascent developments around the world.

We would like to thank all the contributing authors for lending their expertise to make the book truly unique. They have played a crucial role in the development of this book. Without their invaluable contributions this book wouldn't have been possible. They have made vital efforts to compile up to date information on the varied aspects of this subject to make this book a valuable addition to the collection of many professionals and students.

This book was conceptualized with the vision of imparting up-to-date information and advanced data in this field. To ensure the same, a matchless editorial board was set up. Every individual on the board went through rigorous rounds of assessment to prove their worth. After which they invested a large part of their time researching and compiling the most relevant data for our readers.

The editorial board has been involved in producing this book since its inception. They have spent rigorous hours researching and exploring the diverse topics which have resulted in the successful publishing of this book. They have passed on their knowledge of decades through this book. To expedite this challenging task, the publisher supported the team at every step. A small team of assistant editors was also appointed to further simplify the editing procedure and attain best results for the readers.

Apart from the editorial board, the designing team has also invested a significant amount of their time in understanding the subject and creating the most relevant covers. They scrutinized every image to scout for the most suitable representation of the subject and create an appropriate cover for the book.

The publishing team has been an ardent support to the editorial, designing and production team. Their endless efforts to recruit the best for this project, has resulted in the accomplishment of this book. They are a veteran in the field of academics and their pool of knowledge is as vast as their experience in printing. Their expertise and guidance has proved useful at every step. Their uncompromising quality standards have made this book an exceptional effort. Their encouragement from time to time has been an inspiration for everyone.

The publisher and the editorial board hope that this book will prove to be a valuable piece of knowledge for researchers, students, practitioners and scholars across the globe.

List of Contributors

Martin Jonáš and Jan Strejček
Masaryk University, Brno, Czech Republic

Andrew Reynolds and Cesare Tinelli
Department of Computer Science, The University of Iowa, Iowa City, USA

Andres Nötzli and Clark Barrett
Department of Computer Science, Stanford University, Stanford, USA

Markus N. Rabe
Google, Mountain View, CA, USA

Radu Iosif and Xiao Xu
CNRS, Verimag, Université de Grenoble Alpes, Grenoble, France

Heiko Becker and Eva Darulova
MPI-SWS, Saarland Informatics Campus (SIC), Saarbrücken, Germany

Magnus O. Myreen
Chalmers University of Technology, Gothenburg, Sweden

Zachary Tatlock
University of Washington, Seattle, USA

Sicun Gao and Nima Roohi
University of California, San Diego, La Jolla, USA

James Kapinski
Toyota R&D, Gardena, USA

Jyotirmoy Deshmukh
University of Southern California, Los Angeles, USA

Armando Solar-Lezama
Massachusetts Institute of Technology, Cambridge, USA

Nikos Arechiga and Soonho Kong
Toyota Research Institute, Cambridge, USA

Aina Niemetz, Mathias Preiner and Clark Barrett
Stanford University, Stanford, USA

Martin Brain
University of Oxford, Oxford, UK
City, University of London, London, UK

Jake Silverman and Zachary Kincaid
Princeton University, Princeton, USA

John Backes, Catherine Dodge, Andrew Gacek, Temesghen Kahsai, Bill Kocik, Sean McLaughlin, Neha Rungta, John Sizemore, Mark Stalzer, Preethi Srinivasan, Carsten Varming and Blake Whaley
Amazon, Seattle, USA

Byron Cook and Pavle Subotić
Amazon, Seattle, USA
University College London, London, UK

Evgenii Kotelnikov
Amazon, Seattle, USA
Chalmers University of Technology, Gothenburg, Sweden

Alan J. Hu
University British Columbia, Vancouver, Canada

Sam Bayless
Amazon, Seattle, USA
University British Columbia, Vancouver, Canada

Jure Kukovec
Amazon, Seattle, USA
TU Wien, Vienna, Austria

Jason Reed
Semmle Inc, San Francisco, USA

Gidon Ernst
LMU Munich, Munich, Germany

Toby Murray
University of Melbourne, Melbourne, Australia

Ahmed Bouajjani and Constantin Enea
Université de Paris, IRIF, CNRS, 75013 Paris, France

Rachid Zennou
Université de Paris, IRIF, CNRS, 75013 Paris, France
ENSIAS, University Mohammed V, Rabat, Morocco

Mohammed Erradi
ENSIAS, University Mohammed V, Rabat, Morocco

Nick Giannarakis and David Walker
Princeton University, Princeton, NJ 08544, USA

Ryan Beckett
Microsoft Research, Redmond, WA 98052, USA

Ratul Mahajan
University of Washington, Seattle, WA 98195, USA
Intentionet, Seattle, WA, USA

Shuling Wang, Shenggang Ying, Tao Liu and Yangjia Li
State Key Laboratory of Computer Science, Institute of Software, Chinese Academy of Sciences, Beijing, China

Junyi Liu, Naijun Zhan and Bohua Zhan
State Key Laboratory of Computer Science, Institute of Software, Chinese Academy of Sciences, Beijing, China
University of Chinese Academy of Sciences, Beijing, China

Mingsheng Ying
State Key Laboratory of Computer Science, Institute of Software, Chinese Academy of Sciences, Beijing, China
University of Technology Sydney, Sydney, Australia
Tsinghua University, Beijing, China

Index

Printed in the USA
CPSIA information can be obtained
at www.ICGtesting.com
JSHW051409221024
72173JS00006B/1322